Nine Months in Tibet

RUPERT
WOLFE MURRAY

All the best

Ballater 2016

Scotland Street Press
EDINBURGH

Published by Scotland Street Press 2016

2 5 7 3 12 9 7 5 1

First published in Great Britain in 2016 by
Scotland Street Press
7/1 Scotland Street,
Edinburgh, EH3 6PP

www.scotlandstreetpress.com

Cover Design by Tudor Matei
Cover photo by Uli Zimmermann
ISBN: 978-1-910895-03-0
www.wolfemurray.com

Typeset in Scotland by Theodore Shack
Printed and bound in Poland

This book is dedicated to Hu Yaobang, who made my journey to Tibet possible, as well as Lara and Luca, who inspire me, and everyone who wants to overcome their fear of travelling alone.

"I would hate to tell you what this lousy little book cost me in money and anxiety and time. When I got home from the Second World War twenty three years ago, I thought it would be easy for me to write about the destruction of Dresden, since all I would have to do would be to report what I had seen. And I thought, too, that it would be a masterpiece or at least make me a lot of money, since the subject was so big."

Kurt Vonnegut, *Slaughterhouse-Five*, 1969

"During the last ten years literature has involved itself more and more deeply in politics, with the result that there is now less room in it for the ordinary man than at any time during the past two centuries. One can see the change in the prevailing literary attitude by comparing the books written about the Spanish civil war with those written about the war of 1914-18. The immediately striking thing about the Spanish war books, at any rate those written in English, is their shocking dullness and badness. But what is more significant is that almost all of them, right wing or left wing, are written from a political angle, by cocksure partisans telling you what to think, whereas the books about the Great War were written by common soldiers or junior officers who did not even pretend to understand what the whole thing was about."

George Orwell, Inside the Whale, 1940

Foreword

There is something very compelling about a memoir of a journey made in the early years of adult life. The world at that time lies at one's feet. Everything is possible, and remoteness, the exotic, and indeed the forbidden all beckon. It is a call that is hard to resist. In that spirit, Patrick Leigh Fermor set forth on his extraordinary walk through pre-War Europe, or Laurie Lee embarked on his own famous walk. There are many other accounts of similar journeys.

Rupert Wolfe Murray's story of his time in Tibet belongs in the same company. He has written a highly readable and engaging book about going off to Tibet in the late nineteen-eighties, with little money in his pocket, but with all the optimism and determination that goes with being twenty-three. In a world that is now so accessible to visitors, it sometimes requires a leap of the imagination to understand just how closed and impenetrable some parts of the world then were. Tibet remains relatively isolated even today, but when the author of this memoir was there it was even more so. As it happened, his visit coincided with a very difficult time in the country's history, and Mr Wolfe Murray's account of being caught up in that is both tense and enlightening.

This is a fascinating and thoroughly engrossing tale of a strange time spent in a strange place. Like the best travel writing, it conveys just what it must have been like to have the adventure of a lifetime. We are there with Mr Wolfe Murray, experiencing his discomfort and anxiety, but sharing, too, his insights. He would be a great travelling companion, I suspect, because of his sympathy and his instinctive understanding of those amongst whom he spent time – qualities that make him a fine chronicler and a fascinating guide.

Alexander McCall Smith

NINE MONTHS IN TIBET

Prologue

While taking a shower 26 years after the event I realise that there is an irony about my experience in Tibet, an irony I was unaware of until this moment: I was thrown out of Tibet because the Chinese police suspected I was involved in organising a violent protest.

A human rights lawyer who was there at the time of the 1987 uprising in Lhasa told me your name is probably at the top of the police list of instigators. You speak Tibetan, lived in the centre of the old city and they needed scapegoats.

No wonder they threw me out. I am still grateful that they didn't treat me like a Tibetan suspect and hang me from the ceiling in Lhasa's notorious prison.

The irony is that I was expelled for instigating a protest, even though I was the last person in Lhasa to find out about it. I was living about two minutes from the centre of old Lhasa, where the protest was taking place, so I should have known.

I remember vividly, as if it were yesterday, when an English friend burst into my room in Lhasa. He stood there in amazement, unable to comprehend how I was sitting so calmly while the city was in uproar. For a long moment he was speechless.

- What are you doing here? he said.

- Teaching English, I replied, pointing to the Tibetan girl who sat next to me in the tiny room.

I was in no hurry to leave my cosy position. I didn't want to stand up, go outside and see what was going on. I was happy in my cocoon with my fantasies of a happy life in Tibet, a country I had fallen in love with and planned to stay in forever.

But how could I ignore my friend's news of the first major protest that the Tibetans had staged against the Chinese since the sixties?

This is the story of the two years that led up to that moment.

CHAPTER ONE

We lived in a white house on the Firth of Forth, the estuary just north of Edinburgh. It was called Society House and there was a sign at the top of the road which read Private Road to Society. It was so close to the sea that in rough weather waves would crash into the sea walls and throw spray over the hedge and onto the windows. We would explore the rocky beach and the woods that people rarely visited, climb the walls of Bo'ness Castle, only a few miles down the coast and sometimes sleep rough in the garden.

One day I was standing on the sea wall when my elder brother Kim turned up. He had left school under a cloud of bad behaviour a year earlier and had gone to France and Switzerland. We hadn't heard from him in ages but we knew from occasional letters that he had learned French and got some work.

There he was, standing in front of me with a big grin on his face. The thing that impressed me most was his jacket: elegant, dark grey and beautifully designed. It had thin red piping along the seams and a large unusual collar which looked like it could be wrapped round your neck in a blizzard. There was no sign of luggage, just a small leather bag.

- Where d'you get the jacket? I asked.

- Switzerland. It's a postman's jacket. I was thrown out of Switzerland for working illegally. I'm home.

To me this was the definition of cool. This was someone with courage. How could I be like him? How could I get out of this place? The idea of travelling abroad on my own was scary. I just didn't have the courage to do it. I had never jumped into the unknown to such an extent and – worst of all – I didn't know how to overcome this fear of travelling alone.

It was 1982 and I had managed to scrape my way into Liverpool University where I studied history and politics. I chose Liverpool because it was easy to get into, thanks to the nine-day riot that had taken place in 1981. The riots had stunned the nation as it was the first time since the nineteenth century that Englishmen had risen against the state. The names of the inner city areas where the riots took place – Toxteth in Liverpool and Brixton in London – were burned into the nation's consciousness.

My Mother was a book publisher and she encouraged us to follow our dreams. She had separated from my father who, in the sixties and seventies, had written a couple of great novels. My Dad now drove a truck between Edinburgh and London, carrying paintings and artworks. His company was called Moving Pictures and it was a chaotic one-man-show. He took great care of the paintings, was always on the road, couldn't delegate and often didn't send out invoices. I would help him load furniture and I learned to pack paintings into a truck without breaking them; each painting had to be wrapped in a blanket and then tied to the side, making sure that the edges of one painting couldn't puncture the canvas or glass of another. It was an art form and my Dad was the best in the business.

My Mother lived with a young builder called Stewart Anderson, an ambitious and inquisitive man whose black moustache was a source of mockery to my three brothers and I. He was interested in what I was reading in history and we talked about Napoleon, the colonies, Latin America, Asia and the world wars. Stewart renovated old houses in Edinburgh and every holiday I would get a job with him as a labourer. I learned to manoeuvre a wheelbarrow full of rubble up a narrow plank into a skip and how to take abuse from the other workers.

In the summer of 1984 the British Council invited my Mother to go on a tour of the People's Republic of China – which back then was just coming out of the grip of Mao Tse Tung's dictatorship. The idea was that a delegation of British publishers would meet their Chinese counterparts. She later told me that most of the Chinese publishers insisted that they met up in her hotel as they were too ashamed to show their offices. After the China trip she had booked a flight from Beijing to Thailand where she was going to meet up with Stewart for a romantic two week break.

My introduction to Asia was totally unexpected. I was working as a labourer for Stewart, renovating a terraced house in Edinburgh. My job was to break up big stones, shovel the rubble into sacks, carry these to the street and empty them into a skip. It was hard, filthy work but there were plenty of jokes (and joints) floating around and I imagined it was making me tougher. I remember seeing a street sweeper pushing his brush, enjoying the sunshine, and me thinking: Now that's a cushy number.

I wasn't earning enough on the building site so I got a second job – washing dishes in a restaurant. My boss was the sous-chef, a dictatorial Turk who enjoyed shouting at me. By the second night the sous-chef was no longer there and the chef yelled at me as soon as I walked in:

- Where the hell is that useless Turk?
- No idea.
- Can you cook?
- Me?
- Get over here and start making salads!
- I'm just the dish washer.
- Screw the dishes, get over here. Now!

He grabbed a handful of lettuce and threw individual leaves, very precisely, onto a line of plates that were neatly lined up on the stainless steel counter. Then he showed me a huge jug in which the salad dressing was kept. My task was to prepare these side salads, drip a blob of vinaigrette onto them, wait for the main dish to be dropped on the plate and then get them out to the waitresses. The speed, atmosphere and swear words were exhilarating.

After that second night in the kitchen I decided to celebrate my promotion by going out to get drunk. There was no way I could go straight to bed after working until 2am and Edinburgh has always been a great city to go boozing in. Later that night I ran into Najma, a beautiful dark-skinned former girlfriend of my brother Moona, and we ended up drinking far too much beer. We both staggered back to my place, singing and swaying and shouting.

We got into the house and I put an LP on the record player. My brother Moona popped his head into the room and said:

- What the hell are you doing?
- Come and join us? We're gonna make a joint.

Moona, my youngest brother, was only about 16 at the time – and that night he started behaving like an adult. He calmly turned off the music, sat down beside me and started talking, as if giving a pep talk at a sports game:

- You know Stewart is going to Thailand tomorrow morning?
- Yeah...
- And he'll be there for two weeks, with the Boss [our Mother]. This is

the first time in ages that we will have the place to ourselves.

- Yeah, s'pose so.

- And you're blowing it. Coming in here at this time, making that racket. You're gonna wake him up and freak him out. Either shut up or get outta here. Please.

But it was too late. Stewart's face then appeared through the door with an intense look that said I'm wide awake, fully alert and haven't slept a wink. He asked me to come upstairs and then told me to get into the bath. I protested. I didn't want a bath, especially with him watching. And what about the beautiful drunken girl that I'd left downstairs? He told me I needed to sober-up fast. I said I needed to go to bed. He ran the bath and went to get me a cup of coffee.

Then he hit me with a bombshell: he wanted me to go to Thailand instead of him. My befuddled brain couldn't comprehend this so I got into the bath and listened:

- I have a plane ticket for Bangkok leaving at seven this morning [Stewart paused and looked at his watch]. We've got less than three hours. Rupert, I want you on that plane instead of me.

- What?

- I've been thinking about it all night. I can't leave Moona on his own here, he's only 16. You're in no state to look after him. Your Mother would enjoy a holiday with you, and you want to travel. I'm giving you a free ticket.

My brain stopped working. I couldn't think, couldn't come up with the right words and couldn't stop the room swaying. I was pickling in a hot bath, trying to stay awake and vaguely aware of conflicting feelings: the opportunity of a free ticket to Asia; depriving Stewart of his holiday due to my irresponsibility; lumbering Moona with a guardian just when he thought he could have a moment of freedom. These thoughts weren't coming together, they were like different coloured liquids that weren't mixing properly in a glass. I couldn't speak and I couldn't resist Stewart's determination. Next thing I knew I was sitting in First Class, flying over Europe and wondering how on earth I had managed to get there.

- Where's Stewart? asked my Mother when I met her in Bangkok Airport.

She had no idea that I was coming out to Thailand instead of Stewart. There were no emails or mobiles in those days. I was so excited by the turn of events that I didn't notice if my Mother was upset at finding out that he hadn't turned up. My explanation of what had happened the night before didn't make a lot of sense, but it was the truth and I didn't want to dwell on it. I wanted to explore Thailand, a country I knew absolutely nothing about.

My Mother had been told that the Oriental Hotel in Bangkok was the best hotel in the world and she was expecting Stewart to take her there, at least for a night. I'd talked to Stewart the night before about money:

- Have you got any money on you, Rupert?

- Er... no...

- No problem. I've got a fifty quid note you can have.

- Fifty quid. Is that enough?

- Do you have a credit card?

- Yes.

- Good. What's the credit limit?

- A thousand pounds.

- Excellent. Spend it all. I'll reimburse you. Give your Mother a good time.

A thousand pounds was a lot of cash in 1984. My Full Grant at university, for rent and living expenses, was £2,000 a year. I felt like a rich aristocrat who had the world at his feet; with these funds we could go anywhere. We spent our first night in the Oriental Hotel, which was impressive, but I kept wondering why it was considered the best hotel in the world.

I had never seen anywhere as crowded as Bangkok – a vast sprawl around a big dirty river that was full of little wooden boats, each one packed with exotic fruits and mysterious looking boxes. The sky was overcast and the air was humid and smelt of spices and petrol. It was so hot that we sweated continually. Each street was blocked with cars, each pavement was full of people hurrying along and I was glad to find that the Thais are a friendly people.

What do people do on holiday in Thailand? We found out that tourists' head for the beach or the hills and because we were fabulously wealthy we did both. We flew south to an island called Phuket, a hilly paradise covered in forest, beaches and bulldozers. We hired a motorbike and a grass hut by the beach.

We soon realised that Thailand is riddled with prostitutes; not the middle-age toughs that used to patrol my street in Liverpool but young and enticing beauties. I was afraid of getting tangled up with them but they assumed my Mother, who was attractive and young-looking, was my girlfriend and they left me alone. But when I was on my own these pushy young women would follow me and hustle like drug pushers.

I went to the beachside disco one night, was given juice and spirits, got totally smashed and went into a blackout. I came to my senses in a shower with a young man washing my back. How the hell did I end up here? I realised what was going on and felt a stab of fear; I was being prepared for homosexual sex. In a panic I got dressed and hurried out past a group of young men who lay expectantly on mats.

Many of the prostitutes I had seen were transvestites. The best looking woman in the disco turned out to be a guy, which I found out by being in his powerful grip on the dance floor. Thailand had developed this type of economy because of the huge numbers of American soldiers who would come over the border to Rest and Recuperate from their pointless war in Vietnam. I was told that there were over one million prostitutes in Thailand and that sex plays an important part in their economy.

We got the bus back to Bangkok. The southern part of Thailand is a thin strip of land covered in forest and when passing through the thickest part of the forest the bus was stopped by a squad of heavily armed soldiers. They swarmed onto the bus and checked my passport and the ID cards of the locals. I was surprised to see that the soldiers were friendly and that I wasn't terrified.

We didn't hang around in Bangkok. We got a modern sleeper train to the northern city of Chiang Mai. I was most impressed by the fact that our wagon had a shower, something I had never seen before on a train. We found a guide who took us trekking through the jungle of the Golden Triangle – a vast area covering parts of Thailand, Burma and Laos and said to be the world's second biggest area of opium production. We would hear the odd explosion but none of the locals seemed even to notice them and I knew nothing about the struggles taking place between national armies, drug smugglers and liberation fighters hidden in the jungle.

We had been sold a Jungle Trek but the trees seemed rather thin and ordinary. There was no soundtrack of chattering monkeys, screaming parrots and the other sounds that accompany all televised presentations of the jungle. We could have been in France.

But when we reached the first village I realised we were in another world. I'd seen primitive villages in books and films but only at that moment did it strike me how attractive they are. Everything about these villages was magical: the surrounding forest, the lack of roads and modern communication, the simple houses and especially the half-naked people who were curious and so different from anyone I had ever come across. They would watch our every move with a patience I had never seen before, in a manner that felt unthreatening.

I was intrigued by these people and particularly by their feet. Because they never used shoes their feet were much stronger than ours, with well-developed muscles around each toe. It was almost as if each of their toes had a personality, unlike our toes which are crushed into one ugly shape by constantly being trapped in tight shoes. Some of them had sores and fungus and I dispensed tiny amounts of anti-fungal cream that I happened to have in my bag for athlete's foot. They seemed very grateful, word spread and soon there was a queue of people wanting a dab of cream.

The villagers' houses were inspiring. A simple wooden frame would be covered with grass and leaves. Thin strips of split bamboo were used to make floors and these flexed every time you stepped on them – with bare feet of course; entering with muddy walking boots would have been criminal. The buffaloes lived downstairs, on the earth under the hut, and the family above. You could see, hear and smell the animals but it all seemed quite natural. They would invite us in and give us glasses of milky coloured alcohol, strange food and sometimes opium – which we smoked from pipes while lying on our sides – a narcotic that made the place seem like paradise.

They used tiny candles and I was really impressed that even the young children were aware of the risk of fire; as the candles guttered and burned out a small child would nimbly manoeuvre across the bamboo floor and, in a single movement, grab it and extinguish it. I was also impressed that my Mother entered into the spirit of all this like a young traveller; gone were the worries of publishing and running a big unruly family in Scotland. I had never seen her so relaxed.

Back in Bangkok the money was running low and my Mother was quite happy to stay in a cheap hotel. She had shared in my enthusiasm for the villages and encouraged me to visit somewhere else on the way home. My fear of travel had been replaced with a thirst for discovering Asia and a wonder for primitive lifestyles.

I changed my return ticket so that I could stop off in New Delhi and spend a month in India. The ticket didn't cost much but I was down to my last hundred dollars and surely this wasn't enough for a month in India? In

Thailand I had spent over a thousand bucks in just two weeks but we 'd been living well and India was said to be really cheap.

It turned out that a hundred dollars was more than enough to get round India in 1984. Everything seemed to cost a dollar or less: a delicious spicy meal from a street hawker, a bed in a cheap hostel or a train ticket to Agra, location of the Taj Mahal. I got a bus into the Himalayas, for not much more than a dollar, and ended up in Kashmir. The journey over those mountains was the most terrifying trip of my life and a useful opportunity to exorcise my fear. The bus was packed to the gunnels and just when I thought it can't posibly get any fuller, it would stop and more people would push their way in. The noise -- people yelling, and Indian music blasting through tinny speakers – was deafening but strangely inspiring. I held a place by the windscreen and the more full the bus got the more bodies pressed me up against the front windscreen. Eventually I was held there like an insect squashed against the glass, unable to move.

I had a bird's-eye view of the Himalayas which were unfolding before us – wave after wave of high, black ridges. The road was narrow, twisted and steep. The black-bearded driver gunned the vehicle to its top speed until the engine screamed in protest. When he hurled his vehicle round the first sharp mountain corner the front end of the bus was momentarily suspended over open space. I caught a glimpse of a bottomless chasm, hundreds of feet deep – and I knew we were were all going to die. I closed my eyes and imagined the bus was already flying through open space and in less than a second we would hit the ground.

Somehow we were still driving. We had survived although nobody but me seemed to notice our miraculous escape. And then the same thing happened at the next corner, and the next. The driver, who was obviously insane, showed no sign of slowing down. I had the same shock when oncoming trucks would hurtle down the road towards us, each one of which would be taking up more than half of the road – as was our bus – making an impact inevitable. But neither driver made any sign of slowing down and they would pass each other smoothly.

Gradually I realised that we weren't going to die and this was just how they drive buses in that part of the world. The driver and the passengers showed no sign of fear so why should I? What would be the point of worrying? All I could do was get off the bus and walk but it was a cold, hostile environment out there and it was getting dark. On that journey I felt as if I was looking death in the face and I learned to accept it, to not fear it, and as soon as I did this I started to enjoy every moment.

The bus drove through the night and we would stop for short breaks now and again, at tea shops in the middle of nowhere. Rickety wooden beds were laid out on the road and huge kettles of tea were bubbling on charcoal fires. The next day we passed a small mountain town and the bus stopped. On the pavement opposite the bus was a man in a white jacket pulling at the teeth of another man in a chair. The man in white was presumably a dentist and he was pulling with all his strength. The man in the chair made no sound. Eventually the tooth came out and the dentist held it up triumphantly. The seated man bent forward and spat big gobs of blood into a white metal bowl that was placed between his feet. Half a dozen other men were seated in a semi-circle, looking on approvingly.

In Srinigar, the capital of Kashmir, I stayed in a House Boat on Dal Lake, where high cliffs seem to climb directly out of the water. I spent an evening with the boathouse family, who stayed on a small wooden vessel behind the one I was in. Crossing from one to the other involved walking along thin planks suspended above the water. We sat on the wooden floor of a large room that had no furniture whatsoever, and the evening's entertainment consisted of watching the smallest children play. The toddlers were responsible for the infants and the older kids were in charge of them. It all seemed to make perfect sense.

Many years later I realised that I had visited India during its curious period of economic isolation, a period that lasted from independence in 1947 until the early 1990s. Before getting entangled in globalism and becoming the back office for capitalism, India occupied an unusual position between the global blocks of Capitalism and Communism. They used to describe themselves as a Non-Aligned nation, along with Yugoslavia and a few other countries, and as Fabian Socialists who aspire to socialism without the hassle and violence of a revolution.

You could see small shops and individual businesses on every street – so they obviously weren't Communist – but the leadership believed in Marxist ideals and western investors were kept out. The cars were ancient British models, and the roads were full of buses, bullocks, hand painted trucks, ancient British Enfield motorbikes and tiny home-made motorised trikes they called phut phuts.

It was the only non-Communist country that refused the Coca Cola Company the right to sell its fizzy drinks. I felt particularly close to India as my grandfather was born here, as were his parents. For hundreds of years my ancestors were soldiers in the British Army in India and I felt this gave me a special connection to the place. In a way I felt like I was coming home.

Getting back to Heathrow airport in London was one of the most depressing moments of my life. I was missing Asia as if I had left my lover behind and I didn't want to be in this freezing, mechanized, impersonal, unfriendly hell. I saw a couple of tough English lads, bursting with pent-up aggression, standing at the entrance to the airport. They looked at me as if to say: Look at that hippy! He needs a good kicking! and it struck me how I had never felt fear like this during all my recent travels in Asia, where people are a lot poorer.

I was so badly underdressed – sandals and shorts and my ridiculous looking leather jacket -- that I felt real humiliation. All I could afford was an undergound ticket to North London where I stood on the M1 motorway, held up a piece of cardboard that said Edinburgh and waited to get a lift home.

I had no idea that home could be so depressing. I was suffering from culture shock and talked about Asia continually, sharing my travel experiences with anyone who'd listen. Then my brother Gavin, who has always been honest to the point of brutality, said: Here he goes! Talking about Asia again. It struck me like a physical blow, a shock, a stab of shame, as I realised that perhaps not everyone wants to hear all about my travels! I learned something very useful that day: don't talk to people about your travels unless they seem genuinely interested; and it soon became clear that most people are not.

Although I loved the city of Liverpool I found the university itself really boring. What helped me stick it out was mixing with ordinary people. In my first year I had hung out on a building site – there was too much drinking and fooling around to say that I actually worked. I was one of the few students with the opportunity to get to know working class Liverpudlians, or Scousers, and this felt like a privilege.

In my final year I worked as a travelling salesman for Canongate Publishing, a struggling publishing company that my parents had set up in 1974. My job had started out as a challenge by Dave, a bearded Australian roughneck, who always had a rollup sticking out of the side of his mouth. Dave was in charge of distribution which meant he spent his days wrapping up books and muttering at anyone who walked past. When I told him I was studying history and politics at Liverpool University he laughed:

- Liverpool! They're illiterate down there!
- How can you say that?
- There's not one bookshop in Liverpool!
- But I've been to some really interesting bookshops in Liverpool. There's an interesting one called News from Nowhere…
- Humph. Well they've never ordered a single book from us!

One thing led to another and I ended up working as a book rep for them in Liverpool. I bought a silvery suit from an Oxfam charity shop for two quid and a plastic yellow bag, with Kodak branded all over it, into which I could fit plenty of new Canongate books, most of which were by obscure Scottish poets. My training consisted of Dave reluctantly showing me how to use an invoice book.

The bookshops in Liverpool did buy from me and I was delighted to be sent to sell books in another unknown area of the map – south west England – where I honed my camping skills. By day I was wearing a suit and driving a decrepit old Vauxhall Viva that I had bought for £200, and in the evenings I would change into jeans, carry a rucksack, cook dinner on a petrol stove and sleep in a waterproof sleeping bag on a beach. I loved the idea of changing from a besuited sales rep into a backpacker sleeping on a beach.

The final year of university dragged on and I couldn't wait to make my grand escape. I had a flat in the centre, in Toxteth, and my routine was fairly nocturnal. When I went to lectures I tended to fall asleep, and during one particularly boring seminar I fell asleep as I was talking.

We were limbering up to leave university. Big companies and public institutions came to make fancy presentations and size up the best students. This was called the Milk Round and my friends saw it as the logical next step, the obvious way to plug into a career. The idea was to choose what branch of industry suited you and friendly career officers would give advice. The top spot was diplomacy but you needed a First in your finals just to get an interview. If you weren't sure what to do with your life you went for accountancy and the lowest of the low was sales. The secret intelligence services were recruiting too; they hired the biggest ruffian I knew, an alcoholic brute of a rugby player, on the basis that he was studying Russian.

I had my own plan: I was going to hitchhike to Shanghai. At the university's Careers Office they weren't impressed with this; China was unknown to them as a career destination as it was under hard-line Communist rule. They said that good jobs in the financial sector were available in Hong Kong – still a British colony at the time – but I had been a mathematical disaster area in school so that conversation didn't go anywhere. But they did come up with one useful suggestion: perhaps the People's Republic of China needed English teachers? The address of the Chinese Embassy in London was located and I wrote them a letter.

The Chinese Embassy wrote back, confirming that they needed English teachers and asked me to undergo a series of blood tests and fill in a massive form. This is my big chance, I thought, surprised at how easy it was all turning out. I went to a local clinic and the nurse was amazed at how many different blood tests the Embassy wanted but she proceeded anyway and filled up five different syringes with my blood – until I passed out on the chair. The embassy never replied to my application but this just made me more determined to get to China.

There was also a political angle to all this. Much of the northern hemisphere was under Communist control at the time: the map was red from the China Sea to the Adriatic and I was attracted by the fact that this red blob on the map was considered a dangerous no-go area by most people I knew. I wanted to get away from the comfort and security of bourgeois life and get a job without the assistance of my parents' good reputation. Every job I had had until then was due, in some way, to family influence and I wanted to prove to myself that I could get a job on my own. My grandmother was a Conservative voter who hated Socialism and Communism and all things left wing. Anyone who votes Labour, she would say, should go and live in Russia. That will show them what it's like. When I was a kid this kind of talk would scare the wits out of me but later on it was an inspiration.

At sixth form college in Edinburgh my politics teacher had been a true Communist and he converted me to look at the world through the prism of Marxism. Although the effect didn't last very long – how can you hand over absolute power to the Dictatorship of the Proletariat and expect them to share it? – it did encourage me to go and see what it was like to live in a Communist country. Marxism is a useful analytical tool for seeing the world from the perspective of the underdog; it helped me understand it better and build-up my confidence to explore.

One of my best friends at University was a Northern Irish charmer called Peter Morgan. He studied architecture and only came to life at night. His room was on the ground floor of a student block near the best pubs in Toxteth, the city centre area that became synonymous with the 1981 riots. Drunken friends would knock on his window at all hours of the night and he used to say he hated being interrupted but whenever I showed up he was keen to chat, drink and smoke. One night he taught me what it's like to experience fear.

I knocked on his window after a late night boozing session and he invited me in. He was drawing with intensity on one of those huge draughtsman tables that can be moved to different angles. There was a single anglepoise lamp that lit up his work but left the room in darkness. I saw a tube of lip moistuiriser and rubbed it on my lips. Pete's face suddenly dropped and after a long pause he spoke:

- Did you use my lipsalve?

- Yeah. So what?

- You shouldn't have done that.

- Why not?

- Have you got little cracks on your lips?

- Yeah.

- Oh dear. You know I've been away a lot recently?

- Yeah.

- Well, I haven't told anyone yet but I've been diagnosed with AIDS. I've been getting intensive treatment for it but I've not got long to live. I also have little cracks on my lips and I just used that lipsil. That means I've probably passed it onto you. I'm really sorry Rupert.

I stood there in the dark and the silence for what seemed like an eternity as his words sank in. I was going to die. I didn't have long to live; a year, maybe two, perhaps just months. How long do people with AIDS survive? It was a newly discovered disease at the time and the media used it to put the fear of God into my generation.

I was overcome with fear, as if I had been hit by a train. I could see my life flashing by. My body became instantly weak and I couldn't stand up any more. I wanted to projectile vomit across the room and the contents of my bowels felt ready to burst out onto Pete's floor. I was gripped by terror, frozen to the spot and it took all of my energy to focus on one simple task: to lie down on the floor and try desperately to control my body. I was wrestling with an overwhelming feeling of panic that I was about to die – not in six months time but right now. Marijuana can contribute to these feelings of panic and I had smoked several joints that evening.

I felt as if I was lying in my grave. Gradually I accepted the fact that I was going to die and I realised I must stand up and deal with it: I would face the last days of my life like a man. The feelings of uncontrollable sickness passed and I stood up and faced Pete, shook his hand solemnly – as if for the last time – went home and lay in bed wondering what I should do with the time I had left. By now I had found a sense of calm and had the wild feeling of fear under control. The next few days passed in a blur. I couldn't think of anything special to do with the rest of my life and neither was I ready to tell anyone; I knew they would react with horror and make a big deal out of it. I just wanted to ignore it and get on with my life.

A few days later I ran into Pete and he casually told me that the whole thing was a wind-up: he didn't have AIDS but he had got a lot of laughs out of convincing me that I did. He had told our group of friends and they were all smirking at my strange behaviour.

Pete knew it was a cruel trick but I was grateful to be alive – I felt like he had given me a new lease of life. To move from the fear of death to the knowledge that I could live my life to the full was a powerful and liberating experience.

Sometime later Pete drove up to Edinburgh in a hired car. I met him in a tiny village just outside of Edinburgh where I had been walking in the hills; we had agreed to meet at a particular spot on the Edinburgh road and I was going to guide him to our family home. By the time he showed up it was dark and I got into his car. We started chatting intensely and he was driving slowly down the narrow country lane to my place.

Suddenly he turned into a huge field, stopped chattering and stepped on the gas. The grass was wet and he pulled on the handbrake, spun the steering wheel and went into a long skid that seemed to go on forever. I was used to his reckless driving and knew that he was quite competent behind the wheel. It was unlikely that he'd take us through a drystone dyke and, even if he did, a spot of bother with the police was exactly what he needed.

Then he stopped the car and asked if I would like to drive. What young man can resist an invitation to drive a car recklessly? So I stepped out of the passenger door to make my way round to the driver's side. Then he zoomed off, leaving me standing alone in the darkness. What's this all about? I wondered calmly. Pete reached the far end of the field, turned round so the headlights were pointing at me, stopped and gunned the engine. I felt like I was in a bad movie but there was no script, director or stunt coordinator.

He started driving towards me and built up more and more speed. One option was to run to the edge of the field but it was so far away that I couldn't even see it. I would stay exactly where I was and jump out of the way at the very last moment. He was getting closer and closer, faster and faster, still heading directly for me. I didn't panic; my mind was calm and adrenalin was keeping me alert.

When the car was just a few metres away Pete steered to the right. But he was going too fast, the grass was too wet and the car didn't steer as he wanted. It started to skid directly towards me. I waited until the last possible moment before moving and, when the time came to run, I slipped and fell on the wet grass. The car made a whooshing sound as it passed by my legs. He missed me by a matter of inches.

The car came to a shuddering halt not far away and Pete got out. He was ashen-faced, shaking and kept apologising. He realised that his prank had almost resulted in his friend getting killed and this really shook him up. What haunted him most was the idea of having to tell my mother, with whom he got on really well, that he had killed her son. He was surprised that I wasn't upset but he was so angry with himself that what good would it have done? There was a certain satisfaction in seeing Pete being humbled by his own recklessness.

Having finished university and gone back to Edinburgh, the big challenge was to raise enough cash to get to Shanghai – my target destination. Every job I'd ever done had only paid peanuts; washing dishes, selling books and working on building sites had been useful experiences but none paid more than was needed for booze, food and smokes.

Up in Edinburgh an opportunity soon presented itself. I had often helped out my father in his trucking business and I knew the ropes: I could pack valuable antiques and large paintings into the back of a truck without breaking anything. I knew how to drive his Three Tonner truck and was used to his non-stop hours. Trouble was he only paid the going rate for unskilled labour, about twenty quid a day, and I needed a lot more.

My father had a business partner called Gerry, a smooth talking Irishman who had an impressive moustache and, as my Grandmother would say, he could talk the hind leg off a donkey. Gerry fancied himself as an antique dealer, and would go off on important business trips. He was also a heavy drinker and womaniser. My father would get really angry when he didn't show up for a job and I would be sent to pick up his truck and stand in for him.

Then Gerry announced that he was going to Texas as he had some big deals cooking; he mentioned antiques but refused to share any details. Would I be willing to look after the truck for two weeks? This was my opportunity to make some big money fast. Being in possession of Gerry's truck meant that I could make the transition from driver and unskilled humper to equal partner. It meant that I could charge the full fee that my father would normally charge the client. If I worked like a slave over the next two weeks maybe I could earn enough to hit the road.

What I didn't know was that Gerry was up to his eyeballs in debt and was, in fact, doing a runner. We never saw him again and I'm pretty sure that his story about going to Texas to stitch up an antiques deal was another of his eloquent fairy tales. I also didn't know that his Mercedes truck was on hire purchase and a payment was expected every month; he hadn't left me any instructions about debt payments. Just the key. For two miraculous months I was able to make big money – £500 a week, which was a fortune in those days – and not once did anyone ask about debt repayments, taxes or the whereabouts of Gerry. It seemed too good to be true and I soon realised that this was my chance to earn enough cash to get to China.

I worked at fever pitch past the original two-week term and carried on for two months. I would drive down to England every week, pick up paintings from artists living in remote cottages, deliver them to galleries in central London, sleep in the back of the truck, sometimes drive for 18 hours a day and go for drinking sessions when I was in the vicinity of friends. I learned to get through the city at high speed, to intimidate taxi drivers (the bullies of London traffic), to park and unload in impossibly narrow streets, reverse down alleyways with inches to spare and sweet-talk policemen, traffic wardens and officious porters. It was a great job and within two months I had saved £2,000 and was ready to go to China.

Then I had to overcome the biggest challenge of all: complacency. I was earning up to £500 a week and having a great time with my girlfriend in London who would give me full body shiatsu massages. The reasons for not going anywhere were building up fast. I could settle down in Britain! My father wanted to give up his fine art transportation business and part of me wanted to take it over. But my father was dead against the idea: You don't want to work 18 hour days for the rest of your life, have no friends and sleep in the truck! Hit the road. Travel. Live your own life.

Finally I got the impetus to get up and go. My best friend from school, an artist called Christian Anstice, reminded me that we had planned to meet in Berlin on February the 20th (1986) and he called to say: You'd better be there.

It was time to finally tear myself away from the comforts of life in the UK and do the rounds of saying goodbye. Everyone asked me when I was coming back but I really didn't know. My father told me to park the truck near the garage where Gerry had bought the van. They'll know what to do with it, he said. And that was it.

Berlin back then was entirely surrounded by a high security wall and guarded round the clock by dogs, landmines and thousands of heavily armed soldiers. The whole thing was a bizarre hangover from the Second World War. In 1945 Germany had been occupied by the allied powers and in the areas controlled by America, Britain and France free elections were allowed – and that part became known as West Germany, or the Federal Republic. The Russian army controlled the eastern part of the country – East Germany or the Democratic Republic – where Russian-style elections took place and Communism was imposed.

As Berlin was located deep within the Russian zone, one would have thought it should have become a Communist-controlled city like Dresden or Leipzig. For some reason that I never really understood, Berlin was divided up between the allied powers and this resulted in the western part of Berlin becoming an island of Capitalism in a sea of Communism. The status of West Berlin was backed up by American military muscle, and their nuclear arsenal. By the time I got there the political situation was relatively settled and the city functioned well. It was connected to West Germany by an airport and a fenced-off motorway that was so heavily guarded that you couldn't stop anywhere without East German troops appearing.

My impression of West Berlin was that it was populated by artists, gays and drifters. If you wanted to avoid the military draft in West Germany you moved to Berlin where that particular law didn't apply. The West German government was worried about the city becoming depopulated so it offered incentives like this so people would go and live there. Christian and I stayed with a Scottish artist called Fiona, a friend of my skateboarding brother Moona. We visited art galleries which I got bored of pretty fast. I was more interested in the nightlife, which started after midnight and went on until nine in the morning. I had never seen anything like it. In Britain the pubs all closed at 11pm, thanks to a law from the First World War that was designed to keep the workforce sober, but in West Berlin there was no such thing as closing time. And the pubs weren't the smoky, crowded, noisy pits I was used to – they were more like art galleries with smoked-glass tables and great music. They served beer in large, elegant brandy glasses.

Christian was gone after a few days and I was left on my own, feeling a bit disorientated and not quite sure how to start my epic journey round the world. Fiona lived alone in a big flat and said I could stay as long as I wanted.

The most interesting part of the city was East Berlin, the Communist controlled sector, where the architecture was verging on the grotesque. Getting there was exciting. You had to pass through what was probably the most famous border crossing in the world: Checkpoint Charlie. On the western side there were no passport controls at all, just relaxed American soldiers. On the eastern side there were scores of armed military officials who checked passports, searched bags and took the whole thing very seriously. Anyone caught trying to escape from the Communist part would be hunted down by dogs, blown up by landmines or shot. There was an exhibition at Checkpoint Charlie documenting some of the more dramatic escape attempts. People used to dig tunnels, hide in cars and risk their lives to escape the restrictions of East Germany.

One evening on the Eastern side I passed a pub – a thin room, full of smoke, packed with people and roaring with voices – and it reminded me of pubs in Scotland. So different from the smart but staid pubs in West Berlin. The only thing I missed about Scotland was the pubs. To me they represent community.

Berlin has a big underground railway system, the Metro, which was built before the city was divided up by the Allied Powers. An agreement had been made at some point whereby the western side controlled the metro system and the Communist side blocked access to it for their citizens. I wasn't aware of any of this at the time but I was stunned when the train didn't stop at an underground station that seemed to be lit with just one fluorescent strip and looked like it hadn't been swept in years. I saw soldiers in stylish grey jackets which reached down to their hips, thick belts round their waists and high black boots. They each carried a short machine gun on a strap round their shoulders and stood menacingly on the platform with their legs apart, looking at our carriage intently. The Metro had been a popular escape route – people would hang onto the bottom of trains so that they could find freedom in the west.

One of the main reasons I spent so much time in Berlin was to get visas for all the countries I planned to go through: Poland, Czechoslovakia, Hungary, Romania, Bulgaria, not to mention Iran, Pakistan, India and China. I had started this process over the previous few months – visiting spooky embassies in London. The Romanian Embassy was in a huge Victorian villa and looked like something out of a Dracula movie. Getting visas is a time consuming process but the one thing I didn't have in the UK was time, as I was so busy making money driving that truck. I suspect that if my friend Christian hadn't insisted I come to Berlin I might never have left. Berlin proved to be a useful staging post where I could prepare for the next leg of my journey. I didn't need to think about a Chinese visa until I got to Hong Kong -- if I ever got there; it still seemed so impossibly far away and the money I had brought with me no longer seemed like such a vast hoard.

The first challenge was to get a visa for the Islamic Republic of Iran, a country that stood right in the middle of my planned hitchhiking route. Iran had been taken over by Islamic Fundamentalists in 1979 and they didn't have a very good impression of us Brits. Our colonial history there is a shameful one and I wasn't sure they would give me a visa at all. But I had to try. Several weeks later I stood in the snow outside the Iranian Embassy, clutching my passport with a fresh visa in it. It was time to move on.

Just before leaving Berlin I had an attack of fear and paranoia. It happened late one night in Fiona's flat, which was large and empty. Fiona was out, as she was most nights. The rooms were cold and dark and the street lights were casting strange shadows. I was smoking a joint on my own and contemplating the future. I had smoked a lot of pot over the last few years and I believed it had made me more aware, but I knew it had also made me lazy and disconnected from university.

I started to feel paranoid. The more I smoked the more scared I became – a horrible, crawling feeling in my stomach and on my skin. The Iranian visa was the spark: around the visa stamp was a lot of Arabic writing and I became convinced that this was my death sentence which said This is a British spy! Arrest him immediately! I imagined being hauled off to a crowded dungeon, put in chains, starved, screamed at, flogged in public, tortured and eventually decapitated.

The Iranian fear was avoidable as I had a choice: I didn't have to go there. I could fly over Iran. No sooner had I decided to do just that the next shock came marching in: I was trapped in this city and it was surrounded by the Red Army. What if the Russians decided that I was not allowed to leave? Maybe they had talked to the Iranians? Surely they would lock me up and throw away the key?

Fortunately, I managed to sleep and by morning my living nightmare was just a memory. Something good came out of this episode: I gave up smoking cannabis. I realised that if I was going to hitchhike across Europe and Asia it wasn't in my best interest to use a drug that could make me feel so scared. It wasn't until that morning in Berlin in 1986 that I realised the importance of giving up dope. I tried some many years later, in the basement flat of a doctor friend in London, but the demons of paranoia came on strong and I realised that I must give up this shit for good.

It was time to hit the road but I was running out of cash. I had spent too much time in this damned city. Even though I was living frugally and wasn't paying rent, the cash was dripping through my fingers as if it were sand. What could I do? How could I earn some money? The last thing I wanted to do was call home and say Mummy! Please help! I've run out of money. It would have been so humiliating. I didn't know enough German to be able to get a job in Berlin and I wanted out of this town. It was becoming suffocating. I looked at the map and considered my options: Poland, Czechoslovakia, Austria, Hungary; not much chance of getting a job in those parts. The only modern capitalist city on my route was Vienna: Hmm...I wonder...Could I get a job there? I had to find out and I got the train to Vienna.

Now that I was finally away from home I had so many questions. Why was I planning to travel by train? Wasn't I supposed to be hitching? Why was I planning a route through South-East Europe? Wasn't that a long and complicated way to get to China? How much would all the visas cost? What about exchange rate losses? Why not get the train to Moscow? I could get the legendary Trans-Siberian Express, stop off in Mongolia, and then arrive in Beijing dusty and experienced in the ways of the traveller. I didn't have a neat answer to my choice of route but I did want to see as many of those strange East European countries as possible.

If I didn't make some money soon there was no way I would get anywhere near China. I had underestimated how much things cost. I was down to $200 and I needed to build up my stash to over $2,000 before proceeding eastwards. This became my formula: when the cash dropped below $200 I had to get a job; when more than $2,000 was saved – hit the road. Would I be able to get a job in Vienna?

German words are so long, the language seemed impossible and I doubted I could ever learn it. I was also studying Mandarin Chinese with the aid of a book from the 1930s and I remember thinking: Chinese is easier to learn than German – it's just a series of monosyllables; whereas German words are really long and almost impossible to remember.

Germany has one of the best railway systems in Europe but the trains it deployed for going east, into the Communist world, were old and run-down. My impression of the Communist Bloc, a vast stretch of the northern hemisphere, was that all the nations were the same. They were all toiling under Moscow's rule, uniformity in all things was the order of the day; they wore the same clothes, drove the same cars, did the same things, learned the same Communist-inspired history and took their orders from Russia. If you had asked me: Why on Earth would you visit such a boring place? I would have told you that I wanted to see for myself how dreadful it really was and if this impression of uniformity was really true.

I finally made my move and got a train ticket to Warsaw. After a few minutes the train stopped in East Berlin's hauptbanhof (main station). There was a wild bustle of activity as hundreds rushed for the carriages, clouds of steam rose into the black metal roof arches; uniforms everywhere; a terrific noise of people and engines; announcements were barked out in an officious tone. The only colour in that station was black and the steam and condensation made the surfaces shine.

That stop in East Berlin was short but the compartment I had been sitting in alone now filled up with noisy passengers, each one of whom seemed to be carrying twice his weight in bags, boxes and jerry cans. (I never did work out what was in those jerry cans but I saw scores of them that day). They quickly packed away their contraband, removed the seats and skillfully filled all the spaces underneath. When they were finished and we all sat down I felt like I was in the store room of a grocer's shop. I looked at the grinning faces opposite, tried to decipher their incomprehensible language and realised that the Polish people can be really friendly.

Poland was the second Communist country I visited and even before I got there I realised that it was very different from East Germany. This might seem like stating the obvious, and today would sound ignorant, but I was struggling with the stereotype that all Eastern European countries were the same. But the people from Poland seemed to be different to those I had seen in East Berlin, where they seemed unfriendly and scared. I wondered if the East Germans took Communism more seriously than the Poles? My new Polish friends in the carriage were determined to have a blast; as soon as the journey started they whipped out bottles of vodka and a collapsible metal tumbler and poured a drink. The tumbler was handed to me as if I was part of the gang. There was no polite sipping as we might do in Scotland, it was down-in-one every time followed by a cheer and then a high-pitched discussion. Each round was preceded by a toast and all I could understand was: to you...to us...to our parents...to Poland...to Germany (I'm sure fallen comrades was in there somewhere too). The more I drank the better I seemed to understand their language. By the time we reached our destination we were blind drunk and I felt like we were blood brothers.

The other difference with Poland was the border guards: the man who came to check our passports at the Polish border didn't seem to mind that we were so rowdy. He had white curly hair spurting out from under his cap, rather like horsehair bursting out of an old mattress. He had the tired, resigned air of a grandparent who knows he can't control the kids and has given up trying. He seemed bored but friendly and didn't check my passport or visa too carefully. This was very different from the East German border guards who examined my passport as if it was fake and looked at me as if I was a spy. They looked like they would enjoy torturing me. Their uniforms were well laundered and intimidating but they seemed to have absolutely no sense of humour. I wondered if cracking a joke would land me in jail – at school we had plenty of sick jokes about Germans, Jews, French, Irish, Americans, Pakistanis and Italians. They carried curious square cases over their shoulders and when they opened these the front and top part would fold down and be suspended by little leather straps. This formed a miniature table where they could place the suspect's passport and scrutinise it carefully.

Unlike many travellers I don't like to research a country before visiting it. If you arrive somewhere in a state of ignorance then everything is waiting to be discovered. And I would rather find out what's worth visiting from local people rather than guidebooks. At university I barely studied the Communist countries and so it made sense to head East, to learn about an unknown area. But I did know that Poland had once been erased from the map by their Russian, Austrian and Prussian neighbours, that the Nazis had given them a particularly hard time and that there were rumblings against Communism in the port city of Gdansk. But I knew nothing of its geography and looking out of the train window it looked very flat. In fact, my impression of Poland is that it's a big flat plain stretching into Russia, with a mountain range on its southern border.

Not everyone was as welcoming as my friends on the train. I went to change money at a big bank in the centre of Warsaw and came across the stereotypical Communist woman; a big bully of a beast, oozing irritability. In those days you had to change about $20 a day, at the official exchange rate, for every day you were staying in Poland. This was a way of getting hard currency from tourists, as the official exchange rate was really low compared to what it was on the street (wherever you went men would hustle up to you and whisper change money, showing thick wads of zloty). In fact, the official exchange rate was so artificial that you would get five times more for your dollar on the street than in the bank. It was frustrating to hand over hard-earned cash to an officious hag who gave a fraction of what you could get outside. And the problem with Polish money, or the money from any Communist country for that matter, is that it was totally useless outside that particular country. Everyone in the region wanted US dollars and would grimace at the sight of Polish Zloty, Czech Crowns or Hungarian Forints.

But there was a loophole: every time you exchanged money officially they would give you an elaborate handwritten receipt. I got chatting to a fluent English speaker in the queue at the bank and he told me:

- If you have any zloty left when you leave Poland, show your receipt at the border and they are obliged to exchange it at the original rate.

Maybe this would be an opportunity to get even with a system that seemed intent on cheating me out of my US Dollars. We're not talking about a lot of money here – I only stayed a week and had exchanged only $140 – but it was the principle that mattered. Getting ripped off is a humiliating experience, however small the amount is. When I left Poland I handed over a wad of zloty – that I had exchanged illegally – and had the exquisite pleasure of being given a stash of dollars by a Communist official.

The woman who handed me those dollars could have been the same thickset peasant I had come across in the bank in Warsaw: surly, uncommunicative and wearing a peaked hat that looked as if it never left her greasy scalp. When I asked if I could change money I thought she would laugh dismissively or make a sarcastic comment. Citizens of these countries were strictly forbidden to possess hard currency – a law that didn't seem to stop the money-changers flashing their wads of cash on street corners. It reminded me of parental rules to stop kids drinking and smoking, rules that inspire them to do just that.

She remained expressionless and opened a drawer in a battered wooden table that stood between us. Inside the drawer was Aladdin's cave. It was packed full of banknotes that were scattered all over the place. I saw English Pounds, Swiss Francs and Italian Lira – and plenty of US Dollars – and wondered why someone hadn't robbed them of this treasure by now. She rummaged among the notes, gathered up some dog-eared dollars, tossed them onto the table, closed the drawer and wandered off. She didn't even glance at me as I gathered up the loot. The idea of grabbing what I could from that drawer crossed my mind. In one movement I would have enough cash to get me all the way to China; no need to find a job in Vienna or crawl home in disgrace.

But it was only a thought. These Communist officials may have looked unfashionable but they were formidable – after all, they had managed to stop the use of illegal drugs in their territories, an impossibility in the west. The butch woman who was now picking her teeth on the other side of the room looked like she had wrestled for Poland. Or had she been a champion weightlifter? Overweight people can sometimes move surprisingly fast and she would have caught up with me in seconds, coshed me on the back of the head and slung me in a shallow grave.

I stepped out of the ramshackle customs house and realised that I was the only person there. Where were all the cars? I had taken the scenic route from the southern city of Krakow and from there followed a lonely road up into the Tatra Mountains, a road that led into Czechoslovakia. The border crossing seemed to be at the top of the mountains but I wasn't sure as a thick blanket of mist had descended and all I could see was a bit of

road and a curtain of pine trees. An excellent place for a murder I thought
as I wandered into Czechoslovakia, a country that no longer exists.

Perhaps the most significant thing for me that day wasn't my triumph
over Communism in the form of the money change scam, but the fact
that I had started hitchhiking. It had been my intention to hitch hike from
Scotland to China but I had made a pretty poor job of it so far. I had only
been on trains, planes and buses. When I left Krakow I finally overcome my
complacency and did what all hitchhikers have to do: get to the outskirts
of town, find a good spot by the side of the road, stick out your thumb and
wait for ages before getting a lift.

CHAPTER TWO

- You want a job? Here? In Vienna! Are you mad? You don't even speak German!

My new friend Andras was most amused. He was short, athletic, handsome and spoke fluent English. His family were obviously rich; he had his own flat in the centre of town and didn't seem to work. He also had a small but incredibly fast car – a Peugeot 206 – which he raced round town and in rallies. Andras had studied English in Edinburgh; I had got his number from a friend and invited myself to stay.

Andras pointed to his girlfriend, a long-haired blonde with a perfect figure, a languid aristocratic manner and a beautiful face. Just looking at her was a pleasure.

- Look at her! She's been searching for a job for two years! And she can't get one. How on earth do you think you can?

- Er...I dunno...but does she go out there and ask for work?

- Actually no, she just sits around here all day, and then has me drive her to the shops. Don't you baby?

- Fuck off darling!

- But how on earth are you going to get a job?

- I'm going to walk the streets for three days and go in every shop, restaurant and building site and ask for work.

- Hmm. I've never heard of anyone doing that.

- If I can't find a job within a week I'll have to go back to Edinburgh, and I really don't want to do that. My plan is to travel overland to China.

- Well I think you're absolutely mad but you're welcome to stay here for a couple of nights.

- By the way, how do you say in German: Do you have any work?

- Haben Sie Arbeit?

We were in a small, exquisite flat high up in an old block in central Vienna, overlooking St Stephen's Cathedral – one of the most beautiful buildings I had ever seen. Arriving in Vienna was one of the most memorable moments in my life: never before had I seen such incredible buildings, such gorgeous networks of narrow streets, beautifully preserved houses that you could sometimes glimpse inside – such stylish and well-lit interiors – and well-dressed and handsome people everywhere. The whole place was magical and I couldn't think of anywhere better to live. Andras didn't share my enthusiasm for his home town:

- Vienna is populated by students and old ladies. Budapest is more beautiful and more fun, and it's only down the road.

The next morning I got up early and started looking for work. The unbearable thought of going home motivated me to go from door to door – shops, cafés, cinemas, restaurants, hotels, building sites – and say the magic words: Haben Sie Arbeit? Although I didn't understand the replies, their body language and facial expressions were enough to let me know the answer: no, we don't have any work for you! I dealt with this series of rejections by comparing it to hitchhiking; thousands of cars pass the hapless hitchhiker before one will stop. Working as a sales rep for publishers is similar; most of what you present to the bookshops isn't wanted. Being rejected is a part of everyday life.

After three days I had a success – a hotel where the young manager must have recognised the hungry immigrant's look in my eye. He was vague about what I would do and I didn't like his laid-back manner. When I saw a topless girl in a leaflet saying Come with me! Come on me! Come in me! I decided not to come back unless there was no other option. Fortunately there was.

One of the first places I'd done in Vienna was to visit the British Embassy, where I asked for a job helping set up a British Arts and Crafts exhibition:

- How did you know about the exhibition? asked the friendly young diplomat.

- I met a Scottish artist in Berlin called Gwen Hardy. I asked her advice about getting a job and she advised me to go to Vienna. She told me she was exhibiting down here, at the Künstlerhaus, and that I should ask for a job helping to set it up.

- Hmm, very interesting. And you came all the way here, from Berlin, looking for a job?

- Yes.

Three days later they called the number I had left them – at Andras' flat – and left a message telling me to show up at the Künstlerhaus. In a flurry of excitement I rushed down to the city art gallery and, without any formalities, got my first job abroad. The job only lasted about a week but it banished the pessimism that had been gathering like storm clouds. I threw myself into that job with such energy that the organisers from the British Government's Central Office of Information offered me a job back in London, but I was heading east and had no intention of returning.

My job involved humping paintings around, something I knew all about, and setting up the information desk. But there was plenty of spare time to sneak off and go round more shops and building sites asking for work. One day we were told that Prince Charles and Lady Diana were going to show up in a few hours and officially open the exhibition. The whole place went into a frenzy of excitement. A tough looking crew of security men came round the building looking for bombs and we were all herded into the basement.

The others seemed quite happy to sit around underground and take a break, but I wasn't. I snuck back upstairs, saw the security people leaving and thought I should stand behind the information desk which I had helped to set up. What was the use of an info desk without someone behind the counter? The gallery was deserted – the Austrians were all in the basement drinking, smoking and playing cards and the Brits had disappeared. I had a moment to appreciate the imperial architecture of the building, the light that flooded the place, the windows all along the ceiling and the dramatic paintings that had just been trucked in from London. Künstlerhaus means House of Art and I suspected it was one of the most impressive galleries in Vienna.

There was a commotion coming from the front door and suddenly Charles and Di appeared, as if they were in a real hurry. My first thought was: How can they be so small? They don't look small on TV!

But they looked open-minded, attractive and keen to get away from the crowd of sycophants, officials, and posh hangers-on who came surging through the hall after them; people with excited looks on their faces, delighted to be in contact with British royalty and chattering like monkeys. Not one of the entourage even noticed me or took a second look at the Information Desk – but Charles and Di did.

Prince Charles walked straight up to me and said:

- You from Vienna are you?

- No, just passing through.

- Really? And he was gone.

- Would you like one of our brochures? I said, holding them out to the departing couple and feeling rather ridiculous.

- I would, said Lady Diana. She took a few steps back to where I was standing, took a brochure, walked off and gave me a backward glance and a seductive flicker of the eyelids.

I was smitten. Like everyone else of my generation I had seen hundreds of photos of Lady Diana, and who didn't know about the Royal Wedding of 1981? But I hadn't thought much of her and found the media coverage excruciatingly boring. I was neutral when it came to royalty; they seemed rather harmless and people say they attract tourism – which is rather odd if you think about it; the best argument we can come up with for justifying royalty is that they're a tourist attraction. But seeing her in the flesh was another thing altogether; she was not only beautiful but she looked rather lost and vulnerable. I fell in love instantly, was head over heels, fantasising about what we could do together, plotting about how I could entice her away from Charles.

I crept into the grand room where Prince Charles was giving a speech to the officials, artists and hangers-on. He was reading slowly from a series of elongated cards but I don't remember a word that he said. Lady Di was standing to one side like a beautiful Japanese doll and I wondered if she was bored out of her mind. Does she have to listen to this sort of stuff every day? I wanted to go up behind her and whisper in her ear: Let's get away from this place! I'm going to show you the delightful backstreets of Vienna! But I noticed the beefy men with well trimmed beards and plain clothes who stood at strategic points around the gallery, legs apart, watching everything. Each one carried a little handbag that contained, I was sure, a pistol. These men were calm and motionless and they blended into the crowd, and they had surely spent time honing their killing skills with the Special Forces. It would be a matter of about four seconds to knock me to the ground, stick a pistol in my back and lock me up.

Andras and his girlfriend were astounded that I had managed to find a job, and I took advantage of their surprise to ask if I could stay a few more nights (which stretched to three weeks). Although I was technically employed I knew the job wouldn't last for more than a week, I hadn't seen any actual cash and wanted to avoid paying rent at all costs.

I made a lifelong friend at the Künstlerhaus: Bettina Tucholsky. Bettina always seemed to be smiling; she had chubby cheeks, a mischievous nature and we had conversations that never seemed to end. She had been brought up in London by Jewish parents who had fled the Nazi persecution in Russia. They had set up a small shop and taught their children to speak German, English and Russian. I had never met someone before who could speak as fluently as a native in three languages, and I was intrigued. We would hang out with Paul, a giant of a man with a black moustache and an unhappy marriage.

I soon realised that I wasn't being supervised at all and, as long as I did what was asked, I could disappear off for a few hours and nobody at the gallery would know. I was pounding the streets again, saying Haben Sie Arbeit in every shop, cafe and restaurant I came across.

When I walked into Café Central on Herrengasse in central Vienna I knew my chances of getting a job there were non-existent. There was no point in even asking. I was getting nowhere. Andras would kick me out before long, I'd run out of cash and I'd have to make a humiliating call home begging for a loan so I could crawl back to Scotland in disgrace. A feeling of failure and guilt, for sneaking off for so long from the Künstlerhaus, settled over me as I admired the interior of the Café Central, which was located within a palace – Palais Ferstel. It made me feel small, weak and pathetic.

The gothic interior of the building was more beautiful than anything I had seen yet and the waiters, in tuxedos and bow ties, glided around as if trained at the Bolshoi Ballet School. How could they even consider offering me a job? I didn't know their language, didn't look the part, had never worked as a waiter and surely they already had someone to take out the garbage. This was the place where Hitler used to hang out when he was a penniless artist, so presumably it had been a cheap place for a cup of coffee at one point. Not any longer. Now it was full of grand ladies in fancy hats and there was no way that I could afford the espresso which I craved. So I sat on a chair in the empty hallway and contemplated my situation.

Suddenly a door burst open and a short, fat man in overalls stepped into the hall. He was covered in dust, carrying a piece of wood and seemed oblivious to the fact that his scruffy presence was lowering the tone of this grand location. He slammed the door with a deft kick and shuffled up some steps, leading away from the grand world of Café Central. As if pulled by a string, I stood up and cautiously followed him up the steps and along a marble-floored corridor. He opened another door and disappeared inside a big room with pillars and arches and the familiar sounds of a building site. My heart leapt: here was a building site right under my nose. I had been so pre-occupied with my own misfortunes that I hadn't even noticed. This was more like it! I felt at home on a building site, and what a building site this was! The feelings of unworthiness that I had been wallowing in two minutes earlier were banished like mist in the morning sunlight.

- Haben Sie Arbeit? I asked a kind looking man in a beard. He didn't reject my question immediately, as was the norm, but he looked at me and seemed to be thinking. Perhaps he was wondering why I had a silly grin on my face.

- Upstairs go, he said, in broken English. Go see artists. Maybe have work there.

Artists on a building site? I thanked him profoundly, bounded up the stairs and stepped into a room that was as spacious as a skating rink and as tall as a cathedral. The floor was made of antique wooden tiles that were beautiful. Tall arched windows reached up to the full height of the room and flooded it with light. Halfway up the wall was a narrow balcony, a mezzanine, fronted by elaborate wrought iron railings with imperial eagles painted in gold-leaf. High above where I was gaping, was the pièce de résistance: a wooden ceiling, with elaborate coats of arms painted onto huge roof beams. Later, I discovered that this had been the stock exchange of the Austro-Hungarian Empire, an entity which had controlled much of Central and Eastern Europe until the First World War. I was so stunned by this room that I had forgotten to ask for a job. Just standing there and basking in its beauty was enough.

- Can I help? asked a thin bearded man in fluent English. I snapped out of my daydream and looked at him. He didn't look like the usual roughneck you find on building sites, he wore a white coat and had intelligent, penetrating eyes.

- Er, I'm looking for a job.
- What kind of job?
- Anything.
- Hmm. He was silent for a while and seemed lost in thought. I wondered where he was from as he spoke English fluently, without the tell-tale German-speaker's accent.
- Have you worked on building sites before?
- Yes, in Edinburgh. I am from Scotland.
- Good. You tell him that.

- Tell who?

- Professor Fastl. He is the boss. He's not here. He comes tomorrow. You must come back and tell him you are a student of art, that you studied his work, and you came here from Edinburgh for the great opportunity of working with him. He will like that. Come back tomorrow morning.

- But I can't say that! I'm not an artist. I can't draw anything. And I didn't come here to see him.

- Just come tomorrow and you might get a job.

- But I'm not an artist.

- Not a problem. I'm not an artist. I am a doctor from Poland. I came here to get away from Communism. I will go to the USA soon.

And with that he was off. He walked back to a group of scruffy but handsome artists, at least I presumed they were artists, who were lounging around. They were painting a huge piece of fabric and looking over at me with curiosity. They looked totally out of place on a building site. They also looked bored.

The rest of that day was a torment. It would be a dream come true to get a job in a place like that but I would have to tell a story that was untrue. I didn't know if I had the courage, or if I could keep it up in the face of my interrogator. Wouldn't he see through me at once?

Professor Fastl seemed like a kind man. He was tall, handsome and pre-occupied. He had renovation projects going on all over Austria and wasn't going to look too carefully at this scruffy applicant. He had no reason to not believe my story of studying art in Edinburgh, of working in restoration in that great city – and there was an element of truth here; I had worked on building sites in Edinburgh, and they were renovation jobs – for Stewart Anderson -- builder, climber and my Mother's boyfriend.

- Have you heard of the restoration work of Professor Stewart Anderson? He is the leading expert in the restoration of ancient buildings in Edinburgh. He always praises your work.

- Humph, said the professor.

- It has been my ambition for the last two years to come and see your work.

- Hmm...said the professor, not really listening

- And if there is a chance to experience your restoration work more closely...

- Come here tomorrow morning. Have a trial. We will see then.

On the one hand I was euphoric – I was going to work in the most beautiful building in Vienna. On the other hand I was a fraud and I couldn't bloody paint. How on earth was I supposed to do anything? I was in a panic as I left but Krzysztof, the Polish doctor who'd landed me in this, told me not to worry:

- I will show you how to do this job. It's easy. You will see tomorrow.
- Er, but, I can't paint. I never could.
- It's no problem. Just come tomorrow. It will be fine.

I worked harder than I ever did in my life, desperate to keep this job and cover up my deceit. To my relief, the job was a lot simpler than I'd imagined. A huge renovation project was going on at Palais Ferstel and we were dealing with a relatively small part of it: painting huge pieces of fabric with a simple floral design. Each piece of fabric was about six metres long and two metres wide and took weeks to complete. When it was done we would attach wooden blocks to the back of the fabric, climb up scaffolding that was erected inside a series of huge arches and screw the fabric into the arch. The idea was to make copies of the original floral design that had been painted on the wall, inside the arches, and then cover them with this new fabric. Apparently this would improve the acoustics, as the room was destined to become a concert hall.

It was a bit like drawing in a children's colouring-in book: you just need to make sure you don't spill paint, which is easy if you concentrate. The tricky part was drawing straight lines. I was a nervous wreck: surely everyone could see that my lines weren't straight, my hands were shaking and that I wasn't an artist. My new colleagues, the real artists, seemed happy to have someone new to talk to and they were patient and kind. One of them was a sultry, attractive Hungarian woman called Beata whom I soon fell in love with – a hopeless case as her artist-boyfriend was working alongside us. There was also a small Turkish lady who offered me a room in her spacious apartment, an offer I jumped at.

Her flat was located at the Schottentor (the Scottish Gate) which was five minutes from the job, very central and next to the Sigmund Freud Park. It was an old and spacious flat, the most elegant place I had ever lived in. She used to give me coffee in delicate china cups and then read my fortune in the leaves; one evening she described my father in chilling detail and then showed me the cup and there he was, in outline, among the tea leaves.

I couldn't believe my luck, although I was dreading the moment when Professor Fastl would next visit as he would look at my work, realise I was a fraud, and fire me instantly. My denouement became even more likely when an American artist showed up and managed to paint at twice my speed, whilst gabbling on about his jealous Austrian girlfriend. I was convinced that this friendly, long-haired American would get congratulated and I would get the sack. To my amazement the opposite happened: the American was shouted at by the professor and fired on the spot. He had used brilliant white rather than the magnolia colour the rest of us were using and the professor, who had been very mild-mannered until that point, was furious. I was so nervous about my own performance that I hadn't even noticed what colours we were using; I had simply copied what the other artists were doing.

Gradually I mastered the art straight lines and filling in colour. Once I'd cracked it I started inventing ways of doing the job more quickly. Krzysztof, the silent Pole, was like a foreman in that he organised the supplies. He was also in charge of hanging the huge pieces of fabric in the arches, the trickiest part of the job. I could see that his was the least artistic role of them all and realised that this is what I needed to be doing. I watched what he did, helped him constantly and slipped into his unofficial position by the time he emigrated to America – about a month after I started. I also loved the part that everyone else hated – climbing up the scaffolding and screwing the massive piece of fabric into the wall. I had found my niche.

Three months passed quickly. My love affair with Beata got nowhere, but it was nice being in love and I would amuse her trying to pronounce impossible Hungarian words like eggy-sheggy-dray (which means cheers). Her boyfriend noticed my obsession for his girlfriend but didn't seem to mind, he even made the odd joke about it; was he bored of the relationship or did he trust her totally? The work was going far better than I had expected, all thoughts of going home were banished and I even managed to get a job for Bettina Tucholsky, my new friend from the Künstlerhaus. My apartment never ceased to impress me with its big windows, wooden floors and beautiful art on the walls and I kept thinking: What have I done to deserve all this?

It was time to go. I had over two thousand dollars in my money belt and this time I felt determined to keep going until I reached Shanghai. When I asked Professor Fastl for a reference letter he gave me such an excellent one that I considered staying on indefinitely. But it was time to go. I organised a going away party in my apartment and the next morning I was on the road, hung-over, with my thumb out and a cardboard sign that said Budapest.

In Budapest I met up with Bettina for a weekend together. While I was hitchhiking she was getting a ship down the Danube. We had become closer and closer over the preceding months and we would go out for long beer drinking sessions. My definition of a friend is someone you can talk to about anything, indefinitely, and never get bored. We had managed to keep the whole thing platonic – avoiding romantic entanglements is an essential part of my type of travelling – until the combination of alcohol, closely packed bodies and dancing at my going away party had somehow ended up in bed.

Budapest had a special status within the Soviet bloc. I could feel it as soon as I arrived in this most beautiful of cities. Its architecture was similar to Vienna's but it had a sinister atmosphere I couldn't explain. I was told that Budapest was more open than any of the other Soviet bloc cities in the region: the service in restaurants and stations was friendly and efficient, people spoke English, there were foreign tourists everywhere and someone told me: this is the city that Russia uses as a place to meet with westerners. It's their window to the west. They also offered a service I had never heard about before: a list of families from whom you could rent a room. In other words you could officially stay with families. We stayed in a big, nineteenth century room belonging to an elderly couple.

I had a small camera with me but I took very few photos in those days. Film was expensive and you could buy professional photos, very cheaply, in the form of postcards. I kept one black and white photo of Bettina in a bikini, laughing, in an old fashioned outdoor pool (lido) for which the city is famous, where old men played chess on floating boards, enjoying the hot water. In the background was a line of concrete dolphins, water spouting from their mouths.

In a crowded bar we bumped into a young, chatty American with a neat beard and a loud voice. He turned to me and said:

- So, you're going to China?

- Yes.

- Which way are you planning to go?

- The usual way, in through Hong Kong. It's the only way in as far as I know.

- Not any more. Things are changing fast over there.

- What do you mean?

- I'm just back from Asia and I met people who got into China through

Kathmandu, Nepal.

- You mean they got into Tibet?

- Yeah, they've just opened up Tibet to tourists.

- Wow, it would be incredible to visit Tibet. I'd never thought about going there.

- Go for it man! Go to the Chinese Embassy in Kathmandu and ask for a tourist visa. They're giving them out.

Heading for Nepal and Tibet seemed like a much better plan than working my way through South-east Asia where there were bound to be border problems, expensive visas and other hassles. I'd already spent enough time in Eastern Europe and I didn't want to waste more time by picking my way through small countries like Burma and Thailand. On the spot I decided to head for the Chinese Embassy in Kathmandu, from where I could discover a land I knew precisely nothing about: Tibet.

There were still too many East European countries to get through and I was getting impatient. I wanted to be in the wide open plains of Turkey, Iran and India – getting nearer to my destination – but I was stuck in this patchwork of small, complicated, repressive, dark countries. I didn't feel I was actually getting any closer to China and over four months had passed since I had left home. If things carried on like this I would be an old man before I reached Shanghai. It was like a dose of the flu – I had to be patient and work my way through it.

Next on the agenda was Romania, the biggest country in that part of Europe. I had been interested in Romania since university because it never appeared in the media. All the other Communist Bloc countries got mentioned now and again, but Romania seemed forgotten. All the Hungarians I met hitching across their country warned me about visiting their eastern neighbour:

- You go Romania?

- Yes.

- Why you go Romania?

- It's on my route to China.

- China? But Romania not near China. I do not understand.

- I'm on my way to China. Romania is in the way.

- You no go Romania. Not good country. No food in Romania. They steal everything. Bad people.

These warnings made me even more curious to see Romania, but I did take the advice about the food situation seriously. Could it be true that there was no food in Romania? Surely that would have been a news story at some point? I had some space in my old canvas rucksack and I went to a grocer's shop and filled it up with tins of grim-looking beans and a big leg of smoked ham. The shopkeeper asked where I was going and shook his head in sympathy, as if I was off to the front.

The border crossing was deserted. There was space for trucks and cars and people, and men in uniform everywhere, but the only form of transport I saw going in or out of Romania that day was a single car, surrounded by armed soldiers who were patiently going through all the driver's possessions, and a lone cyclist. None of the uniforms seemed interested in my appearance – I presume they were geared up to search vehicles and interrogate drivers – and they seemed rather bored. I had a brief chat with the cyclist, who was an American. He was middle-aged, skinny and didn't seem to have any luggage at all. I wondered if he was some kind of undercover missionary. I asked him what it was like in Romania and he said:

- It's exotic.

I tried to hitchhike but it didn't work. I walked from the border crossing point and eventually got a lift from a tractor driver, black with grease, to the nearby city of Oradea, a horrendous looking dump that had been disfigured by grotesque architecture. In fact, Communist architects had ruined the entire country. I walked through the city, saw greasy looking cakes in a shop – there was food but it looked inedible – and tried to hitch towards Bucharest on the road south. I stood on the outskirts for the rest of the day but none of the drivers would even look at me. On the street nobody would make eye contact with me and I couldn't understand it. Nowhere else had I encountered unfriendliness on such a scale. They also looked incredibly shabby, as if they had been wearing the same clothes for months. That night I walked back into town, found the railway station and got a ticket to Bucharest and thought: What a horrendous place. I can't wait to get away from here.

I was travelling in terra incognita and the only contact names I had were reluctantly given by the boyfriend of Gwen Hardy, the artist I had visited in Berlin who had given me the tip about the Künstlerhaus exhibition in Vienna. Gwen's boyfriend was a dark, brooding, silent Romanian called Marian. He didn't say much when I visited their apartment – was he jealous I had come to visit Gwen? When I found out he was from Romania I asked for some contact names, and he reluctantly gave me a scrap of paper with

two names and two numbers. The names were Lolla and Vlad and there
was no mention of a surname, address or any other information.

I was standing in Gara de Nord, the main railway station in Bucharest,
the capital of this accursed country, holding that scrap of paper in my
hand and wondering if I should call the numbers or get the next train
to Bulgaria. The thought of leaving was most tempting but something
made me hesitate. I found an antediluvian phone box and some grubby,
aluminium coins and made the call. No reply. Vlad wasn't in. Things were
looking up: one more phone call and I could hit the road. I was keen to
get away from the oppressive atmosphere of this station. And then I called
Lolla – what kind of a name is that? – and a grumpy female voice shouted
Alo and I was at a loss for words. I hadn't learned even one word in the
Romanian language and I had no intention of doing so. Marian hadn't told
me anything about this Lolla character. Was it male, female or animal? Did
it speak English? What was I supposed to say?

- Do you speak English?
- Poftim!
- Sprechen Sie Deutsch?
- Moment! barked the female voice. There was a long silence. After
what seemed like an eternity I heard footsteps approaching the phone.
- Alo, said a male voice.
- Do you speak English, oder Deutsch?
- Ja, the voice said, followed by a long pause

I explained in my kindergarten German that I had got this number from
a friend of his in Berlin, Marian Stoica. There was another long silence on
the phone and I could hear a frantic, whispered conversation going on at
the other end. This is ridiculous, I thought, deciding to get the next train
to Bulgaria and be done with this Godforsaken place. Eventually the voice
said:

- You wait in station. We come! The line went dead.

I wouldn't have been surprised if a squad of policemen had dragged me
off in the next half hour. Maybe it was true what the Hungarians told me,
that half the population were informers for the dreaded Securitate, the
secret police. Had this Lolla character called them up and told them there
is a dangerous foreign spy lurking in the station? And was Lolla the woman
or the man? Maybe Lolla was the acronym for the Secret Police? Should I
go and get my ticket to Sofia now? What was I doing here?

The scene that followed could have been from a romantic film. I was standing in the station looking at the collection of people walking by, wondering why everyone looked so depressed, as if we were in a massive psychiatric ward not a busy European railway station. And then the sun burst through the gloom, lighting up the station for the first time and, just as the orchestra struck up, a handsome looking couple appeared. It had to be Lolla and his sister, or was it Lolla and her brother? I just knew it was them as they looked so different from the mentally disturbed crowd that I had been observing.

- Guten Tag, I said, addressing the tall and handsome man. I was so pleased to meet normal people that I couldn't get the huge smile off my face.

- I am Laurentiu. This is my sister Cristina, introducing me to a beautiful young lady who had a perfectly formed round face and long, flowing black hair. Her smile was enchanting.

- But who is Lolla?

- I am Lolla. My name is Lolla. And Laurentiu.

- Aha, so Lolla is a nickname?

- We must go from this place.

- You speak good English, I said to Laurentiu on the way out of the station.

- I do not speak English. I speak German.

- But you are speaking good English.

- I never speak English before. I watch English films.

Laurentiu was a maths teacher and a film buff and he had watched all the classic old films at the National Film Archive, the Cinemateca, learning English, French and Russian in the process. German was the only language he had studied formally and he knew it so fluently that when I tried to speak it he would wince in pain as he knew my pronunciation was appalling. He was incredibly good looking but seemed a bit sad and I presumed this was to do with the repressive country he lived in. Why didn't he go to Berlin like his school friend Marian? But he didn't want to talk about Romania, emigrating, the Securitate or the dictator who overshadowed everything – Nicolae Ceausescu. In fact, he didn't want to talk about anything – but he was warm and understanding and silent communication worked fine.

We drove off in their father's Wartburg, an ancient East German car with a two-stroke engine, leaving behind a cloud of blue-grey smoke. We went to their house in the old town, an apartment in a street of beautiful nineteenth century town houses. They welcomed me in and fed me. I handed over the leg of smoked pork I had carried down from Hungary in my rucksack but they refused it. I insisted and so did they, but when they weren't looking I put it in their ancient fridge and it wasn't mentioned again. Later on I learned that Romanians are the most welcoming people in Europe and if they take you into their home they will refuse payment and share all their food with you, however little they have.

Bucharest felt scary, especially at night when each street seemed to be lit up by a single street lamp. It felt good to have a friendly base in such a hostile location. The next day I walked the streets alone and saw the biggest queues in my life. I passed what seemed to be a grocers shop but noticed that instead of fruit and veg on the tables outside the shop they were displaying books. When I looked closer I noticed they were all the same books, all with the name Nicolae Ceasescu on the cover. This was strange; I understood the Communist Party urge to sell the great words of the leader, but to sell them on the street like fruit and veg? Didn't that lower the tone? Later on I came across the Museum of Romanian History, one of the few buildings with an English sign on it, and noticed that the whole upper level of the building was dedicated to Nicolae Ceausescu. There was a big sign that described in glowing terms his personal contribution to Romanian history. This didn't feel right, the creep wasn't even dead yet and already he's got half the National History Museum. Needless to say my new friend Laurentiu didn't explain any of this.

But he did take the weekend off and show me round town. Gradually, I realised it wasn't as grim as I had first thought. We met with Victor, his sister's boyfriend, who had smiling eyes, a stylish 1930s moustache, a devil-may-care attitude, and a car. We went to a park that was wrapped round by a lake, shadowed on all sides by trees, where we played ping-pong on concrete tables outside and drank strange fizzy juice from glass bottles. Laurentiu took me to a screening of a new Russian film called Come and See and we sat in a small, grimy but totally packed cinema watching scenes of butchery as the Nazi army invaded Belarus and proceeded to burn, shoot and destroy the local population. The film was in Russian, the subtitles in Romanian, but I didn't need to know a word of either language to understand it. Never before or since have I seen such a powerful war film. I later found out that the director of Come and See, Elem Klimov, decided that all he wanted to say was in that film and he never made another.

I only stayed four days in Romania but it felt like months. I was glad to be sitting on the train to Sofia, the capital of Bulgaria, to be gradually moving on. Laurentiu and Cristina had brought me to the station, insisted I take some chunky sandwiches and waited on the platform until the train left. Their hospitality belied the image of hostility, fear and repression that had I felt on the streets of Bucharest. The train crawled out of town, made its way across a flat plain to the Danube. I was saved from excruciating boredom by a big, bouncy black woman from West Africa who was studying physics in Sofia and had been visiting her African friends in Bucharest.

- Why would you come and study here? I asked.

- There aren't enough university places in Nigeria.

- But Bucharest? Sofia? Don't you find these places dark, repressive and dull?

- Not at all, she replied cheerily. The place looks bad but the people are very friendly. They know how to party and the authorities leave us alone. The education here is very good and very cheap. Much cheaper than it would be in Western Europe or America.

We talked all the way to Sofia and when we arrived in that strange capital city she invited me to come and stay with her African friends in a block of flats, a student hall of residence. That evening I was basking in the euphoric friendliness of Africa, soaking up the human contact which acted like an antidote to the hostility of previous days. I hardly noticed the city of Sofia. I had no time or energy to look around yet another East European city. I was desperate to get going and first thing the following morning I went straight back to the station and bought a ticket to Istanbul.

When my train rolled up to the Turkish border I was in a deep sleep. Sounds of people shouting woke me up as I lay on the comfortable bench, not wanting to move. It was night outside and I lay there wondering why I was doing this journey. All of a sudden the whole journey felt pointless and I didn't want to go on. I felt sad, lonely and bored and I had a powerful urge to go home. I was at the border and I had to get up, grab my rucksack, go outside and submit myself to questioning by the Turkish border guards. For the first time since I left home, I just couldn't be bothered. A sense of doubt quickly started to grow and I could feel my purpose melting away. Then I heard a high pitched oriental song blasting out of a distant speaker. All of a sudden I knew why I was here. The Orient was calling, sweeping away all sense of doubt. I jumped up, grabbed my stuff and got off the train.

The travel agent in Istanbul looked like he never got out of his seat. He was friendly, helpful and spoke English but was so overweight that I wondered if he could even stand up. Everything he needed was right in front of him – telephone, reference books, airline catalogues, adding machine, cashbox – and I wondered if he slept there at night. I had noticed a lot of skinny people on the streets and wondered how this one had got so huge.

- I would like to fly to India, I said, not mentioning my fears about going overland through Iran.

- Hmm, let me see. The most comfortable route is through the Middle East but it is rather expensive.

- I want the cheapest ticket possible.

- Hmm...in that case you must go to Athens. I have a very good offer here of a flight from Athens to Bombay but you have to pick up the ticket in Athens.

- Greece? But I thought Greece and Turkey were enemies? Can I cross the border? There are so many newspaper reports about hostilities between your countries.

- Someone has been filling your head with a lot of nonsense, he said with a laugh. Indeed, the politicians and newspapers on both sides of the border do make a lot of noise, but when it comes to business we just carry on as normal. Do you want this ticket? You have a two day stopover in Athens.

- Yes.

I didn't appreciate Athens with its infernal traffic, ugly modern buildings and westernised people. I had adapted to the gruff but friendly Communist citizen and was looking forward to the noisy chaos of India. I didn't want to be in Greece but I now had a ticket for Bombay in my money belt, squashed up against my sweaty collection of US dollars, and I had to do something for two days.

The closest island to Athens is called Aghina and I got there by a short boat ride. All the buildings round the harbour were restaurants, hotels or something to do with the western tourists I was trying to avoid. It was the height of the summer holiday season and there were tourists everywhere. Aghina is a small island and I decided the best way to escape from the tourists, and to get some exercise, was to walk across it. It was less than twenty kilometres to the main beach resort on the other side. In my hurry to get away I forgot to take water and several hours later I felt I was dying of thirst in the middle of dry and barren hills. The heat was intense and I cursed my own stupidity.

Eventually I found a small village with old ladies walking around in long black dresses, with black headscarves, as if they were in mourning. It was the first place in Greece I had seen that wasn't modernised; finally I was seeing the ancient stone buildings that travel agencies use in their enticing brochures. Perhaps I could enjoy Greece's traditional culture? Maybe they would feed me something delicious? I had heard that the Greeks were hospitable. The village looked totally cut off from the tourist circuit and I wondered if any westerners had ever made it up here. I staggered through the village, feeling like Laurence of Arabia, and walked up to an ancient looking house with an outside well and an old crone sitting on a bench.

- Water, water, I pleaded. She looked at me stonily but didn't reply.

- Water, wasser, l'eau! Can I have some water? I made drinking gestures and she finally got it, stood up and shouted:

- Cola, Fanta, Sprite?

CHAPTER THREE

Bombay's main railway station is vast, Victorian and teeming with people. I stood there feeling at a loss as to how to navigate through the crowd. Bombay is the biggest city in India and I didn't have the energy to explore it. I stood in a queue, requested a ticket for the next train to New Delhi and was told they were sold out. I stood at the head of the queue wondering what to do next until the ticket seller took pity on me and said:

- Speak to Station Supervisor. Only he can help you.

The Station Supervisor's office felt like a museum about Britain in the 1930s: shabby old cardboard files were stacked against each wall, from floor to ceiling; each file was bulging with paperwork, tied with string and covered in dust. An endless stream of small, thin men dressed in white cotton pyjamas came into the room to consult with the supervisor – a hugely fat monster who sat immobile behind his desk. He would give everyone a few seconds, look at their note, stamp or sign their paperwork, exchange a few words. He was like a spider sitting at the centre of a vast web. I wasn't sure how to approach him, how to interrupt the constant flow of people. Nobody seemed to notice me, so I just stood there and watched. Time seemed to stand still.

- How can I be of service? the fat man asked, without looking up.

- I would like to get the next train to Delhi, but the ticket office says they are sold out. They also said if I came to the supervisor perhaps you could find me a ticket.

- Who on earth told you that? These Ticket Wallahs are acting very cheekily. They will have to be punished. If the tickets are sold out they are sold out. There is nothing I can do. Tell me please, where are you from?

- I am from Scotland.

- Ah, Scotland. I am very fond of your Scottish whisky. I don't suppose you are carrying any on your person?

- Er...No.

- Well you can just stand there for a while and we will see what developments arise.

Eventually the penny dropped and I realised he was waiting for a bribe. I had never bribed anyone in my life and I had no idea how to do it. Isn't it illegal? Maybe he would report me and have me thrown in jail? More time passed and I knew the Delhi train was about to leave. Desperation drove me on and I fumbled around in my money-belt and pulled out a Scottish five pound note, went up to him and said:

- I would like to give you this.

- What on earth is this?

- A Scottish five pound note.

- And what am I supposed to do with it?

- You can exchange it for ten rupees.

- That is not a great sum of money.

- It's a gesture of my appreciation.

- I beg your pardon.

- I want to show my appreciation for getting me a ticket on the train to Delhi, which I simply must catch.

- I see. It's urgent is it. Well, it all boils down to the same thing in the end. This train or the next one?

He barked orders to one of the nearby Ticket Wallahs and within minutes a ticket was produced, more money was exchanged and I was escorted across the station by a cheery old man in a white pyjama suit. He indicated a third class carriage that was packed to bursting point. There was no way that I would be able to get on there, but he shouted an order, an opening was made in the crowd and I squeezed through the railway carriage to my compartment.

It wasn't the usual railway compartment with six individual seats, it was a sleeping compartment with three levels of beds on one side and three on the other. They weren't beds with mattresses, they were simply hard wooden surfaces, like shelves in a store room. People were crammed into every available inch of space, there were faces in front of me, above me and even below in the narrow space under the bottom bunk. There must have been over thirty people in there and all of them were staring at me. Indians can stare at you all day and I always appreciated the absence of hostility. They seemed interested in everything about me: my clothes, my rucksack, my movements, anything I took out of my pocket. They had welcomed me in and I felt safe. I leaned forward and immediately fell asleep.

When I woke up the train was moving and my fellow passengers were still staring at me. Time passed slowly. I had a book to read and a diary to fill in – every day I wrote one page – but the others had nothing to do but stare. Then I pulled out a packet of Shag tobacco and rolled a cigarette. There was a murmur of excitement in the crowd and they moved a bit closer. Each of my movements was scrutinised but it didn't bother me. I finished rolling the cigarette, handed it to the person sitting in front of me and then lit a match. He was delighted and he puffed away happily. The others had become agitated with excitement and they all wanted a puff – but they didn't ask me for more, they asked him to pass it round, which he did. This little act of sharing sealed our friendship.

I felt protected by this group and when I squeezed my way through to the toilet I didn't think twice about leaving my rucksack with this group of poor Indians. I trusted them and knew that if anybody even touched my bag the others would have lynched him. When we arrived in Delhi I met a serious German couple who described how they had chained their rucksacks to themselves as they slept on the top bunk – but still their stuff had been stolen. I wondered if trusting people was the key to having a safe and stress free journey.

At every station we stopped at skinny old men in loincloths would stride up and down the platform swinging a huge aluminium kettle in one hand and a pile of tiny cups in the other. Gup Dee! they would shout. Gup Dee! Gup Dee! Gup Dee! These were the Chai Wallahs and they would appear whenever the train stopped. I crowded up to the barred window of our compartment, held out one rupee coin and was given a beautiful hand-made clay cup, full of hot milky tea. It was delicious, very sweet with a hint of cardamom. Best cup of tea I've ever tasted, I thought. I carefully handed back the precious clay cup, assuming I was doing the old man a favour as he could use it for the next customer, but he threw it down onto the tracks with a look of contempt as if I had given him a piece of rubbish. This was their form of disposable cup.

India doesn't look very big on the map – especially if you compare it to Africa – but when you cross it by railway you start to realise how vast it really is. It took over 24-hours to reach Delhi and another day to cross the northern plains to reach the border of Nepal. By this time I had developed a sense of momentum and wasn't hanging around in every city I came across. After Delhi I started hitchhiking on trucks that were so overloaded that they would swing from side to side like ships at sea, and motorbikes, jeeps and cars that had been designed in the 1950s. Soon enough I reached Nepal.

Kathmandu was the first Asian city I had seen that wasn't built of concrete. This small city seemed genuinely ancient and the centre was full of Hindu temples, each one a hive of activity. Some were covered with elaborate stone statues of Hindu Gods penetrating their consorts with massive stone penises. The streets were narrow and packed with crowds, people selling fruit and all manner of foods, sacred cows wandering freely and helping themselves to the produce of the fruit sellers who would get infuriated but were unable to do anything. There were more hippies per square yard than I had seen anywhere in my life and their expressions told me there were plenty of cheap drugs available. Everywhere you looked Nepalese men would be hustling, offering hotel rooms, cheap restaurants, tours to the mountains, rupees, precious stones, antiques, temple visits and, of course, hashish. It was pouring with rain and everything felt damp.

At 70 pence a night, the Trekkers' Lodge was the cheapest place I found to stay. The boys in charge of the guesthouse walked me up some dark stairs, along a gloomy corridor and showed me into a small grubby room with three beds. The boys thought they were doing me a big favour by putting me in a room with two Englishmen. We entered the room and two shabby looking travellers glanced up from their fat paperbacks and tried to look welcoming. Mosquitoes circled the sole light bulb and a towel was stuffed into the small, broken window. I took the free bed by the door.

Richard was dark and good-looking and he had the bed by the window. He sounded like an upper class Englishman but he claimed to have worked as a brickie before going to study at East Anglia University. He fervently believed in the British Labour Party and put all his energy into convincing us that Neil Kinnock, the leader of the party, was different and would transform society when he became Prime Minister. His diatribes were fascinating and I learned more about British politics than I had done at university, where I had studied the subject, but I didn't believe in party politics, or ideologies of any stripe. I told them that my view of parliamentary elections was based on some graffiti I once saw in Liverpool: Whoever you vote for, Government wins!

Adrian was in the middle bed. He was thin, witty, had a whispy beard and was a seasoned traveller from the West Midlands. He showed me a photo of his mates back home, lined up outside the pub, a grotesque glimpse into another world. Adrian had lived in Greece where he had witnessed the Socialist Party getting elected based on a promise of expelling the American troops from their country, a promise they had failed to deliver. Nothing could convince him that any political party delivers on its promises, Neil Kinnock being no exception, and so they had endless material for debate.

We would go for meals together in cheap restaurants with pastel drapes and nice decor, endlessly talking about world politics while eating westernised food at a tenth of the price. Prices are a big topic among travellers and I noticed how our understanding of money changed to suit local prices. The restaurant we frequented most often sold delicious bean burgers, with all the trimmings, for just twenty rupees which is one British pound. If we went to another restaurant and saw bean burgers on the menu for thirty rupees we would consider it extortionate and leave in disgust.

I had to get a Chinese visa and I wanted it quickly. Neither of my roommates had a clue where I should begin, but across the landing a chatty Chinese American girl with chubby cheeks and a bright smile told me where to go. At the Chinese Embassy, an inscrutable official sent me packing: I didn't have the relevant papers and couldn't possibly get a visa for China. They told me to get one in London. This isn't what I was told in that bar in Budapest.

I then ran into a haggard looking American journalist who told me how to go about it: send a telex to Beijing requesting permission to visit the People's Republic of China and to issue the visa in Kathmandu. Then send a telex to the Bank of China, New York branch, to pay for Peking's reply. Whatever the reason behind this ludicrous procedure it took ages, cost far too much, and left me twiddling my thumbs in Kathmandu for the next two weeks.

My new Chinese American friend had travelled overland from Tibet with a horde of young people from Hong Kong. I noticed that Hong Kong Chinese people, when travelling together, can be incredibly loud and also rather exclusive: they seemed to ignore everyone around them and are self-contained in a rather selfish way. I had tried to share a dormitory with them, as they occupied the biggest and cheapest room at Trekkers' Lodge, but they had specifically told the boys in charge that they didn't want to share with anyone. I later noticed that Hong Kong Chinese people behave totally differently from their compatriots in the People's Republic, where people seemed more friendly and humble.

But my Chinese American friend was different; she had all the openness and warmth of the Americans and was keen to talk. She had been brought up by an American family in the Midwest (I presume she had been adopted) and only learned Chinese when she went to live in Taiwan for two years. Her recent trip from Hong Kong through China and Tibet was the most potent experience of her life. She described her best moment as watching the Potala Palace, a vast and ancient structure that overshadows Lhasa, at sunset, while listening to country and western music on her Walkman. Her description of Lhasa's street life was far more vivid that anything I had read in the guidebooks. She talked of playful monks, cuddly dogs snoozing on the streets, the infectious friendliness of the people, children running alongside the tourist buses and demanding sweeties. She told me that Tibet was quite backward compared to China proper but the effect of western tourism was spreading fast.

Our conversation inspired me to find out more about Tibet and as I began devouring guidebooks, with their short potted histories, I realised my knowledge of Tibet was virtually non-existent. My only source had been Tintin in Tibet, a cartoon book involving a plane crash in the Himalayas, some amusing encounters with Tibetan monks and a showdown with the Yeti, the Abominable Snowman.

I learned that Tibet had been a medieval country until the 1950s. Neither China, home of ancient technology, nor Britain, the scourge of Asia, had introduced anything more than a radio set to this ancient abode of Lamas, or Buddhist priests. It seemed inconceivable that such a strategic country, located between the Chinese, Russian and British Empires, had managed to evade colonisation for so long. Tibet's policy towards its imperial neighbours had been simple: ignore them. Incredibly, this policy had worked and they had been left in relative peace for almost a thousand years. When a Chinese dynasty got powerful it would install an ambassador in Lhasa and encourage trade in silk and tea, and when the dynasty grew weak their influence would wane and the ambassador would go hungry. Not until the 1950s did China conquer Tibet and incorporate it fully within their border.

By the nineteenth century Britain was raping China, selling them vast quantities of Indian opium and setting up fortified trading ports where huge profits could be made. Meanwhile, to the west, Russia was expanding into the vast deserts of central Asia, butting up against the outer rim of the Chinese area of influence and conquering the ancient kingdoms that had ruled the region for centuries. China's ruling Ching dynasty couldn't cope with all this. For hundreds of years they had considered themselves to be the centre of the universe – they called themselves the Middle Kingdom -- as their land was between heaven and earth. When foreign kings would visit they would be expected to kowtow: prostrate themselves on the floor in a gesture of total submission. Unlike the Japanese, the Chinese were unable to adapt to modern technology and, as a result, the western powers were able to humiliate them. The Chinese didn't know how to cope with the arrogant Brits who not only refused to kowtow to the emperors, but undermined Chinese society with opium, made a mockery of their armies and destroyed the exquisite Summer Palace in Peking, a vast playground of parks, pagodas and ponds, in an outrageous act of vandalism.

As the twentieth century approached, Tibet's importance as a strategic buffer zone grew. In 1904 a British force marched into Tibet, fired a few volleys against medieval troops and met virtually no opposition. They found that rumours of Russian influence had been exaggerated, there were no foreign representatives in Lhasa, and they quickly withdrew. But they did sign a treaty, lay a telegraph line and install a trade representative in the city of Gyantse. The Tibetans started to realise that they couldn't go on ignoring the rest of the world and they tried to sign a treaty with China, but the Ching Dynasty was disintegrating at the time and they were unable to make any progress in this regard.

The chaos of the Second World War enabled Mao Tse Tung and the Communist Party to seize control of China and by the late 1940s they turned their attention to Tibet. They considered Tibet to be another part of the Chinese Motherland that needed to be liberated. They didn't need to fight their way in as they made a promise that Tibet's autonomy would be honoured, that the Dalai Lama could remain as leader and that its unique cultural integrity, including a distinct language, would be respected. A treaty was signed in 1951, under duress, and for the first few years the Communists did carry out some useful reforms. By 1959 Chinese heavy-handedness had become unbearable to the Tibetans, and especially to the Dalai Lama, who was nominally in charge. It became clear that the Chinese would only tolerate Tibet's culture for as long as it took to install the Red Army and their oppressive system of administration.

In 1959 there was a general uprising in Lhasa. The Tibetans didn't stand a chance thousands were killed. The Dalai Lama, followed by about 80,000 Tibetans, fled over the Himalayas and eventually set up a government-in-exile in the Indian village of Dharamshala. The darkest period in Tibet's history was still to come: in the 1960s over a million were displaced or killed, villages starved, collectivisation was brutally installed and, during the Cultural Revolution, Tibet's vast network of monasteries was destroyed and the monastic way of life abolished.

But this had all changed when China's new leader, Hu Yaobang, visited Tibet in 1980 and publicly apologised to the Tibetans for the mistakes that had been made. He decreed that Beijing's grip on Tibet should be loosened and that Tibetans would have a say in its governance. Part of the reform process that followed included the opening up of Tibet to international tourism.

At that point I still retained some faith in Chinese Communism, which I believed to be more benign than the East European and Soviet variety. I wanted to believe that Communism could work somewhere on this planet as it is such a great theory. I became fascinated by Tibet and refused to believe all the horror stories I was hearing. I wanted to find out the truth for myself.

The more I found out the more questions I had: why wasn't Tibet even mentioned at university where, in my final year, I had studied The Western Powers and Asia? Why did all the other tourists in Kathmandu seem to know the history of Tibet back to front? Did people in the west know this story? Was I completely wrong in thinking that the Peoples Republic of China was the one place where socialism hadn't been so terrible? Were the guidebooks wrong? Was the potted history I had just learned nothing but capitalist propaganda? Was Mao Tse Tung really such a baddie?

Kathmandu seemed seedier than ever as I waited for my Chinese visa. I had to keep busy, I couldn't sit around all day or I would get depressed. It was August and the weather was hot, too hot, and by mid-afternoon I would feel slimy with sweat, as if I had been digested by a frog. I forced myself to have cold showers, hot water being unavailable in the Trekkers' Lodge. The showers in cheap hostels doubled up as toilets: this was where you went to relieve yourself of diarrhoea and the smell, and the slime on the floor, was appalling.

One day I went for a trek (fashionable travellers don't go for walks, they go for treks) to the nearest hill, just a few miles away. The atmosphere felt different as soon as I got out of the city and I could feel the tension ebbing out of my brain. While Kathmandu had been modernised, to a limited extent, by the influx of tourism, the countryside felt totally untouched.

By now I was at the bottom of a hill which, according to a sign, was a Royal Nature Reserve and contained wild boar and tigers. A high fence stretched out in both directions and I could see Nepalese soldiers patrolling it. They charged me two pence to enter. The path led through light woodland that reminded me of England, the air became cooler and within a couple of hours I had reached the top. I stood panting under a large, spindly observation tower, observing a laughing group of Gurkhas who seemed to be on their lunch break. My plan was to see the view when the mist lifted and see if I could scrounge some lunch from some unsuspecting visitors.

The soldiers were friendly and offered me a glass of chang, a milky-coloured and quite disgusting home-made alcohol, from a jerry can. I gratefully swilled down a cupful and asked for another. An important question was pressing: where would I get lunch? I hadn't brought anything and my stomach was rumbling. The chang helped relieve the hunger pangs but something more was needed. I climbed the observation tower and noticed a rather odd-looking couple sitting nearby. I walked over to them and tried to look friendly. The girl was white and seemed to resent my appearance, he was Nepalese and older and invited me to sit down and join them. The picnic was small but she had constipation and couldn't eat a thing. He invited me to tuck in while she asked me if constipation is worse than diarrhoea.

The man introduced himself as Shankar and started talking about his uncle who, he claimed, had been Prime Minister of Nepal and good friends with the king. It sounded very unlikely but I made I'm impressed noises as I bolted down their picnic. He had been educated at one of the English-style public schools that are dotted around India and had the behaviour, accent and witticisms that are typical of people who get educated in these places. As I started on the hard boiled eggs Shankar said:

- My uncle went to China and returned to make Nepalese history. I nodded with interest, looking forward to a good yarn.

In Beijing the uncle had opened negotiations with Zhou Enlai, the Prime Minister, and signed a trade agreement that resulted in cheap goods flooding into the Nepalese shops and the opening up of the land border to traders and international tourists. However, this created a problem with India, which had always considered Nepal to be within its sphere of influence and had never forgiven China for stealing a huge chunk of its north-western borderland – the Aksai Chin – in the early 1960s. China had briefly invaded northern India in 1962, but quickly withdrew. My new friend told me that there are other disputed areas along the Himalayan frontier and war between India and China was always on the cards. I kept nodding enthusiastically, trying to keep his attention away from my real priority: finishing off their picnic.

By the end of the conversation my head was spinning with names and borders and strategies and once I had eaten my fill I started to note it all down in my diary. Shankar seemed impressed that I was so interested in his knowledge and as we were leaving he whispered to the girl conspiratorially, they both glanced at me, and he said grandly:

- We must meet up again. Do call me tomorrow.

The following day I checked with the Chinese Embassy to see if my visa had been approved and, having heard the same answer I got every day, I called up Shankar. He had been very friendly on the hillside the day before but now he sounded quite distant and remote. Had the girlfriend pointed out that I had greedily consumed the bulk of their picnic? But he invited me to come and meet a fellow Scotsman, which sounded interesting. Later that day the three of us drove out of town, heading north, towards Tibet, on the first bit of decent tarmac I had seen in Nepal. We passed a series of concrete poles by the side of the road which supported overhead cables. Shankar explained that this was Nepal's first electrified bus line, built by the Chinese.

We parked by the end of the flat plain that Kathmandu is located on and looked up at the vast wall of mountains, the Himalayas, that towered above us like a tidal wave. We went up to a tall, newly-built house, saw a well kept, English style garden and were greeted with great warmth by an old couple from Forres, Scotland: Mr and Mrs McLellan. They were a pair of bright- eyed Highlanders who had come to retire in Nepal. He was a tough cookie, thin and friendly, and a great storyteller. His wife complemented him perfectly – warm and sympathetic with a voice like a soft highland breeze – and kept our teacups full as he blethered on into the evening.

Mr McLellan began life in a croft, a miniscule farm in the Highlands, got called up for the Second World War and then got a job washing dishes in a hotel. He then learned the hotel business, worked his way up the management chain and eventually set up his own business. During the 1970s the McLellans moved to Nepal and he established himself as a hotel consultant. Because tourism is about the only thing that makes cash for Nepal, apart from drugs, they desperately needed a Mr McLellan, who loved telling people how to run things. He described Nepal as somewhere between autocracy and democracy and told us that corruption is rife. Comparing the running of a country to the management of a Scottish hotel, he saw himself as a source of practical economic advice, leading the region into the next century.

Some years before, the Chinese leadership had invited Mr McLellan to come and advise them about the hotel business. Due to some canny diplomacy on Mr McLellan's part he managed to get a personal audience with China's top leader.

- What, he asked, is the precise population of China? The Chinese leader thought for a moment, scratched his head, looked in his file and then admitted he didn't know the precise figure but thought it was approaching a billion.

Mr McLellan was not impressed. He informed the leader that not having high quality demographic information is a major handicap for a government, and he explained the value of a detailed census as a building block for good government – especially when it comes to planning, which is something Communist governments take very seriously. The Chinese leader apparently took all this in good faith, spoke to someone on the phone about it and thanked Mr McLellan for his advice. He concluded his tale by telling us that their next census, taken in 1982, was the best that had been carried out since the Communists' took over in 1949. We were impressed by Mr McLellan's storytelling and even Shankar felt outclassed. On the way back to Kathmandu that evening he hardly said a word and I felt sorry for him when he glumly said goodbye.

After repeating the tale to Adrian and Richard that evening and imagining an audience with the Chinese leadership in the sumptuous Forbidden Palace in Peking, Trekkers' Lodge felt grottier than ever. Sleep was impossible because of the buzzing mosquitoes dancing round the windows and the endless howls of the stray dogs that roamed the streets at night. My tolerance for the travellers' life in Kathmandu was ebbing and the one idea that gave me cheer was the knowledge that the Trekkers' Lodge was luxury compared to what would be available in Tibet.

Just as I had come to the grim conclusion that the Chinese weren't going to give me a visa, or an explanation, and certainly not my money back, they promptly told me that I had a one-month visa to visit the People's Republic of China. I was delighted and I dashed off to inform my new friends of the great news. Then I started to ask myself if one month is enough time to visit Tibet, get through China and reach Shanghai? Is it possible to get visa extensions in Tibet? But I didn't dwell on these future challenges; this was my ticket out and I was delighted to be leaving.

I was full of optimism the next morning as I walked through the golden fields outside Kathmandu, enjoying the warm sunshine. It was one of those moments of such complete beauty that I momentarily forgot that I was doing something that often feels depressing: standing by the side of the road and trying to hitch a lift. There wasn't much traffic: a tractor now and again, some trucks and the occasional official zipping by in a shiny Japanese jeep. A kindly man on a small motorbike gave me my first lift. He didn't mind the extra weight even though his back springs screeched over every bump. The wall of mountains ahead got closer and closer and at the foot of them my companion stopped, said he had to turn off the road and I had to get off. I started walking up and up. A lorry carrying sacks of grain picked me up and we made good time; it was a Mercedes and the driver easily overtook the Indian-produced trucks that seemed to be crawling along. Within a few hours we had reached the Nepalese side of the border, which is located in a steep gorge.

A torrential rainstorm had started and I didn't have a raincoat. The driver stopped by the Nepalese customs house and I dashed in before getting soaked. The customs house was actually a shed perched on a thin strip of land between the road and a river that was powering through the gorge with a deep roaring sound. There were a few more sheds stuck to the customs house, a teahouse, a primitive shop and some shanty type accommodation. The whole shambolic construction looked like it would get swept away by the river at the next monsoon. A few hundred yards up the road was a ramshackle bridge that marked the border between China and Nepal.

Inside the Nepalese customs house was a noisy group of Italians who were all talking furiously at the same time. Their gear had been soaked and was spread all over the small room. An attractive woman with short black hair, glasses and a mad look in her eye pointed a finger into my chest and said:

- You go to Teebet?

- I'm going to Shanghai, I admitted sheepishly. There is something fascinating about furious Italian women and this one reminded me of the raging torrent outside. She looked at me askance, tapped her temple vigorously and launched into a tirade:

- You can't go! No transport! We try to go to Lhasa. We get nowhere. Why? Because no transport, no nothing, only the stupid donkey and cart. Three days we wait. No car, no bus and no food! We get so wet. You like adventure? You have big adventure. You must be crazy!

- Is there no bus service on the Chinese side?

- You no listen to me! I say you there is no bus, no nothing. We order private bus from Lhasa, we spend thousands of dollars and what happen? Nothing. We wait like stupido. Now we go to Kathmandu and complain to Chinese Embassy.

- So there's no bus service on the other side? I repeated, more to myself than the enraged Italian, thankful that I was hitching and able to walk if there was no transport.

Pools of water were forming on the mud floor of the customs house and I noticed that the Italians had hung their raincoats and capes all round the bamboo walls. The only person who was completely detached from this chaos was the customs officer himself, an emaciated Gurkha who was calmly ironing his khaki drills. I quietly waited until he had folded away his trousers, caught his attention, showed him my passport, got an exit stamp and walked out into the pouring rain.

Standing on the shaky bridge, I looked up at the Chinese village and realised it was quite close as the crow flies. If you were to climb directly up the gorge it wasn't more than a mile away, but the road must have been four times that length as it switched back and forth, forming a zigzag pattern up the mountainside. There was no traffic of any description and I presumed the road had slipped off the edge at some point. Suddenly I saw a fountain of brown earth thrown up into the air and heard a sharp explosion echoing off the gorge walls. A group of men in white helmets appeared on the hillside above, Chinese engineers trying to tame this wild hillside. Rocks spasmodically cascaded down the mountainside and bounced off the road. The whole mountain seemed unstable, as if annoyed by the impudence of cutting a road into its surface.

A line of what looked like Sherpas passed me on the bridge and disappeared into the undergrowth on the Chinese side of the border. I later learned that Sherpas would never do such lowly portering work (the

Sherpa's domain was Mount Everest and the foreign climbing expeditions – these people were local Tamang tribesmen).

Assuming this was the shortcut, I followed. The porters were barefoot, wearing only loincloths and each one carried on his back a huge pack, wrapped in canvas, about the size of a bale of hay. The packs were held on their backs by a single strap that went in front of their foreheads. They moved fast and silently, up a steep, muddy track that was covered in various sizes of boulders, effortlessly carrying the huge packs that seem to have been glued to their backs. I struggled to keep up with them, conscious of the fact that I was carrying a puny little rucksack, a handbag compared to their loads. Eventually they stopped for a two-minute cigarette break and I begged one of them to sell me his raincoat – a square of thick polythene, probably from a construction site. Even though I was already soaked to the skin, this scrap of plastic seemed to help against the cold that was seeping into my bones.

Was I the worst prepared traveller to have reached Tibet? With a slight sense of shame I realised I didn't have any warm clothes, waterproofs or a sleeping bag. I had been put off by the smugness of some travellers who knew exactly where they were going, how they would get there, how much they'd spend, the political situation; they had the whole thing worked out, they were executing a plan with a complete lack of spontaneity.

Khasa is the Nepalese name of the Chinese frontier village and it was dominated by a big, white customs building and a new hotel. It is located halfway up the gorge and the only place where construction is possible is right by the road. The street was full of people milling around: porters waiting patiently with their huge loads, pushy Nepalese traders whispering Change money! Change money!, western travellers checking their maps and trying to look purposeful, Chinese soldiers in green uniforms, rifles slung over their shoulders, not seeming to notice what was going on around them and dark-looking Tibetans who were joking with each other and didn't seem to have anything to do. There was a whiff of anarchy about this town, it was like something out of the Wild West. I went into the new customs house and was struck by the almost clinical hygiene and calm, the automated politeness of the uniformed officials and the speed with which my passport was stamped.

Food was my first priority and the smell of Chinese cooking was drawing me towards a ramshackle wooden construction a few hundred yards up from the customs house. Smoke billowed out of an improvised chimney; there was a trail of black slime on the cliff directly under the shack and the place was packed. As I got closer I could see that it was built in mid-air. They had somehow fixed poles into the cliff below and built a platform on the poles. The walls consisted of scraps of wood that were roughly nailed up to keep out the elements. It looked as though it could disappear off the edge at any minute.

I learned one of the secrets of Chinese cooking that day: the worse looking the establishment the better the food. It looked like Satan's boiler room inside the shack: packed with rowdy, hard drinking groups of Chinese and Tibetans, all talking furiously. The walls were black with sticky grime and the air was thick with tobacco smoke. All the Chinese I had seen thus far seemed to be chain smokers. There was no kitchen, it was just one big room, and if you needed the toilet I supposed you went outside and did it over the edge (hence the trail of black slime below). In one corner was a small man in a cloud of steam, standing over a flaming wood fire, handling a wok with a speed I had never seen before. I went over to watch and he didn't seem to mind. Cooking a dish took less than a minute: he held the wok in his left hand, a metal ladle in his right and he would start by ladling some oil into the wok, holding it over the flame until it spat, then use the ladle again to toss in the finely chopped meat and vegetables that were neatly arranged in a series of bowls. He would then squirt some evil-looking sauce into the fray, and ladle in a big quantity of what looked like salt – while continually moving the wok over the flame in a tossing movement.

Then I realised the brilliant logic of it: he had to keep the food moving constantly or it would burn, it had to be tossed to ensure that the sauce and meat and vegetable would all blend. When he wasn't cooking the wiry little chef would step over to a huge tree trunk that stood behind him – his bloodied chopping block – grab a metal cleaver and hack away furiously at chickens, fish and vegetables. I stepped closer to see what sort of mess he was making of the ingredients and to my surprise everything had been chopped very precisely; he was using the big cleaver with the delicacy of a French chef, but with much more force and speed. I felt quite comfortable amidst the chaos, ordered a dish by catching the cook's attention for a moment and pointing at a nasty-looking concoction he had just produced. It was the most delicious Chinese meal I had ever tasted.

CHAPTER FOUR

The road from Khasa was surfaced with gravel and clung to the gorge precariously. Soon it became clear why there was no traffic: as I walked along I could hear boulders crashing down from the forested gorge above, bouncing over the road and plunging into the abyss below. It was still pouring with rain but the little square of plastic I had bought from the Tamang porters was keeping me dry and happy. After a few hours a Chinese man bounced along in an old car and gave me a lift. He was middle-aged, friendly and the seats were covered in some sort of carpeting. Even though he was only going for a few miles it was wonderful to relax in a comfortable chair. Our conversation consisted of single words:

- You? America? He said. America good! You go?
- Me? I replied. I go Shanghai!
- China! He concluded with disgust. No good! No money!

We finally reached the top of the gorge. On a nearby hillside was a miserable settlement of low houses huddling from the wind. The driver indicated that this was where I had to get out. I happily complied, grateful for the lift. I waved goodbye and to my outrage noticed that he didn't turn off into the village at all, but drove on towards Lhasa. The swine! He just wanted to get rid of me. Maybe I should have offered him money. I walked on.

Hours later I saw a tiny shack by the side of the road – a tea-shop – and went in. The tables and stools were so small, and so low to the ground, that it looked like a kindergarten. I sat down on a stool that wasn't much bigger than a cigarette pack and looked at the big, pretty, round-faced Tibetan girl who was standing over me. She looked nervous and kept saying momo which I assumed was the Tibetan word for steamed dumplings. Tea and momos were the only thing she had on offer, apart from hot chili sauce. They were delicious, invigorating and cheap.

Back on the road I was starting to feel light-headed because of the altitude. The colours were changing: in the gorge it had been dark green, brown and grey but now the predominant colour was yellow, the sort of browny yellow you associate with the desert, or lions. The air was incredibly dry and dusty. There were no people around, no settlements, no cars, no animals. I was feeling optimistic and not at all lonely in this wilderness.

Suddenly a Tibetan man on horseback appeared. He looked weather-beaten and far bigger than the pony he was riding. He looked at me with interest, jumped off his pony and came over to sniff me out. He made appreciating noises about my rucksack, my sunglasses and my boots, smiled broadly and then indicated his stirrups, boots and hats. Would I like to swap? He took my sunglasses, put them on and squealed with delight as the whole landscape changed colour. He moved towards his horse and I was sure he was going to shoot off with my specs, so I grabbed him and we wrestled and laughed like a pair of teenagers. As he rode off with a wave I was struck with the harmlessness of the incident – if this had happened in a western city it could easily have turned violent. I walked on.

Am I on the right road to Lhasa? I thought. Surely there should be more traffic on the main road from Kathmandu to Lhasa?

I hadn't actually asked anyone if this was the right road but it was the only one leading out of Khasa so it had to be. I trudged on, enjoying the atmosphere, talking to myself and not caring where I was going. Some time later I noticed a dust cloud in the distance, coming up the road behind me, and then a small new minibus appeared. I stuck out my thumb. If there's one thing I learned from hitchhiking it's that the more expensive the vehicle, and the better dressed the occupants, the less likely you are to get a lift. To my amazement, the minibus stopped some distance in front of me and I raced up to it. But something was wrong: a kind-looking Tibetan man was blocking the door:

- I'm sorry, he said, in good English, but we can't give you a lift.

- But didn't you stop for me?

- No. Driver have problem. You cannot come on bus. This is private bus, hired by Japanese tourists. I am guide and translator.

I pushed onto the step of the bus and looked at them: waxwork models, expressionless. They didn't seem to notice me and I realised this was an opportunity; they weren't objecting to my presence. They were probably embarrassed by the incident but didn't want to speak out. I knew how to exploit this.

- I go to next village, I said to the guide, staying fixed in the door frame.

- There are so many empty seats, I continued with as much charm as I could muster, moving inside another fraction.

- Okay, at next village you get out, said the guide unhappily. I jumped on and gratefully dumped my rucksack. The bus moved off and I found a seat near the Japanese tourists, appreciating the luxury for every minute that I could.

- Where you from? I said to the nearest Japanese. No response, not even a glance in my direction.

- You from Tokyo? I asked again cheerfully, not caring if they replied or not.

- I'd like to go to Tokyo. I continued. Nice place.

At the next village I watched the minibus disappear into the horizon, followed by its faithful cloud of dust, I realised that the landscape had changed again: I had passed through the mountains and reached an endless plain. Much of Tibet is a flat country, a high plateau, with mountain ranges around the sides. The unique thing about this plateau is its height – thousands of metres above sea level – no wonder they call it the roof of the world. India also is relatively flat, with the Himalayas along the north and a range of hills running through the centre. I remembered my geography teacher saying:

- India crashed into Tibet and the impact formed the Himalayas. The Himalayas are a barrier between the two plateaus. Wolfe Murray, boy! Are you awake? What plateaus are we talking about here?

- Er, um. I'm not sure sir.

- Stupid boy! Never pays attention. I've been talking about India, which is more or less a flat country, a plateau, which crashed into Tibet, which is also a plateau.

- And what mountain range was formed by the impact?

- Er...um...not sure.

- I don't know why I bother. Does anyone listen to me? The Himalayas, boy! Have you heard of the Himalayas?

- Er, yes Sir. Highest mountains in the world.

- Sometimes I don't know why I bother.

The plateau stretched out across vast distances, with each horizon serrated by mountains. It was an uninhabited desert, alive with colours and strange sounds made by the wind, much more inspiring than the static photographs one sees in the National Geographic magazine.

The village I had been left in was a small collection of low-slung mud buildings, ideally suited to resist the wind and dust. You couldn't actually see any houses as they were all surrounded by walls which, I guessed, act as a wind, dust and snow barrier. I could see goats and children and assumed I could scrounge a cup of tea, or some water. A barefoot child ran up to me and then dashed off in terror after I made a gesture meaning drink. He came back with a crowd of noisy kids and a strange mime act followed: me pretending to drink, and the kids screaming with laughter. They were filthy, dressed in rags and scraps of animal furs but they looked happy, fit and healthy. Eventually they realised what I wanted and two of their members were sent racing off across the dust. A woman appeared carrying a gourd. She was wearing a long leather coat, with fur on the inside, belted at the waist. Her face was dark brown, filthy and weather-beaten but her teeth looked perfect. She passed me the gourd and I sucked at it desperately while the kids clapped and screamed with joy. It contained sour goat's milk and felt like the best thing I had ever drunk in my life. I felt invigorated. I thanked them in Chinese and walked on. The kids followed me for about a mile down the long dusty road.

The landscape was empty as far as the eye could see. Every hundred yards stood a wooden telegraph pole and the wire stretching between them made strange humming noises in the wind. It felt like someone was trying to talk to me in a language I didn't understand. I examined an ancient stone wall by the side of road and compared it to the ones I knew from the lowlands of Scotland. This wall was made up of large round stones, as if from a river or sea, not like in Scotland where stones for drystone dykes are dug from the earth. I got so lost in these thoughts that I almost missed the truck that was approaching. Then the roar and dust cloud was upon me. The truck was slowing down. What joy! I ran along the road, waving to the driver – who took one look at me and accelerated. But he had slowed down just enough for me to race after him, grab the tailgate and get into the back of the truck. I lay face down enjoying a moment of rest, grateful to be moving, enjoying the comfort of a wooden floor. And then I felt a hand on my arm. I looked up and saw a row of western faces.

They asked the usual questions:

- Where are you from? Where are you going? My answers were short and simple:

- Scotland and Shanghai!

It felt strange being able to talk normally with people who could understand me and I wasn't sure I liked it. The more time I spent in the wilderness the less I felt the need to talk, and the more I felt the power of silence. On my right was the guy who had touched my arm and helped me up. He was from Denmark and his face was tanned from travelling. He looked kind and had a blonde moustache. He seemed to be with the thin Englishman with a red face, clutching his camera and staring out of the open back of the flat-bed truck. The Englishman didn't want to miss anything and kept taking photos. On the other side of the truck sat an emaciated-looking Australian who seemed to be staring at the spare tyre. He was the only one who seemed unimpressed with the spectacular view that was unfolding behind us, as if to say this is nothing! You should see the places I've been to! The wooden floor became uncomfortable and we all stood up for long periods with slightly bent legs, in the surfing position, trying to absorb the bumps, chatting like a group of commuters on the train into London.

The sun was going down and the evening light illuminated the dust cloud behind us with flashes of gold. The road started climbing again and we continued uphill for hours. The Englishman told us that soon we would reach nineteen thousand feet and I wondered why these travellers feel the need to know all sorts of facts and figures before they go anywhere. I could feel the altitude fiddling with my brain. Despite the headache I felt a wild freedom welling up inside me. I wanted to cry, to weep, and scream with joy – all at the same time. By the time we reached the high pass I was slumped over an oil drum, fast asleep.

There was no movement and the stillness woke me from a deep, dreamless sleep. The truck was empty. I looked outside and saw them standing in a group talking with the driver and looking at the sun going down on a jagged horizon. The air was incredibly clear and you could see for miles. I jumped down and wandered over. The young Tibetan driver and his mate were animated and friendly and it was difficult to imagine that they had been quite happy to leave me by the side of the road earlier on.

- That's Mount Everest over there, said the Dane, pointing to a ridge of mountains on the distant horizon. It looked impressive but it was hard to make out which one was the biggest as they all looked roughly the same size. I looked again and saw that one was slightly bigger than the others.

That was the tallest mountain in the world?

- Chomolangma, said the driver with a smile.

- That's the Tibetan word for Mount Everest, said the Englishman. To the Tibetans it's a holy mountain.

There was a pause and I was glad to see nobody was encouraging this annoying Brit to spout any more of his schoolteacher-ish knowledge.

- He says we should take photos, said the Englishman, who took another. There was no way I was going back to the truck, to rummage through my bag, find my camera and waste a precious shot on a vast plateau like this – even though the colours were rather incredible. I had a crappy camera and only one film; I wanted to remember the feelings on this trip, not rely on photos to remember what happened.

- I only have black and white film I said, feeling as if I had to justify myself.

- The driver's inviting you into the front, said the Australian with a trace of resentment. He lets us all ride in the front for a bit. Go for it mate!

Now I understood why nobody seemed to want the front seat: there was so little space between the dashboard and seat that your legs were constantly crushed. It reminded me of a story I had heard about the Russian T34 tank that was built in huge numbers during the Second World War. Apparently the Soviets saved huge amounts of steel by building the tank for small people and, so the story went, the Russians only recruited short people for the tank brigades. I wondered if the same designer had worked on this truck.

Darkness fell with surprising speed. Blackness spread out in every direction. I leaned forward, looked out through the grimy windscreen and saw that the sky was lit up by bright stars. The driver was talking to me in Tibetan and pointing up, but I couldn't understand a word. The stars shone so brightly that I wondered if they were the same stars that we sometimes saw at home. They had to be, but these ones looked so much bigger and brighter. They seemed to illuminate the ground in the same way that moonlight would.

I decided to make friends with the driver and his mate so I rolled them a cigarette. Soon the cab filled with Dutch tobacco smoke and it seemed more cosy. They were chatty and I started to practice some Tibetan words with them. After much confusion I worked out that Dro is the Tibetan word for go. I pronounced it again and again, raising a few laughs from the driver's mate, and eventually found the right tone. As we ploughed on into the night I worked out how to say: Lhasa. Go. You. Me.

We drove on and on through the night and I realised the driver wasn't going to stop. My headache was getting worse and I felt exhausted too. I couldn't cope with any more Tibetan words or jokes I didn't get. Why didn't the driver feel tired? He had been driving all day but he just seemed to get more cheery. We stopped a few times in the wilderness to get out, stretch our legs, have a pee and stare up at the sky. The Ozzie was getting restless and said I had been in the front for long enough; I came out of that warm cocoon and he jumped in. In the back I noticed the others had brought out puffy down jackets and Arctic sleeping bags and were looking very snug. I had nothing but a hat, a thin jacket and the plastic sheet I had picked up at the border. I started to freeze.

At the next stop an old woman wrapped in rags emerged from a low mud building. She was carrying a metal flask and she handed us each a hot cup of tea. The driver gave us all a packet of Chinese noodles and we dissolved them in the tea and ate greedily. Nothing had ever tasted better! Then I realised that I needed to stop, to get some sleep, to try and deal with my pounding headache. I told the Dane that I wasn't going any further with them and he seemed disappointed, as if to say: don't leave the cosy protection of the gang. I gestured to the driver, pointed to the mud buildings and indicated sleep. He understood, shouted what sounded like orders to the old woman and she disappeared into the darkness. There was a flurry of activity: parting greetings, headlights spearing the blackness, a roar of engine and the build-up of their dust cloud. I was left standing alone by the side of the road, hoping the old woman hadn't barred her gate and left me to freeze. A few minutes later she re-appeared with another cup of tea, led me inside her low, dark, smoky abode and pointed to an ancient metal bed covered with a filthy carpet that would serve as my cover. I was so tired and in such pain from the headache that lying down on a surface that wasn't bouncing up and down was pure unadulterated pleasure. I lay there with a smile on my face, trying to work out what the appalling smell coming from the carpet was and thinking that I really needed to get one of those high-tech sleeping bags. But none of this was important and within minutes I was fast asleep.

The next morning my head was still splitting with pain but the exhaustion had been replaced by a determination to hit the road. The old woman was standing over an open fire and she handed me a wooden bowl with Tibetan tea in it. I swallowed hungrily. Tibetan tea is made with sour yak's butter and salt – it's more like soup than tea – but at this altitude it's the perfect energy drink.

I walked into a wide, barren valley with no houses, fields, people, animals or traffic; a completely different landscape from yesterday. I was determined to just keep walking, hoping that a steady rhythm would help me forget about the headache. I concentrated on the sound of the wind and kept going for hours. As I approached a low rise an old flat-bed truck appeared as if from nowhere. It swept past in a cloud of dust and stopped on top of the hill. I raced up to the parked vehicle, jumped on the running board and made an enthusiastic gesture to the driver who looked at me angrily, shouted and indicated that I should get off. I knew that if I could just hang on he would take me.

He moved off and I climbed into the back of the truck which was open to the elements and full of empty oil drums, so many of them that there was nowhere to sit. As he built up speed the drums started to move and shake and jump up and down in rhythm. Even standing was a struggle as the drums were bumping against my legs, as if trying to push me off. I found some string, tied up my rucksack to the board behind the cab, strapped on my furry Russian hat to keep out the noise and climbed on top of the barrels. The only way to do this was to spread out my arms and legs as far as they would go, touching as many barrels as possible, in a star shape, trying to relax with the rhythm. It was a curious sensation, and quite pleasant. I imagined this is what flying would be like.

Hours later the truck pulled into what looked like a military base, with skinny Chinese soldiers in bottle-green uniforms. None of them paid us the slightest bit of attention. The driver jumped out, looked at me lying on the barrels and laughed. He pointed to my rucksack and, in sign language, indicated that I should bring it in case someone stole it. Then he led me into the first modern canteen I had seen in Tibet: smooth concrete floor, plenty of space, few people and large windows. He ordered tea and noodles and was so friendly that I couldn't believe this was the same man who was cursing and shouting and telling me to get off his truck. The thick steaming noodles were delicious and spicy. By the time I had slurped my portion down I noticed the driver had gone, his noodles untouched. I looked around but couldn't see him anywhere. I could hear an engine revving and then I saw the old truck pulling out. My only thought was: Great! Now I can eat his noodles too.

The landscape was becoming greener and there was vegetation growing round the villages. A miniature two-wheeled tractor appeared, so slow that it hardly produced any dust. It was a curious contraption, consisting of an engine above two small wheels and two long handlebars that could be held by the driver, who sat on the trailer. The trailer formed the back half of the vehicle and provided the second pair of wheels. The old farmer was carrying a few barrow loads of potatoes and he had a twinkle in his eye, which seemed to suggest hop on. I ran alongside, threw my rucksack onto the potatoes and dived in after them. He didn't even have to slow down. I lay in the trailer for a few minutes of pure luxury, enjoying the view of the mountains rippling into the horizon and glad to be resting from endless walking. A few minutes later the farmer was shouting and pointing down a small track; he turned off the main road and my break was over.

The rest of the day was spent in a haze: getting into a dreamlike trance of walking, walking and more walking; a hot burning sun that had vaporised all cloud cover; an endless and empty road; mountains and telegraph poles; burned face and lips – but no face cream; almost no traffic, only six vehicles passed that day; and a terrible thirst quenched at a dirty river. Then I noticed a dust cloud in the distance and my heart leapt, the demons of enthusiasm and hope were awoken. It was two army jeeps but one look at the dead eyes of the officers within told me there was no way that this little convoy would be picking me up.

I walked into the evening and pangs of hunger started to bite. I passed another mountain and came across an old man and three children tending a flock of dirty sheep by a small lake. I approached them, waved and the old man waved back. I slumped down nearby. The three children raced over and we observed each other. They stared in fascination: was I the first foreigner they had seen up close? I noticed their bright eyes, perfect teeth and skin, tremendous energy, rags held up by string, matted hair and wild screams of laughter at anything I did. The old man walked over with a large thermos flask and gave me a cup of hot tea – salty, oily, rancid and totally energising. He sat down nearby and said, in sign language: Sleep? You! Where? I communicated back with my palms raised upwards, as if to say I have no idea, hoping that he would invite me to his place.

The sheep had wandered far and some had strayed up the nearby mountainside. At a signal from the old man the kids raced off in different directions, whistling and hooting and pulling out their slingshots. I got up, joined the old man and started walking slowly in the direction of the village. The children were herding the sheep into an increasingly tight group that formed up in front of us. I was surprised to see no sign of sheep-dogs, it was all done by the kids. Their main instrument was the slingshot: they would load a stone, swing it hard round their heads and with a tremendous cracking sound the stone would fly like a bullet for several hundred yards, landing with a booming sound in a puff of dust. These missiles would land with incredible accuracy just in front of the straying sheep, shocking the animal into running in the opposite direction. In this way they gathered up the strays in no time. I thought it looked like fun and asked one of the children for a go on their slingshot. I couldn't believe how long the woollen straps were, over two yards, but it was impossible to use. In my hands the stones just flopped out in front of me. This amused them enormously.

The village contained about twenty houses, each made of stone and enclosed by walls. The buildings had been painted with a pleasant brown colour and I realised that the houses were plastered with mud. We approached a wooden door, covered with moon and star symbols, and entered a yard with two low buildings, a cow, some chickens and a storage space under a lean-to roof. The kids ushered me inside the house which was pitch-black and smoky. I couldn't see a thing, but I could hear the kids jabbering away excitedly. Were they telling their parents about their newly discovered foreigner? A candle was lit. I stumbled around and found somewhere to sit on the floor. Gradually my sight came back and I noticed the woman of the house, wearing a long woollen dress, standing over a fire, shouting at the old man, probably saying:

- Who the hell is this? What are we supposed to feed him?

I was introduced to the father of the household, a bulky but friendly presence, and he solemnly poured me a cup of yak butter tea, and kept filling up my small wooden bowl for the rest of the evening. He offered me some tsampa, a dusty brown flour made of barley that they mixed up into dough-like lumps in their tea bowls. I copied what they are doing but ended up producing a slimy pancake mix; they laughed at my incompetence, pointed to the leather bag of tsampa on the table and, by adding more flour to the mix, was able to get the right dry consistency. I ate the tsampa mix but it had no taste at all. I rummaged in my rucksack, brought out an old can of tuna, flourished it in front of them and shouted:

- Dee yag bo doog, which means this is very good.

The father handed me a dagger and I cut open the can, and solemnly gave everyone a small spoonful. They regarded the tuna with suspicion and their faces said that stuff is disgusting, smelly and probably evil. With a sniff, a taste and a curse each one of them threw their portion of tuna into the fire – and stared in delighted horror as I wolfed down the rest and made humming, appreciative noises. I became the evening's entertainment, making them laugh by attempting to pronounce Tibetan words, showing them things from my rucksack, and singing half-remembered Scottish songs.

It had been a long day and I was exhausted. Where could I sleep? The room was tiny, the floor filthy and there were six of them but only one bed. I didn't dare ask about sleeping arrangements, nor did I know how to, but I did feel at home with these people and trusted that something would work out. Just when I was nodding off I noticed that everyone climbed into the only bed and I wondered if they would all sleep in a heap, which seemed quite a natural thing to do in the circumstances. The father beckoned me to follow him outside into the yard, where he pointed to the lean-to. He cleared a space under the rickety roof and exposed a hardened mud floor. It wasn't the Ritz but at that moment it was ideal. He handed me a couple of smelly old blankets and I got under them, fully dressed. Moments later I was dreaming of stars and wind and strong smells and walking and wishing I had some face cream. The dream transformed into a dark underground world where hot, steamy air was being blown on my face. I felt something warm and slimy rubbing against my face and woke up with a shock: there was a yak standing over me, exhaling steam in the cold night air and licking my face. Yaks are big black long-haired brutes but they're surprisingly gentle considering the long, deadly horns they have. It didn't object when I herded it out of the yard, and blocked the gate with an old sack.

By dawn the yard was full of sheep, many of which were walking just inches from my bed and looking at me with suspicion. I got up and noticed that the children were running among the animals, stark naked, and I wasn't sure if they were playing with the sheep or checking them. Each of the kids had a small wooden bowl with tea in it and when they saw I was awake they fetched one for me too. As I got ready to leave the father came over and asked for five yuan – fifty British pence. I was rather shocked, wondering why he was charging me to sleep in his yard, and refused. There was a bad feeling in the air and I realised they had been generous, they had shared everything they had and I was being mean and ungrateful. So I handed over a five yuan note, said goodbye and left.

It was another day of walking and there were very few vehicles; about one truck every hour, none of which even slowed down. Storm clouds approached, the temperature dropped and I was walking up a long, seemingly endless hill. Rain had started to pour down and the wind blew hard and drove the rain into every part of my clothing. I stared back down the mountain, willing a vehicle to come this way. Any vehicle! As if in answer to my prayers I realised that something was chugging slowly up the road. Eventually an old tractor appeared and the driver gave me a look of sympathy. He was going so slowly that I easily jumped in the back and sat silently with three other Tibetan men. We ground our way up a high pass. At the top the tractor stopped, turned off the engine and the Tibetan men went over to a pile of stones by the side of the road and offered it blessings.

The tractor wouldn't start. The driver tried the ignition, we all had a go with a crank handle but nothing would get the engine to start. We then tried pushing it but it was too heavy to move. There was no shelter anywhere from the wind and rain and I realised that if I didn't get moving I would freeze to death. So I said goodbye to my glum companions, grabbed my soaking rucksack and started walking down the other side of the mountain. The next valley was rocky and deserted but it felt good to be on the move. Just when I was getting into my rhythm the tractor reappeared and the men in the trailer waved triumphantly. I jumped back on and we bumped along for what seemed like an eternity, through vast open spaces, mountain ranges, some containing ruined monasteries, and new colours that had been highlighted by the rain. There was no talking in that freezing trailer but when we stopped at a quarry, where they lit a fire and made tea, I felt that they appreciated my presence. The feeling was mutual. In darkness they dropped me in a big town.

Shigatse is an ancient Tibetan town that has become a Chinese garrison. I checked into a big green, concrete hotel and met a tall Australian in the lobby who told me he was on his way to the Holy Mountain, pointing to the west and assuming that I knew what he was on about. I didn't and was too tired to listen. I just wanted a real bed, a real mattress, real sheets. By the next morning I was wallowing in luxury and got up late, washed my socks, went out and ate delicious Chinese food on the street and then visited the big monastery that dominates the town. I noticed the strange smells, the atmosphere, and looked at huge statues with red faces, but didn't have the energy to take it all in. I went back to that wonderful bed to build up some energy for hitching the next day.

The key to hitching is energy. If you have the energy it's easy to cope with the walking, the standing around for hours and the constant rejection by thousands of heartless drivers. Without energy I just couldn't do it. Hitching out of Shigatse was easy as there were more vehicles than I had seen in all of Tibet: tractors and trailers going to a nearby quarry, hundreds of cheery horsemen, some of them pulling trailers, all of them smoking and dressed in black, and the odd truck. I jumped in the back of a slow-moving tractor filled with boys with shovels. After a few minutes they gesticulated that I should get out (which I had no intention of doing) and then I saw why – they turned off the main road and into a quarry. Soon after I got a lift in an old Toyota Landcruiser and haggled hard with the Chinese driver to take me to the next city, Gyantse, for five yuan (50p). He offered to take me all the way to Lhasa for another five yuan but I decided to check out Gyantse. When we arrived in the evening he dropped me outside a rough tourist hostel and said he would be back to pick me up in the morning. I never saw him again.

The hostel was newly-built but it had been ravaged by the elements and looked shabby. It had a big concrete courtyard at the back that was full of broken vehicles, building materials and other junk. I could smell the low toilet building on one side of the courtyard. A surly Chinese family demanded money, took me upstairs to a balcony that led to a large, crowded and dingy dormitory. I noticed the windows were unusually big for this country, where local houses seem to have no windows at all, but the curtains were thin and grimy. All the beds but one were taken by foreign travellers.

There was a good buzz in the room. The centre of attention was a tanned Chinese American girl and her Danish boyfriend. They told good stories, were popular with everyone, and were having a good laugh with a group of hippies from Holland. They welcomed me into the discussion. They were laughing about the two Englishman who were camping on the balcony, just outside the door:

- What's so funny about those English guys? I asked.

- They're crazy, said one of the Dutch hippies. They come to a hostel, pay for a bed and then sleep on the balcony. I think they just want to show us how tough they are and what good camping equipment they have.

- Maybe they got a discount, I said.

- No, explained the Chinese American girl. I talked to them. They're loaded. The one with the aristocratic Brit accent is an officer with the Ghurkhas and the other one is a stockbroker in Hong Kong. They're doing this fake camping thing so they can tell their buddies back home: I went camping in Tibet.

That evening we stood on the other end of the balcony, watching the stars over the wave-like formation of hills. The friendly American girl was talking about her plans for the next trip to Tibet, which would be by horseback (I asked her if she had ever done anything like this before and she said she'd ridden a donkey on a Mexican beach). A small Tibetan man joined us and asked endless questions; this was the first Tibetan I had met who spoke good English. All the travellers had been to Lhasa and one of them, the Dane, had spent four months there:

- What did you do for four months? I asked.

- It takes that long to get to know the place.

- Really? I get bored of a town pretty fast, unless I get a job. Maybe I'll get a job in Lhasa.

- You can't get a job in Lhasa. The only foreigners who work there are at the Lhasa Hotel, which is run by the American company Holiday Inn. That was part of some high-level government deal. You can't just rock up and get a job.

- I know, that's why I'm heading to Shanghai.

- What are you going to do there?

- Teach English.

- Aha, that's possible. I guess you've already arranged it?

- No, I replied, feeling slightly embarrassed that I had arranged nothing in advance. What kept me going was a blind, dumb faith that things would turn out well.

The next day, before leaving, I had a quick look at Gyantse Monastery. It looked small on the outside but was vast inside. The inner walls were painted with big faces of black demons, creatures that Tibetans believe protect them from evil, and Buddhist statues everywhere. The place was deserted and there were marks of desecration everywhere, holes in the wall that looked like they had been made with pick axes or bullets. A small fortress sitting on top of a low hill dominated the town, but I didn't have the energy to visit it. It was time to hitch to Lhasa.

A big group of Italians, who had been staying in another room, had assembled in the yard, awaiting their transport. They seemed rather like the Italians I had seen at the border: noisy, well-dressed and unable to hire a bus. Some time later a flat-bed truck turned up with a canvas-covered back and a Chinese driver. The Italians seemed delighted even though the truck was dusty and they were in fashionable clothes. Once they were all loaded, the Chinese driver sealed the back of the truck (was it illegal to pick up foreigners?) and got in the cab. He was joined by two cheery Italians who took the other front seats. Just before the truck pulled out an old Tibetan man ambled over to the cab and stared blankly at the Italian passengers. The nearest Italian thought this was amusing and he leaned out and pinched the old man's cheek between thumb and forefinger and declared in a loud voice:

- Ciao bello.

The next day I walked out of Gyantse in the direction of Lhasa. After a few hours I came across a scruffy old bus that was full of Tibetans and parked by the roadside. I stuck my head in the door, pointed eastwards and said Lhasa. They nodded and so I climbed aboard. The Chinese driver demanded twenty yuan and I grudgingly paid, assuming this would get me all the way to Lhasa. Later on we pulled in at a run-down concrete truck stop at the side of a lake and trooped inside to get some food. The place was in uproar. There was a shouting match going on between the Chinese cooks and the Tibetan clientele. My fellow passengers immediately joined in the fray and the noise increased. I sat down and waited, wondering what all the fuss was about. When things had calmed down I went into the kitchen, ordered some food and was given what looked like grass fried in grease. It was disgusting, inedible, and I too became an angry supplicant, demanding my money back. Back at the bus the driver refused to let me back on board. My rucksack had been flung into the dust and he was preparing to leave. There was nothing I could do, nothing I could say. I'd been ripped off and this made me even more furious. I wandered back to the truck stop, feeling lost, angry and demotivated. Hmm, they have rooms here, I thought. I will get myself a little room and read from my book Siddartha. That should be relaxing.

Later on that evening I wrote a letter to Bettina in Vienna: Tibet is too hard. I want to come home. See you soon. I was feeling lonely and miserable and sorry for myself. Time to go for a walk, through this village with no name and maybe up a hill. I passed an official building with a huge red banner showing stylised images of the revolution: sunrise, stars, tractors, abundant harvest, strong handsome peasants and a feeling of hope. I walked up the nearest hill and found a curious network of sticks at the top, each one adorned with scores of little flags with strange symbols on them. I remembered the annoying Englishman from the truck telling me that the Tibetans put their prayers into little flags, place them in a windy place, usually on top of hills and mountains, and believe the winds carry the prayers up to heaven. That made sense, as much sense as believing in an old man with a white beard living in the clouds.

The view from the top was stunning – a long and thin turquoise lake out of which steep mountains rose, topped by dark pointed peaks. Huge black crows were circling above ominously. I could feel my anger and frustration and loneliness being lifted up and carried away by the wind.

The next morning I set off early and within an hour reached the massive turquoise lake I had seen from the hilltop the previous day. Some time later an old truck rattled past and ground to a halt ahead. It had big rounded wings at the front, in the pre-war style, and a windscreen made up of two separate panes. It was probably based on a German design from the 1930s. One of the travellers had told me that the Russians had stolen entire factories from Eastern Germany after the Second World War, sent them into Russia by train and, in some cases, passed them onto the Chinese. That was why pre-war German vehicle designs seemed to be the order of the day in Tibet. My favourite was the motorbike and sidecar combination.

A tough-looking Tibetan jumped out of the truck and sauntered over to me. He was dressed like a warrior from a children's fairy tale book: strange boots, tribal hat, black cloak and a big sword strapped to his waist.

- Lhasa, he said with a smile, pointing east.

- Yes, I go to Lhasa.

- Twenty yuan.

- Twenty yuan? I said with a sense of shock. Two quid! I could fly for that price. I knew this was what they charged foreigners and was far higher than locals paid.

- Five yuan, I offered. The warrior laughed as if I had told a hilarious joke, then started acting out how good the truck was and what a great driver his friend is. The driver wandered over and stood there meekly. Unlike most truckers, this pair weren't in a hurry.

- Fifteen yuan, they offered, making it clear this was their final price. I walked off in disgust, in the direction of Lhasa. Some minutes later the truck appeared alongside, going at walking pace, and the grinning warrior stuck his head out the window and shouted:

- Ten yuan.

Having strapped my rucksack onto the top of the vast pile they were carrying in the back, I took the seat by the window, admired the lake and felt quite at home, as if I had earned my place among them. The Khampa took on the role of court jester and a good atmosphere soon developed. He kept telling me he was a Khampa as if I should know what this was and be in awe of him. The more I shrugged in incomprehension the more he tried to explain. When I took out my map he jabbed at the eastern part of Tibet and kept repeating Kham! with a look of pride. Aha, the penny dropped: Kham is a region and the Khampa are a people! From the way he was talking I guessed that Khampas look down on the rest of Tibetans and I wondered if they were similar to the Sikhs of India, a proud warrior people who live in the Punjab and don't think much of the rest of the population. It was obvious that the Khampa couldn't drive but he had put himself in charge of the truck and the Tibetan driver.

At the end of the big lake the road started climbing and I looked up and saw that it went up for mile after mile and that we had to cross a massive mountain pass, bigger than anything I had crossed thus far. I wondered if this overloaded heap would make it but one of the great things about hitching is that you don't need to worry about the reliability of what the Americans would call your ride. If it breaks down you just get out and walk. I was heading to Lhasa and I was grateful if any vehicle – truck, jeep, tractor or cart – could take me just some of the distance. Getting a lift was doubly satisfying because I would be moving in the right direction and getting a rest. Just before we started the long climb we stopped by the lake and the Khampa strode down to the waterside with a bucket, filled it up and poured it into the truck's radiator. Clouds of steam rose from the engine. I started to skim stones and wondered why the lake looked so ordinary from close up but when seen from afar it had an incredible turquoise colour. I took the bucket from the Khampa, filled it up and drank as much of the gritty water as I could, assuming there would be no water up the mountain.

The engine started with a roar and a cloud of exhaust smoke, the gears were crunched into first – and we were off. A few minutes after starting the long climb the engine stalled and we ground to a halt. We all got out. The driver lifted the bonnet, swearing continually, and studied the engine with a look of fury. I realised that the carburettor was the guilty party and I watched in fascination as the driver gave it the kiss of life: he took a swig of petrol from a filthy bottle he had in the cab and squirted the fuel inside a thin fuel pipe he had disconnected. I could see the carburettor filling up with yellow fuel and clear bits of saliva. I felt sick at the sight of this and took a swig from the bucket that was hanging from the side of the truck and still had some water in it. I offered some to the driver but he wouldn't drink. He stank of petrol for the rest of the day.

An hour later we were on the move again, chugging upwards. It took half a day to reach the mountain pass and the view of the turquoise lake, and the bottomless drop below us became ever more spectacular. At the top we stopped for a leak and then began the steep, twisted descent. Surely he was going too fast? Did the brakes work? Would I be able to leap out if disaster struck? What about my rucksack? Suddenly a truck appeared in front of us, in the middle of the road. The driver reacted quickly, showing none of the sickening panic that was welling up inside me, and veered towards the abyss. I closed my eyes and waited for the plunge, and then opened them and everything was back to normal. Joy surged within me after this brush with death. I was alive!

When we reached the valley floor we drove alongside a huge river. I looked at my pocket atlas and identified the Tsangpo, which flows all the way across Tibet, getting bigger all the time, and finally drops down into northern India where it becomes the Brahmaputra River. This mighty river goes through Bangladesh, joins the Ganges and empties into the Bay of Bengal.

It was evening and we stopped at a roadside shack that served food. The Khampa ordered something to eat from the Chinese cook, who threw her hands towards heaven and launched into a tirade. I didn't need to know Chinese to understand her message: no food. The Khampa went into the kitchen and entered into a shouting match with her. Five minutes later he emerged triumphant, carrying a tray full of strange looking biscuits. They were greasy, rock-solid and sugary and he insisted that I eat. I tried one but it was so vile that I couldn't get it down. Further discussions followed and it was decided that I would sleep on a grimy bench in the cafe, for a cost of five yuan, and they would sleep in the truck. I wondered if they would sneak off in the night but I was too tired to care.

The following day the road became real asphalt for the first time since I had entered the country. It felt strange not hearing the rattling sound of truck on gravel and the rhythm of constant bumps. Presumably we were getting near to Lhasa, the capital of Tibet. There were scores of villages, cultivated fields and military bases. At one point we passed a new bridge, guarded by a soldier in green, standing motionless by his little sentry box. The Khampa started acting out an aeroplane and pointing over the bridge;

presumably an airport was located across the river. The closer we got to Lhasa the more miserable I felt; I didn't want to end this journey. I had got used to being with people like this and I liked them, I wasn't ready for a big city and I had no idea what I would do when I got there. Maybe I would just keep going onwards to Shanghai? But shouldn't I see more of Tibet? The weather was warm but cloudy and I dozed in the truck, feeling like a schoolboy in the morning, saying to his mother: just a few minutes more.

Now that we were on luxurious asphalt the truck had picked up speed. Lhasa was approaching fast and my companions seemed pleased with the prospect. I was missing the wilderness and wishing I had spent more time in it, wondering what I would need in terms of equipment if I were ever to go back. Suddenly the Khampa shouted, pointed towards the left and the driver turned off the main road and bumped along a gravel track towards the foot of a huge mountain. The Khampa became animated as he was trying to explain where we were going, but I understood nothing.

The truck parked in front of a huge monastery that was surrounded by a high whitewashed wall. The Khampa hurried me out of the cab and insisted I follow him into the compound. The driver stayed where he was, pulled his cap over his eyes, leaned back and seemed to fall asleep in an instant. The atmosphere inside the high wall felt strangely intimate and quite different to how it was outside. Young monks stood around in purple robes and shaved heads. They had grins on their faces and were far more welcoming than I had imagined they would be. We entered the main building to the sound of monks chanting and I noticed the musky smell from hundreds of butter lamps. I fell into step behind the Khampa and watched him perform a series of rituals – kneeling and chanting and touching his brow on the floor – in a way that was practised and natural. Gone was the happy-go-lucky persona I had come to know in the cab, the bandit-warrior image he projected. Here was a gentle, warm and spiritual person. Some of the monks seemed to know him and they offered him some strange-looking cakes. The Khampa introduced me with a sense of pride and soothing words of welcome were said. I felt that I was being blessed.

Back at the truck the Khampa gave me one of the cakes and I tasted it. Yuk! I could taste sour milk and the dusty barley flour the Tibetans eat, and it had a disgusting sticky texture. But it seemed disrespectful to reject such an offering, after all it came from a holy man in a monastery, and the Khampa seemed to be enjoying them. When his back was turned I

threw mine into the dusty roadside. We woke up the driver, hopped back
in and drove back to the main road and the river that seemed to follow
it everywhere. My companions were humming with pleasure, unable to
contain their glee and I supposed that Lhasa was their hometown.

Suddenly the Khampa shouted Lhasa and pointed ahead, but I couldn't
see anything: just a narrow plain and surrounding mountains. Then I
started to notice ugly, low concrete buildings everywhere and vast numbers
of soldiers. Lots of questions came to me: Is this city populated by soldiers?
Do they live in those concrete bunkers? Isn't there an old part to this city?
As if in answer to my question I could see an old building, a huge white
building, sitting on top of a little hill. Potala! Potala! shouted the Khampa,
pointing to the vast white palace that stands over the whole city, an image
that seems to be on the cover of every guidebook to Tibet. It didn't look so
impressive from where I was sitting; there were too many featureless new
buildings cluttering up the foreground.

We drove into the centre of what looked like a very ordinary little town
and the truck stopped. The Khampa put his two hands to his ear, bent his
head to indicate sleep and pointed down a side street. He was obviously
saying that's where the hotels are for you foreigners. This is where you get
out. I didn't want to go but neither of them looked too sad at the idea. I
handed over some banknotes, got out and said goodbye glumly. The truck
drove forward, unusual in that it didn't produce any dust, and I walked
around the unimpressive centre looking for somewhere to stay. Eventually
I ran into some bronzed westerners who pointed me towards what they
called the Guest House Ghetto, where I reluctantly settled in with a crowd
of Hong Kong Chinese, Japanese and western travellers.

CHAPTER FIVE

As I looked out of the window of my dormitory I thought this must be the smallest capital city in the world. The only traffic was an occasional tractor, or a truck, moving at walking pace, and lots of bicycles. There was so little traffic that pedestrians didn't bother looking left or right before crossing and people were standing in the middle of the road, chatting. I saw crumbling old Tibetan buildings with new constructions tacked on shakily to the front, forming a higgledy-piggledy mess of shops and cafes, each with a hand painted sign.

Around the hostel was a rash of Sichuanese restaurants, each with a little crowd of foreign travellers, and I noticed that they all seemed to congregate in a tiny area on the Beijing Road, the main route through the city. I ate noodles in one of the Sichuanese places and eavesdropped on a group of travellers:

- Tourism will soon ruin Lhasa! Just like it did to Kathmandu...I wonder where we can score some hash in this town?

The people in my dormitory were friendly. They shared stories, books, chocolate, maps and teaspoons. They had formed into groups and the singles gravitated towards one another. So many questions: Have you been to....? Do you want to go to...? How much is....? The most frequently discussed issue was prices; they would quiz anyone who walked in about how much they paid for this or that and then compare, comment, complain and evaluate. All of them were on strict budgets so they could only spend a limited amount each day. They were carefully planning their time in Tibet: studying lists of monasteries that had to be visited; time and cost estimates; bus timetables; organising food, wash bags, water filters and purification tablets, first-aid kits and appropriate reading material. This approach to travelling looked stressful and I felt that in their zealous attempt to understand Tibet they were somehow missing the point. All this planning removed the spontaneity and joy of discovery that I thrived on.

- I am from Zurich, said an attractive girl with a big smile. My name is Christina. Would you like to come with us to visit the Potala?

Christina was travelling alone but she had attached herself to a group of Australian backpackers. I could sense that she was looking for a male travelling companion but I wasn't ready to join their comfortable clique. I was drawn towards a group of Hong Kong Chinese who didn't seem to want any contact with us westerners. They looked horrified when I first spoke to them but I persisted. Their English wasn't good but one of them asked me:

- Where are you from?
- I am from Scotland.
- Ah, Scotland, he replied, not really knowing what to say next.
- I am from the city of Aberdeen, I said, knowing that Aberdeen is the name of the port in Hong Kong.
- Ah! Aberdeen! You from Hong Kong? They laughed. My little white lie seemed to have broken the ice and from that moment on they tolerated my presence.

I think the Hong Kong group were intimidated by the close proximity of so many westerners, but within a few days they had built up their confidence – as well as the amount of noise they were making. Their concept of conversation is totally different from ours. They all talked at once and if someone wanted to stress a particular point they started shouting, and inevitably someone else would shout back, and then they would laugh and the whole place would be in uproar. They could keep this up for hours and I found it entertaining. The westerners didn't know how to deal with the noise they were making – in fact they hated it – I could feel the tension between the groups.

I noticed the Hong Kong travellers had organised themselves into groups and when I asked what was going on they told me they were looking for a cheaper place to stay. I was keen to get out of the friendly embrace of the western travellers and I asked if I could come along. To my surprise, they agreed. They divided into small groups and systematically searched the town for cheaper accommodation. Within a few hours they had re-assembled and were engaged in a noisy discussion, I presume about which option to choose. We all packed our rucksacks, paid up and left. I had no idea where we were going but I was delighted to be joining this group of nine.

The new place we went to was a grimy truck stop with Tibetan pilgrims from all over the country, people who looked weather-beaten and dangerous in their long woollen coats. Some of them had swords. The manager was a barrel-chested bandit with a laugh that could have awakened the dead; he didn't want us there and he entered into a long and noisy argument with my Hong Kong friends in Mandarin. They overwhelmed him with arguments and paperwork showing they were Chinese citizens and therefore eligible to remain. He reluctantly agreed and the group started trooping up the steep, wooden, outside staircase. Suddenly the manager roared out in anger – he had seen me – and evidently this was too much for him; he screamed a volley of abuse in my direction. I knew he wasn't allowed to receive foreigners in this place, we were all supposed to stay in specially designated hotels. But my friends were on a roll and the manager's hysteria seemed to amuse them. They trooped back down to the yard, surrounded him, and insisted that I too was from Hong Kong, from Aberdeen, and therefore I had a right to stay too. The argument raged and the manager could see that he was heavily outnumbered, and they weren't giving up, so he stomped off in disgust, cursing. We were in.

We went up a steep ladder-type staircase, along a slimy corridor and into a room at the top of the house, a room that took my breath away: each of the four walls had a window and we had a panoramic view over the old town. We could see the golden roofs and incredible colours of the Potala Palace. It was also the dirtiest room I had ever seen in my life. The floor was so sticky that my shoes stuck to it and the beds looked flea-ridden, sagging and flimsy. It stank of feet, stale sweat, unwashed bodies and rancid cheese. The manager's face was no longer red with fury, he now had a wry grin as he knew his new Hong Kong guests would be appalled. This was his revenge. There were twenty small beds in the room, each one more horrible than the next, but before long my friends had taken over and the place was full of their noisy chattering.

Our truck stop was called Pemba and the atmosphere was raucous. Although people were yelling at each other, their look showed that they weren't shouting in anger; they were teasing, taunting and mocking. Someone told me these people were pilgrims, had travelled far to see Lhasa's Jokhang temple, but all I ever saw them do was shout, drink, gamble and joke. Every night a gang of big Tibetan women would come round the dormitory with buckets to collect the rent. Everyone paid two yuan, twenty British pence, but some of the Tibetan men tried to refuse payment so that they could provoke a wrestling match with the women. The women wouldn't hesitate to throw themselves onto a disobedient male, pin him down and, while he roared with laughter, search his pockets.

The Pemba truck stop was located in the city centre, on a street that didn't seem to have any traffic apart from people wandering by. Underneath the hostelry was a teahouse that faced onto the street. It was just a room with four tables, thin benches and full of noisy Tibetans who looked so different from each other that I guessed they were from all over the country. The noodle chef had a big grin on his face and was covered in flour. He would walk around the teahouse as if he were in his own kitchen, ignoring the invisible barrier that most chefs observe between the kitchen and the restaurant. He would tease and wrestle with the sweet tea waitress at every opportunity and engage in shouting matches with the clientele. When he saw me he came over at once, sat down on the bench next to me and with a beaming smile proceeded to search me: he wanted to feel my clothes, to see what I had in my pocket, to try on my sunglasses, to show the others my diary. He was rude and outrageous but he made me feel welcome and that evening I wrote in my diary that he had introduced me to the casual exuberance that is Lhasa.

This seedy little teahouse became my base as I explored Lhasa, but I was careful not to tell the western travellers about it or they would have spoiled the atmosphere. I drank sweet tea by the gallon; sticky and milky, invigorating, served in small glasses, only costing a penny a cup. Fooling around with the people there and looking out on the town made me feel part of the local scene.

One morning, before dawn, the Hong Kong Chinese were getting dressed in a hurry and preparing to leave. I asked them where they were going and before they all trooped out one of them casually said we go see dead body. I later found out that they had been to see what travellers call the Sky Burial, a ritual that takes place every day on the outskirts of town, under one of the high mountains. Dead bodies are laid out on a huge rock and then chopped up by body-cutters, a class of men whose profession is to crush the bones with rocks. The pieces were then thrown onto the ground where flocks of vultures and other birds of prey devour them. This ritual was one of the main tourist attractions in Lhasa and every morning the backpackers would march off towards the hills to see it for themselves I found it hard to believe that this way of dealing with dead bodies had anything to do with Buddhism, the religion that pervaded all aspects of Tibetan life. I wondered if it came from ancient Tibet, before the spread of Buddhism, or was to do with the lack of topsoil needed for burying people? I didn't want to see the ritual and felt that the crowds of tourists who went to watch were similar to the vultures who swooped down to get their breakfast every morning.

The best way of finding unexpected places in a new city is to get lost in it, and getting lost in Lhasa is inevitable considering that street signs were in Chinese and Tibetan and the very concept of city maps was completely unknown – not only here throughout the Communist world, where detailed maps were considered classified military information. Lhasa was like a doughnut in that the old centre was Tibetan and wrapped round it was a swathe of newly-built Chinese buildings. The old buildings were simple, single-storeyed, stone-built and whitewashed, The new Chinese buildings were also quite low and unobtrusive – but ugly, built of concrete and unpainted.

The market was the centre of the old town and was divided into two parts: the modern fruit, veg and meat section, and the ancient Barkhor. The Barkhor was a network of old streets that made a circuit round the Jokhang, the city's main Buddhist temple. Each of these streets was stone paved and packed with stalls selling hand-made curios, grimy old antiques, Tibetan clothes, shoes, candles and ceremonial gear. There was a constant flow of pilgrims walking round the Barkhor, chanting, fingering their rosaries, prostrating themselves and oblivious to the world around them.

I came across a narrow street that the travellers referred to as Yak Alley. It smelled of stale piss and, curiously for the old town, was paved with asphalt. A yak walked by and an old woman greeted me with great warmth. There were traders squatting down both sides of the lane, in dark filthy coats, with a wild look about them, as if they had just come down from the hills. Many of them were holding long knives and sitting next to piles of freshly cut meat, yak's heads and trotters, separated from the pavement by old scraps of leather and cloth. Scores of Tibetans were haggling with these traders and I could pick up the good-humoured banter. At the far end of the lane beefy women were unloading big heavy blocks that were wrapped in badly treated leather – still covered in hairs. I looked closer and saw that these blocks contained rancid butter, the stuff that went into Tibetan tea, and the smell was overwhelming. There was always a big crowd around the butter sellers.

I began to absorb the atmosphere of the city. There was a reckless humour about the people that appealed to me and I began to realise that behind their raunchiness was immense warmth and a spirituality that was spontaneous and without any of the self-righteousness one comes across among religious people in the west. A feeling developed that I should stay here in Lhasa as long as I could. I began to lose the drive to push on for Shanghai although I knew there were no jobs for foreigners in Tibet.

Every day I would go to the Barkhor and walk round the temple with the pilgrims. It was like getting into the flow of a river. Many of the pilgrims were in rags and I was struck by the contrast between their obvious poverty and the joyous expressions on their faces. The Jokhang is the central point of Tibetan Buddhism, a sacred place in their culture, and getting there was a lifetime achievement for poor villagers. From the outside the Jokhang didn't look that impressive: stone whitewashed walls about one-storey high, sloping slightly inwards (an ancient earthquake precaution), with black-painted window frames and white cotton curtains. Inside was another world of murals, statues and yak butter lamps. The experience of visiting the Jokhang was, for me, deeply moving but also accompanied by a feeling of bewilderment: I felt like the only one who didn't know what to do with myself. The Tibetans would approach each statue, stand in line and address it with a prayer and a ritual – they had a circuit to follow – and the foreign visitors had guidebooks open and were ticking off, and photographing, the various statues and images before them.

The inside of the temple was overwhelming at first and I found my way onto the flat roof, where I found something I was familiar with – construction work. I started comparing building techniques with what I knew from back home in Edinburgh. A team of Tibetan joiners, in blue Chinese cotton clothes, was working on a big tree trunk and I observed their tools, their methods and their banter. I was particularly intrigued by the adzes they were using to whittle down the massive piece of wood. An adze is a short axe on which the blade is at right angles to the shaft, so it forms a T-shape and is suited to whittling down tree trunks. The action required lots of gentle but accurate strikes, chip-chip-chipping away at the wood. The tree trunk they were working on had big bulbous lumps at either end and these would become the elaborate, splayed carvings that I had seen at either end of the pillars below in the temple. The work looked easy and the workers were friendly; they saw that I was interested in what they were doing and they offered me a cup of home-brewed chang. I wondered how to say in Tibetan have you got a job?

Back at the Pemba truck stop I realised with horror that my hat was missing. It was a dark blue Mao-style hat that had only cost two Yuan, about twenty pence, at the border but it had been useful protection against the sun on the road. What gave it sentimental value was a little tin badge that I had picked up in Warsaw, a badge that said Solidarnosc (Solidarity) and had helped me get the mural painting job in Vienna, where the foreman was a Pole. Somehow it felt like an important part of my identity and I just had to get it back. I retraced my steps and found myself back in the Jokhang Temple. The monks on the front gate were amused when I acted out my message:

- Hat...lost...here...inside...please...

One of the young monks ran off, his maroon robes flapping behind him, and then reappeared with an excited look on his face. He beckoned me to follow and we walked quickly into the temple. The search was on! Whenever he questioned a monk or a worker they would send us deeper and deeper into the interior of temple, and all over the building sites on the roof. Just after I had given up hope a young worker led us through a labyrinth of wooden scaffolding and pulled out a dusty old trunk from a cupboard. It looked like nobody had been in that cupboard for years. He opened the trunk, rummaged around inside and, to my amazement, pulled out my hat. I couldn't believe it. But there was a problem – the little badge was missing. Another hunt began and after more searching and questioning it was eventually found in a dank cubbyhole.

Before the end of my first week Lhasa had me hooked and I knew I should stay, settle down for a while and find something to do. The finding of my hat impressed me deeply. I hadn't expected to find it, since all my experience told me that when something is lost or stolen you don't get it back. It made me re-think what is and isn't possible. Could I apply this experience to something that seemed equally impossible, like getting a job? I needed to work, not only to make money but also to give a purpose for my presence in Lhasa.

But what could I possibly do in Tibet? I liked the idea of working on the restoration of a monastery and imagined myself filling in the holes that rampaging Chinese had made in the murals during the Cultural Revolution, but the Chinese are a bureaucratic lot and I knew that I would fulfil none of the requirements if a job was actually on offer. Also, it was obvious to see that the restoration work was being done by local tradesmen, who seemed to know exactly what they were doing, and the idea of them hiring a foreigner, even a volunteer, would have raised gales of laughter. The only relevant qualification that I possessed was a certificate in the teaching of English but the only experience I actually had was correcting the essays of a student in Vienna.

One of the advantages of being a foreigner in a place like Tibet is that people will let you in where you shouldn't really be. I would walk into the various hotels and hostels and everyone working there would assume I was just another guest. In one such hotel I found myself in a corridor that was lit by a single light-bulb. Light was coming out of an open door and I looked in to see a large, thin, middle-aged man writing on little pieces of paper. I stood there watching him, noticing the white streaks in his long blond, thinning hair. He stuck one of the little bits of paper onto a small basket with a lid on it. The word STOMACH had been written on the bit of paper with a red marker pen.

I stepped into the room and tried to attract his attention, but he was deeply concentrating on the next label:

- What are you doing? I asked. He glanced up with a look of annoyance; I had interrupted him.

- I help foreigners who get sick or need help, he snapped in an upper class English accent. Was he some kind of doctor?

The next day I returned to the same room and the scene had changed: there was no sign of the man with the long thinning hair but there was a lady talking fast in an English accent to a room packed full of foreign travellers. I also noticed that the room was lined with shelves, each one full of books. What was this place? The foreigners were bombarding the lady with questions about travelling in Tibet and nobody noticed as I squeezed through and found somewhere to sit on a disused bed. She was middle-aged, and kindly looking, with long blonde hair, spectacles and faded flower-power clothes. She was talking loudly to the assembled mob about monasteries, opening times, prices, bus tickets, routes and what to do about diarrhoea.

I wasn't interested in any of this information but I found the whole scene bizarre and fascinating and realised that she was running some sort of information centre. I listened carefully to the endless flow of information and joined in one of the conversations, involving five people, and managed to steer it in the direction of finding work locally. She explained in an aside that she was an underpaid, overworked English teacher in Lhasa and I popped the question:

- Any English teaching jobs?

- No, and there are unlikely to be any in the future but if you leave your name on a bit of paper we'll get in touch if anything comes up.

Back at the Pemba truck stop things were getting chaotic. Now that the hot summer weather was over the real pilgrim season had begun, and crowds of tribesmen were turning up on overloaded lorries, many of who would appear at the Pemba demanding a bed for the night. The din at midnight was incredible and I remembered how noisy my brothers and I had been after moving into Edinburgh from the Scottish countryside; people with no neighbours have no concept of keeping the noise down. Somehow I managed to sleep. The Hong Kong group were bristling with irritation and I could tell that they didn't find these newcomers as interesting as I did; they obviously saw them as a noisy rabble. When they started complaining to the manager about the noise and the filth I started to distance myself from my former allies.

My dreams became powerful and vivid. I dreamt that my skin had been destroyed by fallout from the Chernobyl nuclear accident, an event that had shocked the world a few months earlier. A vile apparition – a skinned camel – appeared in my dreams as an argument raged nearby and doors were slammed. I admired the audacity and freedom of these Tibetans but realised that, as a foreigner, I was at a great distance from them. In my dreams I rode with them across the prairie and shared their wild women.

I would recover from the chaos of Pemba by spending a bit of time every day in the middle-class calm of the travellers information centre – a place that was known as The Travellers' Co-op. I persisted in hassling the talkative blonde, whose name was Isabella, about a teaching job and she introduced me to an old American professor called Robert Morse – a Tibetan scholar, polyglot, veteran world traveller and English teacher at Tibet University. He explained that Tibet University was a very new creation; it was small, underfunded, badly managed, had very few students and the two English teachers were recruited in Beijing. At last I felt like I was making some progress, finding out some information, sowing seeds. If I was patient and persistent things would work out.

The ongoing drama at the Pemba took a new turn when the irate manager and his harem of rent-collecting women appeared in the dormitory early one morning and ordered the Hong Kong group to leave immediately. The beefy women moved in on their rucksacks, with every intention of throwing them into the street, and the Hong Kongers leaped up, screamed hysterically and started struggling with the women for the possession of the baggage. I was watching all this from under a dirty sheet, trying to remain as inconspicuous as possible, hoping I wouldn't get the heave too – and with absolutely no intention of helping. Pandemonium reigned but the Tibetan women were winning and the Hong Kong group were gradually forced out of the room, with sleeping bags trailing after them. Suddenly my sheet was roughly ripped off and I was exposed; fingers were pointed and a volley of abuse hurled my way but I stayed put and for some reason they didn't grab my rucksack, hurl it down the stairs and order me out. The woman standing over me was called over to the main struggle, which was now taking place on the staircase. They never came back for me.

That same night a violent storm hit Lhasa and, with four windows overlooking the town, I was ideally placed to observe it. Bolts of lightning lit up the landscape and the roar of thunder, echoed by the surrounding mountains, was louder than anything I had ever experienced. It rocked the building and shocked all the noisy pilgrims in the room into a timid, cowering silence. Torrential rain was hurled against the windows with a demonic fury that seemed intent on destroying us. The wind tore at the roof and battered the windows until one of them exploded in fragments of glass. Energised by the storm, I moved from window to window to get the best view. The street outside had become a river and water was pouring off our roof in furious, spitting arcs, from gutters that were extended about a metre from the edges of the roof. Water was spraying through the broken window and nobody else was making a move to stop it so I found a blue cotton sheet and held it to the window to try and stop the rain pouring in. I got soaked immediately, as did the sheet, and the wind seemed to grab and shake me as if I were a rag doll. Floods had formed all over the floor and other windows were being burst open. We were helpless.

As the storm reached the height of its fury a huge lightning bolt, far thicker than anything I had seen yet, shot down. Unlike the other lightning bolts, this one didn't go into the ground; it shot back up towards the clouds and formed a massive u-shape in the sky. The whole landscape was brilliantly illuminated for about half a second. The image that was forever burned into my retina was the building directly under the u-shaped bolt of lightning: the Potala Palace, revealed for a moment in a mosaic of gold and red and white colours, a massive fort-like structure that was sitting on its own little hill.

The following day I was surprised to see that the city was still intact and not much damage had been done. I felt we had survived an aerial bombardment, but the Tibetans were going about their business as if nothing had happened at all. Presumably they were used to this kind of weather and I wondered what a big storm meant for them spiritually; their temples were full of demons and dragons and I imagined we had met one of them the previous night.

Lhasa was becoming surprisingly hectic and I needed some silence. I became more aware of time: my visa was running out and if I didn't make a move soon there wouldn't be enough time to reach Shanghai, or see anything more of Tibet. I had done my best to find a job but was under no illusions that I could actually get one. Where could I go and visit? I should try and see some of Tibet before leaving. I started asking the travellers, all of who were keen to share their knowledge. There seemed to be two main options: the Everest Base Camp, back down the road I had already travelled, and a big lake up north. The Everest option seemed too touristy so I opted for the lake, which was on a huge plateau populated by nomads. I borrowed some camping equipment and walked out of town.

Unlike the road I had travelled along from Kathmandu, the road north into China was paved with tarmac. It was also full of military convoys: lines of trucks, each one packed with soldiers or covered in green tarpaulin; none of who ever stopped for me. Lhasa is located on a narrow strip of flat land but it is surrounded by mountains and once you cross these you reach a high plateau that stretches out into the horizon. They call this plain the Changtang, the Northern Plateau.

Other foreigners were heading out of town that day and I was determined to get ahead of them so I marched as fast as I could, across the short plain and into the hills. Eventually a flat-bed truck stopped and I climbed up, noticing that a middle-aged foreigner had already installed himself. I stood on the tailgate for a while, holding the metal bar, feeling the wind on my face and enjoying the fact that I was on the move again. Then I went to talk to the foreigner, an elderly Austrian:

- Nettles, he said, are the only survivors in this area of overgrazing. There are no wild flowers up here anymore and the grass is disappearing. The Chinese have doubled the population of yaks and this fragile ecosystem can't take it. Soon there will only be dust.

The road into the mountains got steeper and the truck got slower. As we approached the high pass we were crawling along at walking pace. The sky was covered with clouds but at the pass we got a glimpse of the sun before the truck began a reckless plunge down the other side. We were being shaken around so much that I felt we were two dice in a cup. The driver stopped at a lonely truck stop on the other side, at the start of the endless Changtang plateau.

The Austrian stayed at the truck stop and I carried on walking northwards, enjoying the mesmerising monotony of the flatlands. Eventually I was picked up by a bus, a knackered old claptrap, and chugged along the few miles to the next village – where the track to the lake began. I was told it would take two days to walk to the lake from this point on the main road, and it involved crossing a high mountain pass to the west, before dropping down onto another flat plain. There was a lively truck stop in the village where I ate delicious Chinese noodles, chatted to a friendly American couple and found a bed for the night. The Americans told hair-raising stories about travellers who had been savaged by dogs and advised me to take a strong stick in case of attack.

The next morning I was full of energy and, after finding an old axe shaft as protection against the dogs, I set off early. It took half a day to get up the mountain pass, from where I could see the plateau stretching out in all directions, with distant mountain ranges forming a jagged horizon. The lake I was heading for was visible – it looked huge – but after a full day of fast walking it didn't seem to be getting any closer. I passed some nomads who were skulking around a black woollen tent and noticed that they were dressed in rough fur coats, belted at the waist and reaching the ground. Their huge guard dogs were barking viciously but were held back by ropes tied to stakes in the ground. Tibet was full of barking dogs and Lhasa was full of strays but these dogs were vast and they looked deadly. I wondered what they were protecting the nomads against? Wolves?

By early evening I had covered a huge distance but the lake still didn't seem any closer. I stopped to rest near a nomad's tent, not getting too close in case the dogs got angry enough to burst their bonds. The wind grew colder. A young nomad, wearing a one-piece fur belted at his waist, walked by and invited me into the circular tent, which was made of thick black wool. I could see penetrating eyes and when he smiled brilliant white teeth. He took me inside the tent and introduced me grandly to his petite wife and an old woman I presumed to be his mother, and a couple of naked children who were half hidden behind big wooden boxes. Apart from the granny, whose hair was white, they all had long, wild, matted, pitch-black hair. The wife was slim and attractive but there was a strange lump on her lower back, some sort of deformation I assumed. Moments later the lump moved and suddenly a shock of black hair appeared, two eyes, a nose and a mouth: it was a baby, living in the top part of her leather coat, held in place by a tight belt: a way of keeping the baby close all day, while allowing the mother complete freedom to move around.

I left my boots and socks outside the entrance flap and stepped onto a mosaic of rugs that covered the whole area inside the tent, except for a little circle in the middle where a small fire burned. There was a hole in the top of the tent where smoke lazily poured out, but much of the smoke lingered and started to penetrate my clothes and hair. Wooden boxes and sacks were stacked all round the outer rim of the tent, forming a barrier against the cold and creating a cosy, cave-life feel in the middle. I wondered why they had so much stuff, what was in those boxes and how did they move them? And surely they moved frequently? They were nomads after all, living in a tent. Did all of this stuff go on the back of yaks?

Around the fire was a circular, narrow rim that was the only clutter-free area. This was where the family moved nimbly around and where we sat. The old woman seemed to be the busiest; feeding lumps of dried yak dung into the fire and shouting at the children. A large loping hound nosed its way into the tent, sniffed at me suspiciously and went back out again. Now that night had fallen, the dogs had been unleashed and were allowed to wander freely, providing a roving security barrier against intruders. The man produced a long wooden tube like a thin barrel, about four inches wide and four feet long. He filled it with hot tea, threw in a lump of rancid yak's butter and some salt and started to mix it up and down with a long plunger, a stick with a flat round bit at the bottom – making sure that the tea and butter and salt were all mixed up well together. I was licking my lips in anticipation: this was dinner.

Darkness was approaching and I had to make a move: head out into the wilderness and find some shelter, or hope to get an invitation from this lot. I didn't dare ask about staying the night but I gave my new friend an entrance ticket to the Potala, with a crude sketch of the palace on it, and his face lit up. He placed it on the family altar, alongside a small Buddha and a photo of the Dalai Lama. The old woman handed out bowls with disgusting looking black sausages but I refused mine, sticking to tsampa and tea. The man asked where I was going and when I acted out lake... birds...over there. He jumped up, pulled out a dagger and hacked the neck off a dead goat that was in one of the sacks. He presented me with this bloody, bony, grisly present with a huge smile – I could see it was an act of real generosity – and I wrapped it in a cloth and put it in my rucksack. They hadn't invited me to stay as they had assumed all along that I would, and when the time came I lay down in my borrowed sleeping bag on a soft pile of dried yak dung and fell fast asleep. During the night I was awoken by a sound and I saw the man hopping nimbly over the clutter and out for a pee. He was stark naked and didn't seem to notice that it was freezing outside.

The next morning I walked out towards the lake and reached it by the middle of the day. I then realised that Bird Island wasn't an island at all, it was a peninsula; a huge lump of rock that stuck out of the plateau like a lone thumb. It was surrounded by water on three sides and was connected to the mainland by a narrow neck of land, an isthmus. The lake is called Namtso and it was as smooth as a mirror that day, deep blue and stretched out towards the horizon. An Austrian couple were camping by the lakeside and, hungry for conversation, I went over and sat by them. He was a middle-aged ecologist and I soon bored of his monotonous and rather depressing talk. His girlfriend was half his age, beautiful but not very chatty. This couple were seriously well-equipped and I admired their tent, boots, waterproofs, dehydrated food, rucksacks and cooking equipment, wondering if I would ever be able to afford gear like that. I told them that I didn't have a tent and he suggested I walk to the other side of the rock where there was a small cave.

From where we were sitting it didn't look far to the rock, but time and space had assumed a new meaning on this plateau and it wasn't until evening that I found the cave, which had a rounded entrance hole about a metre off the ground. Even though the sun was going down it was warmer than it had been all day and the rock, which had been soaking up the rays all day, now shared its warmth. It had a soft carpeting of dried sheep dung, considerately arranged on a space that was just perfect to take my sleeping bag.

Some days before, in Yak Alley, the meat market in Lhasa, I had met a scruffy Englishman who had walked across Pakistan and Tibet and was en-route to Australia. His hair and beard were unkempt and he looked more grimy than the poorest Tibetan. His eyes were sparkling and he looked at peace with himself. His feet were black from the home-made sandals he had fashioned out of an old tyre – footwear that had lasted him thousands of miles. We got chatting and he told me that he never needed to spend money as people would give him food and shelter for free:

- Here in Tibet, he said, the people are the most generous I've come across anywhere. In the market they give me food – and money. He gave me some advice about cooking that I was now trying out in the cave:

- Take an old tin can and half-fill it with sand or dried earth. Pour in a small amount of petrol, light it and then cook your dinner. It worked perfectly; a small pot of water quickly boiled and before long my noodles were ready.

I was being watched. Outside the cave was a young, weather-beaten face staring at me. I finished my noodles, made some tea – and he was still there, still staring. I wondered if I was the first white man he'd seen? Was this his cave? I could see sheep grazing around him so presumably he was a shepherd. I started to get irritated as I realised that he wasn't going to leave me in peace, he wasn't going to be satisfied until I got into bed and it was too dark to see. I had to accept his presence. I realised that living in those tents, in such close proximity to one another, it's understandable that nomads have no sense of privacy. What was strange about this character was that he made no attempt to communicate; he didn't say a word, or make any gestures, and this was unlike most Tibetans I had come across. I wondered if this is typical of people who spend their whole lives with sheep and goats. Resigned to his presence, and realising he represented no threat, I made a show of taking out my sleeping bag, making sure he could see it properly, and settling down for the night. Before falling into a deep sleep I listened to the noises drifting across the plateau: animals moving far away and the wind playing strange games in the rocks.

The next morning I explored the area. What I thought had been one big rock at the side of the lake was actually two, looking like massive dinosaur eggs. Most of the part facing the plateau was a low cliff and as I walked towards the lake – about an hour away – I could see that there were more caves, and all sorts of intricate carvings made by the wind. Suddenly I came across two army trucks and a group of soldiers in green uniforms – all Tibetans – eating their breakfast. What on earth are they doing up here? I wondered. Giant crows were circling around overhead, making ominous cawing sounds. The soldiers were as surprised as I by the encounter and they beckoned me over. I didn't hesitate, making a beeline for the trestle table that was laden with Chinese beer, cooked meats, cakes, fried biscuits and boiled sweets. It was an orgy! They had enough food to last a nomad family for months.

All afternoon I explored the lake side of the peninsula. There was a rocky beach and caves that were inhabited by serious, well-equipped foreigners. Two couples were lying in the intense sun, covered in white sun block cream. All they were wearing was sunglasses. None of them looked particularly friendly. That night I lay on my back on soft, golden dust and watched the stars. The sky was clear, we were at fourteen thousand feet and the stars were far brighter than I had ever seen them before. It was mesmerising.

Back at the cave I noticed that an intruder had been going through my things. My precious biscuits had been half-eaten and my stuff was scattered around. I've been burgled I thought, that thieving shepherd bastard! So that was his game! I frantically searched my rucksack and nothing was missing. Someone had told me that nomads are known for their honesty. Of course I realised, it was the sheep, they were the intruders – although they probably consider me to be the intruder as this is obviously their cave.

I spent almost a week up there, wandering around, acclimatizing to the altitude, trying to climb the rocks, relaxing. After a while the intense quality of the place became too much and I felt I lacked the experience needed to truly appreciate all this beauty. Part of me wanted to stay forever but I knew I had nothing to do and that boredom would soon come visiting. Whenever I saw couples who were travelling together there seemed to be a heavy atmosphere between them, as if they were still angry with each other since the last argument. When couples live together in an urban, western environment they both do their own things during the day. Out here they were stuck together all the time and it's no surprise that they got thoroughly sick of each other.

I set off from Bird Island long before dawn, picking my way through the strange rockscape by the light of the stars. There was no moon. Walking in the night felt incredible and it was giving me extra energy. A grey light slipped over the distant, serrated horizon and gradually I could make out the shape of the landscape. I looked back with a smile and a feeling of affection at the bulbous shape of Bird Island, thinking I'll be back here soon enough.

I came across a marsh and had to take a slightly longer route in order to avoid it. No problem I thought, I've got plenty of time and energy today. A nomad's tent was blocking the short cut back to my route and I didn't think twice about walking near to it: the nomads are friendly, honest and they like me. I noticed a big dog looking at me suspiciously but he didn't move and I wasn't afraid. I was still carrying the axe handle I had found at the truck stop and I wondered, why was I carrying this lump of wood? It was heavy, too short to be used as a walking stick and the dogs can sense that I'm a friendly presence and so they were leaving me in peace. Why don't I just throw it away, I thought, the nomads will put it to good use.

Then all hell broke loose. Three dogs came running towards me, making low growling noises. I spun round and instantly knew this was serious; when dogs bark at you it often means they will not actually attack; they know that just barking will keep most people away. But when a dog runs towards you without barking it's a sign that it really means business. And these dogs were huge Tibetan mastiffs, bred to protect the nomads against goodness knows what threats, and they were almost upon me. Adrenalin flooded my system and enabled me to move with a speed and precision that I had never been capable of previously. I started swinging my stick back and forth with vicious energy and screamed at the top of my voice Back! Back! Back!

Oblivious to my defensive tactics the dogs charged on. The first one to reach me leapt at my face. I could see that his paws were stretched out in front of him and they would hit my chest with the force of a battering ram, knock me to the ground from where they could rip me apart at their leisure. My Guardian Angel was on his toes that morning and my first desperate swing with the axe shaft connected with the skull of the oncoming dog with a deep thud. Any lesser dog would have been killed instantly. This one just yelped once, shook its head and withdrew from the attack. The two other dogs didn't even glance in the direction of their wounded comrade; they had no intention of giving up their prey. Having seen that their frontal charge had failed they instantly changed tactics: one of them stayed at the front of me, probing and barking viciously; waiting for a gap in my swinging bat so he could leap in for the kill. The second dog started running circles round me, looking for an opportunity to attack from the rear. While screaming and swinging and turning to keep an eye on the circling dog I was constantly stepping away from their territory, hoping to get away before they got me.

A figure appeared out of the gloom, raised a cry of alarm and raced over in a long leather coat. It was a nomad woman and, considering the whole incident had taken place in a few seconds, she had got out of her tent with remarkable speed. She ran up like a rampaging harpy, screaming at the dogs and wielding a long stick. The dog that was facing me paid her no attention and she whacked it hard with the stick. It yelped in pain and ran off into the darkness. The other dog was too fast for the woman and it wasn't giving up: it continued to circle me and both of our eyes were locked onto one another; and both of us knew that if either one of us made a mistake it would be fatal. Both of us ignored the woman. I carried on stepping backwards, turning round constantly to keep my eyes on the dog, swinging the stick in front of me and shouting at the top of my voice. At some point I crossed an invisible line, where the dog's jurisdiction ran out, and it gave up.

I had been driven mad by a powerful rush of fear and rage. Even though there was no longer any threat I swung at imaginary attackers, cursed loudly into the wind, vowing to always carry weapons and avoid nomads' tents at night. The flood of relief and joy to be alive were mixed with a powerful sense of fear and for the next few hours my thoughts were manic and obsessive – about death, fighting, lying wounded in a ditch – and I jogged on, half expecting to be attacked again; on guard for wolves, dogs, bandits or mythical beasts. By lunchtime I was starting to calm down and I remembered what a Buddhist scholar told me about death:

- Buddhist monks are encouraged to think about death every day.
- Why's that?
- So they are reminded of the transience of life.
- That sounds depressing.
- Not at all, by thinking about death every day you appreciate life more. The idea is that you should live in the present, for the moment, and not worry about the past or the future – or death.

The incident had given me a tremendous energy boost and I crossed that plain in record time. I concentrated on my pace, got into a fast walking rhythm and felt myself going into a trance-like state, oblivious to the view or the aches and pains that come with walking. All that mattered was getting through the landscape in the fastest time possible. I didn't feel like an outsider any more, I felt I belonged here and was somehow becoming part of the countryside. At one point I passed a hungry-looking fox, presumably trying to hunt the little picas – tail-less mouse-hares – that had made holes everywhere.

By lunchtime my stomach was in agony and I made a little fire in my old tin can (a dash of petrol on a handful of dried earth) and heated up a delicious can of Chinese pork-fat in gravy.

Night was falling and if I hadn't seen a friendly looking foreign couple beckoning me over I probably would have marched on into the night. I had overcome any sense of exhaustion, hunger or time. The couple were Belgian and they had made friends with a nomad family. I went over to the big black tent, warily eyeing the dogs, sat with them and greedily drank several cups of yak butter tea. I felt a sense of pride at having walked to this point from Bird Island in just one day. It had taken them three. The Belgians retired to their neat little foreign tent and the nomads invited me to stay with them. I pulled out my sleeping bag and settled down by a stack of strong smelling yak skins. The man of the house came over and laughed at my sleeping bag, as if to say how can you sleep in that pathetic thing? He rummaged around some sacks, hauled out an old carpet which he threw over me; it was so heavy that for a moment I couldn't breathe but I knew it would bring warmth. According to the Belgians, the nomads were en-route to the meat market in Lhasa, with their yaks, and the tent was surrounded by the big, black, peaceful beasts. During the night I was woken up by the animals' stomping, chomping and heavy breathing.

Before dawn the next day I jumped up and quickly got ready. I knew it was Friday and there was an early morning bus to Lhasa, the last one that week, and I was determined not to miss it. I didn't have any energy left for hitchhiking. The nomads were already dismantling the tent and packing boxes and sacks onto the backs of the patient yaks. They would continue their journey towards the meat market in Lhasa over the coming week. The village with the bus stop was about two hours distant and, energised by a cup of Tibetan tea, I marched there at top speed; maybe the bus hadn't left yet? But the closer I got the more convinced I became that I had missed the bus.

I noticed the village was built by the Chinese – uniform concrete walls surrounding each house, a thicket of antennae poking out of each roof. I walked past a school where all the children were lined up in military formation; the red flag was fluttering in the dawn light and the teacher started to sing the Chinese national anthem, quickly followed by all the young voices.

By now the sun had risen and I knew that the bus was supposed to leave well before dawn. I went to the bus stop just in case and, to my surprise, it was still there. A crowd was there for the same reason as me – to get to Lhasa – and more people were arriving every minute. There was no way all of us would fit into the small, battered, dust-covered old banger that they had surrounded. After some time the driver and conductress appeared, and the crowd opened up a gap for them to pass through. The conductress stood in the bus doorway like a colossus, shouting aggressively at the crowd, trying to prevent us from storming the bus, while letting on a select few. Grinding noises could be heard as the driver tried to nurse the old engine to life. The crowd pulsated impatiently, we were all desperate to get on board. I had an advantage compared to the Tibetans: I only had a rucksack and wasn't carrying large numbers of cumbersome bags.

I managed to push past the conductress, as she was shouting at someone else, and get on board. She turned to me with a face of fury, screamed and pointed at the door, but I had already settled down in the first chair I had experienced in a week and I knew she couldn't leave her post at the door, as it would give the mob instant access. She could shout as much as she liked, I wasn't going anywhere unless they hauled me out and I reckoned it would take at least two of them. We left in a storm of curses and banging fists on the window and I thrust some notes in the harridan's grimy fingers. Grateful that she didn't heave me out at first stop, I appreciated that bus journey more than any other I can remember – sitting in a comfortable chair and moving along at the same time. What a miracle! Waves of heat from the engine wafted over us and I slept all the way to Lhasa.

As if in a dream I got off the bus in the outskirts and walked into Lhasa. I had started to get used to life in the wilderness and coming back to a big town felt alien. I felt real appreciation for what we normally take for granted: food, running water and a bed. My top priority was food: I hadn't had a proper meal in a week and the thought made my mouth water.

Many months before I had heard about Jill Kluge, a girl from England who worked in Hong Kong and had just got a job at the new Holiday

Inn in Lhasa – a big, white, American looking spread called Lhasa Hotel. I stood outside it, wondering if they would let me in considering that I hadn't washed in a week, was covered in dust and had the hairdo and beard of a tramp. There were scores of Toyota Landcruisers and smart minibuses in front of the hotel and to my surprise nobody challenged me when I wandered in and stood in the lobby, gaping. The guests all looked smart and wealthy and some wore trekking gear as if they were heading into the mountains, but their boots and trousers looked brand new and unused. I asked about Jill Kluge who was, to my surprise, in the hotel. She was running the restaurant and seemed delighted to meet a fellow Brit. She bought me a Yak Burger with all the trimmings. As my taste buds were running wild with new sensations. We talked:

- You know where I found your name? I asked
- No.
- In Vienna. I was working on a restoration project in a historic building which had been emptied out. One day I explored and found an empty office. There was a telephone in the room and to my surprise it had a dialling tone. I immediately thought who can I call? and I remembered Matthew.
- How do you know Matthew?
- I don't. My brother Kim was at school with him at the Edinburgh Academy and he gave me his number in Hong Kong.
- You called him in Hong Kong?
- Yes, and he replied. We must have talked for half an hour. I told him I planned to hitchhike to Shanghai and he told me about you, your schooldays together in Edinburgh, your work in Hong Kong with Holiday Inn and this new job in Lhasa. I never thought I'd make it here so I didn't think much more about it at the time. I wrote down your name in my diary, and here I am.
- You're hitching to Shanghai? How long will you stay in Tibet?
- Not sure. My visa will run out soon. I was hoping to get a job here but...
- A job? Here? Not much chance of that I can tell you. You wouldn't believe what a palaver it was for me to get this job. I applied for it in Hong Kong, got interviewed and accepted there, but then it was months and months before my application was approved by the bureaucracy in Beijing. The Chinese are very wary about hiring foreigners, each hire needs to be approved by a ministry in Beijing and they like to hire people abroad, not

on the ground. And they're very fussy about having the right academic qualifications.

- Hmm. You know what? That little story makes me all the more determined to get a job in Tibet.

- Well good luck to you. And you're always welcome here. Fancy another Yak Burger?

- Yes please! I've never tasted anything like it before.

CHAPTER SIX

I was surprised that they let me back into the Pemba truck stop and even more surprised when they gave me my own room. It wasn't a room, more of a glorified corridor – a tiny space, enough for two beds and a sticky patch of floor that allowed constant passage to the people staying in the big dorm next door – but it felt great to have my own space. If the Tibetans saw me lying on the bed and reading they would grab the book, look at the cover for a few seconds, toss it back and laugh. Their rude behaviour didn't bother me as something significant had taken place: I had been accepted by them.

I had to deal with my priorities: getting a new visa and a job. The visa issue was starting to get worrying but there was no shortage of foreign travellers who were happy to advise. The visa extension procedure was laughably simple; all you had to do was go down to the PSB (Public Security Bureau), sit under a tin roof while they stared dumbly at your form, pay five yuan and get a big, wet square stamp in your passport that said One Month Extension. The green-clad policeman – overbearingly formal, bored out of his brains and speaking pidgin English – told me that I could get two more extensions.

Next stage was to find a job. Although the atmosphere in Lhasa was both laid-back and dynamic, it wasn't the sort of place you could hustle for a job. It seemed that only three foreigners were working in Tibet and two of them, Roger and Isabella at the Travellers' Co-op, were presumably not approved by the Beijing bureaucracy. Considering my chances of getting hired were almost nil, I tried my most unlikely skill first: restoration work. It seemed worth a try. I had heard that the monasteries were being rebuilt and repainted – slowly, lovingly and voluntarily by local Tibetans – why couldn't I join in?

I racked my brain for someone who could help and remembered Robert

Morse, the sixty-year old son of an American missionary whom I'd recently met at the Travellers' Co-op. He had offered to help me and I sought him out and asked if he had any relevant contacts. He reluctantly admitted that he knew the Minister of Culture and promised to introduce me if I met him the next day at noon.

- But remember, he said, bring a bike – it's the ubiquitous form of transport in Lhasa.

The next day a friendly Chinese waiter reluctantly lent me his old bike. It was ruggedly built and, having been used to transport sacks of flour, was covered with white dust. I met with Morse as agreed but he didn't say a word. I wondered if he was annoyed at being dragged out on this pointless search for a job? I didn't dwell on it. We bypassed the crowded maze in the old centre and cycled along the new Chinese road, wide and deserted, to the south. The rainy season had been killed off by the big storm and I wallowed in weather that felt just perfect. The sky was a deep blue azure and the sharp sunlight was an inspiration. However hot the sunshine became the air was always cold. I had read in one of the guidebooks that in Tibet you can get sunburn and frostbite at the same time.

That's the university, said Morse, breaking his silence, and we turned off, went down a windy road, passed a long wall and there we were – in front of the minister's house. It stood in a yard, behind a big wooden gate, and didn't look very impressive. For a long time I had wanted to see inside a high-class Tibetan house. Nobody answered our banging, so we stood in the dust and talked. Robert Morse was well-proportioned, smiling and old – one of those people who embodied the Buddhist ideal of harmlessness. He beckoned me to the wooden gate and spoke in conspiratorial whispers:

- See the house in there? Look through this crack.

- Yeah.

- It was built by Heinrich Harrer, you know who I mean? The Austrian who lived here during the war and wrote Seven Years in Tibet.

- Hmm. I didn't want to admit that this was one of the many books on Tibet that I hadn't read.

- He lived here for years and planted a lovely garden.

I was wondering if this were really true. Morse struck me as rather eccentric, the sort of person who could make up stories like this. Then we heard a noise and the wooden gate was opening. A lovely old Tibetan woman's face appeared. Morse spoke to her in fluent Mandarin:

- We've come to see the minister.

- The minister? Here?

- Yes, he invited us here.

- Well you can come in and have some tea but he's not here. He may come tomorrow. He doesn't live here anymore. He's moved into that new block by the Post Office, the block where the government officials live.

As we were led through the garden I noticed a flash of unusual colours and a wealth of flowers and shrubs. I realised that I hadn't seen any flowers since I came to Tibet. In the house I greedily absorbed all the impressive details: polished wooden floor, unusual icons on the wall, colourful hand-made rugs, wide wooden windows through which you could see climbing flowers, an intimate little porch where, I imagined, Mr Harrer would sit and write his diary. As I took all this in, Morse and the old lady were talking in high-speed Mandarin.

A servant appeared and placed little ceramic bowls in front of us and filled them with golden-coloured tea. It was similar to the salty, greasy tea I had drunk on the plateau but in this environment it tasted totally different – smoother and more refined. Biscuits and snacks were offered to us and as soon as we had eaten and drunk our bowls were refilled. They kept insisting we have more. This was done with charm and exuberance. The old lady and her servant seemed delighted to have foreign visitors and I was pleasing them by wolfing down everything they put in front of us. Leaving was complicated as Morse had to implore and explain that we were required elsewhere, that we didn't want to detain her any longer but were eternally grateful for her generosity and hospitality. We slowly retreated towards the door, walking backwards and repeatedly saying

- Thank you so much. You are the best hostess in Lhasa. We will be back soon.

The following afternoon Robert Morse didn't show up at our meeting place – I assumed he was well and truly fed up with helping me – and so I went to the minister's house on my own. The chance of seeing that house again, and its enchanting garden, overcame my sense of doubt about getting a job and the weather was too perfect to worry about work. The grandmother took me in and kept me full of tea, an excellent substitute for lunch, while I flicked through ancient copies of National Geographic. Then a small man with bright, sharp features appeared. He spoke some English and introduced himself as the brother of the minister. I explained what I was looking for and he shot off on his bike, in search of his brother.

I sat around contentedly, watching the afternoon drift by. After a small meal of deliciously fried shredded meat and vegetables, and more tea, the minister himself appeared, on his bike, puffing from the exertion of cycling home in a hurry.

I had always assumed that government ministers were fat, pompous and had big jowls from too many boozy dinners. The man who stood in front of me was slim, unassuming, good looking and in his mid-thirties. He was full of warmth, friendliness and interest in my quest. He asked about me, my past, my interests, my plans – in a mixture of basic Tibetan, which I was still struggling with, and monosyllabic English. He was genuinely interested in my idea of working in a monastery and his bright face seemed to be searching for possibilities, opportunities. His response was negative in the most positive way possible; honest about my slim chances and yet hopeful for the future. He said they desperately needed to restore more monasteries and the best scenario would be if I could organise a restoration project at a national level, and get funding from a donor. Although I had no idea about how to go about such a task I was deeply encouraged by the meeting. It gradually became clear that he didn't really have much influence at the Ministry of Culture – where the main priority was to open up more sites for the visiting foreigners – and all he could really offer was advice.

We exchanged addresses – I used the Travellers' Co-op as mine – and agreed to meet up again in the New Year when mural painting and restoration projects would be taking place in certain Buddhist monasteries. I was impressed that this man had put so much time and thought into helping me with friendly advice. It didn't matter that I would almost certainly not be in Tibet the following spring – how could I get a visa for that long? – but what was important was that I had been welcomed into a Tibetan home and treated with such respect. I wondered how I could repay it. The old lady and the brother came out into the yard and, in the warm evening sun, they warmly said goodbye. I slowly cycled back to the Pemba, treasuring my good fortune at having met these people.

Even though the Pemba was a dump, I appreciated it as a crash course in Tibetan culture and language. I was learning new words every day, making a fool of myself when practising them in the teahouse, something I could never do in front of other travellers as I would feel a horrible sense of embarrassment. It felt fine when the Tibetans would laugh and mock when I tried to speak their language – it made the exercise fun – but if I tried to speak Tibetan in the presence of foreigners they would become analytical, start asking questions and I would become self-conscious. This was especially true of those who knew some Tibetan.

The Pemba had been an ideal place to immerse myself with Tibetans but the honeymoon was over: travellers had discovered it and they had obviously worked out that the fat manager's protestations, that foreigners are forbidden, was nothing but bluster and hot air. I bumped into an energetic American couple I had last seen by their tent at Lake Namtso and there were two strange Englishwomen who were making cheesecake, which they would then sell to other travellers. Their salesman was Jake, an emaciated Englishman who was full of strange wisdom and stories of travelling around India. Although their presence was annoying – I felt they had invaded my private space – I did appreciate the travellers for the fresh information they sometimes had. They were a far better source than the guidebooks, which were okay for maps, photos, basic words and historical background but out of date when it came to what was going on and how to get around.

I got talking to an American:

- Have you been to Samye Monastery?

- No, I replied.

- Check it out man, it's awesome. It was totally trashed by the Chinese during the Cultural Revolution – you know about the Cultural Revolution I guess?

- Er, yeah, I heard about it.

- They sure trashed it, man. Now it's being renovated by Tibetans. Totally awesome project. You can go in and see them painting mandalas.

- What's a mandala?

- Man, you really don't know nothing do you? A mandala is an intricate icon painting thing. Religious, Buddhist. You'll see.

- How do I get there?

- Best way is to walk. It takes five or six days from here, over those mountains to the south. We hitched back and got a truck.

- Do you think I could get a job there?

- A job? You outta your mind?

At the Kirey Hotel, the most expensive place to stay in the old town, I met a charming Tibetan who had been educated at an English-style private school in the Indian city of Chandigargh. Hundreds of thousands of Tibetans had fled their homeland since the 1950s and they were well established in India. Now that Tibet was opening up a few of them were coming back as traders. They all spoke Tibetan, and English with an Indian accent but not a word of Mandarin, which is China's official language. My new friend was called Lobsang and I managed to remember his name by thinking of the word lopsided. Not only was he charming and interesting – he told me about India's English-style education system with their elite private schools – but he seemed well connected in Lhasa too. I asked him to find the phone number of Samye Monastery and to call them to see if they needed some extra labour.

Lobsang was happy to help but where would we find a telephone? The only places that had phones were the units – the Chinese Communist term for companies, schools, factories and any other organisations,– but it was highly unlikely that any one of them would let two suspicious foreigners in the door, let alone use their phone. There were no telephones at the Post Office, or hotels, as far as I was aware, and I had got used to doing without them.

Lobsang turned his charm on the pretty young Tibetan receptionist at the Kirey. He leaned seductively on the counter, stared deeply into her eyes and got chatting. She tried to be hostile and frosty but failed miserably and within minutes had told him the crucial information:

- There is a telephone in the hotel, in the accountants' office...cross the yard and up the wooden ladder.

Seized with excitement, we abandoned the receptionist, climbed the ladder and found the accountants drinking beer and playing cards. There was a large abacus on the desk and a messy pile of paperwork. Lobsang asked if we could use their phone and they waved lazily in its direction. He made some calls, found the number for Samye and entered into a shouting match that seemed to last for half an hour. The accountants had paid no attention to our intrusion up to that point but eventually they were listening to every word. At the end of the conversation Lobsang said:

- They have an office in Lhasa and say you should go and see them tomorrow. I will come and translate for you.

The next morning I discovered the downside of Tibetans: chronic unreliability. From that day onwards Lobsang could not be found anywhere. He had disappeared and I couldn't understand it: he had been so warm in his encouragement and I was sure that his offer of help was genuine. I was desperate and I ran around town looking for him. He had arranged an interview with the representatives of a monastery that may be willing to hire a foreign mural painter. I had to meet them. I returned to the Kirey Hotel and turned my attention to the pretty young receptionist who seemed, I was glad to note, rather bored. This time it was I who turned on the charm, doing all I could to make her feel special before popping the question: Will you come with me to the Samye office?

She was shy and small and laughed at my suggestion, but when she saw that I was serious she said she couldn't possibly leave her work and that her English wasn't good – which was true. She was my last hope of getting a translator (or a job) and I hung around for hours, begging and persuading and imploring. Eventually she agreed to accompany me, but not for another two days.

It felt strange walking through the maze of backstreets next to a pretty Tibetan girl. She stared at the ground all the way and her face was red with embarrassment. The passers-by stared at us in surprise, some made comments and the young men whistled and laughed – giving me the thumbs up as if to congratulate me on my conquest. We reached a newly-built arched entrance with Chinese characters written on the right hand pillar and Tibetan words written on the left. We went through the arch and found ourselves in a deserted builders' yard – sacks, bricks, metal pipes scattered everywhere – and moved towards an impressively restored Tibetan building. A huge dog looked at us lazily through one eye, pondered for a moment and then charged at us in a fury of barking and snapping teeth. The receptionist screamed hysterically, unable to run, frozen in terror. A millisecond later the dog's charge was violently stopped by the thick rope that was firmly anchored into the ground. Recovering quickly from its temporary strangulation the dog kept on barking. The girl recovered from her paralysis and tried to run back, but I had a firm grip on her wrist and pulled her towards the main building.

Two bored youths were lounging in the hallway – neither of whom had reacted to the dog's outburst – and they grinned widely when they saw me with the girl. They pointed upstairs and said third door on the left. Dark stone steps and dragons painted in fluorescent colours. A thick blanket hung over the third door on the left, presumably to keep the draughts out. We entered a large room with two huge wooden desks and some plastic chairs. At the sight of Tibetan officials staring at us, the girl had another panic attack and tried to retreat but I was still gripping her wrist and I whispered fiercely to not abandon me at this stage of my quest.

The two Tibetan men watching us were a harmless looking old man and a young cynical-looking one in a Mao cap. They waved us to be seated in the only armchair, which I gallantly offered to the receptionist, while I sat on one of the plastic chairs. There was an embarrassing silence as I fumbled for the dog-eared reference letter that I had preserved carefully since my mural painting job in Vienna. I passed the shabby bit of paper to the receptionist, trying to get some enthusiasm into the girl and stop her sinking deeper into the armchair. The paper ended up in the hands of the man in the Mao hat who looked at it blankly and was obviously confused about what the hell we were doing there. When the girl reluctantly explained that I was looking for a restoration job at Samye Monastery they said I would have to speak to the boss, who was directing operations down at Samye Monastery and is far too busy to interview foreigners. The girl perked up as she realised this wasn't working and we would have to leave, but I pressed on, trying vainly to get a name, a phone number, some sort of commitment – but in vain. Soon we were hurrying down the stairs and heading back to her hotel where I thanked her profusely, hoping I hadn't compromised her reputation and put her through a traumatic experience.

Back at the Pemba all the foreigners were packing their stuff. I spoke to one of the Americans:

- What's up? I asked, are you being kicked out?
- No, they've just opened up the Cheese Factory. Why don't you join us? Get outta this dive!
- What's the Cheese Factory?

I helped them move their gear about ten minutes up the road – turn right at the Kirey Hotel and go past the smelliest toilet in Tibet – and saw the Cheese Factory, a Tibetan style construction made of square blocks of stone and leaning inwards to save itself from earthquakes. The building was austere and you got to the rooms by climbing up steep, fixed ladders which led onto wide wooden balconies. There was a rich smell of bread coming out of a noisy unit on the ground floor. We passed some unfriendly looking Tibetan traders on the first floor and eventually reached the third floor where eight rooms had been taken over by foreigners.

I dumped the couples' gear on a surprisingly clean concrete floor and took in the fact that in this room there were eight beds, each one of which was taken, and two windows. The travellers seemed to take themselves quite seriously and some were dressed in Tibetan clothes, which looked ridiculous. There was a lot of demand for beds and they had developed a dog-eat-dog system to cope with it. As soon as the word got out that a free bed was available, travellers in the more expensive hotels would hurriedly pack their rucksacks, rush over and throw themselves onto the free bed.

I was told there was a free bed in Ron and Cherry's room and so I ran back to the Pemba, packed my rucksack, hitched a lift on the back of a bicycle, got back to the Cheese Factory only to find that the bed had already been taken by some other swine. There was nothing I could do except go back to the Pemba and get my room back, but they didn't want to know; a horde of pilgrims were disembarking from a truck. The fat manager shouted at me, pointed up the street and made it clear that I was no longer welcome. By now I knew the layout of the Pemba and when the manager's back was turned I raced up the ladder, pushed through the crowd of smelly pilgrims, found an empty bed in the big dorm, dumped my stuff on it and asked those nearby to hold it for me. They grinned and seemed amused to have a foreigner in their midst.

Confident that my bed was booked and my stuff would be safe with the friendly nomads I went back to the Cheese Factory where some Americans from Arizona had asked me to eat with them. We drank and joked late into the night and at midnight, like some debauched Cinderella, I remembered the Pemba and my bed. Through dark and empty streets, silent apart from the howling dogs, I raced back to the Pemba: too late, the three metre high metal gate was closed. I silently climbed it and saw the night guard was asleep – his feet were sticking out from under a truck. I also knew he was a light sleeper and sure enough he woke up when I landed, cat-like, on the inside of the yard. He roared at me in rage, reached for his metal bar and started to get up. I put my fingers to my lips to urge him to shut up and hissed some words at him: Nga Injee (I am the Englishman). This was fine by him, he recognised me, and settled down again for the rest of the night.

I crept upstairs as silently as I could, anxious to not wake the volatile management, heard muffled noises of people drinking and talking from a first floor room, reached the big dormitory at the top and found, to my horror, that my bed had been occupied by two pilgrims. I began protesting and people started to wake up and look on with interest. The two men on my bed looked at me blankly but had no intention of moving. They shrugged their shoulders as if to say bad luck. Then the manager's women appeared and the lights were on. Get out they screamed and moved in on my gear. I screamed back at them and a struggle began for my rucksack.

I knew the game was up; I had already been told to leave and was unable to stop the forced move towards the big metal gate – which I had to climb back over as they cackled and laughed.

It was after two in the morning and the town was totally dead: not a soul to be seen, not a light on anywhere, even the dogs seemed to be asleep. I wasn't sure what to do. I wandered in the direction of the Kirey, which was all barred up and dark. At the Cheese Factory there were some lights on the top floor and I climbed the wall and looked in at the yard for a few minutes, scanning the area for guards or dogs. There was no sign of either but just to be on the safe side I didn't jump down into the yard, but climbed up the wooden frame that held up the balconies. All was quiet on the first floor, which was fortunate as the Tibetans who stayed there looked like they could be dangerous and who knows how they would react to finding a foreign intruder on their doorstep at this time of night. I crept over to the ladder up the next landing and found a room full of drinking, smoking foreigners, none of whom seemed surprised to see me. I told them my story, which raised a few laughs, and a redheaded girl from New Zealand asked if I would like to share her bunk. Thanks a lot I replied and then spent the night carefully keeping my hands to myself, not wanting to touch, hug or get involved with a woman. In the morning she had her arms round me but when she saw that I wasn't reacting said:

- The Scots aren't very affectionate, are they?

The next morning I hung around the Cheese Factory and kept a sharp eye on proceedings. I put a reservation in with the management and when someone left I was on their bed like a shot, and I stayed on the bed for most of that day to make sure I didn't lose it. A sense of exhaustion came over me and I realised that all the hustling, optimism and hope that I had put into finding a job was more tiring than my exertions up on the plateau. I decided some down time was needed and for the next two weeks I hung out with a crowd of New Yorkers who had taken up residence in the Cheese Factory. I became good friends with a skinny couple called Frenchy and Diane, the best conversationalists I had come across in Asia. There was also Larry who said he spoke better Spanish than English and looked like a character from New York in the 1920s. Larry's travelling companion was Adrian, with whom he had shared a flat in the Bronx. Adrian was loud and annoying, but entertaining in a twisted kind of way.

Diane and her boyfriend Frenchy were the first travellers with whom I formed a real friendship. We spent lots of time talking, walking and eating together. They both enjoyed hanging out with Tibetans in the daytime and drinking with the Chinese at night, and neither of them were judgemental about the politics, poverty and other heavy issues that travellers tended to know so much about. They entered into the spirit of things, joined in, rather than observing from the sidelines.

I related to Frenchy and Diane so well because they were living on their wits – rather than executing a carefully worked out travel plan. They appreciated spontaneity. They only had five hundred dollars each and they knew that if they didn't find a job soon they would be stuck. They were more realistic about working in Tibet than me; they knew it was impossible and had set their sights on teaching English in Hong Kong or Taiwan, where people like us could get hired relatively easily. I told them that my destination had been Shanghai but now I'd seen Lhasa I wanted to stay, and I was doing all I could to find a job. If not, it was Shanghai and if that didn't work out I would probably head for Hong Kong or Taiwan. Maybe we'd meet up there? For the next few weeks I felt like taking it easy, hanging out with Diane and Frenchy and seeing the town from a different perspective. It was a period of indulgence, topped off by a joint birthday party that Isabella, the woman at the Traveller's Co-op had organised for Roger, her boyfriend, and me. Our birthdays were only two days apart.

I was surprised that Isabella had arranged this party as she saw so many people in her Co-op that I wondered how she even remembered me, but there was something else going on: she was using this party as a means of introducing me to her students and the boss of their English language school. She really did want me to get a job with them! With a bunch of people from the Cheese Factory I entered a big, whitewashed room with carved pillars that had been painted red. It was the classroom, located in a curious old building that surrounded a yard.

- Oh, it's Rupert, shouted Isabella when we came into the room,
- Say hello everyone.

I felt a rush of embarrassment and almost turned tail and fled, but a group of smiling young monks were approaching and it would have been disrespectful to run out on them. The monks were each carrying a white cotton scarf and they each laid these over my neck, saying some kind words that I didn't understand. There were other Tibetans in the room, some Chinese as well as some of the more intellectual looking travellers. Isabella took my arm and led me round the group, introducing me to them individually. Some of the Tibetan students couldn't stop themselves from giggling:

- This is Rupert. Injee teacher. Very good teacher.

We approached an older man with sallow cheeks, sunglasses and pockmarked skin. He had probably been handsome once but now he had a haunted look.

- He was in prison for 20 years, Isabella whispered into my ear, and it was him who set up this language school for 40 people. He's with the Tibetan Peoples' Consultative Conference. It's important you meet him in case a job comes up here. We approached him and shook hands sincerely. He smiled and said in old fashioned English:

- Thank you for coming here, my very good fellow. Here is a present for you.

He handed me a small package that was wrapped in newspaper. I thanked him profusely, unwrapped it and found a modern Chinese tea strainer. A bit later the monks all trooped out and went back to their monastery, some alcohol was produced and Roger put on some funk. By midnight I was dancing with a crowd of young students, all of whom were scrutinising my every move, sharing jokes and squealing with laughter. They were good dancers and I got into the spirit of it. The only bores were the foreigners, especially the bearded guidebook author. They sat around the edges of the room, observing, smoking and making wise comments to each other.

Over the next few weeks I developed a routine with Diane and Frenchy. We would get up late, savouring the warm beds and waiting for the sunlight to heat up the frozen room. Diane would take ages to get ready while I would hustle them impatiently so we could get breakfast, usually consisting of cold rolls and yoghurt from the market, with Chinese jam, all eaten sitting on a wall or doorstep with plastic spoons and penknives. The main attraction of the afternoon was sunshine and once settled in comfortably on the balcony at the Cheese Factory it was hard to go anywhere else.

We had a stunning view of the Eastern mountains from this spot and as evening approached the sun would throw strange shapes onto the mountains. By this time the cold was back and so were our appetites and it was time to go and find dinner. We would go to the shacks that functioned as little restaurants, sit around miniature tables or on dirt floors, within a lively buzz of multi-lingual chatter. The food was greasy, delicious and always took ages to arrive. I would get impatient and harass the cooks to speed things up a bit. I preferred to eat in the Chinese places, with their finely sliced meat and veg, plus a bowl of rice – ten yuan in total – while they preferred the Muslim noodle house where we'd pay just two or three yuan for a plate of boiled noodles mixed in with fresh garlic, and sit with a local crowd on tightly packed benches. After dinner, when the cold had descended, we would search out somewhere warm to drink Chinese beer, which the Tibetans call Pee Jew, and chat late into the night.

One of the things that kept reminding me how great it was to travel alone was that almost every couple I saw travelling together through Asia seemed to get on badly with each other. Diane and Frenchy were different; they didn't get on with each other better than other couples I had met, if anything they got on worse, but they let me in to their disputes. I found myself becoming their mediator, a role I enjoyed, and worked out ways of defusing the insults and barbed comments they would hurl at each other. They hardly spoke to each other but both of them talked profusely with me. Frenchy shared his frustration about sleeping with her:

- Whenever I show any affection she calls me a pervert.

Frenchy was running low on cash and Diane would continually mock him for not saving more when he was earning good money in Boston. He was always on the lookout for ways to earn a few bucks and he would haggle with the Khampa tribesmen in the marketplace, buy their hand-made trinkets and sell them to gullible American travellers as antiques. There were plenty of other Americans haggling in the marketplace, buying up old silver antiques, for prices well out of Frenchy's league, and I disapproved of the trade as I knew these valuable objects would end up being sold in the USA for twenty times the price.

One day Frenchy took me to the sky burial site on the outside of town. I could see the bloodstains on the big rock that was used to smash up the bodies, and hundreds of vultures flapping around expectantly, but there was no activity that day. The body-cutters were having a day off. The best antiques that Frenchy had found were in the huge mound of clothes that lay by the sky burial site; I didn't want to join in his business but I did think that anyone bold enough to rob the dead deserves whatever they get.

It was October and Frenchy's birthday was approaching. With Diane and some disco-crazed Tibetans from India we organised a big party for him in the restaurant at the Snowlands Hotel. There was no charge as long as we promised to bring a crowd and consume lots of beer, an easy problem to solve with my new-found friends. The problem with organising parties is the anxiety one feels at the beginning – will anyone come? – and it took about a gallon of beer for me to feel sufficiently relaxed to join in the frenzied dancing. I got so drunk that night that I ended up taking a beautiful blonde German girl to bed in her room at the Snowlands. The next morning I had a vague memory of frantic undressing but no recollection of the actual act, but one look at the German girl the following morning – tight-lipped, cold, furious – made me squirm in shame and get out as quickly as possible. I scurried back to the Cheese Factory and guiltily confessed all to Diane and Frenchy. They mocked me about it for weeks.

I became friendly with some of the Tibetan exiles; young, well-dressed and handsome men from India who had returned to the land that their fathers had escaped from. They didn't share our appreciation of Lhasa's backwardness; they saw it as provincial, boring and desperately in need of some good nightlife. I doubted their trading activities were legal but the Chinese authorities seemed to tolerate them. The local Tibetan men despised the exiles as lechers who were corrupting their women, and neither the local Chinese nor the foreign travellers trusted them. I was keen to learn Tibetan from them and enjoyed their company.

Their priority was having a good time and their passion was organising big discos, in large modern halls, where they could show off their superb disco dancing skills – making the locals and the travellers look like ridiculous puppets in comparison. My best friend among the exiles was called Pemba and he could break-dance so well that he would bring the whole dance floor to a halt as we watched on in amazement. Diane and Frenchy would smuggle in beer and watch from the sidelines, never dancing. Some of Isabella's English students would come to the disco and one of them, the sexiest mover in the place, was known as the Disco Queen. One night she asked me to dance and although I failed miserably to perform to her high standards, I was honoured to have been asked. I got lots of jealous looks that night.

Elliot was another New Yorker who lived by his wits and slipped into our scene. He hunted deals by day, was a boozing socialite by night and spoke with a drawl. There was something fascinating about his contemptuous manner and I appreciated the honesty of his behaviour: he made no attempt to be pleasant. His main scam was to buy cheap bus tickets from Lhasa to the Nepalese border and sell them to fresh travellers at twice the price. He had a stash of slide film, which he would also sell at a huge profit. I would berate him for his rapaciousness but he would dismiss my observations as if to say who gives a shit? Elliot was the only one of us who could afford a decent hotel room; he stayed in the newly-built Plateau Hotel where a single room cost ten yuan (£1) – four times what we paid.

One night some Tibetans had accosted Elliot and Diane and begged them to teach English. Apparently the last English teaching volunteer had disappeared without trace and these young folk were desperate for someone, anyone, to teach them basic English. The group had organised itself spontaneously and everyone chipped in for the teacher's fee – but there was no contract. In fact the whole thing was illegal. I thought it ridiculous that untrained half-wits like Elliot could be invited to teach English when he could hardly string a sentence together. Some days later Elliot announced that he had a headache and asked me to teach for him that evening. I wasn't quite sure and he took advantage of my hesitation and said:

- Nine thirty. Friday. Disco Hall. Be there! And then he was gone.

At nine thirty on the Friday night I approached the disco hall and realised that all my struggles with conquering fear had been in vain. I was terrified. The memory of the terror I had felt when I first taught English came flooding back: Norwich 1986, the final test in the most intensive educational experience I had ever endured, a one-month course in Teaching English as a Foreign Language (TEFL); a group of adults looking at me expectantly and the tutor lurking at the back marking me down for being a nervous wreck.

As I made my way through the dark, deserted hall I could see light coming from under a door and heard voices. I wanted to run, hard, in the opposite direction. I can't teach English I told myself, I'm a phoney. All I've ever done is help one girl in Vienna correct her essays. I've forgot everything I learned on that TEFL course and I never understood grammar anyway. I looked through the door into the room and saw row upon row of bored faces staring at Elliot. Before I had time to flee they spotted me and I knew there was no escape. Elliot was already heading for the door and before he disappeared into the night he handed me a children's book and said commandingly:

- Make 'em repeat.

What followed was a nightmare. I could hardly control my feelings of panic and confusion; how was I supposed to make a lesson out of this ridiculous kid's book that Elliot had thrust into my hand? And the students weren't making it any easier by sitting there silently, staring at me as if I knew what to do. It was the longest hour I ever lived through and what made it worse was the news that the pay was only five yuan an hour. After the class I protested and said I wouldn't go on unless they raised it to at least seven yuan an hour. Surely such a big group could scrape that much together? I sought Elliot's support but he had washed his hands of the situation by now and didn't even want to discuss it. It's your baby now was all he would say. I waited for them to agree on a raise but, perhaps realising how hopeless their potential English teacher was, they presumably decided to forget about the whole thing and I never heard any more about it.

I was living a double life in those days. With Diane and Frenchy I was a drunk, a hooligan, someone of whom decent people would disapprove and keep away from their daughters. With Isabella, who was a textbook definition of a decent person, I portrayed myself as a clean-living, enthusiastic English teacher who didn't swear, spit and drink too much beer. It seemed to work and I felt sure that Isabella would give me the first job that came her way. I was glad to be getting the best out of both these worlds but was always careful not to get too close to one group or the other as I didn't want to be pigeon-holed as a boring English teacher – or as a drunk.

After a few weeks this exhausting, debauched lifestyle was getting me down. All those late nights and all that booze was starting to burn me out. As the New Yorkers would say, I needed to bag the scene, do something else, move on. I was starting to feel rotten inside. I was getting hooked into this routine of sloth and alcohol and while I knew I should clean up my act, there was nothing else going on in my life – no prospect of a job, nowhere else to go and the idea of hitching all the way to Shanghai seemed like a drag.

During this time I was sustained by the optimistic belief that something good would eventually happen to me in Tibet. This sentiment led me to believe that I had better see some of Tibet now, while I still had time on my hands, as who knew how busy I would become in the future. I built up my determination to get out of town for a while, to give the decadence a break and look for a job restoring murals at Samye Monastery, whose representatives in Lhasa I had recently met.

I found out as much as I could about the route from Ganden Monastery, which was about an hour away from Lhasa by bus, to Samye Monastery, which was about four days walk to the south. I thought this sounded feasible and I geared up mentally to overcome my sloth. I hung out at the Travellers' Co-op just long enough to scrounge a sleeping bag and some tinned food supplies. I wondered if I could find a travelling companion who wasn't a crashing bore. Of course, I realised, Diane and Frenchy can come with me. They liked the idea but the reality of walking further than the nearest teahouse was anathema to them. When I pushed them about it they called me a Limey dork. The weather was getting colder and this made it impossible to get either of them out of bed in the morning, and I realised that I would never be able to drag them on a four-day hike. I was on my own.

What gelled thought into action was a particularly decadent night at the Lhasa Hotel, the place where I had enjoyed a Yak Burger when I came back from the plateau. Diane had booked a triple room for the reduced winter rate of thirty yuan (£3) and we all chipped in. Six of us crowded into the room and we took turns to luxuriate in the bath. We were astounded by the crisp cotton bed sheets and the firm mattress and the deep pile carpet was more comfortable than my bed in the Cheese Factory. Heat kept pouring into the room as if by magic. We drank a bottle of Old Suntory Japanese whisky, several crates of beer and played poker in clouds of cigarette smoke until dawn. When I woke up on the floor I had a powerful feeling that the age of endless hangovers had just come to an end, and with a fresh sense of determination, I left the room before anyone else was awake, went back to the Cheese Factory, packed my rucksack and started walking along the road towards Ganden.

It was afternoon. I had missed the early morning bus by over seven hours but I was so determined to get out of town that I would have walked all the way. Fortunately a truck picked me up and dropped me off, a couple of hours later, at a small village underneath the mountain that Ganden Monastery sits on. It was evening by now and I felt tired, thirsty and hungover. I was glad to have left my American friends behind and I hoped I would never drink alcohol again. I looked at the muddy road leading up to the monastery and decided to try and find somewhere to stay in the roadside village. Soon enough I found an old couple who took me in and gave me a cup of tea, and just as I was getting comfortable and hoping to settle down for the night they said sharply:

- You've had your tea. Now get out.

It was pitch dark and the muddy road was steep and endless. I plodded up and lost track of time. A wild howling of dogs mixed in with the sound of the wind and the higher I got the louder the barking sounds became. There must have been hundreds of stray dogs up there and I imagined they were passing the word round that some new meat was on its way up. Ganden Monastery was said to be vast but there was no sign of it, no lights or sound (apart from the dogs). Had I come up the wrong mountain? Was it invisible? I was staggering, parched with thirst and frustration. Why hadn't I organised this properly? Why hadn't I brought a bottle of water? Where was the monastery? Will the dogs attack?

An old building with thick, stone walls came into view. Weak candlelight was coming through the windows and I rushed towards it, hoping to reach safety before the dogs got me. I banged loudly on the wooden door and then screamed. No reply. The barking was getting louder. I reached down, grabbed some stones and started throwing them as hard as I could at the beasts, missing but momentarily keeping them at bay. I knew that when they had built up enough numbers they would charge.

The door of the stone building burst open and three young monks came rushing out and ran, screaming, towards the dogs. The dogs just melted away. Then the monks turned to me and invited me inside. I was safe. They all seemed to be teenagers and their chief, to whom they showed great respect, couldn't have been more than twenty. They gave me tea and food and seemed delighted to have me in their midst. Was I the first foreigner they had entertained? They were laughing and chasing each other around the room, not the sort of behaviour one would expect from a Buddhist monk. By now I could communicate in basic Tibetan:

- The Guest House is over there, one of them said.

- Can I stay here for the night? I asked, pointing to the floor.

- No, you have to go to the Guest House. You're not allowed to stay here.

- Please, I asked, I would much rather stay with you.

They argued about this for ages. The chief monk wanted to stick to the rules but the three teenagers obviously wanted me to stay. Eventually it was agreed that I could stay and I settled down for the night on a wooden bench. The three teenagers lay down on the floor and the chief monk on a bed. We were all in the same room and they joked late into the night. I slept like the dead. The next morning I woke early and everyone was gone.

I stepped onto the porch where pale sunlight was coming through frozen, misty air. The three young monks were all sitting cross-legged, chanting furiously. Was this a way of staying warm? Each one of them had a curious collection of papers on their laps and they seemed to be chanting from what was written on them. I looked more carefully and realised that these were books with mantras, or chants. Each book consisted of about fifty or sixty thin strips of paper, all covered with ornate Tibetan script, and the covers of the books were made up of long pieces of wood. They would flip each page over after they had chanted it and each monk had two piles of paper in front of him – the pages they had chanted and the remainder. When they were done the monks gathered up the papers, closed them in their wooden covers and then wrapped them up in cotton – presumably against the dust. They piled these sock-like packages into a cupboard where hundreds more were stacked. When they had finished their chanting they gave me tea and tsampa, and started to mock fight with each other.

The ruins of Ganden Monastery are majestic. There are hundreds of gutted buildings, spread out on top of a crescent shaped mountain. It looked like the remnants of a small town. Seven thousand monks had lived here before the whole place had been dynamited during the China's Great Proletarian Cultural Revolution of 1966 to 1968. During that period, when much of China's cultural heritage was destroyed, Mao Tse Tung encouraged the population to attack the Four Olds – old customs, old culture, old habits and old ideas. In Tibet over six thousand monasteries were razed and thousands of monks were killed or sent to prison camps.

The effect of seeing these ruins was numbing and I wondered what it took for people to destroy such a spiritual place. Some of the buildings were being rebuilt and I could see Tibetan workers heaving great oblongs of chiselled stone and there was a boisterous atmosphere on the building site. Most of the monks were young and allowed to run around and play like kids; nobody seemed to mind their shouting and pranks. It had the atmosphere of a school-yard. I was introduced to a monk who must have been in his eighties and his room was an ocean of calm and solitude. His floor was covered in rugs, his walls filled with icons – and a poster that seemed totally out of place: the Central Committee of China's Communist Party.

He tried to talk to me about spiritual matters but my grasp of Tibetan was far too basic to understand anything. He showed me a photo of Ganden before the Communists had got to it and it looked like a full-sized town. I felt honoured to be in this man's presence and I could feel the goodness and wisdom emanating from him, to such an extent that it didn't seem important that I couldn't understand his words. I never found out who he was. He asked if I would like to stay in his room but I politely declined as I felt more comfortable with the rowdy teenagers. I spent the rest of the day wandering around the ruins, catching a bit of sleep when I found a sunny spot, and by evening I was with the boys again, shouting, singing and laughing.

The following morning I was full of energy and ready for anything the heavens could throw at me. I got up at dawn, said goodbye to my young friends and confirmed with them that the narrow path heading into the mountain above Ganden was the right track for Samye.

When I'm walking alone over a long distance, with no need to adjust my pace for other people, my subconscious takes over; it works out how far I have to go and then sets my body at the optimum speed – usually pretty fast. I felt myself powering over that mountain as if driven by some other force. I reached a small village on the other side of the mountain, had a short break, crossed a small river and strode up towards a distant pass. One of the foreign travellers had told me that this pass was 18,000 feet high but this was no problem as I was flying up. I would arrive in a jiffy. Unfortunately it was a false summit that I had reached so quickly – and then there was another, and another. It was evening by the time I reached the pass and the weather was taking a turn for the worse. Dark clouds were being churned around by a strong wind and it felt like snow was on the way.

I was in need of shelter and was surprised to note that there weren't any nomads around. I had been told that this was a common route for nomads to reach Lhasa from the south-east. Confident that I would come across somebody soon enough I charged on into the night, oblivious to the fact that I had walked about sixteen hours that day. Eventually I gave up on finding any nomads that evening; I found a spot between mounds of moss, in rough grass and stones, and settled down for the night. I started heating up some water for noodles with my petrol in the tin can trick, and laid out my sleeping bag and plastic sheet.

Suddenly there was a clash of thunder and a violent storm came crashing up the valley, with demonic energy. I forgot about the noodles and whipped out my plastic groundsheet – the Tamang porter's raincoat that I had bought at the border – and tried to make a shelter. Just as hailstones started to spit furiously I got my boots off and crawled into the sleeping bag. The temperature dropped rapidly and I could feel water soaking into the bottom of the sleeping bag. The storm built up to a climax of fury and noise and was hurling down big hailstones. As long as this plastic sheet holds, I thought, I'll be fine, and I stretched it to cover my feet. With an awful ripping sound the square of plastic ripped in half, exposing the sleeping bag to the elements. For some reason I started laughing; it served me right for being so unprepared, for sneering at the well-equipped travellers, for becoming so decadent. This was my punishment. It also felt like a test, as if the Storm Demon was saying: So, you want to stay in Tibet? See if you like this!

I tried to ignore the dampness and cold that was spreading into the sleeping bag from all sides and told myself I'm not cold! This isn't so bad! Could be a lot worse! It's not even winter. The nomads would laugh in the face of this storm. With thoughts of sunny days and warm childhood afternoons in Scotland by the River Tweed, and babbling continually to myself, I managed to get to sleep.

I woke up as soon as the grey light started creeping under the horizon. I was buried in snow. I couldn't see my rucksack, boots or any of my possessions. I forced my way out of the sleeping bag, which had been frozen solid underneath. It took over an hour to dig out my gear. My hands – which I had used as snow shovels -- were so cold that it was almost impossible to tie my shoelaces and pack up my rucksack. I kept motivated by running a dialogue in my head: This isn't cold! This is nothing. What would the nomads say about you now? They'd call you pathetic! Get on with it!

Eventually I started walking and the movement brought welcome relief as my limbs got some heat into them. The snow was knee-deep and I had to wade through it slowly, each step was an effort and the valley in front seemed endless. It took all day to cross it and by nightfall I was lucky enough to find a cave where I fell asleep instantly. By the third day I reached Samye Monastery and the first thing I noticed was that it was surrounded by sand and I imagined for a moment that I was a French Foreign Legionnaire who had just survived an impossible march through the Sahara Desert.

Samye had been destroyed during the Cultural Revolution and was being rebuilt, but the atmosphere was totally different from Ganden: the place was overrun with pilgrims from the eastern part of Tibet, the unruly Khampas, and there was a reckless feel in the air. I was buzzing, delighted to be alive, and I was sure that this feeling would be crowned by the offer of a job helping with the restoration work, perhaps even on the murals. Before visiting the monastery I spent time in the workers' tearoom, a huge space run by a cripple who leaped around the place with incredible energy. I made repeated visits to a vast cauldron that held delicious sweet tea. Then I wandered through the half built monastery and saw scores of brightly painted statues, each one more terrifying than the next. These were the guardians of the faith.

A wild family from the east took me into their makeshift room that night. They were gambling and drinking late into the night and people were coming and going constantly. Over the course of the evening I started to piece the story of Samye together: the monastery was a vast three-storey structure before its demolition during the Cultural Revolution; each floor represented Buddhism from a different country. Tibetan Buddhism was on the ground floor, the Indians were on the first floor and the Chinese at the top. The whole complex was built in the shape of a mandala – a tiny circle surrounded by bigger circles and squares. By the end of the evening I got the name of the man in charge of the restoration work and my confidence, fuelled by drinking too much chang and my luck at surviving the snowstorm, was at stratospheric levels. Surely they would be delighted to offer me a job? I would be an honoured guest, a respected advisor, a foreign expert living with the monks.

The next morning the wild family who had taken me in, and who shared my enthusiasm for my imminent employment, sent their youngest daughter scurrying off to find the boss. Soon she returned with him and I realised, to my horror, that he was none other than my drinking partner from the night before – in other words, he'd seen me at my drunken worst. He was young and businesslike and seemed unimpressed with my reference letter, which had been badly stained during the storm. He didn't offer me a job. I pleaded with him to hire me, soon running out of the vocabulary needed to argue my case. He seemed unmoved and then had an idea; he searched his pockets, pulled out a picture of a Tibetan mandala, passed me a scrap of paper and a pencil and said copy it. The family crowded round noisily, expectantly, but I knew the game was up. I couldn't do it, all I had learned in Vienna was to draw a straight line. What was I thinking? Who was I kidding?

I tried to recover from my humiliation by offering to show what a good labourer I could be, but the workers seemed to be under orders to ignore me. I watched lines of cheery Tibetan women wearing traditional, multi coloured aprons picking up baskets of sand, walking along networks of rickety wooden planks and dumping them in a pile. They had a good system going, they were working hard, and I started to realise that perhaps it would be inappropriate for me to try and insert myself among them. I would look totally out of place. There were plenty of children running around and they were used to fetching and carrying stuff for the women, and taking messages around the building site. They didn't need me.

Not sure what to do with myself, I went into the monastery and climbed the stairs. I wandered into a huge room where a group of young monks in purple robes were sitting in a circle. They were printing text onto strips of paper, which they then rolled up and stuffed into small statues. When they saw me they jumped up and insisted I join them. One of them went off to get a cup of tea but it was tepid and too buttery (if Tibetan tea isn't piping hot you notice how greasy and disgusting it really is). One of them said What do you have in your pocket? and I pulled out the Swiss Army Knife I always carried around with me. They asked if they could look at it and each one of them examined it carefully. When one of them found that it had a small magnifying glass they leaped up in excitement, forgot all about their work and took it in turns to examine the murals that were painted on every wall of the room.

I left Samye with a good feeling. Although the boss had humiliated me, I felt I had deserved it. That particular avenue of employment was now closed. It was time to return to Lhasa but there was no way I was going back over those mountains. I walked down to the main road and spotted a truck that had slowed down. It was packed full of pilgrims and I raced after it, grabbed hold of the tailboard, started climbing up. Strong hands grabbed me and hauled me aboard. Smiling, sunburned Khampas surrounded me and there was a carnival atmosphere on the back of the truck – they were heading for Lhasa, their holy city.

The truck only went as far as Tsedang. We reached a truck stop and everyone got off. The pilgrims started walking towards Lhasa but I wasn't in a hurry and went into the town to see if there was an old Tibetan quarter. There wasn't. Tsedang looked like a small Chinese settlement but I ran into some travellers who told me it's one of the biggest cities in

Tibet. They also told me there was a friendly PSB (Public Security Bureau) nearby where I could get my visa extended. I had completely forgotten about my visa and I quickly checked it, glad to see that the storm hadn't totally destroyed my passport, only dampened the edges a bit. Oh my God! I thought, My visa extension has run out! I cursed my laziness and stupidity. What do they do to people whose visas run out? I thought as I hurried to the PSB, I expect they will fine me. They might even expel me from the country. The policeman who dealt with me was polite, dressed in a uniform, and Tibetan. He gave me a one month extension without fuss and didn't seem to notice that my visa had expired.

Back at the Cheese Factory the scene was the same, but more Americans had moved in and it felt like they had colonised the place. Diane and Frenchy had stayed longer at the Lhasa Hotel, until they were thrown out for not paying their bill. Frenchy had seen a bucket full of aborted babies and felt nauseous for a week. My short trek had purified me of my previous decadence and I felt in a different mood now, healthier and determined not to binge. I would have to focus on getting a job or facing up to the fact that I would have to leave. I checked my money supply – just over $200 left – and knew it was time to move on.

I managed to get my own room at the Cheese Factory – a tiny, vile hole with black walls – but I was delighted as it put some distance between me and the Americans, a breathing space. One evening two hitchhikers from California pushed their way into the room, sat themselves down on the bed and started telling me their story. They talked for hours and I wasn't interested; I wanted them to leave, but they were determined to tell me about their route (which they pronounced rout) of hitching from Chengdu, which is the next province directly east of Tibet. They went into minute detail about avoiding police checkpoints at night, walking through mountains and jungles and beating off savage dogs. Although their tale bored me I did absorb the information that it was possible to leave Tibet by that route and it did sound more interesting than going through the northern desert. But I wasn't so interested in going into China, or my initial destination of Shanghai, as my new priority was to stay in Lhasa. If I needed a new visa I could get one in Kathmandu.

The next days were spent asking everyone I had ever met if they knew about a job. I spent hour after hour walking from unit to unit, asking for a job. I asked Tibetan exiles, Chinese leaders, secretaries, teachers if they had any ideas. Nothing. Isabella was keen to help but she couldn't produce a job out of a hat, she had had to wait four months before finding hers. Diane and Frenchy thought I had gone insane:

- Man, you can't get a job here! This is China for Chrissake. Communism. Duh. Just relax and go back to bed.

It was Wednesday and I set myself a new deadline: if I don't find a job by Saturday I will leave. I would hitch down to India and make my way home. Every moment became precious as I realised this might be the last time I saw Lhasa, a city I had grown to really appreciate. I spent the mornings hustling for work and sat around gloomily in the evening with Diane and Frenchy, trying to savour my last moments in Tibet. I packed my tattered rucksack. I didn't have much and was careful not to accumulate stuff, like the beautiful silver antiques in the market, as when you're walking you regret every bit of extra weight and start thinking of what you can jettison.

On the Friday night I was psyched up to go, I had done my best to find a job and had failed. With a friendly Mexican I had just met, I went to the restaurant in the Snowlands Hotel and got into the party atmosphere coming from the neighbouring table – where ten well-dressed Tibetans were celebrating. They spoke some English, we got chatting and they invited us to join them. We said cheers in every language we knew (this is the one word I learned in every country I had visited). They were a handsome looking bunch and they told us they had just returned from two years in Beijing where they had been trained to come and work for the Tibet Import Export Bureau.

- Do you have an English teacher? I asked
- No.
- I am an English teacher. I am looking for a job. Could I come and be the English teacher at the Tibet Import Export Bureau? They talked furiously among themselves for what felt like ages and then said:
- We see leader. We say you good English teacher. You come Monday.

I couldn't believe my luck, I jumped for joy, raised another glass, I had managed to get a job in Tibet. I didn't need to leave after all.

CHAPTER SEVEN

Although the Import Export people didn't give me a job everything started happening at once. Life seems to work this way; once inside the magic circle you'll find anything is possible, but getting inside it often seems impossible. The key is coming across the right people and impressing them, but quite how one goes about that is something of a mystery.

Things really started moving after meeting Asheya, whom I was introduced to at the new Kailash restaurant – the first place in town that played music. Asheya was extremely small, but he was solidly built and had a round face and warm, beaming eyes. He was middle-aged, lived in Kathmandu where he dealt in carpets and antiques and spoke fluent English. His family was from Lhasa and, for the first time in decades, he was able to visit them. He was much warmer than the other exiled Tibetans I had come across and was a different generation to the disco-dancing crowd I had met thus far. Initially I was suspicious of his interest in me, although taking full advantage of it, and wondered what his ulterior motives were. Did he want something? If so, I never found out what it was.

He listened to my plea – I want to stay in Lhasa but I need cash, a job, and also a place to stay so I can get away from some annoying Americans. Although my demands were simple enough most people I spoke to seemed to have a problem understanding me. Maybe they didn't want to? Perhaps helping a foreigner was too risky? Asheya got it in one go, thought about it for some time and told me to come back to this same restaurant the following evening.

When I returned the next evening I wasn't expecting anything and I wouldn't have been surprised if he hadn't turned up at all. Not only did Asheya show up, he came into the restaurant with two attractive young ladies. These lovely ladies, he announced grandly, are your new students. They were Tibetan nurses from the big Chinese hospital on the north side of the city, both wanted to learn English and were willing to pay seven yuan an hour fee – each. I couldn't understand why these two could pay me when Elliot's whole class had refused. This was a real break; I knew that the big hospital had at least one English teacher and maybe this was a way in. Maybe I could get hired there? I thanked Asheya, spoke to the ladies and arranged to meet up with them three times a week.

The second amazing thing that Asheya did that day was to arrange my accommodation at his sister's place. This was going beyond kindness as I knew it was illegal for Tibetans to accommodate foreigners and I had never heard of it happening in the city. He assured me that it was no problem, nothing special and wasn't a risk. It was with a sense of glee that I went back to the Cheese Factory that evening and met Diane and Frenchy:

- Guess what? I'm moving out!
- Moving out? You can't move out. You've just got your own room.
- I'm sick of it here. I'm sick of you guys.
- Hey, we like it here. We like this Little America.
- Well, I'm outta here.
- You Limeys are crazy. Where the hell ya' going anyway?
- I can't tell you.
- Why the hell not?
- Because.

Asheya's sister was called Joga and she lived down a stinking alley not far from the Cheese Factory. The following day he led me down the narrow alley and we followed the open sewer, which led into an earth-covered courtyard which had a ramshackle well in the middle. Asheya cheerfully pointed to the well and told me it was the only source of water. Did the sewage water leak into it? There were four low, shack-like houses around the yard and Joga lived in the smallest of them. We went into a tiny room with a mud floor, two small benches and a dresser. It was so low that I had to bend almost double. We sat on one of the benches and Joga served us drinks.

Joga was much smaller than Asheya. Although he never talked about it I could see that she was disabled: her spine was only about six inches long and twisted. She had a kind face and served us drinks with no trace of self-pity. She could walk around with a strange limp and she managed perfectly, walking round with her own particular gait. She spoke no English but seemed happy enough to have me to stay. She pointed to the narrow bench that we were sitting on and said that would be my bed. I was delighted. Even though the place was a dive – even my Tibetan friends said so when I invited them over – and the smell from the sewer was appalling at times, I was so glad to get in with a Tibetan family that I would have put up with anything. I had been hoping to get a job but had never even thought that I would also be able to live with Tibetan people.

Joga and Asheya were Khampas, he explained, from the Kham region of Tibet which used to stretch far into the Chinese province of Sichuan. The curious thing was that the Kham people tend to be huge, and they make themselves seem bigger by their bulky cloaks, their big hats, their big mouths and their swaggering walk. When I first turned up with my rucksack I was introduced to three burly Kham warriors who were sitting on the benches drinking chang. They all had big grins on their faces and insisted I share a drink with them.

A constant stream of Kham visitors came to Joga's place and even though they were a noisy, drunken rabble they always treated her – and me – with the utmost respect. They would shout and curse at each other constantly, sometimes even strike each other to emphasise a point; but for them Joga was a princess. Every evening the room was full of chattering Khampas who had no intention of leaving. Not only was my bed inaccessible but when they sat on it they lifted up the blankets and sat directly on the sheet which, as a result, was always grimy. There were usually about six people in the room every evening, a mixture of big Khampas and Joga's local women friends. Their main activity was telling jokes, none of which I could understand but I got into the atmosphere and appreciated the burst of laughter and applause at the punch line. The murky white drink they call chang was being poured constantly and every time I would take a sip of the sour brew my cup would be immediately refilled, even if I refused insistently. I learned that if you didn't want to drink you simply don't touch the stuff.

Joga's place was always dark – the room had only one tiny window and it was usually blocked by a huge Khampa. This was a sharp contrast with the Chinese hospital where I would teach English in a room full of light. The nurses' room had features I had never appreciated so much before — big windows, a clean concrete floor, running water and a kitchenette. There was only one student when I got there, the other one was apparently busy with her new boyfriend. No problem, this one was friendly, attentive to my basic lessons and would always make me a delicious lunch. She was pretty in a natural way but she ruined her appeal by applying too much make-up. I wondered if she fancied me? Did she put make-up on for my benefit? What was I supposed to do? The idea of sex with a local scared me, I had never heard of a foreigner doing it and hated to think what the consequences would be. The suppressed sexual tension between us contributed to a good atmosphere in our series of lessons-cum-lunches.

The next thing that happened was that Isabella gave me a job, as if by magic. She had a new evening student, a Chinese tailor called Sir Woo, but she didn't have time to teach him because every evening she was running the Travellers' Co-op. Would you be an angel and teach him for me? she had asked.

Without hesitation I accepted, delighted to have added another student to my slowly growing list. Sir Woo was small and lively and came from the great city of Shanghai, my eventual destination. He lived and worked in a small box that had been knocked together in the Chinese part of town. It was a space about the size of an entrance hall, enough to have an opening to the street and do his tailoring work. His bed consisted of a board that had been tacked under the ceiling. This space doubled up as our teaching room and the only way in was through the hatch that opened up towards the street; I had to climb in, which was fine by me. Despite the miniscule scale of his operation Sir Woo seemed to make plenty of money, most of which he sent home, and he always paid my fee on time. He later told me that he made 30,000 yuan a year which was ten times what the average Tibetan earned.

Teaching Sir Woo was fun because he was desperate to learn and animated in his responses, even though his pronunciation was appalling. It was also an opportunity to get an insight into the Chinese side of the city and learn some more of their language. His hatch was open to the street and, during our lessons, crowds of his friends from Shanghai would crowd round and watch us in awed silence, trying to hold back their giggles. As soon as we took a short break there would be an explosion of humorous chatter. The idea of Sir Woo learning English made them crack up with laughter. I learned about the textile business in Lhasa and how it is monopolised by people from China's east coast, Shanghai in particular, and I understood that the hopeful traders and exiles who had come up from Nepal and India to trade clothes really didn't have a chance.

One of Sir Woo's visitors stood out from the others. Not only was he taller than the rest but he was quiet and thoughtful and showed genuine interest in what I was teaching:

- How do you do? he said in perfect BBC English. My name is Je Yang, I am a friend of Sir Woo and I too am from Shanghai.

- Hi there, my name's Rupert.

- Glad to meet you.

- Where did you learn such good English? I presume you went to private school and university in the UK. Or Hong Kong?

- Not at all. I taught myself.

- What do you mean? You didn't go to an English school? You must have had a great English teacher. I've never met a Chinese person who speaks English as well as you. How did you do it?

- Like I said, I taught myself. I've never had an English teacher. I've never been anywhere except Shanghai, where I am from, and here, where I work. I did used to listen to the radio and that helped with the pronunciation.

Even in Britain it's unusual to meet someone who speaks English so well. Most Brits have an accent that indicates their class or their region, and however well foreigners master our language – and some know it better than we do – I don't remember ever meeting anyone who spoke it as fluently as Je Yang. Je Yang had been to the technical university in Shanghai and was an engineer. He had a job in the Tibet Electric Company (no, they didn't need an English teacher) and said that getting a job here meant that he got a better salary so it was a good opportunity to save money. He wore old-fashioned sunglasses when outside and when he took them off I could see that he had gentle eyes. He looked rather shy at first but he was full of ideas and concepts that he wouldn't have dreamed of mentioning to the rowdy mob outside Sir Woo's place.

When someone is eager to learn the results can be electric. That was the case with Je Yang. We would meet often and talk for hours. They weren't lessons – there was no lesson plan, curriculum or text books – and I didn't charge him; they were more like wide ranging conversations. I was hungry to learn about China and he wanted to improve his knowledge of English peculiarities. I would think back through my life, searching out all the weird and wonderful expressions that I had squirreled away in my memory, and we would discuss them. He was delighted with the phrase Bob's your uncle!, and especially my story about Sheila, the secretary at Canongate Publishing who would say Mary's your aunt! as a refrain.

Only now were all these expressions coming out and I was amazed at how many I knew. I had a glimpse into the massive warehouse of information stored away in my memory – information that I'm not aware of and barely use. What made it particularly interesting was that I wasn't quite sure if my explanation of each expression was the correct one, so we would debate it, look it up in his dictionary and sometimes accost British or American travellers for their view on whatever expression we were debating that day.

Just when I was starting to form the impression that Je Yang was something of an innocent, he told me he had a private business interest. Private business? In Communist China? Isn't that illegal? He shrugged off the suggestion and told me about his friend in the Government Unit that had access to a bus that had been forgotten about. The bus driver didn't have to report to anyone, didn't have to do a particular run and basically worked for himself. He had made a deal with Je Yang that involved running foreign tourists from Lhasa to the Nepalese border, stopping off at important Tibetan monasteries on the way. He explained that the bus wasn't exactly new but they were able to undercut the official tour operators, and so the travellers were getting a good deal. The tourists could, of course, get the local bus but that was a two day marathon to the border and if you wanted to visit a monastery en route you had to get off the bus and chance your luck hitching through the wilderness. It seemed that Je Yang's bus made everyone happy.

But Je Yang had a problem. He told me that dealing with these foreigners made him unhappy and nervous, especially the French who were always complaining. He said the Americans could also be very difficult.

Some days later I found myself sitting with Je Yang on a hotel balcony outside the Travellers' Co-op, waiting for the thirty people who had signed up for the next bus trip to come and buy their tickets. I was terrified; I had never dealt with so many strangers before and my hands were shaking. This is more scary than teaching I thought. Je Yang was right, the travellers were tough, pushy and suspicious – and his attitude of meek servitude only encouraged them. Most of them had travelled through India or China to get here (the consensus was that it was much harder to travel through China). They were hard-bitten and experienced and all of them had been ripped off at least once. I could understand their reluctance to hand over a hundred yuan to a pair like us. Two weeks later we were doing the same thing and before long I had got the knack of it. I realised that however rude and tough I tried to be, nobody seemed to mind. It reminded me of a quote from Napoleon, who apparently said: If the King is a nice man the reign is a failure.

My routine in Lhasa had changed completely. Most lunch times I was teaching at the Chinese Hospital – doing more eating than teaching – and evenings were taken up with Sir Woo. I was still staying at Joga's place but it was almost impossible to relax there. Many times I wanted to stretch out on my bed for a few minutes but there were always a couple of burly warriors on it, cheerfully insisting I drink another cup of chang. At weekends I would climb onto the flat roof and read novels by Henry Miller, whose description of decadent Americans in Paris in the 1930s seemed to resonate with the life I was currently living.

Perhaps it was due to the altitude, or the fact that I hadn't worked for so long, but I felt continuously exhausted. Often I would go to the Cheese Factory and stretch out on Frenchy's bed for a few minutes. They had finally got their own room, which had become a wasteland of half-eaten food and all sorts of rubbish. The cold was really settling in with a vengeance and their borrowed paraffin heater was in constant use – not that it made any difference as the cold air leaked in through the windows, the ceiling and the thick stone walls. There was nobody on the Cheese Factory terrace anymore, everyone was inside trying to keep warm – many of them crowding into Diane and Frenchy's room in the vain hope that a large number of bodies would result in warmth. They were all eager to know what it was like staying with Tibetans but I didn't tell them much; I didn't have much to tell, and I certainly didn't invite any of them round in case they tried to muscle in on my space.

Diane and Frenchy both seemed obsessed with health matters. She was convinced that AIDS was a major epidemic that would end up destroying everyone. She said that if you slept with one person it could bring you into contact with over a thousand people, a claim that didn't make much sense to me. My view was that the media had distorted the risks of AIDS, as they had done with herpes before that, but she dismissed me as an ignoramus and shut me up by quoting statistics. Frenchy was more concerned with hepatitis, an illness that was much closer to hand, in fact just next door four people had it. We called the next room the Hep Ward and noticed that everyone who went to stay in it seemed to catch it – not that this stopped the never-ending stream of travellers looking for a cheap bed. Jake, an English guy we had known for months, was now called the Yellow Man. Italian Paola, who had sad eyes and long black hair, claimed to have been cured by Tibetan medicine.

- Nonsense, cried Frenchy. Hepatitis doesn't have a cure. Everyone knows that. Paola's bullshitting herself. With hep you just stop eating oil and alcohol and sit and wait. That's all you can do.

Larry, another American with an opinion, said he'd heard that a lot of people had been cured of hepatitis and other illnesses at the Tibetan Medicine Hospital. He said that Tibetan medicine is an ancient tradition that seems to get really good results. I didn't pay much attention to these discussions and Frenchy dismissed it out of hand – he dismissed Tibetan medicine as alternative, and all alternative medicine as hocus-pocus. I would make the occasional provocative remark to try and keep the discussion going.

Paola was different from the Cheese Factory crowd in that she didn't hang around in the rooms all day, moaning and groaning. She was intrigued by Tibetan religious culture and seemed to know a lot about it, although she rarely spoke. Her favourite spot was right in front of the Jokhang, the main Tibetan temple in the centre of the old town, where she would spend hours talking to people in fluent Mandarin. As a relaxing contrast to my other activities, I was spending more and more time at the Barkhor, walking the network of streets that surrounded the temple, as the pilgrims did. It was a good place to have conversations; you could walk and talk. One evening I was walking past the front of the Jokhang with Frenchy and we saw Paola, who turned to me dreamily and offered us a sliver of dried cheese – white cheese that had been hardened to rock and then cut into little slivers, probably with a cleaver considering how hard the stuff was. I had seen this stuff before but never tried it so I took one, thanked her, popped it in my mouth and tried to get some taste out of it. We walked on and Frenchy hissed into my ear:

- You idiot. She's had hep! I laughed off his suggestion and thought how sad it must be to go through life with this kind of hypochondria.

A few days later I got hit by a terrible feeling, a shockwave of illness, and it was so bad that I was convinced I was about to die. All I could do was lie in bed and drink water. Fortunately Joga's place was empty that day and I tried desperately to convince myself that I was fine, but the signs of hepatitis were hard to ignore: brown urine and yellow eyes. For two days I lay there, trying to get used to the feeling of being so ill, trying to accept it, trying to convince myself there was nothing wrong with me. This was the worst possible time to get sick: Roger and Isabella were both going off on a trek together and they had asked me to be Roger's replacement teacher;

it was the best job opportunity that had come up yet so I couldn't stay in bed. But I was too weak to get up.

A day before the appointment at the class I staggered up to the Chinese Hospital – a Herculean feat – and sat by the window of my student's room. I was too exhausted to teach and could barely talk. She assumed I was hungry and offered a plate of thick curry and pickles, but the smell turned my stomach even though I hadn't eaten for days:

- You no eat?

- I can't eat. Today I can't teach! I feel very sick. I must see a doctor.

- Okay, we go see best doctor man in hospital.

With a sense of purpose that I found exhausting, she led me out of her block, up the road and into the Chinese Hospital – which I hadn't actually visited thus far. It looked modern enough from the outside but inside it looked terrible: dirty, chaotic and with a cold, unwelcoming atmosphere. The doctor took my pulse, told me I had a common cold and gave me some aspirins. I returned to Joga's, feeling like it had been a wasted journey and was so burned out by the exertion that I spent the rest of the day asleep. Joga's place was full of her middle-aged lady friends who made sympathetic noises, but Joga was both sharp and sensitive and she knew what was needed: she shooed her friends out and banned others from coming for the next few days, giving me some welcome relief. I still couldn't accept the fact that I had the dreaded hep. I was in denial: This can't be happening to me!

The next morning was the job test and I dragged myself over to the Shata building, an ancient courtyard where Isabella and Roger lived and where the classes were held. I slowly made my way up the stairs, knocked on their door and was invited in to join them for breakfast. The smell of frying food was too much; I went straight to the toilet, located at the end of the landing and puked violently into the slit in the floor, inhaling a terrible smell from the cesspit that filled up the room below. Nothing came out. My body went through the heaving gesture of vomiting but there was nothing to puke except some watery gobs of sticky phlegm.

- You look rough, said Isabella back in the apartment. You don't have to do this you know?

I didn't know her well enough to know that she meant it. I had spent days working up the energy and determination to go through with this test, which was crucial – I was convinced that my very survival depended on it.

Downstairs in the big classroom the students were lively and pleased to see me. They were laughing and expecting me to join in but I just slumped into a chair, croaked out some words to explain my state and asked them to be quiet and read their books. They understood immediately and settled down to read. I felt they were on my side and that maybe I could actually pass this test. Towards the end of the class the head teacher came in and I stood up and started teaching some parts of the book. This seemed to satisfy him and he left. I slumped back down again thankfully and the rest of the class passed by uneventfully. For a moment I thought I was beating this illness but when I got back to Joga's place I felt worse than ever and I knew there was no way I could maintain this charade of pretending to teach. On the way back I bumped into Paola who noticed the yellow eyes immediately and said:

- You look horrible. You go to Tibetan Hospital. They will help you.

I had considered going to the Tibetan Hospital but I was sceptical. Wasn't it based on the medieval system of wind, bile and phlegm? How could it possibly help? But Western medicine has no cure for hepatitis so why not try Tibetan medicine? I was too exhausted to even think about it. I had seen the Tibetan Hospital and it was big and crowded. I didn't have the energy to hustle my way in there and I would need a translator. I tried to think about these problems in Joga's place which was now deathly quiet, but I couldn't focus and I drifted off into a long state of delirium.

Joga took action. She had met my Chinese friend Je Yang, who had come round to see the place, and she was impressed with him. While I slept she sent out her lady friends to search the town and locate him. I was awoken by a series of prods and there he was, Je Yang, sitting at the end of my bed rather sheepishly, refusing Joga's offer of tea or chang. He said:

- I've come to take you to the Tibetan Hospital. Let's go. I laboriously got up and followed him across the old town.

There was a big crowd in the Tibetan Hospital and we both took up our positions; me by the bike rack where I was dry retching into the undergrowth and Je Yang inside, arguing with the doctors and nurses, trying to get an appointment. Eventually we got to see a doctor, a young man who was speaking in rapid Mandarin to Je Yang. I was told to roll up my sleeve and he took my pulse with three fingers on each wrist, concentrating hard for what seemed like ages. Then he asked about symptoms and everything I said he would just nod as if to confirm his diagnosis. Je Yang translated:

- The illness you have, what you call hepatitis, is a typical illness that comes up at this time of year, at the change from autumn to winter. A lot of people get ill when the seasons change. This one is to do with the bile, you have a bile imbalance. He says your illness is well-known to them and common for this time of year.

The doctor then gave me some evil-looking black pills, which looked suspiciously like dried sheep shit, and sent us on our way. As we were leaving I asked if I needed to follow a particular diet and he said no. I was willing to try the sheep shit pills, I would have tried anything, but I was still sceptical about Tibetan medicine.

Back at Joga's place I sat with my glass of boiled water and chewed the first of the black pills. They tasted horrible – musty, gritty and sharp – but they didn't make me vomit and I swallowed them down faithfully. I lay down on the bed, expecting nothing, and wondering what I could do next; no health insurance, no western doctors here, no hope? Three hours later I woke up feeling fine and by evening my normal energy levels were back. I couldn't believe it, the Tibetan medicine was working – and I had only taken one pill. Was this a dream? Was this possible? I was still sceptical and expected to wake up the next morning feeling as ill as I'd felt all week, but by morning I was better than ever. Complete recovery.

And good fortune had smiled on me on the work front too. I got the job as Roger's replacement. Also – against stiff competition from their old friends – they asked me to look after their apartment which was the ideal convalescence home. Their flat was upstairs at the Shata courtyard which was, I learned, a former palace. The courtyard had been turned into simple flats and the whole place was rather run down, but Roger and Isabella's flat had some of the elegance of the old days; curious wooden beams and a long sweep of windows that stretched the length of the apartment itself. It was spacious, comfortable, full of interesting books and, best of all, private. I couldn't understand why they had gone off on a trekking trip in winter but it was the ideal place to cook the only thing I was able to hold down – boiled vegetables.

There had been a lot of debate about who would be the replacement teacher for Isabella and I had pitched in with my view that Frenchy would be ideal; although I knew him as a reprobate he could make himself look respectable if he had to, and he was great with the students. I had seen him with them at the party and he'd been lively and stimulating. But they chose Big Jack, another depraved American. Big Jack was a pain in the neck and I didn't like him from the start. He styled himself as an intellectual and had spent time studying Tibetan culture at Dharamshala, the capital of the Tibetans in India, seat of the Tibetan Government in exile and home of the Dalai Lama. He was a far bigger know-it-all than any other traveller I had met. He claimed to have trekked across large parts of Tibet and he considered himself the font of all knowledge regarding the country. What made it worse was that he was also a macho man; he was big, had a beard and he wore a Tibetan Khampa cloak, belted at the waist, and a brown woollen Pakistani hat. I think he tried to imitate the style and swagger of the Khampas. Big Jack's problem was that he had no sense of humour – the saving grace of the real Khampas. He was also a bad teacher: rigid, impatient and liable to fly off the handle. I was sure the students hated him, but they were far too polite to say so.

I do have to thank Big Jack for giving me an introduction to Tibetan medicine, one of the many subjects he could drone on about for hours. I was thirsty for knowledge of this mysterious science that had cured me of the dreaded hep so effortlessly. What caught my imagination was the idea that wind, which is one of the key elements, is believed to be a horse which carries the body. A week earlier I would have mocked such an idea but now I was getting stronger by the day I was open to it. Perhaps the most impressive thing about Tibetan medicine is the way they diagnose illness, by reading a pulse. When westerners read a pulse they are simply counting the heartbeats, but it takes a Tibetan doctor ten years to learn how to read a pulse properly. The Tibetan doctors use three fingers and they develop a sensitivity so fine that each of their fingers picks up two separate pulses. In other words, they are reading six pulses at the same time.

When I first heard that they use the ancient classifications (or humours) of wind, bile and phlegm as the basis for their medical system I couldn't take it seriously – this approach to medicine went out in the Middle Ages. This is their method of diagnosing illnesses. When they take a pulse they are reading the wind, bile and phlegm levels of a patient and they detect illnesses by spotting imbalances in one of these humours. The pills are interesting too. I had assumed they were some kind of herbal remedy but their main ingredients are minerals. Traditionally, Tibetan doctors would spend several weeks a year on horseback gathering rare plants, roots and minerals. Mixing the ingredients and making the pills is an ancient science.

I later found out that Tibetan Medicine dates back to a mythical age when eight Medicine Buddhas wrote down about 80,000 different illnesses – from the past, present and future. Tibetan Medicine is well developed in

India, where they teach it in monasteries, and where it has been credited with successfully treating cancer and also AIDS, a disease they claim to have known about for hundreds of years. In India and the in the west Tibetan medical practitioners keep a low profile and make no public claims about its effectiveness.

I went back to the Tibetan Hospital a few times to try to garner more insights, but nobody spoke English. One day I came across an old doctor in robes who must have been in his nineties. He had a spring in his step and a sparkle in his eye. He stopped me in the corridor, greeted me, introduced himself as Dr Puntsok and asked where I was from. When I told him he smiled enthusiastically and beckoned me to follow. We went through corridors, up stairs and into a distant storeroom where he rummaged around and pulled out a little glass bottle that he showed to me proudly. It said Bicarbonate of Soda and was obviously very old, perhaps dating back to colonial times. I took the bottle, looked at it and wondered what I was supposed to do. Translate the label? Maybe he had heard me say I am from Bicarbonate of Soda? I looked round but he was gone.

I felt so lucky to have been asked to look after Roger and Isabella's flat and I was determined to take this responsibility seriously. The flat had two rooms, a huge bedroom-cum-living room, with a wide array of windows, and a kitchen. Tibetans tend to decorate with loud, home-made colours and the wooden pillars in the main room were painted red and blue while the roof timbers were yellow. I recognised the floor as it was similar to the one that I had seen Diane working on for a few hours in the Jokhang – mud and gravel that had been thumped down by women wielding small tree trunks. Not only are these floors warmer than concrete but all the feet that gently rub them make them shiny and beautiful. There were only two stoves and the one in the main room was too small to heat up the space, so I spent most of my time in the kitchen, where Roger had thoughtfully wired up a set of speakers.

Even though I only had three hours of teaching a day I continued to find the work exhausting. I wasn't sure if this was due to the illness or, as I suspected, or because teaching is a very tiring job. It felt more exhausting than carrying heavy furniture up and down staircases in Edinburgh or working on a building site. By lunchtime I would be shattered, but also feeling satisfied. I needed to conserve energy, and it was freezing outside, so I stopped teaching the nurse and cut back on teaching Sir Woo. After a few days I invited Je Yang round and we would spend the evenings talking and listening to Roger's huge collection of tapes. Then I ran into Diane and Frenchy who told me about the police raid at the Cheese Factory: everyone had been thrown out and the manager was carried off to the police station for under-charging foreigners. The Americans had moved to the Plateau Hotel which they hated because it was modern, concrete, cold and expensive. Diane had fallen out with Frenchy and they argued incessantly except, curiously, when I invited them round to my new flat. Both of them were sick with the illnesses that bedevilled foreigners in Tibet: giardia and bronchitis.

When I saw what a rotten teacher Big Jack was I realised that there had been no point in the job test as they obviously chose their replacement teachers on a whim. Big Jack was always late and he'd never prepare his lessons. I found myself helping him out, filling the gaps and trying to cover up for him. He reciprocated by offering me advice on diet, another of his areas of expertise, and he explained the different qualities that vegetables have and how steaming is better than boiling. This was all news to me. I had no idea that tomatoes are full of acid, peanuts are full of fat and milk creates phlegm in the throat. I didn't invite him round to the flat, telling him that I wasn't allowed to have visitors, hoping he wouldn't see Je Yang, Diane and Frenchy coming round most evenings. We would sit round the yak-dung stove cooking a pot of soup and explain to Je Yang that life in the west isn't as idyllic as he'd been led to believe. Je Yang didn't believe the anti-American propaganda he'd been taught; he believed that once you made it to the west wealth and happiness inevitably followed. I was keen to destroy that image and Diane and Frenchy were the ideal means of doing so. They would talk for hours about racism, corruption, inequality and, most extensively, about AIDS.

Je Yang had a morbid fascination with AIDS and Diane and Frenchy's doom-laden prophecies set his mind spinning. On the one hand the disease appalled him but on the other he couldn't help feeling that this was some kind of divine retribution for all the bad things the western world had done. We would furiously debate the AIDS issues every evening, each one of us strongly defending our positions, and the only thing that we all agreed upon was that mashed potatoes taste great.

The sickness I was recovering from must have lowered my immunity –

by the end of that week I had both giardia and bronchitis. These illnesses were nothing compared to hepatitis but I had to get rid of my chesty cough and the appalling stomach. Diane described how giardia had made her stomach swell up to the size of a basketball, she would rush to the toilet and then piss and fart down the hole. They would both explain these gruesome details endlessly. Giardia, I was told, is a type of bacteria that forms cysts in your duodenum (the bit just below your stomach) and when these burst they produce sulphuric gases. The Tibetan medical cure was said to be effective, but time consuming, and the modern cure was two grammes of a powerful antibiotic called Tiniba, a drug that Diane swore by.

- But you gotta remember, she said, to take a second dose a week later in case you've missed some of those fuckers the first time round. They lay eggs you know and you gotta nuke those fuckers before they can get you again.

I didn't have the energy to deal with the Tibetan hospital again so when the basketball belly hit I downed a couple of tabs of Tiniba, which promptly wiped out the infection. Frenchy then gave me two tabs of Bactrim which, he swore, would get rid of the bronchitis. It worked.

Even among the foreign oddballs and eccentrics who would turn up in Lhasa every week, Big Jack stood out. His thick woollen clothes, big beard and Mujahedeen hat made him the butt of all jokes, at least in my circle. But he was so big and fierce-looking that nobody had the courage to say anything mocking to his face. He had latched on to the cheesecake women and was one of their salesmen. He was good at this because he was pushy and intimidating and people thought they would get thumped if they didn't cough up. I knew where he hung out so I was able to avoid him but we came into contact at class time.

One morning I went to Roger's class and was surprised to find some officials from the Tibetan Political Consultative Conference there. These were the people who had set up the class but this was the first time I'd actually seen more than one of them. They nervously informed me that Tibetan TV wanted to come and film us for their news show, was that okay? Until that moment I had no idea that there was a TV station in Tibet and if they wanted to film us that was fine by me. They left and I started teaching. Twenty minutes later another bunch of officials came in, but this lot burst in the door arrogantly, set up their cameras and started filming. I carried on as normal. When they moved next door to film Big Jack we could hear his voice becoming louder and louder; I stopped teaching to go and look and all the students followed. We peered into the next room and there was Big Jack, shouting at the top of his voice as if he was giving the Sermon on the Mount to a gathering of thousands. That evening I went to Sir Woo's place as he was the only person I knew who had a TV set. He was happy to let me in but there was a power failure, so we missed the chance of seeing Big Jack look ridiculous on TV.

Every Saturday we would teach a song. It was simple, fun and they would learn new expressions and improve their listening skills. Isabella would play the Beatles and Bob Marley, and other favourites from the sixties, but I thought Flower Power might be a bit over their heads so I started using jazz songs. The problem was Big Jack; he never prepared for his classes and without preparation you just can't use a song for teaching purposes. I offered to help him and he seemed willing, so I prepared a Fats Waller song for him and explained the technique that I had learned during my English teaching course in England:

- Write the lyrics on a piece of paper, identify any difficult words in the lyrics that they might not know – and teach these words before you play the song. Then write the lyrics on the board with some easy words missing, and write an underscore where the words are missing. Then play the song a few times and tell them to fill in the missing words. It's easy and everyone usually enjoys it.

When Saturday came round Big Jack was late again. When he did show up, looking hung-over, the class were making a hell of a din and they greeted him with a slightly mocking tone as they had obviously come to realise that he was something of a joke figure. This was the rowdiest class that we had and it contained several tearaway monks, all teenagers, as well as some wild girls. I could hear them joking about his beard and hat and hoped he didn't understand (his grasp of Tibetan was worse than mine). Gruffly, he began writing the lyrics up on the board in a handwriting style that was illegible, even to me. The song starts like this:

- Dina, Dina, is there anyone finer?
- In the state of Carolina
- If there is, show her to me.

I could hear the class growing more restive and I put my head through the door. He was in the process of explaining the meaning of Dixie eyes blazing and I could see some of the students laughing openly in front of him.

- Everything okay? I asked.

- Yeah, he hissed, with eyes of fury, I can handle the little bastards.

I went back to my class, not knowing what was best to do. I heard a crashing sound, shouting, a murmur of voices and then total silence. I went in and found Big Jack on his own, all the students had walked out. He was red-faced and furious, stomping up and down the room.

- What happened?

- Those little fuckers! Nobody fucks with me! Next time I'll really beat the shit out of him! You gotta be tough with these guys.

Then he grabbed his stuff and, without another word, threw open the door and marched off in disgust. I went back to my class and carried on teaching the difficult words associated with my song. I later found out that he had grabbed one of the monks, thrown him against the wall and threatened him with his fists. On the following Monday morning the leaders were waiting for him. They told him not to come back.

Frenchy was delighted with the news of Big Jack's downfall. Even though the two had never spoken to each other, Frenchy's expectations had been raised when I tried to get him in as Isabella's replacement, and the more I told him about Big Jack the more he hated him. The leaders had not mentioned a replacement teacher and, considering Isabella was lost in the wilderness with her boyfriend, I felt it would be entirely appropriate if I appointed Frenchy as the new replacement. Nobody objected.

Although Frenchy was as loud as Big Jack his style was engaging; he had humour and everyone seemed to enjoy it. His lessons were lively and sometimes I caught my students listening to him rather than me. He told me his teaching style was copied from his Spanish teacher who would stop people from drifting off by shouting questions at them, just when he thought they were losing interest. The only other person in the school was an old caretaker whose job was to open and close the doors and provide us with flasks of hot water.

The classes took place in a building that had once belonged to the aristocratic Shata family. It was said to be a palace but it didn't look out of the ordinary, just a one-storey terraced house around an earthen yard. During the Cultural Revolution the building had been vandalised, stripped and abandoned. Only a few years prior to our arrival, it had been converted into a condominium of flats. The neighbours now living there were friendly in a superficial way, but more guarded than most Tibetans I knew and none of them invited me into their homes.

As the second week of teaching drew to a close my old problem began to emerge: my visa was running out. This time I was determined to use all my new contacts and get a Resident's Visa, which would give me another six months. Or should I head for New Delhi where my godfather, Andrew Tarnowski, the resident correspondent for Reuters, had invited me to stay? The idea of going somewhere hot, staying in a really comfortable place and eating delicious spicy food was overwhelming. I knew I was onto something here in Lhasa, I had finally made a breakthrough and if I took off for the luxury of India surely I risked throwing it all away. After agonising over this dilemma for several days I decided I would apply for the visa and stay in Lhasa through the winter.

Time was running out, fast. I had only two weeks left on my visa and if one of my contacts couldn't help then I would have to rush to the Nepalese border, a prospect I didn't like to think about. Je Yang thought long and hard about helping me but finally decided that he didn't have the right contacts. I didn't push it as I assumed his friendship with me was already a risk for him. I then approached my school leaders, the important sounding Political Consultative Conference, the group of former nobles and political prisoners who had renovated the Shata Building and set up the language school. They laughed when I asked them to help and said:

- We have no influence, something that I just didn't believe.

The one person who was able to help was the one who I thought would have least influence: Sir Woo. He knew the Chief of Police as he would come to the workshop in person, discreetly asking Sir Woo to repair his underwear. Apparently he was also interested in getting English lessons from me, although Sir Woo had never mentioned that before (and he never brought it up again). Sir Woo confidently took my passport and said he would get me a Resident's Permit very soon. He didn't think it would be a problem. I would visit him every day in the hope of good news, even though I wasn't expecting much, but all he would say was:

- Tomorrow.

Meanwhile, back at the flat, life as I had come to know it was about to end. I had mentally prepared myself for moving back into Joga's crowded dive and I kept telling Diane and Frenchy that they had to move out, but they had become permanent fixtures, and they didn't give a damn about being caught in the act by Roger and Isabella. It was I who was becoming neurotic about their imminent return and our eviction.

With no word about my visa I began making parallel preparations:

thinking about transport options to India and looking for a new flat. I
sent a postcard to my Godfather in New Delhi and said I would try and
visit, but wasn't sure if I could. One of the main reasons against going
to India was that I wasn't sure if I would come back, even though I really
wanted to. Every single foreign traveller I had met in Tibet had said that
they would return but I hadn't heard of anyone who had actually done so.
Perhaps they found things more attractive elsewhere or they couldn't face
the return journey? I could understand that and I wondered if it would
happen to me. Sir Woo still hadn't got a reply from the police chief and the
more time that passed the more I became convinced that I wasn't going to
get a visa extension after all. Meanwhile, I was negotiating with a group of
Americans who wanted to hire Je Yang's bus, all the seats on it, and trying
to make sure that one seat was kept for me. I didn't want to pay for the
seat but the Americans' sniffed out my scam and insisted that I pay for my
own ticket.

Finding a new place to live was getting nowhere. The police were
cracking down on units that charged less than ten yuan a night and even
if I could afford this outrageous price I really didn't want to stay in a
hotel all winter. It was late November, the air was sharp and gusty and at
night it fell below freezing. People were wrapping up but during the day I
enjoyed the piercing sunshine. I noticed how foreigners would strip down
to their T-shirts as soon as it got warm but Tibetans would just ignore the
elements altogether, wearing the same thick clothes all year round. The
Kham people had a curious tendency to take one arm out of their coats
when it was hot but generally they always wore long coats, belted at the
waist, that looked like they would be very helpful in a storm. I always wore
a thin blue cotton jacket, which I could unzip during the heat of the day
and during winter I wore a jumper underneath it.

My Tibetan pills had run out by now and I really wanted more, so I
asked Italian Paola to come with me to the Tibetan Hospital. She agreed,
we went along, found the same doctor who took one look at me and said:

- He's fine, but he needs to take more of the same pills for his bile
imbalance.

There was no sign of Roger and Isabella. They were due back on the last
Saturday of November but it was already the following Monday. Frenchy
and I carried on teaching but I knew that the coming weekend was my
deadline – I only had ten days left on my visa and I would need some days
to get to the border.

I counted every day like a convict approaching his release. I told Sir Woo that I needed my passport back by Friday, and then started worrying about where the hell my passport was anyway. It had been with the police for eons. Maybe they had lost it? Maybe they wouldn't get it back to me in time? Maybe it had been sold. Everyone had advice: Frenchy told me to enjoy the winter here; Big Jack said there was nothing to worry about and that I should just pretend to have lost my passport. Others said my top priority should be to get to Goa, on the Indian coast, as it's apparently the best place on the planet to spend winter. Je Yang wanted me to stay as he didn't believe I would come back. I was worried about money as I had less than $200 left; one wrong move and my last money would be gone and I'd have been unable to travel at all.

I was virtually living at Sir Woo's place by now, constantly bullying him to get my passport back. He was cycling to and from the police station like a messenger boy. Friday came and there was still no word from the police. I became desperate. What would I do if I couldn't get my passport and couldn't get on that bus? It was becoming a nightmare. I spent the day and all that evening pacing up and down in front of Sir Woo's place and at about midnight he cycled off to the police chief's house, where he got my passport – but it had no visa in it.

My friends had spent the evening waiting for me at Roger and Isabella's place. Neither of them had sent word of their whereabouts. I had no idea about where they had gone and I was starting to worry. I got back after midnight and the atmosphere was subdued; Frenchy and Diane were also leaving soon, their money and visas were running out and they planned to go to Taiwan and make some real money teaching English. Je Yang turned up after one in the morning and gave me an envelope. I opened it and there was a note – saying Good Trip. Come back – and three hundred US dollars in cash. This must have been the profits he had made out of the bus trips. It was a blessing from heaven and it changed my perspective. Now I could get to India in style, without having to live like a beggar and worry about running out of cash, in fact there was enough money there to travel round India and get back to Tibet. What made this gift so special was that not only had I not asked for it but I hadn't even thought about asking him for money.

The next morning I joined the group of Americans and we all lined up to get on Je Yang's shabby bus. For the first few hours, before the sun had a chance to work its magic, we sat there and froze – and I felt particularly vulnerable in my miserable cotton jacket and gym shoes. I looked at the Americans' thick boots and down jackets with jealousy. I don't remember it being this cold, I said to my neighbour. But then again I don't usually get up before dawn. He didn't reply.

If anyone thinks Americans are suckers – as I did – easy pickings for rip-off artists, they should go to China and see the brand of yank that travels there. The ones I had dealt with were so sharp it was frightening. They were aware of their reputation as being stupid and wealthy and compensated by being tough, mean and smart. They wanted answers, discounts and everything to be just right. In addition to this, a lot of the ones I met were incredibly well read. I realised that coming with them on this trip was going to be hell as they could pick on me whenever they didn't like something, and they might try and force me to get the driver to do their bidding.

We soon got a friendly banter going but I was dreading the complaints about the grindingly slow pace of the bus or the lack of a heating system. I was particularly embarrassed by the speed of the bus and was expecting a barrage of complaints – which never came. I realised that our warnings about the bus being an old heap had actually worked. We had lowered their expectations and nobody complained. After fourteen hours on the road we pulled into a lively truck stop in Gyantse which was freezing but it had a stunning view of the Gompa (the domed monastery roof). Harry, a loud Canadian, took charge and got everyone to agree that we should stay longer in Gyanste. This was the moment I was dreading. Harry came over, gave me my orders and I meekly went to speak to the driver, who was a mean cookie himself, hoping that he would refuse point blank and be even tougher than they were. But the driver agreed happily to all of Harry's requests, which included a longer stay in the next town too, Shigatse, where we got a good look round the monastery. The real surprise for me was Sakyapa Monastery, which is located quite far off the main road.

The Sakyapa sect of Tibetan Buddhists wear red hats and while this might not mean a lot to outsiders, to Tibetans it is of great importance. They are one of three Red Hat sects, the other two being the Nyingmapa and the Kagyupa. The Gelugpa sect, led by the Dalai Lama, are known as the Yellow Hats, and they effectively dominated the Tibetan political scene from the mid-17th century until the Chinese Communist invasion in 1951. The Red Hats are smaller groups with different histories and traditions, based in different monasteries, but the different groups seemed to get on with each other quite well. The story which really captured my imagination was connected to the Mongol Invasion in the 13th century: when Genghis Khan was conquering Asia and Europe he would give the besieged people the option of surrendering or being slaughtered. The Sakyapa welcomed the Mongols as new friends and as a consequence the destruction in Tibet was avoided. In fact, they got on so well that the Mongols adopted Tibetan Buddhism. Different groups of Mongols kept up the connection with Tibet and its religion, and in the 16th century one of these factions threw its weight behind the Yellow Hats and gave the head of the sect the title Dalai, which in their language means great lake. This all happened over 600 years ago but the leader of the Tibetans still uses the name, Dalai Lama, which means the holy man who is the Ocean of Wisdom.

When we approached Sakyapa Monastery my first impression was that we had driven up to an ancient prison. Huge walls, black at the bottom and purple at the top, reared up before us. The setting – high, grey, barren mountains on all sides – added to the sense of desolation and the small village at the side of the monastery looked windswept and miserable. My first thought was it's going to be damn hard to get something to eat, and somewhere to stay, in this place. As soon as the bus stopped I went into the monastery, had a quick glance at the candlelit interior, shot up some stairs, identified a suitable place to sleep and ran back to the bus.

As the Americans were lumbering out of the bus and wandering into the monastery, I hurried towards the village in search of food. There was no truck stop, teahouse, restaurant or inn – only a dilapidated little shop, stone walls and low mud houses, as if hiding from the wind. Inside the shop a noisy group of men were crowding round a small fire. I knew I only had a few minutes before the other travellers wandered over, as they had seen where I went. Greeting the bewildered-looking tribesmen in Tibetan, I confidently pushed my way in and squeezed onto the narrow bench that some of them were sitting on. The shopkeeper growled in indignation but I knew it was only to show it was his place, and I knew that pushing in rudely like this was the appropriate behaviour. There was a pan of disgusting-looking food being fried on the fire but I could see that it was just a snack for them; it didn't look like a dish being prepared for a foreign clientele. I pulled out a can of green peas that I had procured in Lhasa and their eyes all lit up in interest. I opened the can, put it at the edge of the fire so it would heat up and decided to share it with them.

A few minutes later the other foreigners started to arrive, but it was so unlike any shop that they had ever come across before and they didn't know what to do in the chaotic atmosphere within. It was clear that the Tibetans also felt rather uncomfortable at having all these strangers standing around in their shop. I tried to explain that they could sell the food that was cooking in their pan but they failed to grasp the idea, or I failed to explain it properly, and the Americans probably wouldn't have bought it anyway – they all had dehydrated food supplies in their rucksacks. One of the tribesmen pulled out a filthy antique from his pocket and showed it to the travellers, who all crowded round to look. The tribesman pulled out more curios, thinking he was going to make some money, but the Americans were only interested in looking, they didn't even want to start negotiating, and suddenly they all left at once, leaving the tribesman looking rather disappointed. I spent the next few hours with the hillsmen, feeling very relaxed. I offered them some tinned peas but nobody wanted to try some. I particularly appreciated their light-hearted approach to life and it struck me that the less people have, and the more hardship they face, the more likely they are to be boisterous and fun, and appreciate the things that we just take for granted. It makes perfect sense: if your life is really hard you want to forget about it at moments like this.

Two mornings later I was colder than I had ever been in my life. We had spent the night at a freezing truck-stop at Tingri, one of the highest settlements in Tibet and the nearest to Mount Everest. What really killed me was sitting by the door in the bus so I could get a good view of Mount Everest, not realising until it was too late that the cold draught that was coming in under the door froze my feet into ice blocks. Even after the sun had defrosted the bus that afternoon I still couldn't feel my feet. They had frozen solid. I realised that cold is harder to bear than the worst illness, even hepatitis; the pain goes right into the bone and won't let up for a moment. I tried putting my feet into a borrowed sleeping bag, I tried rubbing them but there's nothing you can do but get them into a warm place and then wait patiently.

In Kathmandu I found myself in a frustrating position. The first thing I noticed was a sweet shop, a glorious sweet shop, with glittering bars of Cadbury and Lindt chocolate. It got worse. As I walked into the tourist area I passed hamburger joints and pizza parlours and could smell the overwhelmingly delicious aromas of Indian, Italian and Mexican food. I knew that I wasn't supposed to eat anything with fat in it because of the wretched hepatitis, and that included chocolate. I almost passed out with temptation, and then cracked: I couldn't stand it anymore; I went into a sweet shop and loaded up with goodies, which I then gorged on and spent the rest of the night feeling ill. I realised that sticking to this horrible diet was relatively easy in Tibet where you're not assailed by temptations on every street corner.

CHAPTER EIGHT

India felt totally different than on my last visit, just a few months before, when the railway system and skyscrapers of Delhi hadn't impressed me so much. What had happened? Surely India hadn't changed? Then I realised that I was seeing India from a Tibetan perspective. I was a village boy in the big city for the first time, soaking up all the impressions with a sense of wonder. In Tibet the night is black and empty and the only sound is the howling of dogs; but you can see the stars and the moon very clearly. In India the night is a chaos of noises – trains, traffic, people shouting and talking, strange music, crowds everywhere – and the smell of spices, delicious food I couldn't eat, diesel fumes, human and cow excrement, urine, many types of smoke, perfume; and lights, I couldn't get used to all the flashing lights on shops, cafes, all night bakeries and sweetshops, buses, bicycles and rickshaws. I felt like I had arrived in civilisation and it took a few days to get used to it.

Delhi is divided into new and old, rich and poor, north and south, Muslim and Hindu, the posh part that was built by the British Empire, and the sprawling poor part. I had an address in the southern, rich, British Empire part of town – New Delhi – where my godfather lived. The quiet streets in that part of town felt a bit artificial even though they were obviously old and well established. It was unusually quiet and each house was surrounded by lawns, walls, trees and guards and each one took up a lot of space. Was this really where my godfather lived? Isn't he a journalist? I didn't know journalists were so wealthy.

The story of my godfather, Andy Tarnowski, and my family is a complicated one – but to cut a long story short, he is the Polish stepson of my paternal grandfather Malcolm Wolfe Murray. My grandpa was a professional officer in the Black Watch, a Scottish regiment, and during the Second World War he was stationed in Cairo with the British 8th

Army. I have no idea what my grandpa did in the war but I'm sure it wasn't anything too dangerous; he was probably a desk officer. Malcolm had married before the war to a beautiful Scottish woman called Grizel Boyle and they had had two boys, one of them being my Dad. For some reason I've never quite understood, Grizel visited Malcolm in Cairo early on in the war and by all accounts they had a good time – Cairo was a British colonial hub where there was a great social life going on even during the war. On her way home, by now pregnant with her third child, the ship in which she was travelling, the Laconia, was hit by a German submarine and sunk. The German commander, realising that he had sunk a ship full of civilians, and Italian prisoners of war, picked up the survivors and towed their lifeboats towards the West African coast. They were then spotted by a patrolling American bomber, which attacked the sub and the convoy of lifeboats it was towing. The German commander then abandoned his rescue mission and told the hapless survivors that they were on their own. The event, which came to be known as the Laconia Incident, led to an order by the German Navy which stated that no survivors would be picked up by U-boats from then on. My grandmother was subsequently on an open boat for 27 days, with very limited food and water. She died a few days before they reached land.

Some years earlier, Andrew Tarnowski was born to an aristocratic Polish couple who had escaped the Nazi and Soviet invasion of Poland in 1939. Chouquette, Andrew's Mother, had made it to Cairo while his father had joined the Free Polish Army which was part of the British Army. Somewhere along the line they had separated and in Cairo Chouquette met up with my grandfather Malcolm. By the end of the war Malcolm and Chouquette were married and they moved to Scotland, where Andrew was sent to Ampleforth, an exclusive Catholic boarding school. He graduated from Oxford University and became a journalist, initially with the Toronto Globe and then with Reuters, who sent him to Beunos Aires, Beirut and then New Delhi.

I was pondering this family history as I stood in front of Andrew's luxurious house, set in a spacious lawn and surrounded by mature trees. For a moment I thought of running off to the travellers' area and checking into a cheap hostel – just $1 a night – but the friendly old guard had already told them they had a white visitor with a rucksack so there was no escape. Andy came running out, full of exuberant greetings and introduced me to his new Lebanese wife: Wafa. She was big, bubbly and full of maternal love and enthusiasm. She ran the house with a loud voice and lots of humour and she brought Andy down to earth when he was being too pompous. They had two young children who were much quieter than their parents. I loved it.

Although the house wasn't that massive by western standards, to me it was a palace and I was fascinated by everything inside it: draught-proof windows, air conditioning, Persian rugs, sofas, ornaments, the lighting, the cooker, fridge and everything in the kitchen; the TV and video collection; running hot water and the incredible sensation of lying in a hot bath. I felt like I was experiencing all this for the first time in my life and it was wonderful. When dinner was served the assault on my palate of Wafa's Lebanese food was beyond description. Andy was disappointed that I wouldn't partake in some of his Claret, his playful glance said go on – it's really good but I told them about my hepatitis, saying that I really shouldn't be eating all this food without checking for its oil content, but how could I possibly resist a feast like this?

There's nothing quite like the sensation of getting between crisply ironed white sheets. I noticed every detail: the quality of the cotton, their coolness, the way the sheets were tightly stretched over the mattress, the pillow, the firmness of the mattress, the sidelight, the book collection. I felt like royalty but I couldn't sleep properly. I couldn't get used to the smooth, firm, clean surfaces and the cooled air. The next evening Andy took me to a Christmas party with Brits, Americans, Brazilians, Arabs, journalists, diplomats and international businessmen and their wives. I felt like a poor relative from the countryside who couldn't fit in to the social scene. I had never met ex-pats like these before, so confident and successful and so unlike the rough foreign travellers that I knew.

On Christmas Eve my aunt Tessa flew out from London, where she lived. Tessa is tall, cheerful and fun and she works as a potter-cum-artist. We have always got on well and we connected immediately. Tessa had a suitcase packed full of presents from home and long forgotten tastes like marmalade and Bovril. We had a British style Christmas, which felt rather incongruous in this part of the world but I appreciated the roast turkey, Christmas tree and rituals more than I would have done at home. By the time New Year's eve came round I felt I had to get away from all this luxury or I would succumb to it – maybe I would start looking for a job in India and never find my way back to Tibet? Andy invited me on a family trip to Jaipur, in India's western desert, but I wanted to travel on my own for a bit and decided to get the bus to Dharamshala, residence of the Dalai Lama and the exiled Tibetans.

After an all night bus trip I arrived in Dharamshala and was shocked to find that it was an ordinary Indian town – not a Tibetan in sight. I couldn't understand it, the name Dharamshala is known the world over as the home of the Dalai Lama and hundreds of thousands of Tibetan exiles. I had assumed that I would see Tibetans everywhere, that they would be in the majority. I went to a nearby tea shop to enquire:

- Is this Dharamshala?
- Yes please, this Dharamshala. You like tea?
- Yes please.
- Here you are. One rupee.
- Where are the Tibetans? I thought this was a Tibetan town?
- Ah the Tibetans. They are on that side. He jerked his thumb behind him, towards the hills that were half hidden by cloud.
- What's that?
- The Tibetans. They live in McLeod Ganj, up that hill over there. You need hotel? My cousin has very nice hotel. Good price. Yes please.

I walked up the hill towards McLeod Ganj, feeling depressed by the drizzly, British weather. I ran into some Tibetans on the way up and they confirmed this was the right way. They were polite and spoke English with an Indian accent, but they seemed to lack the spark of the Tibetans in their homeland.

McLeod Ganj struck me as rather an odd place. It was built on a ridge and it reminded me of one of those sad, British seaside towns that are abandoned for most of the year. There was a line of seedy looking buildings with names like Himalaya Hotel and Shangri La Guest House and reluctantly I booked into one of them. I missed the bad service, the directness, the banter and the atmosphere of every Tibetan dwelling I had stayed in. These places were empty, sterile and boring.

I didn't know what to do with myself so I wandered down the street and looked at the teahouses with their faded posters, cotton drapes and hippy souvenirs. I sat down in the Abominable Snowman Teahouse and ordered a tea, which was sweet and sickly, and some cake. I got chatting to the beautiful, sad, middle-aged manageress:

- Are you from Tibet? I asked.

- Yes, she replied dreamily, as if she'd been asked this question hundreds of times.

- Would you like to go back?

- Of course. The Chinese we no trust.

A drunken Tibetan man staggered in and demanded money. To my surprise the woman produced a few rupees and handed them over.

- My husband!

I tried talking to people on the street and everyone I met spoke good English but nobody had much to say. They would answer my questions about Tibet but they didn't want to talk about it. I started to get bored which is something that rarely happens to me; I always have things to do. The evening slowly came and I met a long-haired American who had the haggard face and lethargic movements of a long-term marijuana smoker. We talked:

- How long have you been in Dharamshala?

- Oh, man, about nine years – pauses, thinks – yeah, about nine years.

- Wow, nine years, you must speak shit hot Tibetan by now.

- Oh sure, I know a few phrases. I've been selling jam. Selling jam for nine years, and a few other things, ha.

Further conversation was impossible because this seemed to be the extent of his life story and he didn't seem interested in listening to me. I wandered on and came across a cinema, paid a few rupees, went in and sat on a wooden chair. The place was full of cynical young Tibetans watching a cheaply-made copy of Rambo: muscle bound white guy firing a massive machine gun at hordes of slant-eyed baddies who were falling like flies. I wandered out again, tried to find someone to talk to but people just weren't friendly, inquisitive or open so I ended up back at the guest house, wondering about these young people. What were they? They were ethnically Tibetan, located in India but their behaviour was western. They were lost.

The next day I went looking for the Dalai Lama. He's not here said the first person I asked, he's away for the season. I saw his point. Dharamshala and McLeod Ganj are not very inspiring places and I wouldn't want to be stuck there during winter. I started to regret having made the trip. Why hadn't I gone to Rajastan with Andy and my aunt? They're probably having a great time. On the other hand I had wanted to see Dharamshala ever since I had got to know Tibet, so I quickly dismissed these regrets. Down the hill from McLeod Ganj is the Tibetan Government in Exile and I wandered down to visit it, passing a new-looking monastery with prayer wheels and old Tibetans wandering around – the first real connection with Tibet that I had seen – but I felt no desire to go in. The government offices looked abandoned and unimpressive, like the admin block for a school. I presumed everyone was on holiday and wondered what does a government in exile actually do? I came across a quadrangle of buildings surrounded by mud and walked past doors with signs on them which said, in English, Indian and Tibetan scripts, Home Affairs, Foreign Office, Ministry of Health, Ministry of Education. I bumped into someone who looked like he had been well educated in the Indian system, and he said politely:

- Please come back next week when all the fellows will be here.

The next day I was on the bus back to Delhi. Bad news awaited me. Andy had crashed his car by rolling off a steep road up to a fortress they were visiting near Jaipur. The car had rolled down a hillside, turned over many times and they were both very lucky to be alive, but Andy had a broken wrist and Tessa had a broken shoulder bone. The happy, family Christmas atmosphere had been replaced by a sombre one and Andy was furious with himself, brooding and consumed by guilt. He went to work with his arm in a sling and I took to visiting Tessa in a private hospital where she had been operated on, trying to cheer her up. I spent a few nights there, sleeping on the floor under her bed. Opposite the hospital was a private golf course and I would go and look through the fence at rich Indians teeing off into the mist, fascinated by this insight into golf as an exclusive rich-man's activity, not like in Scotland where there are golf courses everywhere and the cost of playing can be just a few quid. A few days later Tessa flew back to London and I got ready to go too – but I wasn't ready for Tibet yet. I wanted more of India, decided to visit Calcutta and found that the train fare was pretty cheap.

Port cities have always intrigued me. In my final year at Liverpool University I went to my Asian history lecturer and showed him an ad I had found for a job at the History Faculty of Calcutta University. I was excited by the opportunity but he had said:

- I wouldn't go to Calcutta if I was you. It's the biggest, poorest, most desperate place in Asia. Who knows what diseases you will catch there?

You may never come back.

As soon as I arrived, I was electrified by the atmosphere of the city. It felt like the most exciting, thought-provoking and unusual city I had ever visited. I was expecting a massive show of poverty: beggars, grasping hands and pleading faces everywhere. It was nothing of the sort; Calcutta is a power-house with a curiously gentle feel to it. Of course there were a few beggars around but no more than in other cities; what really made this city unique, at least in my experience, was the sheer number of people on the streets. Every street was packed to capacity with crowds of people coming and going and it was the dynamic atmosphere created by these people – the Bengalis, who have a reputation for being clever – that made the city so special for me. Plus the architecture: an eclectic, crumbling, stained mix of colonial, modern, Mediterranean and Indian styles.

I met a charming black man called Andrew who said he was qualified as a doctor but drove a taxi for a living. Would I like him to show me round? I joined him in his big, old, wide cab and we drove across a massive steel bridge, nudging our way through the swarming crowd of people who were perpetually crossing the Hooghly River. We got to the city centre and Andrew said:

- That is Chowringhee.
- What's Chowringee?
- Mainstreet. Calcutta's jugular. Everything branches off from here. On the right side you can see the Maidan.
- What's the Maidan?
- It's a big public park. Calcutta's lung.

Chowringhee was too vast to be called a street. On one side was the Maidan, a big green open space, and on the other were buildings, shops and the city centre. All along the city side of the road was a solid wall of buses, miles long, each one jostling for pavement space, each one disgorging or being boarded by swarms of people; when a bus was full to bursting at least ten people would be hanging onto the back door, some of them hanging onto other people. The diesel fumes were so thick that a cloud formed over the road. I was restless with excitement, eager to walk around and sample the atmosphere, but Andrew told me he was taking me to an ideal place to stay.

We passed a huge Victorian building that Andrew pointed out as the Museum of Indian Civilisation and drove down a street that was so packed with people that we had to drive at walking pace. I saw small barefoot

Indians pulling huge, wooden, Victorian-style rickshaws, each one with a foreigner in it.

- Why don't they have bicycle rickshaws like everywhere else? I asked.

- Ah, Calcutta is a special case. The rickshaw drivers' union did not agree with the transition to bicycle rickshaws and they voted to keep the hand rickshaw.

- But isn't it much harder by hand?

- I don't know. It is their choice.

We pulled into the courtyard of a big, old, Victorian building – with a chaos of trees growing up from every corner. It was painted in colonial colours: cream on the walls with dark green on the doors and windows. It looked grand and yet simple, as if it had been built as a palace but was being used now as something more ordinary. This is the Salvation Army announced Andrew, this is where you can stay. We shook hands, said goodbye and he gave me his card which I put in my wallet. The rooms were large, whitewashed, shared and cheap. It was winter so the weather was cool.

The next day I travelled round town on the buses, each one more overcrowded than the last. Everyone seemed very slim and flexible and it was quite easy to slip in among them and feel part of the crowd. The only bad smells came from the diesel fumes; the people themselves seemed very clean, much more so than the Tibetans. Later in the day I noticed that my wallet was gone and I soon realised it had been pick-pocketed on the bus. I wasn't too bothered by this as I only had a few rupees in it, and Andrew's visit card. I would keep the real money, as well as my passport, in my money belt and that was always strapped onto my crotch. The only reason I needed the wallet was to store money temporarily, for the day, so that nobody could see that I was wearing a hidden money belt.

For the next few days I tried to explore the city but each street, market, shop and building was so interesting that I was only able to discover the small area around the Salvation Army building. The Bengalis were incredibly open and often great conversationalists. Many people asked me if I had seen the Victoria Monument which I felt obliged to visit, but it was a disappointment – a straight copy of the Victorian buildings in London, and full of curious villagers under the arrogant stare of former imperial governors. The collection of colonial items didn't seem to have changed in years. The signs and labels were in English and the one that caught my eye was a pistol with the label Lord Curzon's Fowling Piece.

I bumped into Jake, one of the English travellers I had met in Lhasa. He
didn't seem very surprised to see me, and he still had the yellowy look of
someone slowly recovering from hepatitis (I had been very lucky in this
regard in that my recovery had been fast, I had adapted well to my diet of
rice and vegetables and hadn't gone yellow). Jake had a nasty-looking foot
infection but this didn't seem to worry him. We sat in a tea shop and talked
for hours. He summed up my first impression of the city perfectly:

- Every city is here. The Victorians went wild and the jungle is bursting
through.

Jake was in love with the city, felt addicted to it; he wanted to get married
here and never leave, but I was sure the authorities would never approve of
him. Calcutta was full of unusual foreigners. I came across an enthusiastic
group of American evangelists at the Salvation Army who wanted to offer
a mission of hope to the poor – and convert them to Christianity. I thought
they had no chance as the Hindu and Muslim religions are too deeply
embedded.

I soon heard about Mother Teresa and her work with the poor and
dying. A friendly group of scousers were doing voluntary work with her
Catholic charity and they offered to take me there. I was curious. We went
to the Kalighat area which seemed even more crowded and vibrant than
the rest of the city. Mother Teresa's hospice was called the Kalighat Home
for the Dying and it was a hospice in a former Hindu temple, right next to
an important and lively temple to Kali, the Goddess of Death. I liked the
idea of a God of Death because what it really means is finishing something
old and starting something new; the main concept is actually rebirth. I
braced myself before entering the Home for the Dying, remembering the
words of Andy, my Catholic godfather:

- I couldn't go to Mother Teresa's place in Calcutta. I'd be overcome
with guilt.

But guilt was the last thing on my mind when I entered. It reminded
me of what I had read about Victorian workhouses: polished stone floors,
thick walls that kept the air cool inside, two rows of camp beds and nuns
in blue uniforms marching around giving orders. What struck me was the
complete lack of sympathy and care in the air, as if these people had bedded
down in the railway station and the objective was to clear them out. The
inmates – people who had been dying on the streets and brought here to
die in dignity – were whining, arguing, grabbing things from one another
and fiercely guarding their meagre possessions. Some were complaining

about the lack of food and nobody seemed to be grateful for having been saved from the jaws of death, and I couldn't help wondering if some of them would have preferred to peg it on the streets. Was it some kind of scheme to get unsightly beggars off the street and give wealthy people a means of soothing their consciences?

I didn't have time to dwell on these issues – I was spotted by one of the tough nuns who didn't ask if I wanted to help, she just gave me a pile of dented aluminium bowls, pointed to a cauldron of lentil stew and told me to get on with it. One of the other volunteers ladled out the stew, added cold rice and greens and I handed them out, feeling like a waiter. It was quite fun. I found it hard to take this place seriously, considering the gravitas of its reputation. After the meal I collected up the plates and was then told to give out handfuls of pills. When I asked one of the nuns what these pills were she shot me a look of irritation and said sharply medicine – for their benefit. I handed out the pills but nobody was keen to take them and some even cowered as I approached.

A quiet moment followed and I sat with a boy who was thinner than the others, more like a living skeleton. I felt protective towards him as he was in a bad way and nobody had paid him the slightest attention, but he didn't know how to cope with my sympathy. His legs were the thickness of bones and he couldn't straighten them out, his body had been curling up into a ball over a long period and he had remained fixed in that position. A French volunteer came over and told me he had been there for six months and had improved a lot. I asked if I should give him a massage, the Frenchman approved so I found some cooking oil, rubbed it into his legs and body and he smiled and seemed to perk up a bit.

I went back to Mother Teresa's a few times and found my vocation: a sign-writer. One of the volunteers was painting a new religious slogan – Redeem and be Saved – onto a pillar but he was making very slow progress. I offered to help and soon became the official sign-writer. It was a good job as it kept me separate from the main chaos of the place and my location, up a step ladder, was an ideal observation point. The slogan I was painting said Only All for Jesus, a slogan I didn't really understand. If I couldn't understand it how could a dying, illiterate Bengali?

At one point I saw two enthusiastic Americans carrying a dead body into the Corpse Room, a cold cellar that was literally full of dead, stiff, dry bodies – a room that didn't smell any worse than the rest of the place.

- Stop! Roared the Indian doctor. The Americans froze, holding the corpse between them, looking at the medic in surprise.

- He's not dead yet. He hasn't had his pills.   .

It turned out that the body they were carrying still had some life in him
– but it was clear he would be in with the other corpses in a day or two.

The nuns were satisfied with my sign-writing work and asked me to do
the same in the women's section, where male volunteers weren't allowed.
The atmosphere was totally different – wild and uncontrolled, and the
women inmates seemed completely mad. Painting the second sign took
much longer as I wasn't left in peace for a moment: one moment I had
to help the nuns force-feed a frail woman who fought them off with the
strength of a demon; the next minute a lithe skeleton leaped out of bed,
ran around screaming and lifting her skirt; an old crone approached my
step ladder and started rubbing her face against my leg suggestively, like a
purring cat – until a nun roughly grabbed her and forced her back into bed.

The female volunteers were having a lot more fun than in the male
section and there was a constant babble of chatter that was much more
pleasant than the bickering that went on next door. I got chatting to one
of the volunteers:

- Why do the women here behave so differently from the men?

- Indian women are as tough as nails. Indian men are wimps. In the
Indian family the wife always cooks and the husband always gets fed first.
Then the oldest son is fed, then the other sons and then the daughters. The
wife eats last and sometimes there's nothing left, but she must survive or
who will keep all the children going?

Calcutta is full of unknown Mother Teresas. I met an English doctor
who worked for sick street children, but he was unable to get official
approval for his work so he had to do his charity work undercover, illegally.
In the Immigration Office, where I was applying for permission to visit the
northern district of Darjeeling, I saw a frail-looking Irish girl. I asked her if
she too was applying for a visa for Darjeeling but she cried No and seemed
offended by the suggestion that she might be sightseeing when there was
so much important work to be done. We got chatting and she told me
she taught English for a tough Irish Catholic nun in a girls school called
Loreto. She offered to show me so we got the bus together.

Sister Cyril had been in India for years but she still had the humour,
intelligence and energy that I have always associated with the Irish. She
was large, boisterous and talked fast; she had come to Calcutta in 1979 and
taken over the Loreto school so that it offered a free education to the poor.

But, she complained, they couldn't rely on the state for funding so they accepted fee-paying children and these fees subsidised the other pupils. I wondered if this social mixing would prevent the wealthier children from growing up with a sense of entitlement – the great failing of private schools all over the world.

- Do many beggars came to the door?

- Oh yes, she replied with a wry grin. We get beggars knocking all the time. I ask them if they want to do some light work in return for food. They look a bit sheepish when I ask this but I don't waste time, I give them a broom and tell them to sweep the yard.

- And what happens?

- They always disappear. These people can't work. They're unable to.

Her face lit up when I told her that I had studied history and had taught English. I was offered lunch, a delicious Irish stew and, without any formalities or a briefing, was then asked to teach a class. I was shown into a classroom but they seemed to be illiterates; they were lively, fun and charming, and they really wanted to learn, but they were almost impossible to control. I assumed their usual teacher was a disciplinarian. As soon as this class finished I was ushered into a room full of senior girls, to teach history. As I tried to explain why various borders lie where they do I realised how much of my education I had already forgotten.

I went back for several days to help out at Loreto – it was much more rewarding than the Mother Teresa operation. Sister Cyril was continually in a rush, she would sweep down the corridors like a battle cruiser and people would jump out of the way, anxious not to provoke her volcanic temper. One day I was asked to stand in for one of her classes and, at a complete loss as to what I should teach, I started telling them a story about a Scottish Hebridean island. Halfway through the story Sister Cyril burst in:

- What on earth are you doing here?

- I was asked to stand in for you.

- What?

- It's true.

- Why didn't you girls come and get me? Well thank you Rupert, you can go now. I'll take it from here.

I was wary of Sister Cyril, always expecting her to get angry with me about something or other. She was an unexploded bomb. So I avoided her, and the staff room as well, where I felt a bit awkward, and would hang around in the playground with the smaller kids, whom they called the juniors. One afternoon I was propping up a pillar in the yard when a slim apparition in blue glided along. All my senses leaped to attention as this lithe, shimmering beauty skipped past, trailing a silk scarf, perfume and long black hair. I tried to pull myself together and not show how I was dissolving inside:

\- Hello, I said. She turned, stopped and smiled. My heart leaped into my mouth. I was enchanted. She was sexy, innocent and perfect.

\- Er, I am Rupert. I am teaching English here..

\- And I am Shongita. Very pleased to meet you. Would you like to come and meet my family?

\- Of course. I'd love to. I couldn't believe it. I'd fallen in love and was being invited to meet the parents already. This doesn't happen in real life.

I followed Shongita down the road to her street, which was called Lenin Sarani, with mixed feelings of infatuation, terror and excitement; fantasising about what I'd like to do with her and pondering the terrible punishments that Sister Cyril would inflict on me if she knew what I was up to. I was helpless, I was in her hypnotic power now and I prayed that nothing disgraceful would happen (but another part of me hoped that something disgraceful would happen). I was being torn by fear and desire.

We reached her house quickly. It was small, exquisite, British-built and surrounded by a dense network of trees – as if the jungle was trying to reclaim it. Inside it was dark, cool and full of curious objects. We took our sandals off and I saw her feet, the most perfectly sculpted feet I had ever seen, as if they had been massaged with oils and loved since an early age. The floors all had a deep shine to them, a shine that must have come from decades of clean, oiled feet walking over them. The parents appeared, surprised and then delighted to see that their daughter had brought home a foreign guest. The mother offered to make tea and the father – a tired shopkeeper who complained of bronchitis – sat with us and shared his wit. He apologised for the old and decrepit house and its lack of modern amenities but I told him it was the most beautiful dwelling I had seen in India and I was honoured to have been invited in. The mother came with a tray of delicious sweet tea and Uncle Caca was introduced – the family comedian and butt of all jokes. Shongita then introduced Raja, her older brother, who was tall, handsome and spoke English with an aristocratic English accent. I tried to keep my eyes off Shongita who moved between them like a sprite. They were friendly, lively, interesting. The ideal family-in-law I thought with a shudder.

She took me to a nearby rooftop where we stared dreamily into the fog. She told me that in the Indian tradition it was impossible for her to have a boyfriend – only a husband. Was this a proposal? The idea of marriage did pop into my mind, but was gone in a flash. I considered myself unsuitable for marriage generally – I didn't trust myself to be faithful for the rest of my life, and what about my travel bug? I wanted to kiss her all over, worship her perfectly shaped form and keep our conversation going but fear held me back from even holding her hand; I knew it would be fatal to get involved.

I became friends with Uncle Caca who worked at the famous arms factory at Dum Dum, just outside the city. He was the only member of the family who didn't speak English but we managed to understand each other perfectly by using sign language, and when he told jokes his behaviour became clown-like and hilarious. Shongita told me that he wanted to show me the local sights:

- But, she warned, don't let him tempt you with his grog. You see, Uncle Caca is a hopeless alcoholic.

The following day when I went to visit them Uncle Caca hustled me out of the house and took me down the road to the local market. He introduced me to his friends, bloated men sitting immobile amidst piles of fresh produce, home-made sweets, live pigeons, fish and spices. Then we were on a busy main road and he showed me a mosque, a Hindi temple and a church – all modern and unimpressive buildings – and then he stopped me and searched around in his memory for the one phrase he knew in English, which he said loudly, with real passion:

- We all have red blood. Same blood.

On the way back he led me down a dirty little alley where emaciated children had gathered. I could sense a chilling of the atmosphere, as if all the humour and vitality had been sucked out. We reached our destination and he said guiltily Grog Shop and went into a small room full of bitter, angry people arguing with each other. He went to the barman and, without a word, was handed a small, unmarked bottle with transparent liquid in it. He threw it back in one long gulp. We left in silence and I knew it would be pointless to say anything about his drinking, I could see the guilt in his face and was convinced he knew what he was doing to himself.

My days in Calcutta were numbered. I had to get away from this wonderful place. I could see that it would be easy to get a job and it was a wonderful place to be, but I knew I had to run from the mesmerising Shongita and get back to Tibet, the place that I was committed to. I had to go to Nepal, get a new Chinese visa and then on to Tibet. Fortunately, my teaching role at Loreto school never really developed and I was sure that Sister Cyril suspected me of being a charlatan. I got a visa for Darjeeling, bought a bus ticket, and came to say goodbye to Sister Cyril and Shongita's family. They invited me in one more time, served me tea and we sat round and talked:

- Uncle Caca wants to read your palm, said Shongita.

- That's kind of him, I replied, offering up my right hand palm for his scrutiny. He studied it for a long time and I started worrying about missing my bus. He then spoke to Shongita, who translated:

- Uncle Caca says that you are a prince with a good heart, but you will have financial and health problems.

Getting to Darjeeling was a hassle. India has lots of areas where rebellions are taking place and tourist access is restricted or totally forbidden. I had waited patiently for a visa and was officially authorised to visit Darjeeling, a celebrated Hill Station – a colonial term meaning holiday resort – and an ideal a place to escape from the summer heat. But I was missing Calcutta and Shongita.

I looked up into the cloudy hills, didn't appreciate the cold and was reminded of the boredom I had felt at Dharamshala. There was a narrow-gauge train that used to take tourists up to Darjeeling but it was out of order, according to the hustlers at the nearby railway station. It seemed that the only option was to share a taxi – I shared the front seat with five others, the back was even more full and the Tibetan driver had so little space he was half out of the window. It was cheap and he wound up the road with great skill.

The town looked deserted, misty and grim. I didn't know where to go or what to do. In the taxi I had been told of a new separatist movement that was recently started by the Nepalese majority, who wanted to assert their autonomy from the Bengalese state government in Calcutta and the first thing I noticed was that they had stuck up little green flags everywhere showing a Khukri, the deadly little sword used by the Nepalese soldiers – known as Gurkhas. I wasn't interested in the local politics but having come all this way I realised I may as well stay a few days. I found the only functioning hostel, where there were some travellers sulking, checked in and then wandered about. Architecturally the town was quite interesting: lots of well-built, colonial-era houses surrounded by overgrown shrubbery (someone told me the rhododendron bush originates here), and nicely laid out parks with bandstands, fountains and formal gardens – all of which looked neglected and run down.

Darjeeling is known the world over for its tea and it had been an economic success story in the past. When I visited there was a bad atmosphere hanging over the place; it was deserted and it felt like the town had died. That evening I chatted with travellers from Japan, England, Africa, Scotland and America but none of them had picked up on the atmosphere that I had felt. They were all focused on hitting the trail the next day and doing their well-organised treks. We all huddled round one open fire – the only source of heat in the whole building –which reminded me of how we used to try and stay warm in the cold Scottish houses of my childhood.

The next morning the mist had lifted and my heart soared, I saw one of the most inspiring views I had ever seen in my life; on the northern horizon was the mountain of Kanchenjunga, covered in snow and bathed in golden morning sunlight. I had seen scores of Himalayan mountains but this one looked far more impressive than any of them. With its three peaks, and looking like a whole complex of mountains rolled into one, Kanchenjunga seemed to stand alone, rising like some epic creature from surrounding hills that were relatively low. It was almost mythical and I was later told it was the third biggest mountain in the world. I had never even heard about it and felt overwhelmed by the fact that – just like that -- I had discovered it in this way.

The other travellers had already left and I had nothing to do but more wandering. Just down the road from the hostel, down a muddy path, I came across a pompous looking sign that stated it was the Headquarters of the GNLF, which stands for the Gorkha National Liberation Front. There was a bored old guard on the door and a small crowd of toughs hanging about outside. They looked at me suspiciously but nobody stopped me from walking straight in. I came across a couple of well-groomed, middle-aged Nepalese men with oiled hair, blue blazers and some kind of military badge stitched onto their breast pockets. They had a rather stiff, ex-military air and they both looked dishonest. In fact, the whole movement felt phoney. They didn't seem very pleased to see me.

- Where you from? One of them enquired.

- Scotland.

- Ah, Scotland. I know Scotland well. I was stationed there with the Gurkhas. Edinburgh Castle, Basingstoke.

- Hmm, yes

- And what is your profession sir?

- Me? Ah well, I am a foreign correspondent. A journalist.

- Very good. So you will be wanting to find out about our liberation movement. That's why you came here I presume?

- Er...yes.

- Well, you see we have been horribly exploited by these Bengalese rascals for many, many years and we have decided to claim home rule.

- What have they done to you?

- You obviously haven't been reading the papers my good Sir. We, Nepalese majority of this area, have been deprived of the profits of our work for generations and...

- What profits? What work?

- This is a very profitable area. The tea plantations, and tourism. The Nepalese workers are paid a pittance while the dastardly Bengalese criminals are living like kings in Calcutta. Also the State Police are very cruel and they kill a hundred of our people every day.

- What? They kill a hundred people a day? Where?

- Here, in Darjeeling.

One of the men in blazers shot me a look of anger. He obviously wasn't used to having his words questioned like this and I could see his temper was boiling. I started to think about Gurkhas and their reputation for bloodthirstiness and was afraid; after all nobody knew where I was and if I was chopped up by the Khukri wielding mob outside and scattered in the tea plantations nobody would be the wiser. I accepted his version of the truth and made a hasty exit. Once I got away safely I started asking local people, whoever I could find, what they thought about this new separatist movement but nobody would talk to me. Were they all afraid? Later on that day I came across a community of Tibetan refugees who were weaving traditional cloth for sale to the tourists. There seemed to be a lot of Tibetans around and they formed another ethnic minority in the area. Remembering that the men in blazers had claimed 100% support from the Tibetan community I tried to test this, but they were non-committal. They too had obviously been threatened in some form. It was all starting to look very fishy, but also confusing. I couldn't understand how the authorities didn't just arrest these ridiculous ex-soldiers and close the whole thing down.

Interested in checking out the claim of people being killed every day by the police, I went in search of the local hospital, eventually finding a crumbling, wooden, colonial structure with the name Eden Hospital on the gate. Patients and staff wandered the corridors aimlessly, like characters in an old sci-fi movie whose brains had been taken over by aliens. Nobody asked what I wanted, who I was looking for or what I was doing there. I could find no sign of any wounded victims but there were a couple of old policemen who were snoozing in one of the wards. On the second floor I got chatting to a schoolboy with a bright and cheeky face.

The boy spoke fluent English. I soon found out that his name was Ramesh, he was from out of town and was bursting with curiosity about life in the western world. He was a great listener and, unlike most people I had met, he was interested in all I had to say about life in the UK. I showed him an old copy of Private Eye, a satirical magazine from London, explained the jokes and we fell about the place laughing. He was also full of interesting observations about his country and what particularly irked him was the complacency that, to him, characterised India.

Ramesh felt trapped between the stifling local politics and his need to stay on at the local school until he got a place at university, from where he could plan his escape from India. He was the first person I had met who spoke freely about the separatists:

- Can you tell me about this Gurkha National Front?
- Absolutely, they are well-known all over the area. They're a bunch of ignorant fascists who bully the local Nepalese into supporting their pig-headed leader. This dabbling in nationalist sentiment is playing with fire.
- What do you mean?
- They will start a destructive process they won't be able to control.
- What's been happening here?
- Darjeeling was the richest part of Bengal, you know? Now the economy is dead. The tea workers who aren't Nepalese are battling with the GNLF goons and the plantations are in flames. The tourists have stopped coming and everyone's going bankrupt. The locals are afraid to talk and the Indian newspapers only report the Gurkha side of the story.
- Is there nothing that can be done?

- Ghisingh, the Gurkha leader, is only really supported by a handful of thugs. Everyone else is just intimidated. If you could organise a group of people with sticks we could chase these hooligans out of town.

- Why doesn't central government do something?

- Good question. The whole thing was cooked up by the Congress Party, the people who run India, as a way to spite the Communists in Calcutta.

- What Communists in Calcutta?

- Didn't you know? Calcutta and West Bengal are run by a Communist Party and Congress hate them and are always looking for ways to undermine them. Note that there is no local Congress Party here in Darjeeling. If there was they could act as an effective opposition to these bullies. I tell you, the whole thing is a set up.

- So what's going to happen next?

- I don't know but I'm afraid of the Punjab scenario playing out.

- What happened there?

- Well, the rumour is that Mrs Gandhi encouraged the Sikhs to rise up as a counterbalance to the Muslim rebels in Kashmir, but the plan backfired.

- What do you mean?

- Well, they had to put the Punjab under Martial Law and then she was assassinated by her Sikh bodyguards. I tell you they're playing with fire.

- They told me they have nine hundred and fifty thousand members.

- What absolute tosh. You mustn't believe a word they say. They're just a pack of liars and reprobates.

- They also told me that a hundred people are killed and wounded every day by the Indian police. That's actually why I came to the hospital.

- And did you find any of these victims?

- No.

The next morning I met an American at the guest house who claimed that he worked for the CIA. He told us he was on holiday from his job in South Africa where he worked in the Israeli Embassy, but it was all very hush-hush. This sounded interesting! As soon as he mentioned Israel we bombarded him with critical questions about the outrages committed by Israel when they had invaded Lebanon a few years earlier. But the American stonewalled us, refused to comment on Israel's foreign policy and said that he couldn't talk about his CIA work as it was classified. This was extremely annoying – to raise our expectations and then leave us hanging – and I concluded this was just a pathetic attempt to impress us. A real spy wouldn't talk about his work to people he'd only just met.

Down at the Market Square something was happening. A crowd was standing in complete silence, watching a young Nepalese man climb onto a rooftop and paste up a big announcement. I asked someone what was going on and he hissed it's the news. A foreigner was taking notes and another one took photos. I looked again at the foreigner and suddenly realised that I had met him at the party in New Delhi and that he worked at Reuters with my godfather:

- Are you Moses? I asked the man taking notes.

- Yes. Oh, yes. Oh, it's you...Rupert isn't it? What the devil brings you here?

- I'm on my way to Nepal. What are you doing here?

- I'm covering the visit of Rajiv Gandhi. You know he's due to arrive here on Saturday, on an official visit.

- I had no idea.

Moses and his photographer invited me to lunch and I took them to a cafe, but Moses was shocked: we can't eat here. The place is a dump. I'm on an expense account and I will treat you to a proper meal. We went to a more up-market restaurant, which didn't seem any better than my cafe.

I tried to ingratiate myself as their local fixer, but Moses wasn't interested in what I had learned about the separatist movement. But he did agree to come to meet the GNLF and after lunch I led them there.

I noticed how well secured the GNLF premises were: it was surrounded by a high metal fence and always guarded. When we finally got to meet the leader he asked who we worked for. Moses and the photographer were used to this and they just said Reuters and produced press cards. Not only did I not have a press card but I had never even been in a newspaper office, let alone worked for one. My only contact with the media was with an Austrian Newspaper for which I had written a travel article about Budapest. So I said Wiener Zeitung and to my relief no one asked me for more information.

We all sat down in a dark room with thick, heavy curtains and bars on the windows. We were alone in the room with Mr Ghisingh but there was a posse of evil-looking bodyguards waiting next door. Soon the questions started:

- I am particularly interested in the books that you have written, said Moses.

- Ah yes, my philosophy books.

- But don't the ordinary people find it hard to read about philosophy?

- Not at all, replied Mr Ghising jerkily, spitting out the answers with venom. They are simplified so that ordinary men can understand. They are very popular.

- Indeed.

Afterwards I asked Moses why he kept going on about Mr Ghisingh's books. Surely the important issue here was the separatist movement? And what about all his absurd claims? Didn't he think the man was a ridiculous, loud and aggressive buffoon?

- Of course he's a buffoon, said Moses with a smile. But I was trying to embarrass the man. I've never met such a bogus writer in my life. You see he is the author of dirty books, pornography.

Five days was more than enough time for Darjeeling and I wanted to get away before Rajiv Gandhi and God knows how many bodyguards showed up. I walked out of town in the bright sunlight and felt glad to be getting away. Leaving a place, hitting the road, always fills me with optimism and I walked away from Darjeeling with a powerful sense of freedom. The town was bathed in bright morning sunlight but a few miles down the road a thick cloud lay over the flatlands below like a huge blanket of puffy white cotton. As I sauntered down the road I was enveloped in cold translucent greyness and the landscape suddenly disappeared.

The town of Siliguri reminded me what a dump India can be: it was hot, noisy, filthy, chaotic and crowded. Some kind of celebration was taking place and improvised fireworks were exploding; crazed-looking men were walking down the street, some carrying burning torches, some dancing grotesquely; one man was pushing a wobbly pram that was covered in gaudy lights and must have contained a car battery. They all seemed to be in a frenzy. I missed the peace and quiet of Darjeeling, checked into the Airview Hotel, a seedy dive, and wrote a postcard to Shongita.

The following day I hitchhiked and got a series of short lifts from one village to the next. Even though the Nepalese border was nearby it took ages to get there and by nightfall I felt I had covered such a short distance that I decided to get a bus to Kathmandu. At midnight, in a small border town with no name, I found myself in a dusty bus station where nothing was moving. There were a few people lying about on string beds, fast asleep, and the only person awake was exactly who I was looking for: the ticket-wallah.

- Can I get a bus to Kathmandu from here?

- Oh yes.

- When does it leave?

- Tomorrow morning. Come back tomorrow morning. Yes please.

- Where can I sleep tonight?

- You can sleep here!

He ushered me into his office that was just a shed with two chairs. We both sat down and he fell asleep in minutes, leaning back on his chair and letting his head fall back at an impossible angle. He was young and fat and his stomach rolled out of his white vest and heaved up and down in time with his breathing. He was sleeping deeply and making strange, irregular snoring noises. There was a powerful noise of crickets outside, punctuating the heavy silence. I sat there, unable to sleep, watching a huge cricket that seemed to be fixed to the wall. A big lizard appeared and with a sudden flick it moved across the wall with lightning speed until it was within striking distance of the cricket. They both remained immobile for what seemed like an eternity. Were they staring at each other? I glanced away and when I looked back the lizard had the middle part of the cricket in its mouth, but the cricket's legs and arms were still free, struggling hopelessly. They remained there for what seemed like hours and I was affected by the stillness of the scene, as if I was the cricket, unable to move out of my chair. It was as if time had stopped and we were all stuck in these positions forever.

The Kathmandu bus was stylish and ancient. As it filled up, an ever-increasing mountain of luggage was piled onto the roof. Even though I had bought a ticket well in advance I hadn't claimed a seat and when we left the only place left to sit was the metal engine block, a seat that got hotter and hotter as the day progressed. The driver looked like an Italian ice cream vendor from a cartoon, with tight curly hair, a thin moustache and a fancy jacket he kept brushing the dust off. He drove as fast as he could, gunning the engine to impossible speeds down the straights and wrestling with the gears heroically on the climbs. The bus would swing from side to side like a ship at sea and the driver – whom I called Luigi – rolled with the machine as if he were a surfer adapting to the waves. He would stop often at teashops, some in beautiful mountain locations, and we would all pour out in a chattering mob and stretch our legs. Luigi was chatty and friendly and a strong camaraderie developed between us; there were no complaints as far as I could make out (nobody shouting and waving his arms about) and I think the others felt as I did which was gratitude at getting a ride all the way to Kathmandu.

I didn't want to be in Kathmandu but I had to apply for a Chinese visa, to go through their bureaucratic hoops again and it was impossible to do so in India as relations between the two great countries was bad. I was determined to avoid the decadent tourist ghetto with tempting foods and drugs. I checked into the Peace Guest House in another part of town and soon started to make friends with a group of friendly Germans who were staying there.

Harpo and Dirk had driven to Kathmandu from Germany, in a truck that was pulling a caravan. They were inseparable. Harpo was only thirty but he had the air of a wise old man while Dirk was thin, hairy and wild. I functioned as their alarm clock and when they emerged from their bed sheets they would bicker at each other like an old couple, Harpo would pump up his old Primus stove and prepare coffee. We were joined in this morning ritual by Bettina Hertzog - a tall, elegant, German woman who was so beautiful that I knew she was way out of my league. She was friendly with me, unlike most beautiful women I had come across, and said she would meet me in Lhasa. She was planning to ride a horse across the Tibetan plateau in mid-winter, a madcap plan I assumed would come to nothing.

As I waited impatiently for my visa, I made friends with a young black guy from London: Isi Amodu. He was someone I could share my deepest thoughts with, things that I had never been able to express before because I hadn't met anyone who could listen and reciprocate with such patience. We had a conversation about the meaning of life that went on for days, and came to the conclusion that the true meaning of life was women – and we both needed to get laid. Then we hired Indian bikes and for several exhilarating days cycled round town, yelling and hooting at the large numbers of attractive girls on the streets of Kathmandu. We fell into a dizzy social life and met with scores of interesting travellers: three attractive Canadian sisters who considered us too wild for their tastes; a group of Indian hippies; an anthropologist called Charles Ramble who liked to party and two Scottish sisters who worked in Nepal and told me:

- Och, it's so much better here than in Edinburgh.

I persuaded Isi to come with me to Tibet and this delayed things further as we needed to wait for his visa too, but eventually they came through and we said goodbye to all our new friends and hit the road. We followed my border crossing routine of the year before – hitching, walking, catching buses when we could find them – and soon we were across the border and walking up the gorge on the Tibetan side. This time I had come prepared: I had invested in a good sleeping bag and had persuaded Isi to do the same. He very nearly turned back when we were confronted by a terrified tribesman whom we had met deep in the gorge: I had spoken to him and assumed he would be as friendly as all Tibetans in the wilds seemed to be, but this man had never seen a black man before and he hid behind a rock, dagger drawn, shouting at us. I found the episode quite funny at first but Isi was mortified. Later on I realised that most of the demons painted on the inside of the Tibetan temples are black. I wondered if Tibetans had ever seen black people before.

I told Isi that we would get a bus if we could or hitch a ride in a truck, although for that first day there was no sign of any bus, even the small private ones that ply the route. When we eventually saw a truck the driver didn't slow down for us but it was going slow and I shouted jump on to Isi and we threw our stuff into the back and scrambled up. The driver stopped, told us to get off. I implored, stayed put and then produced some cash – and he relented. We were all set – the driver was going all the way to Lhasa. The truck was completely open to the elements and during that first night we passed an eighteen thousand foot pass and almost froze solid – our new sleeping bags proved to be totally useless and Isi got altitude sickness. We were continually being sprinkled with white dust that was being blown up from the road. It made breathing difficult and turned everything we owned white. It must have been a nightmare for Isi but he hardly complained. When we reached the Snowlands Hotel in Lhasa the staff didn't recognise me as I was all white, and when Isi washed his hands and face at the tap in the yard the staff couldn't believe that a white man had walked in but before them was standing a negro. We checked into a room which was unheated, but after the truck it felt so warm that it was like being inside a greenhouse.

CHAPTER NINE

We arrived at the end of February 1987, two weeks before the start of the Tibetan New Year festivities. It was Tibet's biggest public event of the year but had been banned by the Chinese for almost 20 years. This was the second year since it had been re-introduced. That gave us two weeks to kill, two weeks to get my act together, get back into work, earn some cash and adjust to being back in Lhasa.

Showing Isi round Lhasa – my town – felt great. I took him to all the strange locations I knew and my only regret was that Diane and Frenchy weren't around. They had moved on and left no forwarding address; I supposed they were in Taiwan by now. The Chinese were extremely polite to Isi, which I found a bit odd considering how rude they can be to each other, but the Tibetans tended to giggle, point and stare and this upset Isi who, as the only black man in Tibet, felt a bit vulnerable. He was lively, responsive and great company and soon an active social life developed around him which, for me, was a bit of a distraction as my priority was to get back to work.

One evening we were eating a sweet and sour dish in a Chinese restaurant when we got chatting with two Israeli women. They had decided to pick us up and the one who zoomed in on me was called Natasha; she told me she trained Israeli soldiers in small arms techniques. Isi was grinning when he saw how intimate we were becoming and he winked lasciviously, egging me on. By nightfall I was in bed with Natasha but my heart wasn't in it. She was a fast mover and had picked me up in no time, but Natasha was emotionally clammed up and the next morning I was full of regret. The fact that she had picked me up made me feel cheap, a feeling that didn't make any sense at all. If I was emotionally attached to anyone it was to Bettina back in Vienna – and I really liked the German Bettina who was heading this way on a horse. What was I playing at? The Tibetan staff, who

I knew well, and really liked, would giggle and whisper every time they saw me.

The morning after, disaster struck: the door of Natasha's room, where I was lying in bed with her, burst open and there stood Big Jack, huge, bearded and ready to kill. I had last seen Big Jack in the Shata classroom where he had disgraced himself. Then he disappeared into the wilderness and would, I hoped, never come back. Here he was on the threshold looking like a rogue yak:

- What the hell do you want in my room? demanded Natasha.

- What's he doing here? said Big Jack, pointing an accusing finger at me.

- None of your damn business, said Natasha, jumping out of bed.

- He's a charlatan, a Chinese spy and he robbed the Travellers' Co-op of all their money. He's a thief, a robber, a spy. He'll...

I lay in bed, naked and humiliated, unsure what to do, expecting to get a beating; knowing I had absolutely no control over what was happening. Within seconds Natasha had crossed the room and, in a blur, using her unarmed combat skills on the creep, she literally threw him out of the room. The rush of satisfaction at seeing my enemy defeated was short lived as I knew Big Jack had his acolytes and I presumed he was building up a case against me. Everyone I mentioned it to said not to worry and by the following evening Big Jack actually apologised to me for his behaviour. I soon discovered, that he was madly in love with Natasha and hearing that I was in bed with her had sent him into a frenzy.

The whole city seemed to be preparing for the New Year rituals and the market was deserted in the mornings. Finding breakfast was difficult as all the food had been cleared out of the shops in preparation for a great feast, and the streets were deserted; everyone was at home, doing stuff with their families. The busiest place in town was the Jokhang Temple where there was a constant stream of monks and delivery people going in and out with supplies. I wondered what they were preparing and tried to sneak in the back door but it was being guarded by a group of burly looking monks and there was no way they would let anyone in. At the front of the temple, in the main square, squads of Chinese police in green uniforms were practising crowd control manoeuvres and they weren't letting anyone near the main entrance.

Isabella was delighted to see me and took to Isi at once. The scene at her place was homely and warm, with good music on Roger's elaborate stereo. She fed us pancakes and introduced us to some of her new students. Work

was on the cards; Roger had been waiting for me to stand in for him so
he could take off with Big Jack and other keen trekkers on a madcap walk
across the northern wasteland, the Changtang.

Back at the Snowlands, Isi and I were chatting with an old Jewish man
who had a young female companion from Vietnam. She told us how her
family, and thousands of others, had escaped Vietnam in boats, just after
the US withdrawal – she was one of the Vietnamese Boat People. Then Isi
and I stopped listening and, without saying anything to each other, gaped
as the most beautiful woman in the world walked by. She was tall and thin,
with long flowing, black hair and really unusual clothes.

- She's just walked out of my dreams, I whispered to Isi.

- She must be Italian, Isi said, Oh God, let her be Italian.

- Why Italian? I asked. He didn't reply.

The woman walked past, noticed us gawping at her like a couple of
school kids and smiled. It was like the sun had just come out. I was in
love, in her power. Then Isi, to my amazement, started speaking to her in
fluent Italian. How the hell does that bastard know Italian? I wondered.
Isi's charm soon resulted in us becoming friends with this Italian beauty,
whose name was Germana, and I was always grateful to be in her presence,
absorbing her beauty like rays of sunshine.

I had always looked down my nose at the Snowlands Hotel and, with
Diane and Frenchy, would make disparaging remarks about the people
who stayed there. My perspective had changed now I was with Isi, who
was delighted to get a roof over our heads after our nightmarish journey
to Lhasa. He wasn't planning on staying long, thought the price was fair
and had no interest in finding somewhere cheaper. The building itself was
interesting: stone built with an interior courtyard; all the external stones
were painted white and the windows were nicely done in blues and reds
– although they did let in a lot of cold air. The rooms themselves were
basic, clean and accessible from wide balconies where we could sit and
soak up the morning sunlight. The best thing about the Snowlands was
the view, something I had never appreciated before, and from our balcony
we could see the white rooftops of Lhasa and, climbing out of them, dark
blue mountains that reached a cloudless, azure blue sky. It was cold but
the air was dry and the sun would beat down and compensate for the low
temperature.

Our lives began to revolve around the beautiful Germana, whom we
had nicknamed AP which was short for Apparition. She told us she was

an artist from Rome and she was the first artist I had met in Tibet. Why didn't more artists come here? We were both smitten but Isi had got closer to her than me. I cursed him for not getting bogged down with the other Israeli; he was unattached, available and I was sure he would end up in her arms. I had tried to end it with Natasha but the more I tried to get away the keener she became. Fortunately she was planning to leave town so an end was in sight.

Meanwhile AP invited us into her room and I felt we had been invited into some hallowed shrine where the public aren't allowed. She had an ordinary double room in the Snowlands – two iron beds, concrete floor, whitewashed walls with no decoration – which she had transformed into an artist's studio. The walls were covered with bits of paper showing multi-coloured impressionistic works, mainly nudes, all of which looked superb; they seemed to throb with personality, passion and life. She had pushed the beds up against the walls and created a space in the middle of the floor where she would crouch in a den of brushes, papers, cups of coloured liquid, teacups and plates with half-eaten bits of food. I slouched on one of the beds and looked at Isi with jealousy, trying to wipe the huge grin off my face, a grin that I couldn't control when in her presence. Then I noticed that she was watching me – what glory – and, hang on a minute, she was sketching me. I felt as if I had been knighted.

There was a knock on the door, her attention was distracted and the magic of the moment was broken. She called out Lie!, which means come in Chinese, and there standing in the doorway was the most striking looking Chinese man I had ever seen: he had a handsome, rugged face and I wondered if he was a Mongolian aristocrat; his hair was long, black and flowing, rather like hers but more wild, as if he'd been riding a horse across the steppe; but he wasn't dressed like a horseman, he wore a white linen shirt and thick, baggy white trousers, slightly scuffed, that tucked into well worn, loose black leather boots that reached almost up to his knees.

- This is Hang Shoe Dan, said Germana. My artist friend that I travel with.

- Ni hao ma, I said, which means hello in Chinese.

She went over and kissed him deeply on the lips, a message that I imagined was addressed to us and stated: I'm not available. Hang Shoe Dan was an artist and seemed to have adopted the open and free approach of artists in the west. He didn't seem to have any of the anxieties, uniformity and shyness that I had noticed with other Chinese men I had met thus far.

There wasn't a trace of jealousy in his face when he came into the room, just curiosity and warmth, and he crouched down by Isi on the floor and blended in.

But Hang Shoe Dan didn't speak Italian or English and AP only knew a few words of Chinese. Despite this, they seemed to communicate beautifully with sign language and lots of hugs, kisses and laughter. He was learning English – why not Italian I wondered? – but was making slow progress. My grasp of Chinese was basic but in this context I was the master of communication and they started using me as a translator. I was delighted to have a role and to be able to impress such beautiful people. Hang Shoe Dan was a photographer, with a fancy certificate from Beijing to prove it, and a special pass that allowed him access to the heavily guarded Jokhang Temple where he had been photographing the preparations.

Hang Shoe Dan seemed impressed with my plan to stay in Tibet; he knew several artists from China who wanted to set up an art gallery in Lhasa and said that Tibet has a more liberating atmosphere than mainland China. He spoke of Tibet as a separate country, a separate culture, and this was touching because it came with a sympathy and respect for Tibet that I shared.

I told him that I was desperate to get inside the Jokhang and see what was going on -- lamas had come from all over Tibet and some had brought elaborate ceremonial robes with them – and he offered to take me in the next day. He passed me a magazine from the year before that showed the Tibetan New Year celebration, and proudly pointed to his photo on the front cover – of a monk blowing a long horn. We agreed to meet outside the temple at twelve and, the following day, I was there waiting in the bright sunlight, under the watchful eye of the Chinese police guards. He didn't show up. I waited and waited and waited and he still didn't show. He must have forgotten. Despite the disappointment, I couldn't feel angry with him as he was a gentle creature and being forgetful was probably part of his makeup.

Isi was into yoga and sometimes I would come into our room and find him curled up in an impossible position on the floor. He said that improving his yoga was one of the reasons he visited India and Nepal and he found it a good way to deal with his excess energy. I knew what he meant as whenever we would discuss a new idea, or our feelings for Germana, the energy and enthusiasm we would generate was phenomenal, as if there were sparks flying between us. Every afternoon he would meditate in his mysterious positions and I would have a short nap. I had adapted some of the principles of meditation and used them when I went to sleep. I used sleep as a means of getting rid of all the stresses and strains of the day – I would imagine that every important idea or problem I had been dealing with was nothing but a little bubble floating up in the air, and then it would burst. I imagined a stream of bubbles coming out of my head, each one looking very impressive for a moment and then bursting. I would awake feeling totally refreshed – even after a couple of minutes of sleep.

When we weren't hanging around with Germana we made ourselves at home at Isabella and Roger's place. Isabella loved Isi from the start and he fitted into their routines quickly and was soon showing off another of his skills: cooking. He would prepare elaborate and delicious meals that tasted so much better than anything in Lhasa. All this good food seemed to fit in perfectly with the Tibetan New Year, which seemed to be all about eating. He needed a kitchen boy and was constantly ordering me around:

- Rupert, can you pop down to the market and get some coriander?
- Coriander, here in Tibet? Are you mad?
- They'll have it. Just try.
- Oh alright. I looked up the word for coriander and then went and found some. As soon as I got back Isi said:
- Oh Rupert, I forgot to tell you, we're completely out of bread.

One morning, we were having breakfast with Isabella and I told her about our new artist friends – Germana and Hang Shoe Dan – and she said:
- They sound fascinating. I'd love to meet them. Why don't you invite them round for lunch? I'll just pop over to the Co-op and see you back here.
- Great idea, I said.
- Rupert, this time you can do the cooking. Just heat up that stew from yesterday and make some more rice, and I'll go to the Snowlands and pick them up.

They both left the flat and I prepared the lunch – but nobody showed up. I waited and waited and as afternoon turned into evening I became angry. Where the hell is everyone? I wailed to myself. I couldn't leave, in case they came at that moment. I was boiling with frustration. Eventually I had had enough and stomped out of the flat to look for them, and there they all were coming up the stairs: Isi, Isabella, Germana and Hang Shoe Dan.

- Hello, said Isabella cheerfully, oblivious to the fact that we had arranged to have lunch that very morning.

- Where the hell have you been? I hissed angrily to Isi.

- Oh sorry, I got chatting to AP and we went for a walk and er, I, um completely forgot about lunch.

- Bastard. But as I served the lunch – now dinner – I forgot about my anger. It was great to see all my friends in one place. Then I noticed that Germana and Hang Shoe Dan were squatting in the corner, looking miserable and whispering to each other. As soon as they'd eaten they hurried off.

- What was up with them? I asked Isi on the way back to the Snowlands. I wanted to talk about it without Isabella listening in.

- It was Isabella. Germana and Dan had never seen anyone like her before. They couldn't handle it. Me and you are used to people like that, the children of the sixties, English eccentrics. I'm not sure they have people like that in Italy.

Germana told us that she was going back to Kathmandu in a week and Isi subsequently decided that he too should go back to Kathmandu – in a week. Hang Shoe Dan and I were miserable; his lover and my friend were leaving town, but we put on a brave face and I tried to say in Chinese enjoy her while you can. We organised a going away party on the rooftop of the Snowlands, dancing to Talking Heads under the stars. The Tibetan staff looked on and giggled at us. Several months later I received a postcard from Germana and the only message on it was: I remember dancing on the rooftop. Germana.

I wanted to show Isi the inside of a Tibetan home before he left, but this was tricky because all the families were gathering together and working on preparations for the New Year's celebration and I was sure that our presence would embarrass them. As if in answer to my prayer I bumped into Jigme, one of Isabella's students, on the balcony of the Snowlands and he invited us to his house for lunch, right then. Isi wasn't too keen, especially when he realised that he would have to sit on the back of my borrowed bike, but he came along quietly. We followed Jigme, who was riding an old Jawa motorbike from Czechoslovakia, through the centre of town and towards the outskirts.

Jigme was a hardworking English student but not very bright, never remembering more than basic phrases. He made up for this by having an extra dose of confidence, which was an unusual and valuable quality in

Tibet. He wore modern clothes – black flares, plastic boots, nylon shirt and a fake leather jacket – and had well-groomed hair that was neatly arranged in a side parting. He was handsome but he walked with a swagger and this betrayed the arrogance of his class: children of Communist Party officials; Jigme's father was a Tibetan bureaucrat who had been entrusted to set up the first English language school in Lhasa – the Shata school – and I was grateful to him because he left us to our own devices and didn't interfere. They lived far from the centre of Lhasa, down a bumpy track at the southern side of town, a quiet residential area where all the roads lead up to the Lhasa River. Opposite his house, which lay within a small compound, stood a white, modern building:

- That be Himalaya Hotel in future, Jigme announced. He had dismounted from his motorbike, opened up the gate and led us in. We politely said hello to his father who was sitting in the yard reading a Tibetan newspaper. He smiled at his son and I could tell he was pleased he had brought foreign visitors home, but he didn't seem to want to meet us.

- This is a typical Tibetan townhouse, I explained to Isi.

- Hmm, he replied. I could see that he regretted coming here and was probably obsessing about Germana. See the small trees they have growing everywhere? They provide shade in the summer and protection against storms in winter. And what I like best is that the house is arranged round the yard.

- What do you mean?

- You know how in a normal house you have the hallway and the main rooms lead off from it.

- Yeah.

- Well, in a Tibetan house you have the room arranged around the courtyard. The courtyard acts like a kind of hallway. That's the kitchen over there and those are probably the bedrooms. Jigme wants us to go into that room which is probably for receiving guests. Great set up when the weather's nice.

- But pretty damn miserable in a snowstorm.

It turned out to be the most boring visit I had yet made to a Tibetan's home; even when my hosts didn't speak a word of English I would have a good time, as learning a language can be fun if you're not embarrassed about making a fool out of yourself. Jigme was desperate to speak English in front of his parents; he didn't want me practising my Tibetan but he didn't have anything to say. Within minutes the situation became awkward, the conversation dried up and Jigme turned on the TV – one of the few I had ever seen in Tibet. We sat and stared at a Chinese made programme about learning French:

- Bonjour: Knee How, the presenter said.

- I can't stand it here, Isi hissed into my ear. He had a look of desperation in his eye.

- I must go. AP will be getting lonely.

- Shut up and drink your tea. You'll offend them otherwise. And eat some of those biscuits too.

- They're disgusting. They're full of grease.

- They have butter in them.

Ten minutes later Isi was gone, riding up the track on my bike. Now I was regretting having come and to think that the whole point of this visit was to show Isi a Tibetan house. The ungrateful swine. Jigme wasn't going to let me go so easily, he wanted to practice his English. A young lady, a servant, came in and cleared away the tea things. She wiped the table and came back with a pile of tatty books. When I saw that they were Learn English books from China my heart sank and I knew I was trapped for the day. I flicked through the pages and saw that language and Communism were mixed up on the page. I read out one of phrases in an ironically enthusiastic voice:

- Little Jang goes to the commune. Her father drives a tractor. She is a young pioneer. They live happily in the New China.

- Have you read these books? I asked Jigme.

- Yes, he said proudly. Then he showed me a thin paperback on engineering and said:

- Teacher. I work on electricity factory. I need learn words, these. Please help me.

- I looked at the words and pronounced: Thermonuclear reactor; geomagnetic survey; thermodynamic technology. I stopped. This was ridiculous. Why would an elementary student want to learn this stuff?

- You are not ready to learn these words, I said.

- But teacher, I must. It is much important for my job. And so we spent an excruciating hour going through a few more pages.

It wasn't only Tibetans who were pouring into town for the New Year's celebration; so were the foreign travellers and Isabella was busier than ever in her Traveller's Co-op. Roger was up north somewhere, lost in the wilderness with Big Jack and his other trekker friends. More and more travellers were showing up, each one of whom would get a detailed briefing from Isabella on where to stay, eat, visit; how to cure their stomach upsets, altitude sickness and relationship problems; and which one of her many books would be suitable for their particular interests. The Co-op's book collection kept growing; the more books she loaned out the more she was given in return and it seemed that travellers would arrive with piles of academic, religious, travel and political books about Tibet. There were few novels but hundreds of heavy-duty tomes about the destruction of Tibet's culture, none of which I could be bothered reading; too depressing. I would flick through the guidebooks – and there seemed to be hundreds of different titles – they had great photos and a page or two of essential words for travellers. It was satisfying to look at these lists and know that I knew most of the words by now. I was learning Tibetan from these lists and by listening to local people talking. I couldn't handle the proper Learn Tibetan books as the complex grammatical rules made me panic, reviving bad memories of French classes in school.

- Rupert, you know how busy I am at the Co-op?
- Yes, Isabella.
- Well, I have this new group of English students from the Potala. They're really nice but I don't have the energy to teach them. Can you help?
- Of course.

The Potala monks were the liveliest bunch I had ever taught. About twenty of them would turn up on bicycles, three evenings a week, and they were all so small that their bikes seemed bigger than them. I wondered if they only hired small people at the Potala? They were very young and cheeky, most of them teenagers. When they filed into the Shata classroom each one of them would have a big smile on his face, and nobody complained about the fact that the classroom was unheated. I expect they were used to it – I can't imagine the Potala Palace was heated – and I was always impressed by the fact that Tibetans didn't seem to be affected by the heat or cold.

They had learned some English at the Potala but when I tested them I realised that their knowledge was rudimentary. We would have to start from scratch, which was fine, and I started with basic sentences that I was learning in Tibetan like I go to the market. I believe if you can learn the numbers and the verbs – to be, to do, to go and to want – you can start communicating and the rest will soon fall into place. I had seen in places like Turkey and India that shopkeepers and street hustlers can make a living by learning a few phrases in English and engaging with foreign tourists.

The loudest of the monks was called Pema. He was bursting with enthusiasm to learn English in the shortest possible time. He had a wide, grinning face that had been pockmarked by some childhood disease, and he would constantly interrupt the class by shouting out the answer – usually incomprehensible and when I worked out what he was trying to say it was invariably wrong. The sharpest of the bunch was a miniature creature called Lobsang, whose voice was so squeaky that I could hardly hear him above the din. He looked as if he was only seven or eight years old. Isabella later told me that he was actually fourteen but a childhood disease had given him a hunchback and stopped his growth. Whenever Lobsang offered an answer it was always right and his presence in the class added a certain spice that made teaching them utterly enjoyable. The monks were wild and carefree in the class, although they did pay attention and learn fast. They kept a sharp eye on the time and by 10pm a signal would go round, they would all jump up and start getting ready to leave. They told me they had to get back before the Potala gates were locked, and it was quite a distance. Others told me that they were afraid of being attacked by marauding drunks and packs of stray dogs. I was always sad to see them go.

The day before Isi and Germana were going to leave a small group of Potala monks turned up at the Snowlands Hotel and asked for me. They asked if they could see our Injee room and when I showed them into our bedroom they laughed and shouted in delight. They came in like a cloud of locusts and examined everything – our luggage, books, clothes, shoes – and each item seemed to be more interesting than the last. Isi wasn't happy with this intrusion but he didn't say a word. The leader of the group was Jigme and he said:

- Today we go Potala. You come too. Both you come.

- Ah thanks. I haven't been to the Potala yet. Isi, we've been invited to the Potala Palace. Let's go.

- Sorry mate. I can't. I'm far too busy, I've got to finish my packing, help AP and then say goodbye to everyone in Lhasa.

- You've got to come. These guys are monks from the Potala Palace. They'll show us round. I doubt they've ever come into town and invited foreigners to visit the palace before. Come on.

- Hang on a minute. Isi left the room.

I took the monks downstairs and we all waited impatiently for Isi. The monks were determined to get us to come and said they wouldn't leave without us. I was getting excited and was wondering why I hadn't visited the Potala Palace until now? After ten minutes Isi ran down to the courtyard with a big, happy grin on his face:

- I'm coming. I spoke to AP and she has a free day so she's coming too.
- Jigme! We're coming.

Jigme started barking orders at the other monks, sending them off to round up the other English students. When we were on the street I told Isi to get on the back of my bike and Germana on the handlebars, and all three of us set off slowly through the streets. The load was heavy but if I went slowly it was fine, and I was happy to be in the slipstream of the sweet-smelling Germana.

When we arrived at the hill on which the Potala stands the rest of the English class was assembled and there, to my surprise, were Isabella and Roger organising the students into a more orderly group. It was becoming like a school outing. I hadn't seen Roger for months; his face looked weather-beaten and red and he had grown a big beard on his long sojourn into the northern wilderness. He had a slightly mad glint in his eye and round his neck were several cameras and a light meter.

Looking up at the huge Potala Palace from below was overwhelming. We were a large and noisy group but when I looked up at the palace above, which sat imposingly on top of its own hill, I felt we were nothing but insects. It was similar to Edinburgh Castle – which also sits on a rock – but so much more impressive than Edinburgh's simple stone fortress. The Potala's walls are made of huge blocks of stone that are painted white and reach up for hundreds of feet. Were it not for the huge windows – each one a multicoloured and fascinating feature in itself – it would have resembled an impregnable fortress. The walls of the building leaned inwards – an earthquake protection feature I had seen on all the old buildings in Tibet – a feature I found fascinating. I had heard that when they built the Potala they used vast quantities of molten copper to fix the building more securely onto the bedrock. The engineering and architecture that had gone into this structure were boggling and it was humbling to think that it was built over 500 years ago when Tibet was totally cut off from the rest of the world.

By this time we were slowly walking up a cobbled walkway, so wide that six people could walk abreast. It was built at a gentle angle and the walk up was easy; it was over before we had time to notice that we had climbed a few hundred feet. As we approached the huge structure I could see that it was divided into three sections, each a different colour: the smallest part was in the middle and painted yellow; the other parts were white and a deep red colour, similar to the maroon robes of Tibetan monks.

We reached some massive wooden doors, passed what looked like a totem pole, went through the outer entrance hall, up some wooden steps, round a corner, reached the ticket office and stood behind a crowd of jostling nomads. The ticket office was a slit in a wall, rather like the slits in medieval castles through which archers could fire on their enemies. The official price for foreign tourists was three yuan – an extortionate sum by local standards – and a row erupted between our students and the hapless monk inside the ticket office. After a few minutes our students brandished a handful of tickets in the air and announced that we had been given tickets at Chinese price, just three mao – a few pennies.

Moving as an overexcited, unruly mob we surged up more steps and emerged into a courtyard where we all gasped at the city laid out below us and five storeys of elaborately designed levels rising up, past decorative windows, to a pagoda type roof and the azure sky above. On either side were lower levels of buildings that had been, long ago, accommodation for the palace guard.

We climbed more steps and were accosted by a wild looking man who demanded to see our tickets. When he saw that we had paid the local rates he exploded in rage and another row erupted with our students. Several of them ran off to look for Pema, who was obviously their leader, as he would know how to deal with this madman. But before Pema showed up the old man retreated into his room, muttering angrily to himself, and let us pass.

We waited for Pema under an inscription which said, in Tibetan, Chinese and English Fifth Dalai Lama's Handprint. The Great Fifth, as he is known in Tibet, was their greatest historic leader – a monarch who got things done. The Great Fifth had been personally responsible for the construction of the Potala Palace and his role in holding together the country politically was so personalised that when he died they propped him up in the lotus position for fifteen years, pretending that he was in a retreat, so that the building work would be finished and the internecine strife that followed the death of a Dalai Lama could be avoided.

When Pema appeared he took charge of the group and led us in. We climbed more steps and he showed us into a grand room full of ancient wall hangings, statues and antiques:

-This is Dalai Lama State Room, announced Pema. He meet foreign ambassadors here, he said, pointing to a raised platform where the Dalai Lamas, the former rulers of Tibet, would sit. It wasn't a particularly fancy throne and the room wasn't too grand.

- Chinese Ambassador! He sit there! Said Pema, pointing to a low stool.

He showed us more rooms and told us that this was the seat of Tibet's ancient government. Each room was full of Buddhist statues, altars and religious images; every wall was a riot of religious murals and there was an altar in each room, with candles and little gold figurines. It looked like the inside of a monastery but Pema insisted that each of the rooms we were visiting had a different governmental function when Tibet was an independent country.

We were like a doughnut: a small group of foreigners – Isi, Germana, Roger, Isabella and I – surrounded by a much bigger group: our enthusiastic English language students. They wanted to hear every word we said so they crushed in as close as possible and we walked around as one cumbersome unit. Roger was explaining his camera equipment to Tenzing, one of the young monks who attended the English class. Tenzing seemed to appreciate the attention but didn't seem to understand what Roger was on about:

- Now, repeat after me: Film Speed Adjustment Lever.

Isabella had assumed the air of a schoolmistress on a daytrip, determined to enjoy herself, learn as much as possible and ensure that all her charges got the most out of it. She turned her attention to Dawa, the monk who was standing nearest to her:

- Dawa, can you tell me what the name of that statue is?

Dawa looked terrified, as if his life depended on the correct answer. Clearly he had no idea and he froze. Someone asked the room's curator – another monk – and the information was passed on to Isabella who wrote it in her diary.

Isi and Germana tried to walk around on their own, but they couldn't shake off a determined posse of students who kept trying to steer them back into the group, as if they were stray sheep. They whispered conspiratorially and were so absorbed in each other that I wondered if they were taking it all in. One of the monks asked me:

- Mister Teacher, is that black man really English?

After a few hours my stomach was rumbling and my mind had drifted towards food and rest. The Museum Blues were settling in – a sense of exhaustion while visiting a museum or gallery. Our group moved slowly towards the exit, through a labyrinth of connected rooms, thin corridors and rickety wooden staircases. We bumped into Lobsang, the miniature monk who was the star of our class:

- Hello, he squeaked.

- Hello Lobsang. Nice to see you.

- Follow me, he said, leading us through several small rooms.

- This is Fifth Dalai Lama tomb, he said proudly, where a massive statue rose about thirty feet towards the ceiling.

This statue was by far the most impressive thing we had seen thus far. The group assembled in the room and we stood there in silent awe. We couldn't tell what the statue was made of because it was covered in gold plate and studded with what looked like precious stones. In front of the statue, at its feet, were scores of smaller statues and several buckets that were filled with molten yak butter and a wick; they let off a rancid smell and threw a mysterious half light over the room. My first thought was incredulity: how was this magnificent, and presumably precious, statue spared destruction during China's Cultural Revolution when almost every old building in the land was destroyed? Lobsang seemed to read my mind; he was whispering to the old man who was the keeper of the room, a wizened old man with bright and funny eyes. Lobsang came to me and said in his squeaky voice:

- Chinese leader Chou en Lai, he say to Chinese: You no destroy Potala Palace.

I had heard stories like this before. In Kraków I had been told that the Nazi commander had somehow prevented that historic city from being trashed in the Second World War, while further to the north Warsaw, the capital of Poland, was razed to the ground. Similar stories can be heard from Italy where the great cities were saved from destruction.

Isi needed the toilet and I asked a monk to take him there. Some minutes later Isi came running up to me with a big smile on his face; he could barely contain his excitement. He grabbed Germana and me and led us to the toilet:

- You've just got to see the crapper!

He pushed me and Germana into the door of the cubicle and I braced myself for the appalling smell that was a feature of every Chinese and

Tibetan toilet I had come across. To my amazement there was no smell. Is that what he wanted to show us? I looked back at Isi's grinning face and he was pointing down. For a few seconds I didn't understand and then it clicked: he wanted us to look through the slit in the floor of the toilet, something I would usually avoid as it's a reminder that underneath the typical Tibetan toilet is a room which only has one function – to fill up with excrement until it gets emptied out once a year.

But this toilet was different. It was perched on the edge of a precipice, one of the huge white walls of the palace and there was a refreshing wind blowing through the crack, a wind that presumably swept away all the smells. At the bottom of the wall, hundreds of feet below, was a big brown stain that looked like the peanut butter we used to buy at the Lhasa market, spread on a piece of white bread.

By the time we had reached the base of the Potala my stomach was crying out in protest; I had to eat something. Roger and Isabella got on their bikes and went home, the students started to drift off and some of them led us to a nearby teahouse:

- But Mister Teacher Sir, here food no good. Not clean.

- I don't care, I said: I'm starving. I could eat a horse.

- Horse? You eat horse? They no have horse here.

From the outside it looked like an ordinary teahouse but as soon as we stepped through the door we realised it was almost the size of a football pitch. It was packed with small, dirty tables each one of which was surrounded by country folk. A terrific chattering buzz filled the air, punctuated by yells as people tried to communicate across the heads of the others. Tibetan women in black woollen dresses and multi-coloured smocks circled the tables with big, blackened kettles that were filled with Lhasa's treat for the country folk: sweet tea.

Despite the size of the place it was hard to find an empty table but one of the students shouted in triumph; we hurried over and squeezed onto a low bench. One of the big waitresses plonked a handful of grimy glasses onto the table and, without asking, filled them up deftly with steaming hot tea. I asked her about food but she didn't hear. I asked one of the students who gave me a look of pity and said:

- You must go see kitchen Mister Teacher, pointing to a door on the far side of the room.

I hurried through the crowd and entered a room where a frantic washing operation was underway; two women were working their way through a mountain of dirty glasses and the place was in turmoil. There was no sign of a fire, a cooker or anything to indicate food. One of the women looked at me, grinned and pursed her lips in the direction of the back door. I stepped outside and walked into what looked like a farmyard; there were pigs snorting around in the filth, but no sign of food or a cook. I kicked one of the pigs in frustration and it ran off, squealing. At the back of the muddy yard was a small shed with smoke coming out of the roof and I stepped inside the filthiest kitchen I had yet seen in Tibet: piles of meat and vegetables lying on a long wooden surface; a cloud of flies was hovering over it, enjoying a superb feast, undisturbed by the smoke and noise. The cook shouted at me in fury:

- Get out of my kitchen!

I ignored her outburst as I knew it was surely a reflection of her general frustration and not directed at me personally. She probably shouted at everyone who came in. I shouted back and demanded food, pointing to the tofu and vegetables. I wasn't going to leave the kitchen until she had made me something and after a few minutes she ladled out an evil-looking soup from a big cauldron, threw in some boiled cabbage and tofu, handed it over and told me again to get out, but this time in a more playful way.

I looked up from my soup, which was delicious, and everyone was looking at me as if I was about to roll over and die. I laughed at them and carried on eating, appreciating every morsel and remembering the words of a traveller friend who had visited China and told me that the best restaurants are the filthiest ones.

- Let's go to the Post Office, said Isi, impatient to get moving.

- Hang on a minute, let me finish this delicious soup and my tea.

- You're sick! How can you eat that crap?

The Post Office was one of Lhasa's main tourist attractions, if not the main one. We didn't go there to admire the architecture – it's a low and ugly building – to examine the peeling paintwork, or to experience the officious service; we went there to pick up our mail (and Isi wanted to send some letters). Most travellers would plot their route, approximate a date of arrival and give their loved ones a Poste Restante address in each city they would be visiting. I hadn't done this until I got to Lhasa because I hadn't known in advance where I would be, and also because I didn't know about the concept of Poste Restante until reaching this part of the world. Having discovered this French invention I became a big fan and all my letters and postcards included my new address: Post Restante Lhasa, Tibet,

China. That was all the information they needed for a letter to arrive.

The hallway to the Post Office was packed with foreigners who were crowding in to use the city's only form of communication. It was always packed because doing the most simple transaction, like buying a stamp, was complicated and time consuming. The central point in all this chaos was a grubby book that had been thumbed through by thousands of grimy foreign hands: the Poste Restante book; it had a hole in the corner and was tied to the counter with a piece of string and inside was an endless list of names – people who had received a letter – and the all important reference number. Each name was crossed out after the letter was handed over. I pushed in among the huddle of people round the book, eventually got my hands on it and – to my amazement – found that someone had sent me something. There was my name in black and white! I enthusiastically shouted out the number that was assigned to my name:

- Lee oo ser shan, which is Chinese for sixty three

The grumpy Chinese lady behind the counter slapped a form in front of me and I filled it in: name, passport number, letter reference number and signature. Then she tossed the letter at me and dealt with the next foreigner. It was a letter from Bettina Tucholsky, full of warmth and news from Vienna. She had started to study at Vienna University and said that the city was boring, a complaint that I had heard from many people living in that most beautiful of European cities. She complained of being broke and wanting to come and visit me in Tibet. I was cynical about her desire to visit, assuming that lots of people wanted to visit Tibet (but very few actually did). When I thought about Bettina I realised that I still loved her in a long-term sort of way; we had had a wonderful friendship in Vienna over several months and then one short passionate weekend. I wondered if I would ever see her again and if I would still feel this way about her in the future. When we parted there were no expectations or promises but somehow that made me feel more committed to her. My feelings for her were totally different from the insane, fiery, explosion of passion that I had felt as soon as I set eyes on Shongita and Germana. In a way I was glad these wild feelings had not been consummated because I knew that love-at-first-sight affairs rarely work out. When you're in the grip of those feelings they seem impossible to resist.

I walked back into town with a warm, comfortable feeling in my gut. I was wheeling the bike and walking with Isi and Germana, both of whom were still whispering to each other in Italian. I was happy to have a few moments alone to gather my thoughts. Then I saw Kaysang Dunyou on the other side of the street. I first met Kaysang in Kathmandu and he struck me as more serene and intriguing than any other monk I had come across. He had been to India where he'd met the Dalai Lama and I didn't understand how he had been allowed back. He was slight and had a bright, intelligent and friendly face. He smiled easily. I shouted a greeting across the road and he shouted back:

- Kaba dro gee yin? which, in Tibetan, means where are you going?

- Lhasa.

- San yee shoga! He invited me to the Jokhang Temple the following morning. That was exciting. When I glanced back I noticed that he had stopped in his tracks as if he had been shocked by something. Was he staring at Germana, or Isi? Was he falling under Germana's spell or surprised to see a black man? I suspected that Germana's beauty was challenging his spirituality. He seemed to snap out of it and he dashed off in the other direction, calling out to me:

- Kali pe! which means See You.

Back at the Snowlands Isi was in a panic. It was his last evening and he was frantic. Rather than folding up his belongings and packing them in his rucksack, he was spreading his stuff further around the room. He seemed disorientated, blocked, unable to pack.

- I'm not ready to go yet, he complained.

- Well don't. Stay on. Everyone loves you and there's so much you haven't seen yet.

- I'd love to stay, you know that, but what about AP? How will she make it to the border on her own? She needs me.

- Don't be ridiculous. How do you think she got here? She didn't have a nanny running around after her before she met you.

- Fuck off!

After a lot of agonising, complaining, arguing and false starts, Isi managed to sort out his luggage and we went on a seemingly endless round of goodbyes; I couldn't believe how many people we had got to know during the short period he had been in Lhasa. Gerd, the old Anglo-American Jew, came into the room and gave Isi a handwritten note that said: We must keep in touch with each other. The Israeli girls came into the room to hug Isi and wish him the best and they glanced at me with icy disdain. Roger and Isabella came round and promised to meet him again, and I wondered if they would.

Hang Shoe Dan had bought a couple of bus tickets at the local price
and everyone was very pleased with this; but they didn't realise what a
nightmare a two day rush to the border would mean in a battered old
wreck that would be heaving with baggage and crammed to the gunnels
with humanity. I tried to impress on Isi that having a ticket wasn't enough;
it was essential to get there early, push your way on and fight for a seat. He
thought I was being neurotic.

Their bus was scheduled to leave at eight in the morning, a ridiculously
early hour in Tibet where the clocks are all set by Beijing time, which is
several hours ahead. In the winter months the sun doesn't rise until late in
the morning. I had got Isi up at 6am and, despite his grumblings, he was
soon ready to go. We went to Germana's room and, to our horror, saw
that she hadn't packed; her room was a chaos of scattered paintings, boxes,
clothes and all sorts of Tibetan objects she had picked up. Germana looked
at us blearily from under the blankets.

- There's no way she's going to get all that crap ready in time, I whispered.
- She'll manage it, said Isi uncertainly. He didn't want to linger as Hang
Shoe Dan was there and he was still playing the role of friend.
- Let's go then, I said.
- Ok.

I had managed to load all of Isi's luggage, and some of Germana's,
onto my bike, which had become so heavy that it was impossible to ride.
I pushed it as fast as I could and annoyed Isi by constantly telling him to
hurry up:
- What is it with you people? You've got no sense of time.
- What are you moaning about now?
- Don't you get it? I keep telling you that the bus station is miles away
and if you don't shift your arse you're going to miss it. And if Germana
doesn't sort out her crap fast she'll definitely miss it.
- AP will make it.
- I wouldn't be so sure.

I flagged down a passing Chinese cyclist and persuaded him to take Isi
on his back rack; leaving him a few miles up the road ahead. That enabled
me to make good progress and I developed a running movement with the
overloaded bike. By the time I reached Isi I could see that his face was
contorted by worry:
- She's never going to make it, oh shit.

We arrived at the bus station before 8am but the whole place was deserted; no buses, no people, nothing except some dogs who looked at us with suspicion. Time stood still and we stood there motionless in the dark. Gradually people began drifting in, and by eight thirty a restive mob had assembled. The door of the bus was opened by two young Chinese women, who looked as if they had barely woken up, and then attempted to stem the tide of humanity that was surging towards the door. They were swept aside by the horde of burly Tibetans each of whom was clutching a vast quantity of luggage. Isi's eyes seemed to pop out of his head at the chaos; he had assumed they would turn up on time with their tickets, join an orderly queue and be assigned a seat. All very civilised. He didn't have the experience of an oriental crowd. He was frozen, like a rabbit in the headlights of an oncoming car.

- Isi, wake up, I shouted.

- Er, what, sorry,

- You take the luggage and push your way through that crowd who are climbing onto the roof. That's where the luggage goes. You've got to climb up. Imagine you're playing rugby; use your strength to push your way through the crowd.

- But, but...

- Just do it, otherwise you'll get left behind. I'm going onto the bus and will hold you a seat.

After ten minutes the mob had settled down somewhat and all the seats were occupied; I was sprawled across two seats and had to shout at people constantly from taking the second seat. Eventually Isi turned up and I said:

- You take these seats. Whatever you do don't let anyone sit down, even for a second or you'll lose your place and have an even more miserable journey.

- And what are you going to do? he asked miserably, waking up to the fact that he would be taking the journey without his beloved AP.

- I'm going to wait for Germana. If she shows up I'll get her on. It's already 9am so I'm afraid she's blown it.

- Oh my God, I can't stand it. Isi slumped forward, put his head in his hands and I left him to wallow in it as I pushed my way off the bus.

I was expecting the bus to leave at any moment but the driver had disappeared. Where the hell was Germana? What was her game? Had she realised she'd missed the bus and not even come? Was she in bed with Hang Shoe Dan enjoying one last, wild session of lovemaking? It was an hour and a bit since the bus should have left and I didn't expect her to show up, but I hung on until the last moment in case she did.

At nine fifteen Germana and Hang Shoe Dan came ambling round the corner. If it wasn't for the bike he was wheeling that was stacked high with awkward shapes, presumably containing her paintings, I would have thought they were going for a relaxing morning stroll.

- Over here, I shouted urgently. The bus is leaving. We've got to get your stuff on board.

I leaped up the ladder at the back of the bus, ignored the shouts from the Chinese women who were protesting because the luggage pile had already been strapped down. Nobody followed me or tried to stop what I was doing. I quickly untied a corner of the vast pile and Hang Shoe Dan passed me up her belongings which I stuffed roughly under the tarpaulin. I re-tied the rope, hopped off the roof, grabbed Germana and pushed our way into the bus which had become more packed than ever. Whole families had come to say goodbye to their loved ones; it took about ten minutes to cover the two yards to where Isi was sitting.

Eventually I got her installed next to Isi but the seats were small and uncomfortable and they both looked miserable. Saying goodbye was awkward, as it always is, and it was impossible to push my way off the bus. There were so many people on board that we had become congealed and nobody could move. The two Chinese women had boarded and were screaming at the top of their voices for non-passengers to get off, but it was taking forever. I felt we were moving like treacle. A quarter of an hour later I was outside, wheeling my bike round to the side of the bus. I found the window where Isi and Germana were sitting, knocked and shouted one last farewell.

I didn't have classes until 11am. It felt good to be out and about so early and I cycled around for a bit, enjoying the lightness of the bike now that I was free of all that wretched luggage. I took a different route back into town and decided to take a hot shower at the public bath house.

Because the air in Tibet is very dry you don't sweat or feel the need to wash very much; I certainly didn't and judging from their appearance the Tibetans didn't wash much either. The Chinese were like the Indians in that they seemed obsessed with personal hygiene and made a lot more effort with washing themselves than westerners; I had been told that they thought Tibetans were filthy, and that being sent to Tibet was like a curse, and I imagined they scrubbed themselves desperately in order to inoculate themselves against local infections. The other reason that we didn't see much action in the shower department was the rarity of them. Only the super posh Lhasa Hotel had en suite showers that worked properly; in places like the Snowlands they had one shower per landing and there was nothing worse than freezing in the dirty concrete cubicle while you prayed that the warm water lasted long enough to get the soap off your body.

But that morning I was determined to clean myself up for the New Year celebration. I locked my bike, walked towards the People Wash Shop and realised that half the transit population of Lhasa had the same idea; there was a crowd of tall nomads and Khampas with months of grime to be scrubbed off. I sat on a crowded bench and wondered if I had the patience for another chaotic queue. Just then the queue started to move quickly and I could see they had a system of letting in groups of people at a time. I joined the jostling crowd but there were so many people in front that I realised I would have to wait in the middle of this mob until other people left. Suddenly a strong hand grabbed me by the scruff of my jacket and, with a strength that felt demonic, pushed me through the crowd and propelled me forward into the hallway. When the hand let go I turned round to see who my benefactor was but I didn't see anyone I recognised, just a bunch of big grinning Khampas – any one of whom could have lifted me up with one hand. I didn't dwell on it, nobody was objecting to the fact that I had jumped the queue and so I hurried into one of the tiny cubicles and started to get undressed.

The great thing about the People Wash Shop was the heat. Steam and hot water was blasting out of tiny leaks in the overhead pipes and it felt like a sauna. When it comes to washing there's nothing I dislike more than a cold bathroom and this place felt wonderful, even though the filth inside the cubicle was unlike anything I had ever seen. All over the floor and walls of the cubicle was green and black slime and I had to hang all my clothes carefully from one of the overhead pipes and make sure nothing fell down and got contaminated. The walls were a disgusting black grey colour that had, I supposed, once been white. Underneath all the slime I could make out the shapes of tiles. There was a handle that turned on the actual shower, and the water was consistently hot, in fact it was almost boiling, and it either came hissing out at high speed or stopped dead. It was impossible to adjust the temperature or control the surges of water so I stood to one side, splashed water onto myself, lathered up, rinsed the suds off in deliberate stages, always being careful not to stand directly under the shower or touch the walls.

When I stepped out of the People Wash Shop I felt reborn, like a completely new person. I was glowing, I felt a rush of happiness, closed my eyes and soaked up some of the bright morning sun. I imagined that this is how rich people feel after wallowing in those luxurious spas. I had never felt cleaner, as if I had been scrubbed down to the bone. I bounced down the street and came across Sir Woo's shop window, which was crowded with early morning customers:

- Look at me Sir Woo, I declared noisily. I'm clean. I've just been to the People Wash Shop.

- Hello Mister Teacher.

I was still glowing by the time I reached the Shata School, in time to teach my first English class of 1987. Roger had gone off to the wilderness the night before and I was going to stand in for him until he returned in about two weeks. The students were responsive and fun. Shyly one of them came forward and said:

- Mister Rupert teacher, Sir. Please do not speak too fast.

The class zipped by and I felt I was getting into my stride, finding my style in the classroom, enjoying it more. Isabella asked me to come up to her place for a coffee but I told her I had an invite from a monk at the Jokhang and it was my one chance to get inside the temple and see what was going on.

The Jokhang Temple was literally round the corner from the Shata building and I got to the back door in a couple of minutes. A tough looking monk stopped me at the door and I could tell he wasn't going to let me in. He was backed up by four other monks, all of whom had determined, tough expressions on their faces. They were obviously taking their guard duties seriously and had, presumably, been selected for guard duty because of their imposing size.

- Kaysang Dunyou, ma rock-ba, which means Kaysang Dunyou invited me.

The atmosphere changed immediately and the hostility dropped. The eyes of the monk who was blocking my way lit up in recognition and one of the tough looking back-ups couldn't suppress a smile. Obviously Kaysang had a good reputation. They glanced around for Chinese policemen and hustled me through the thick wooden door. I found myself inside a yard which, the last time I'd seen it, was stacked high with building materials and other deliveries. Now, however, it had been transformed – cleared – and filled with a number of circular wooden structures that looked like enormous wedding cakes. I wanted to ask someone what they were but there were too many people milling around and the guards had gone back to their door. And then I saw Kaysang, but he didn't see me. I moved towards him but he was gone by the time I reached the place where he'd been.

I looked back at the huge wedding cakes and noticed a group of monks putting yak butter onto the blackened wood. What on earth were they doing? I went closer and guessed they were going to make some sort of elaborate sculpture. Someone recognised me:

- Teacher teacher. You come here please. It was the cheeky young monk from Sera Monastery, one of Isabella's students, the one who was incapable of being serious.

- Excuse me, wait. Can you tell me what these big wooden things are? I pointed to the wedding cakes. He wasn't listening, he was moving up some rickety wooden steps, calling to me:

- Teacher teacher, you must follow me!

I followed him up the steps, along a corridor and through a low door that was carefully closed behind me. The room was full of our English students – they all had huge smiles on their faces and they shouted in unison:

- Hello teacher! How are you today?

- I'm fine, I replied, unable to keep a big smile off my face.

They were the monks from the big monasteries on the outskirts of Lhasa – Sera and Drepung – and I realised that this room had been assigned to them for doing their homework when they came to the Shata School. It was a small, dark and undecorated room with a low ceiling and no tables. Nobody was studying. It was the first day of the Tibetan New Year and I could tell they just wanted to have some fun. Some of them were looking out of the window, laughing at something in the yard below:

- Teacher teacher! Come quick! See big Khampa carrying bigger rock! I caught a glimpse of a huge boulder being lifted in the yard, but there were too many people outside to see properly.

- Teacher, please. We want English lesson. I groaned:

- Not today. Today I have no time. I came here to see Kaysang Dunyou. The mention of Kaysang's name had a similar effect on the students as it did on the guards; they were impressed.

- Kaysang Dunyou. He leader of Butter Sculpture Festival. They could see I didn't understand and Nima Tsering, the most serious of the bunch, explained:

- Kaysang Dunyou is organiser of the Butter Sculpture Festival. Tonight, when sun is gone, they put up big butter sculptures. Then big festivities. Many people come, big crowd all round Jokhang.

Nima then remembered that he had to report to Kaysang and he dashed out of the room and slammed the door. When I realised that Kaysang was playing a key role in the festivities I gave up any hope of seeing him and I had an idea: I would teach them how to tease each other in English.

- You are not a Sera monk! I said sternly to the cheeky little monk from Sera. You are Sera monkey. Your name is Monkey. They all laughed loudly, delighted at my intrusion into their endless teasing of each other. I loved the fact that most of the monks I dealt with were still children – juveniles, teenagers – and they lacked the boring gravitas that most religious people seem to have the world over. This lot were fun to be with.

- Mister Rupert. Mister teacher, I heard being shouted from the yard. It was Nima and he was struggling with a huge tub of butter.

- I see Kaysang. He say you go to his room now. He will come quickly. He then ordered young Monkey from Sera to guide me.

The cheeky monk was delighted with his new nickname – Monkey – as it has a positive connotation in their culture. Monkey is a Chinese demi-God who travels with a priest and has superpowers. The tales of monkey's journeys are a staple of Chinese legends. He took me along a pitch-black corridor that led to the main part of the temple and suddenly we were looking down on the main courtyard, where a huge ceremony was in progress, but we didn't stop; we went round more corners, more corridors and ended up in Kaysang's tiny room, a cell. I looked back at the crowd of people who had gathered on the first floor balcony to watch the monks going through their ritualistic prayers and movements in the courtyard below. There were hundreds of people up there but they weren't making a sound. It was eerily silent. I could hear a deep rumbling sound, rather like a foghorn, and very close. I presume it came from one of those long horns but I couldn't see it; and then it was answered by a host of similar horn sounds as if they were calling to each other.

There was a blanket hanging over the door frame and I was standing under it, with the cloth draped over my shoulder. Inside the cell was Kaysang's old mother from the village and his nephew, who was so small that he made Monkey from the Sera Monastery seem big. He can't have been more than four years old and he had a very serious expression on his tiny face. The old mother was the perfect hostess and while the boy grandly sat on his miniature bed, we were asked to sit down and then offered Yak Butter Tea, sweets and biscuits. Monkey and I tucked in.

By the time Kaysang came Monkey had run off and I was stuffed. He warmly shook my hands with both of his and asked how I was? Was I working? Where was I staying? Did I like Lhasa? We spoke in Tibetan which was easier than usual because he was a natural communicator – unlike his nephew who never said a word – and he really seemed interested in what I was trying to say and would help me find the words. He had brought a bucket of steaming rice with him, the ceremonial food now being offered to the hundreds of visiting monks. Because it was prepared by the monks and contained butter and sugar it was considered a great honour to be offered some, and I had no choice but to eat a bowl of the congealing mush.

We talked some more and he insisted that I finish eating the rice and tea that was still in front of me. He cupped his palms together, moved them towards me and said:

- Choo choo, which means please eat!

I used chopsticks to shovel up the rice, Chinese style, trying not to think about the horrible taste. They were delighted that I finished a full bowl and immediately there was another one in front of me.

- May! Coochie coochie, may! No! Please please, no.

Such pleas for restraint are considered part of Tibetan etiquette and they ignore them. I didn't touch the full bowl of rice in front of me, which is also an accepted part of the etiquette (and it's the only way to stop them feeding you). The blanket over the door was moved aside and a monk's head appeared; he had a fast whispered conversation with Kaysang, who jumped up, ready to go. I also stood up to follow him but he gently pushed me back down and said:

- You wait here. Mama will look after you. I will be back soon.

I waited in the tiny cell feeling very much at home. The mother was busy tidying up and I knew it would have been inappropriate if I had tried to help; the old woman would have been confused and perhaps even offended. She was clucking around like an old hen and I realised that she appreciated my presence there.

When Kaysang had been in the cell his nephew had come to life and was jumping around, behaving like a naughty four year old. Now that Kaysang was gone the nephew had assumed his stern and commanding presence. I tried not to stare at him because I knew how annoying this is for children, but I was fascinated in his every movement. Kaysang had told me that his brother lived in a village and was delighted when Kaysang asked his son to come and live at the Jokhang; this was a great honour. The boy was adorable, he had sparkling eyes, a lovely face and great presence, and I wondered what would come of him when he was of age. I realised that he didn't talk much because he was shy and he compensated for this by walking with a swagger and trying to imitate the adults – an act which amused everyone who saw him.

The afternoon slipped by and there was no sign of Kaysang. I wasn't sure what I should do. The small boy entertained himself by bossily shouting commands at his grandmother, who would laugh and then obey. The afternoon sun had found its peak and it was getting hot in the cell. I wondered who had made the boy's maroon robes; they were an exact copy of those worn by the adult monks. I had never seen such a small child dressed in monastic robes before and I supposed they must have been made especially for him, and a new set would have to be made every year. I noticed his robe had yellow silk borders on the shoulders, something I'd never noticed before on a robe. What did it signify? He even had a small blanket tucked into the back of the robe, an item they all wear in winter, and he was struggling to get it off. He threw his little blanket across the room where it landed on Kaysang's bed in an untidy heap. He threw it with studied indifference, as if he'd been working in the fields all day and it was a brilliant imitation of how I had seen Tibetan adults behave. The grandmother clucked at him for his messiness, picked up the blanket, folded it lovingly. This was too much for the boy who obviously wanted to play; he wrestled with the granny until he got possession of the blanket and then he threw it again across the room where it landed in a messy heap. I wondered if he was doing all this for my benefit? He was deliberately not looking at me and yet there was no way he wasn't aware of my presence. Eventually he fitted the blanket back onto his robe, as if getting ready to go out, gave me a piercing look and said in a squeaky voice:

- I will show you where he works.

He reached up and took my hand, shouted some words at the grandmother and led me out onto the busy corridor. By now the crowd on the balcony had doubled in size and I could see some older Tibetans who

were dressed in ancient ceremonial costumes. Small pieces of paper, tied
to white muslin scarves, were floating through the air, descending slowly
into the courtyard; they landed on the monks who were sitting cross-
legged in rows below, and were passed forward to the head monk, a huge
man who sat impressively on a raised dais, like a throne, facing them. The
bits of paper contained questions from the public and it was all part of an
ancient debating ritual, a method of identifying the brightest monk – who
would then be awarded the title Geshe.

The crowd downstairs was forbiddingly dense. The nephew, who was
still clinging to my hand, didn't hesitate to push his way through and the
crowd parted as if by magic. From his perspective all he could see was
hundreds of thighs and these he thrust aside with contempt. The people
looked at us in astonishment – a miniature monk leading a foreigner – and
then smiled with delight. However rudely he pushed nobody took offence
– on the contrary, they treated him with reverence; they bowed, whispered
prayers and offered their heads to be blessed. He ignored them all and
pushed through to the heart of the temple.

The big central room was surrounded by a network of smaller rooms
and cloisters. On the left hand side was a series of small rooms with
shrines and on the right were elaborate pillars and sculptures. Every wall
in the room was painted with a chaos of murals, some of which showed
a pictorial history of the temple and others the different manifestations
of the Buddha. Every space was crammed with people and I was struck
by how quiet and disciplined they all were; everyone knew exactly what
they were doing -- praying at each shrine and statue and making offerings.
Each crowd seemed more densely packed than the last but all of them
made a passage for the tiny monk and his strange guest. The centre of the
big room was dominated by three huge statues, which reached up to the
skylights above. The middle statue, the largest, was covered in dull gold
leaf and I thought I detected a Mona Lisa type smile as we hurried by. This
was said to be the most sacred object in the land; I had been told it was
some form of reincarnation of the Buddha – although I never understood
how the Buddha could have reincarnated into a statue.

The nephew was so focused on pushing a path through the crowd
that he didn't even look up at the statues. He was heading straight for
them and then I understood why; underneath the statues were scores of
meditation mats that weren't being used, and the crowd hadn't set foot in
that area; we carefully made our way through the mats, underneath the

great statues and got to the other side of the room: it was the short cut. At the back of the space was a little room that housed the Sakyamuni statue and was considered one of the most sacred spots in the land. Tibetans believe that these sacred statues are alive and the Sakyamuni is believed to have saved the Jokhang Temple from destruction during the Cultural Revolution. Kaysang was supposed to be in this room, but he wasn't and so we resumed our search.

We went back to the space with the huge statues and this time I noticed a tiny fence had been put up round the base of them; only about a foot high, just enough to be unobtrusive and to keep the pilgrims out. Thousands of hands had touched the wire and it shone as if it were precious silver. From the main part of the room the spaces between the statues are effectively invisible; you only see them if you know to look for them and most people are so in awe of the statues that they don't realise there is a space there. We moved into the centre of the space and there, to my surprise, was an old monk with twinkling eyes who was muttering prayers continually. The boy spoke to him:

- Kaysang, ma say gee you: Where is Kaysang?

The statue minder seemed amused that the boy had addressed him with such a practical question, shrugged his shoulders and resumed swaying from side to side – his form of meditation and prayer. After a long pause he suggested we look outside. He glimpsed up at me and returned to his original position.

I closed the little wire gate with a sense of reverence, feeling honoured that I had been allowed into such a sacred space and wondered if anyone apart from this little boy would have ever led me in here. I asked the boy where we would go next but talking to him was pointless as he was still too shy to respond, even though he had no problem in pushing people aside whom he had never seen in his life. We made our way across the backyard and up some stairs. When an old lady offered to help him manage the steep steps, that he was negotiating with difficulty, he rebuked her angrily and insisted on struggling up on his own.

We entered an upper room that was full of monks. Dramatic black demons leaped at me from the walls and, as we made our way through to the door on the other side, I caught a glimpse of an ancient monk who was using a thin curved stick with a soft pad on the end to beat a hanging drum. The drum was beating in time with the chanting made by all the monks in the room.

We were back on the roof space, moving quickly, and I noticed that darkness was spreading across the sky. I felt a slight thrill of panic, hoping not to miss the butter festival, and wanted to follow my urge to go downstairs to find the big wedding cakes. The boy seemed disappointed and asked me to come back to Kaysang's cell with him, but I refused as I knew I could spend the rest of the evening waiting there. It was time to strike out on my own.

When I located the yard I noticed with horror that the wedding cakes were all gone. Hoping I hadn't missed the action I asked one of the monks and he pointed to the back door – leading out into the street. I went out and walked round to the front of the temple, to the big public square that was packed with Tibetans. The atmosphere here was completely different from inside, less reverent and more fun; a sense of charged expectation filled the air and there was a roar as thousands of people talked to each other. The crowd was moving and huge numbers of people were walking round the Kora, the sacred circuit of narrow streets that wraps round the temple.

I had been looking out for Kaysang continually. Instinct told me to peel myself off the wall I had been leaning against and join the crowd. It was like jumping into a fast flowing river and I noticed the whirl of energy and laughter and ended up in the middle of the public square where, to my surprise and delight, stood the vast butter sculptures. The wooden wedding cakes had been stacked on top of each other and each layer was stacked with a crowd of dark sculptures and Buddhist symbols. The structure was ingenious; each of the wedding cakes was a different size, from the wide one at the bottom that supported the others to the thin narrow one that formed an elegant point at the top. It was black, covered in candles, must have been ten metres high and resembled a pagoda. How had they managed to construct such an artistic wonder in the last few hours?

I noticed small groups of Chinese policemen in green military uniforms leaning against the walls. Perhaps they were wondering how they were supposed to control such a massive crowd. Most of them were smoking and they looked rather sinister in their peaked caps. As I was swept by in the crowd I brushed up against an officer who was so fat, and had such a serious expression, that I struggled not to burst out laughing. I wondered if they realised that the crowd was perfectly harmless and didn't need policing.

By now I had given up trying to control where I was going and just

allowed myself to be carried along with the mob into the first part of the
Kora circuit. Soon the crush loosened and I could walk normally. It was
refreshing. I looked up at the sky which was now black. The moon was full
and it hung there, vast and silent, throwing an eerie light over the stone
paved street. On each of the four sides of the temple were other big butter
sculptures, but it was impossible to stop and appreciate them properly.

Back at the public square the police had cordoned off a large group of
monks from the thrusting, eager crowd. I squeezed myself into a space
where I could look through the police cordon at the leathery, weather-
beaten faces of the monks who had travelled from hundreds of miles
away. I was intrigued by their air of antiquity and moved closer so I could
examine their robes which were, I noticed, different from the ones in
Lhasa; they were pleated and dyed in different ways from the standard
maroon ones I had seen. They had probably all made their own robes,
using whatever material and dye they could get hold of locally. I caught
the eye of a broad-shouldered lama who moved with the physical grace
of a fencer; he was old and white-haired and had the air of a tyrant, or an
emperor. His face was full of strength. In the short second he glanced at
me I felt he could see right through me – as if I was being X-rayed. I was
sure he had seen my personality and he gave me an imperceptible nod as
if offering a silent greeting.

Suddenly Kaysang emerged from the main door and I shouted and
waved, but to no avail. I was one of thousands of onlooking faces and
he disappeared inside again without seeing me. A few minutes later he
emerged again, leading a procession of monks each of whom was carrying
a tray with burning candles and strange shapes that looked like huge
onions. A gasp of excitement went up from the crowd and we surged
forward as one. The thin police line disintegrated on contact; we got closer
to the procession of monks and were able to get a good look at what they
were carrying: elaborately designed fishes, umbrellas, knots and scores of
other objects – all fashioned out of the golden butter.

The crowd was still pressing forward, threatening to crush the procession
and destroy the delicate structures. The police were standing at the edges,
looking humiliated. The crush of the crowd was incredible and I feared for
the lives of the monks in the procession. They could be stampeded at any
moment.

The old monks from the provinces took charge. They had been outside
all this time and somehow they organised themselves in perfect unison:

in one smooth movement they all turned their backs to us, forming an impenetrable maroon wall. They started chanting in a loud bass voice, a deep booming rhythm. The effect was immediate; it broke the energy of the crowd, which backed off, and I felt the pressure of people all round me decrease – as if I had become an individual again. Silence swept through the crowd as we all listened to the deep, mesmerising chanting.

The monks had laid their sculptures along a wall at the front of the temple and were making their way back inside. As if by magic, and without a word of command, the crowd reorganised itself into two columns which were forming up to file slowly past the display of butter sculptures. Each column approached the sculptures from a different direction and passed each other in perfect order. Every pilgrim around me was muttering a prayer and clutching rosary beads and so many people were doing the same thing that the whole square was filled by a dull roar of prayer.

A space opened up around the green clad policemen, who used the opportunity to re-form into a small, aggressive looking squad. The police were standing stock still as if on guard duty, and this struck me as inappropriate. They seemed unwilling to blend in and unable to manoeuvre. I imagined they were a group of disgruntled fish who had decided they were going to make a stand against the endless flowing of the river.

I found myself at the end of one of the columns, which was three people wide all along its length, and slowly inching forward. It was moving with remarkable precision towards the butter sculptures but sometimes it would swing out wildly to one side, like a river bursting its banks. At one point our column swung into the central space and brushed against the group of policemen, scattering them in all directions.

Their response was immediate. The police group reformed itself into a tight squad and a voice was shouting angry commands in Chinese. Each policeman whipped off his leather belt or produced an electric cattle prod, shaped like a small black bottle. At this display of force the column gasped and recoiled in horror. One policeman marched forward and lashed with his belt at the hapless Tibetans in our column, shouting in fury and pent up frustration. Our column disintegrated, people scattered in all directions and there was a roar of panic. I could see that people were laughing, as if this display of force was just a comedy act. A few seconds later the policeman stopped his attack, folded up his belt and walked away with what looked like a sense of satisfaction, as if he had taught us a lesson. Our column immediately re-formed, order was restored and we resumed our slow crawl towards the butter sculptures.

Gradually we approached the sculptures and the sound of prayers seemed to increase. When we reached them the pressure of the crowd decreased although the hum of prayer was louder than ever. The column circled round and I realised that they were going to visit the sculptures again and again. I became aware of a burly peasant crushed up behind me; I could feel his hand on my back and, hang on a minute, was that his hand in my back pocket? With a rising sense of panic I felt my right buttock to check for my wallet and – shock horror – it was gone. For a moment I didn't know what to do. Then I noticed a man behind me pushing his way out of the column. I soon caught up with him, stopped him and demanded my wallet back. He was wearing typical winter clothes – a long brown chuba (Tibetan fur coat) with sleeves that stretched beyond his hands, held together with a thick black leather belt. He stood there sheepishly, looking guilty. A ring of people had gathered round us to look on. I instinctively ran my hands into his sleeves and tried to search him while he looked on with a sense of bewilderment. Suddenly it struck me that what I was doing was probably humiliating and what if it wasn't him who had stolen my wallet? It didn't matter anyway, it only contained a few Mao, and all the important stuff – the dollars, my passport – was strapped to my waist in my money-belt.

Feeling drained and ridiculous, I moved away from the crowd to the side of the public square, where it was less crowded. I noticed a truck parked discreetly to one side and a Chinese film crew who had set up big lights and two cameras on tripods. Leaning against the truck were two foreigners that I had briefly met at the Travellers' Co-op: Jenny and June. They had recently arrived from Britain with the Voluntary Service Overseas, an agency that places volunteers all over the world on short term assignments. They had been sent here to teach English at the newly-formed Tibet University. They were friendly and open but seemed completely out of place here; they were watching the spectacle with a sense of wonder and incomprehension; I could tell they were fascinated but didn't really know how to integrate with it. Jumping into the crowd and flowing with it had seemed quite natural to me but I already felt a rapport with Tibetans, and realised that most foreigners would probably feel unable to act like this.

Talking to them was a nice break. Jenny was English, chatty and vivacious while June was dry, warm and Scottish. They were a pleasant reminder of life back home, a million miles away. I had seen them before and noticed how they were always together, even though they were totally different from each other. From what I knew, Tibet University was a newly established unit that didn't consist of a lot more than we had at the Shata, but the fact that China was investing in further education in Tibet was, surely, a sign of goodwill.

The place where we were standing had a good view of the crowd and was strangely calm, like an eddy in a fast flowing river. A street urchin came near and I watched him climb onto the front wheel arch of the TV truck, giving him a better view of the proceedings. He called out to his friends and soon there were a group of them clambering up the truck. Suddenly I heard a cry of outrage and what must have been the TV producer strode over and berated the ragamuffins; I didn't understand what he said but the kids scattered like birds, hooting with laughter, and what struck me was how similar the producer's arrogant behaviour was to TV crews I had come across at home. He had the same dress sense, a combination of casual, stylish-but-scruffy clothing, a well thought-out hairdo which was suitably windswept. He was stocky and dynamic, smoked continuously and had the thrusting charm of the TV producer who is forever trying to persuade people to allow themselves to be filmed which, to Tibetans (so I'd been told) would be most invasive: Tibetans consider that a photo takes away a part of their soul. Considering that this man was unlikely to have had contact with the west, or western TV crews, I wondered if this style and behaviour came naturally with the job. A curious thing about the crew was that they tolerated our presence, perhaps seeing us as fellow foreigners who would never be more than spectators, but they didn't talk to us; they didn't even look at us.

I asked Jenny and June if they would like to walk round the Kora with me and they seemed delighted with the suggestion. They were so new to Lhasa that they weren't quite sure what to do. I led them away from the TV truck and into the flowing crowd, like fish in a river. When we got to the start of the Kora I linked arms with them both and we walked round the ancient circuit of streets, and I told them about my experiences in the temple.

The next morning I felt rather groggy and had a breakfast of yoghurt and sweet white rolls. It was the last day of the Tibetan New Year and I wondered what the day would bring. The whole event had been a series of surprises, which made it all the more exciting; there was no sign of an official programme or even a simple promotional poster. Everyone just knew what was going to happen, and where, and they would happily tell anyone who asked.

There were business matters to attend to. I had been selling tickets for the latest bus trip and in my pocket was a wad of US Dollars that needed to be handed over to Je Yang. I met him briefly; we had a short chat and he shot off again. He wasn't interested in the celebrations and I could see why; the crush of the crowds, the chaos, noise and lack of hygiene would have horrified him.

Back at the Snowlands Hotel I heard a terrific noise outside. The street had been empty a few minutes before but now there was a crowd; laughter and excitement were in the air. What was going on? An exhausted looking man was half running, half staggering along the road wearing what looked like the costume of a clown, with sleeves that were far too long for his arms. He crossed a white line that had been drawn in chalk from the entrance of the Snowlands right across the road. As soon as he crossed what was presumably a finishing line the runner collapsed onto the road alongside a bunch of other burned-out Tibetans also dressed in outlandish gear.

I looked around for someone I knew – usually the best way of finding out what was going on – and spotted a skinny Tibetan exile: Norbu. I ask him in my basic Tibetan what was going on and he replied in his Indian flavoured English:

- Today is big horse day. Horse race at Sera. Horse race through Lhasa. Today many horse race. Look! Here come soldier horse!

We looked down a side street and could see a group of horsemen heading our way. They were dressed in brightly coloured costumes, which looked faintly ridiculous on them. They didn't seem to be in full control of their nags; the jumpy movement of the horses and the way they were pulling too hard pulling on the reins told me they were inexperienced horsemen; this may have even been their first time on horseback. They came closer and I could see they were wearing scarlet jackets and Afghani style baggy trousers that were tucked into high black boots. They looked like an irregular cavalry unit from the days of the British Empire wearing a hotch potch of uniforms they had pinched from different army units. They wore wide-brimmed hats, similar to cowboy hats, with a little curtain of red string hanging all round the rim. They looked both splendid and comical and I could sense that they felt embarrassed by the fact that everyone seemed to be laughing at them, even a nearby policeman. The horses were skittering around the road in circular movements, and suddenly one of the riders pulled out his sword and shouted a command:

- Ah! Sera Tan dro: Let's go to Sera.

The horsemen charged off up the street, scattering the crowd and pursued by a pack of barking dogs. Excitement was still hanging in the air and everyone started moving in the direction of Sera Monastery. I could see that Norbu was going for his bike and I asked him to wait while I got mine from inside the Snowlands. When I came out a few minutes later the street was back to normal, as if nothing had happened; a few people were walking and cycling by at the usual relaxed pace. We set off in the direction of Sera but couldn't find the crowd that we had just been part of, or the horsemen. Where had they all gone? We must have taken a different route. Soon we turned off the main road outside Lhasa and were on the long straight road that leads up to Sera. Next to the monastery stands an ugly army hospital, known as the PLA (Peoples' Liberation Army) Hospital, a concrete reminder of who's boss in this country. It was mid-afternoon and the sun was at its zenith; even though it was winter it felt hot and arid and I was tired. I saw one of my students go into a nearby teahouse and I locked up my bike, indicated to Norbu to follow and went in.

The teahouse was large and dingy and I could see groups of Tibetans sitting round tables, looking as if they were hatching plots. No sign of the students. Then two friendly faces appeared at the back door: Tsewong and Shewashen, Roger's two best students. They were beckoning us to follow them and we stepped through into a backyard, which was being used as a makeshift terrace. Empty bottles and crates were scattered around. Five of our students were sitting there, under a tree, with Isabella:

- Sit thee down Rupert. Who's your friend?
- He's Norbu.
- Hello Norbu.
- Good afternoon Madam.
- Did you two get lost looking for the horse race?
- Yes.
- So did we.

I noticed that the students were talking among themselves in Chinese even though only one of them, Shewashen, was Chinese. Isabella rebuked them gently for not using their own language; I didn't say anything as what they were doing seemed a considerate way of keeping Shewashen in the conversation. I had heard that Tibetans speak better Mandarin than many Chinese people because they learn it as a foreign language, whereas most Chinese grow up with strong regional dialects – that even other Chinese people can't understand. Norbu chatted to the students in Tibetan, saying he'd like to learn Mandarin so he could do business between Kathmandu, Lhasa and Chengdu.

Shewashen was chatty, charming and spoke good English. I particularly noticed his teeth, which seemed bigger and whiter and more prominent than everyone else's. He had a wonky smile and treated me like a good friend. I suggested he worked as an English-speaking guide in Lhasa as there didn't seem to be any. There was good money to be made in tourism. Maybe we could do a business together? Problem was that he knew nothing about Tibet's rich heritage and not a word of the language. I wondered if he'd be willing to put in the effort and learn it? I had not yet met a Chinese person who had.

- Mister Rupert, said Shewashen.
- Yes.
- Me and Dicky go see Sera Monastery now. You come?

How could I refuse such a friendly invitation?

- See you at the races, I said to Isabella and Norbu, who were deep in conversation and made no move to follow us.

I was surprised to see that Sera Monastery was completely deserted that day. I wondered where the horse races were taking place as there was no sign of them from the outside. Four of us walked into the huge and eerily silent chanting hall. As well as Shewashen there was Dicky, which means happiness in Tibetan, and a tall attractive girl from Chamdo in the north. The northern girl was so shy that she would have a fit of the giggles if I even looked at her and if I asked a question she would laugh so much that she would bend and sway like a tree in a high wind. Dicky was cheeky and chatty. It felt great being with them.

The hall was spacious, low and dark. The atmosphere was similar to the chanting hall at the Jokhang but I wasn't used to such silence. Elaborately carved and painted wooden pillars held up the ceiling. The walls were covered in murals although it was too dark to make out more than the faint outline of sinister shapes around the edges of the room. We walked past row after row of long thin cushions, where hundreds of monks should have been sitting and chanting. Each cushion had a series of carefully placed maroon robes, some of which had been puffed up to resemble a headless monk sitting in the meditation position. The eerie atmosphere didn't seem to bother our group; they were teasing and prodding each other, giggling like schoolgirls half their age. We went up some steps into a small shrine room and were surrounded by life-sized statues, each one of which was fully dressed in yellow and maroon robes. They had huge eyes, which stared past us into the hall. We heard a yell from a faraway room, an angry voice that was getting closer:

- Sue ray? Sue ray? Who is it?

A manic looking old monk rushed into view and stopped dead when he saw us. His robes were threadbare, his hair was a wild bird's-nest and he had the crazy-eyed look of a hermit or obsessive. A look of bewilderment crossed his face as he looked at us: a foreigner, a Chinese youth and two Tibetan girls. He was clutching a feather duster and seemed to be pondering his next move. We were all waiting for him to say something, and then he screamed hysterically:

- You girls get out! No women allowed in here!

- Please let them stay, I said calmly, making no move to head for the exit. They are the translators for our friend Shewashen. He doesn't speak Tibetan.

The monk stood there and studied us all again, and I knew what he was thinking: What should I do with this lot? I suspect the idea of throwing us out was conflicting with the more benign intention of showing us around and teaching us a little about their traditions. The others felt awkward and embarrassed and were keen to leave. I hissed at them to stay where they were. He had rebuked us, told us the rules, done his duty and we had been respectful, hadn't challenged him or shown disrespect and I knew from my experience at home in dealing with traffic policemen, or public officials, that if you accept their authority, don't answer back and act like you are genuinely sorry for the transgression – you might get away with it.

Seeing that we weren't leaving and that he had nobody to back him up, the old monk shrugged. He was still a bit grumpy and resentful but I could tell it was fading and the charm of my students would soon work its magic on him. He assumed the role of the tour guide and started explaining, with real pride, what the various statues were. He spoke in an unusual dialect of Tibetan that I could only just follow:

- That one is Chenrezi, there are the Dalai Lamas and here is Guru Rinpoche.

Shewashen's face lit up and without being asked Dicky started translating for him. He pulled out a small plastic covered notebook and started taking detailed notes. I looked at his notes and saw him writing an incomprehensible thicket of Chinese characters. Dicky and the girl from Chamdo seemed rather bewildered by the whole experience and I realised that they knew as much about Tibetan Buddhism and culture as I did, which was virtually nothing; and I thought about how closely intertwined, until recently, culture and religion had been in Tibet and everyone, down to the lowest beggar, would have known the names of the main Buddhist statues.

Dicky and the girl from Chamdo quickly grew bored of the monk's talk, which was becoming ever more detailed. It seemed ironic that the only student who was interested was Shewoshen, who was Chinese. I thought about the Chinese propaganda that presented pre-Communist Tibet as primitive, cruel and exploitative. I had always seen this information as a sceptical outsider, in other words I had distance from it. I wondered how it was for children in Tibetan schools. They wouldn't have had the option of looking at these things from different perspectives; under Communism there was only one version of truth and to challenge it was to risk the security of your family. No wonder Tibetans didn't like to talk about what had happened in their country over the last generation.

I left Sera feeling rather morose. I said goodbye to the students and rode back into town fast, trying to sweep away my sad thoughts with a dash of speed. Then I saw that Dicky, who was the only one of them who had a bike, was following me; she was cycling hard to try and keep up. As soon as she noticed that I had seen her she lost control of her bike, fell off and slid along the gravel on her hand, skinning it badly. I felt terrible as this was surely my fault. How inconsiderate and selfish to just rush off without seeing if anyone was following, but I had wanted to be on my own and assumed none of the others would want to join me.

- I'm so sorry, I said.
- It's okay, she grimaced. I could see blood dripping from her hand.
- You must be in terrible pain. Let's go to the army hospital over there.
- No, I am fine.

A look of fear crossed her face and I remembered hearing about the sterilisation programmes the Chinese carried out in Tibet; apparently any woman who came into the hospital for a birth or abortion would also be forcibly sterilised. I wasn't sure if this was still going on and I didn't really want to know any more details; the very idea was so grotesque that just thinking about it turned my stomach.

- You are very brave, I said to Dicky. I was really impressed with her lack of dramatics. She had a nasty cut on her hand and she was dealing with her pain silently and with dignity. Would you like to come to the horse races? I asked, thinking that it might take her mind off the pain.

- Thank you. No. I go home now. She slowly rode off towards town and I cycled off in the other direction.

The races were taking place on a patch of ground that looked more like a desert than the green racetracks I was used to seeing back home. In this part of the world you don't get big expanses of lawn; in fact our type of grass wouldn't have a chance of survival in Tibet's climate without constant irrigation. The races were taking place on a wide, open dusty space and it was difficult to make out where the actual track was; there were no fences or lines drawn on the ground. The only thing that kept the crowd back was when the scraggy nags came charging past, each one with a wild looking tribesman on its back thrashing it continually. The biggest horse looked like a pony and they all looked undernourished and ready to drop. I wanted to leave as soon as I arrived; I have a profound boredom of all organised sports and this race had a cruel feel that I didn't like.

I cycled back into town thinking that I would like to stay in Tibet for the rest of my life. It was hard to understand why I had fallen for Tibet so completely. On the one hand it was a filthy, frustrating, uncivilised dive and the people were unreliable. Getting work was really hard and making a living in Lhasa was probably impossible, or illegal, for a foreigner. On the other hand there was something about the people that I connected to deeply: their dark, unruly, ironic humour; their friendliness and positive attitude in the face of overwhelming adversity. Tibet had got under my skin and I felt completely at home in Lhasa – a feeling that was as difficult to understand as the infatuation one has when falling in love.

CHAPTER TEN

I was becoming established in Lhasa and a simple plan was forming in my mind; I would stay for as long as possible, put down some roots and not hit the road for a while. My daily routine consisted of teaching English to the monks at the Shata School, giving private lessons to Sir Woo, organising buses for the foreigners and helping Isabella with the Travellers' Co-op. I had been unable to find somewhere local to stay and was still installed at the Snowlands, but now I was able to pay for it without worry.

Roger's English class took up more and more of my time and energy. I really liked the students and had become quite close to some of them; I wanted to be their teacher for as long as possible. Roger was due back from the Changtang, the Northern Desert, any day now and he would presumably want his job back. He said he'd be away for two weeks and already a month had passed. On the one hand I wished he would get back soon, so I could make a clean break with this class, but part of me hoped he would never come back so that I could remain with them for as long as possible. I often wondered if he was all right up north in the wilderness; even a small accident could prove fatal in an environment where the nearest habitation was probably days away. I tried to imagine what it would be like to run out of food or water up there.

My days were becoming busier and busier and I always slept well at the end of them. I avoided the Travellers' Co-op as much as possible because providing the travellers with information was an endless and thankless task. So many of them treated it as if it was just another shoddy service of the Kirey Hotel and their attitude was annoying. On the one hand they behaved like they knew it all, and many were exceedingly well read in the history, geography and culture of Tibet; on the other hand they needed the fresh, local information that we could give them – bus schedules and prices, accommodation updates, health advice, best places to eat, dealing with the police and so on. I sometimes felt they were resentful that we had information they didn't already know, as if we were challenging their mastery of all knowledge regarding Tibet. Dealing with the Tibetans and Chinese was so much more straight-forward and rewarding, even if I couldn't understand half of what was being said.

Je Yang's buses were running every two weeks by this point and we established a meeting place on the roof terrace of the Kirey Hotel to sell tickets. Some of the travellers had seen me in the Co-op and were suspicious. Why is a Brit selling bus tickets? Is it legal? Can he be trusted? I had learned to deal with them by now and had become more direct, almost rude, intolerant of rambling questions: I thought about ticket offices all over the world and that you can't stand there unloading your angst on the hapless salesman, and I adopted a take it or leave it approach. It seemed to work, the buses were always full, we were making money and I managed to pay back Je Yang. We never talked about the legality of the operation.

One morning I was teaching at the Shata School when Roger burst in. He had just returned from the Changtang and he looked like a wild man with long straggly hair and a red, sunburned, grinning face. The class all said hello to him noisily. This would mean a change of routine although I doubted he would be ready to resume teaching immediately – he would surely need time to adjust from the wilderness. Maybe he wouldn't want to go back to teaching at all. I told myself to expect nothing and not build up my hopes.

Every other evening I was teaching Sir Woo in his little workshop where the only way in or out was by climbing through the front window. It was freezing and even when we closed up the hatch I could never get warm. Although Sir Woo was one of the hardest working students I had, he never seemed to make much progress and we would plod along. He couldn't master the pronunciation. It was becoming a bore but he paid a whopping five yuan (50p) an hour and this was a lot by local standards and I would often remind myself that beggars can't be choosers.

Je Yang would pop by some evenings and knock at the wooden boards of Sir Woo's hatch. We would open up, let him in and huddle round. We chatted in fluent English, and I welcomed his interruptions although I did feel slightly guilty at using Sir Woo's time to talk to my new friend. I hoped that some of our erudite conversation would rub off on him, like fairy dust. It was obvious from Sir Woo's sullen expression that he felt left out when we talked; I knew it was unfair on him and I was being a jerk. I didn't care. One of the first conversations I'd had with Roger after he got back was to try and persuade him to teach Sir Woo; I told him that this was the one person in town who would probably like to learn all the technical words he used (Sir Woo loved gadgets and technology). Roger thought about it for a few moments and then refused.

One evening Je Yang said he had to go to Xian (pronounced She Anne) in the middle of China to sit some exams to do with his job.

- This is a disaster, I said. What about our business? It's booming. You can't just walk away from it now.

- Why not? It doesn't matter if we stop the buses for a while. Our man isn't going anywhere and he's certainly not going to work with anyone else. He trusts us. And I've already told him we're going to Xian and he was okay about it.

- You said... we're going?...

- Rupert, I want you to come to China with me.

- Me? Come to China? Have you lost your mind? I can't go to China. I've just got back from India and I've got all this work after spending most of last year hustling for it. I can't throw it all away now. There's no way I'm coming with you.

- Please come. I have a friend in the government here and he can get us onto a new Russian plane that is only used by the military. We can fly all the way there, for free.

He had me. At the mention of the free flight across China and the secret military plane my imagination went wild and my sense of commitment to Lhasa faded away quickly. Je Yang was usually reflective and quiet but that day he was really happy – obviously because of his decision to travel. I caught some of this enthusiasm and started thinking of justifications for the trip; it was a chance to see the Motherland and travelling in China was why I had come here in the first place.

Once I had taken the decision to go to China with Je Yang it all came together remarkably quickly: Roger had turned up in the nick of time and could take his class back – I wasn't going to give him the option of passing it onto me – the bus was on ice and Sir Woo would have to do without his English teacher for a while.

- Poor bugger, I said to Je Yang later.

- What do you mean?

- Sir Woo, he's always getting dumped by me.

- He'll survive.

The mysterious military plane never materialised and was soon forgotten, and I did harbour a suspicion that Je Yang had invented the story in order to get me to travel with him – in which case I was grateful as I realised that I might not have made it into China at all. It was so far away and I didn't have any contacts or anywhere to go apart from a vague desire to see Shanghai. Je Yang attempted to negotiate a lift in a government vehicle but I knew from experience back home that government vehicles, and especially planes, would never take hitchhikers and the chances of them giving me – a Capitalist Roader from Western Europe – a lift was quite unthinkable.

- Je Yang, I said.

- Yes.

- Let's go to the bus station at six in the morning and try our luck on public transport.

- Er...um...

- I'd like to show you how I travel, and I know the bus station is a hive of activity early in the morning, and then dead quiet for the rest of the day. If we show up early we'll surely be able to get a bus to Golmud and from there we can get a train.

- Er, um...okay then.

The following morning we met outside Sir Woo's shop, which was en route to the Bus Station. We didn't disturb him as it was pitch-black outside and there was nobody on the streets; even the dogs were still sleeping. I felt like a conspirator and the effect was exhilarating.

It took hours of hassle, delays and arguments in order to get onto one of the big old Japanese buses that was heading to Golmud. Finally we were trundling up through the mountains. I wondered why it had been so difficult to get a ticket considering the bus was half empty. It was old, very long and a lot more comfortable than any other bus I had been on in the country. The idea of sitting on it for the next two days wasn't so bad. We chatted, listened to music and dozed. After passing through the mountains north of Lhasa the landscape was as flat as a pancake and totally bleak.

The road from Lhasa to Golmud (pronounced Ger Moo) was Tibet's main overland link to China. I had read somewhere that Golmud was the staging post for the colonisation of Tibet and the road had been built with Tibetan slave labour in the fifties. It was asphalted all the way and maintained by gangs of workers who lived in rickety little wooden barracks, which we would frequently see by the side of the road. These road workers were the only inhabitants I saw on the Changtang. The plain stretches all the way north from Lhasa to the Mongolian border, across an ethnically Tibetan region called Amdo. China had taken control of this region in the 1920s and re-named it Qinghai (pronounced Ching High). It was a vast area of rocky desert, the size of Western Europe, with a population of about five million.

Golmud is connected to mainland China by rail and our plan was to get the train to Xian. The road never seemed to end, even though the bus was going fast. We passed convoy after convoy of military trucks, many teeming with green-clad soldiers.

- Why are so many soldiers coming into Tibet? I asked Je Yang.

- Everyone says there will be war with India.

- Why?

- I'm not sure. They say it will take place in the border region just south of Lhasa, and they keep sending troops from the Russian border in the north.

After fourteen hours of driving we stopped at a lonely concrete shack in the middle of the vast, windswept plain. It was a dark, filthy dive but we were glad to get the chance to sleep. We all queued up to get a ticket for the unheated dormitory where we settled down on metal bed frames – there were no mattresses – underneath grimy blankets that had been provided by the truck stop. No sooner had I fallen asleep that there was a commotion, shouting and people moving around – we had to get up and go after just four hours.

I was more exhausted than before and stretched out flat on the back seat, which was long, wide and comfortable. I wondered why nobody else had occupied it. Feeling rather pleased with myself I lay down and soon fell asleep. Then I discovered the problem with these old buses, which hadn't been serviced properly for years; the shock absorbers weren't working and when we hit a big bump I was thrown violently up into the roof and then came crashing onto the floor. The sound of me crunching into the aisle attracted the other passengers' attention, many of whom thought it hilarious. I rubbed my bruises, old phlegm and cigarette butts off my clothes, wondering why the bumps had such an exaggerated effect on the back seat. It was as if I'd been catapulted.

By the evening of the second day we were in Golmud, a town that seemed desperate and without character. It was set in a landscape of endless gravel and the sky was a muggy grey blanket with no trace of blue.

We checked into a concrete hotel where the staff were as hostile as the surroundings. Perhaps this was an auspicious start to our journey: things could only get better.

Je Yang's route to Xian was the longest possible, passing through the Gobi Desert and the province of Xinjiang (Shin Gee Ang) first. He had fiddled an extra week of leave from his boss so that we could get a glimpse of north-west China, which was in the other direction to Xian. He reeled off names of places we should visit but I couldn't take it all in – I would forget each unpronounceable name as soon as he said it – and was content to relax, let him make the decisions, just do what I was told, help out when needed and observe the surroundings.

From Golmud we travelled by bus through the northern part of Amdo and entered the Chinese province of Gansu, aiming for Dunhuang (Dune Wang) where there were some caves Je Yang wanted to see. We were still travelling across an endless plain but this one felt completely different from the Changtang, it was somehow more accommodating to human presence. This was the area, I had been told by a traveller, where China had operated big prison camps, where millions had apparently died of cold and starvation. Since Golmud, we had lost the connection with asphalt and were back on the gravel roads I had become used to in Tibet.

The bus was small, overcrowded, cramped and slow. The atmosphere was buzzing with different ethnic groups – the Chinese call them Minorities – talking in different languages; Tibetans heading north, Han Chinese going east and Xinjiang people heading home and shouting at each other in a language that I had heard was related to Turkish. We passed lots of goats, people on camels wearing the white clothing of the Bedouin and I realised that China is a lot more ethnically diverse than I had assumed; they didn't all wear the same navy blue uniforms that everyone in Tibet seemed to wear.

We crossed into the Gansu Desert – a real desert with sand dunes, cacti, goats and people on camels – more exotic and mysterious than the featurelss gravel we'd been staring at for the last few days. As we drove towards the sunset, through the yellow dunes, I felt a quiet longing and deep sympathy for the desert, an inexplicable feeling of compatibility; I was being hypnotised by the sand, attracted by the prospect of being out there, utterly alone. I felt a spiritual connection with the place that I couldn't understand, although it did help me understand what drew people like Big Jack and Roger to spend so much time in the wilderness.

The twelve hour bus journey had all the ingredients of being complete hell but it passed with remarkable speed. Before I knew it signs of greenery and urbanisation became visible. We were approaching Dunhuang. The town was surrounded by fields and my first impression was that someone had splashed green paint across the arid landscape – a mosaic of colours – and when I looked closer I saw an intricate patchwork of fields, separated from each other by thin lines of trees, all of which had been cut to head height, as if they'd had their hair cropped. Every field was a hive of activity, people were moving around busily. I had no idea what they were doing: it seemed like the land itself was full of frantic energy.

The road led past grim-looking factories to a vast, gaudily-lit archway – the whole structure draped with scores of coloured light bulbs, and Chinese characters in flashing neon lights making its concrete pillars illusory. This was the entrance to the town, which was plastered everywhere with huge neon slogans and after the monotony of the desert I found it exciting.

We squeezed off the little bus and I immediately felt a freshness in the atmosphere, a cackling buzz of busy, friendly people and the whirr of continual bicycles passing by. We checked into a hotel, which was breathtakingly clean by our standards, went in search of food and found a simple cafe that oozed quality. Je Yang ordered mountains of food and our taste buds were sent reeling by the spicy, fresh deliciousness of everything we ate. I could see the cook standing in a flickering light over his wok that was lit up by a coal fire underneath. We sat back, feeling replete and asked for the bill. We were shocked: the price was ludicrous, we had eaten like kings yet the cost was about a third of what we would have paid in Tibet. We leaned back in our chairs and Je Yang gave me an affectionate smile and I realised that he had grown in confidence since we had reached main land China; he was losing his sheepishness and becoming more expressive. We wandered happily back to the hotel, savouring every moment.

We both woke at dawn the following morning. I was not got used to the strange sensation of sleeping on clean linen. We had a quick breakfast, hired bikes and rode to the Buddhist caves that were about twenty miles away. After about ten miles the green vegetation that surrounded the town ran out and we were riding through desert; wisps of sand danced across the road. The caves had once been on the Silk Road, an ancient trading route that went from Xian to Constantinople.

In ancient times this area had been green, forested and a popular stopping place for travellers. Over a thousand caves had been in use at one time as temples, shrines and places to store treasures. A small army of Buddhist monks looked after them. Then came desertification, the decline of trade and roving bands of marauders. The most important caves were sealed and deliberately buried, to protect them from robbers, and others were swallowed up by the desert. For hundreds of years the area was abandoned and the caves forgotten – until 1900 when a Daoist monk found a cave full of papers, textiles and paintings. Most of these treasures were bought by Aurel Stein, an Anglo-Hungarian archaeologist who was exploring the area. In Britain he was feted as a hero and knighted for bringing back so much ancient material to London's museums. In China he was branded an imperialist grave-robber, pirate and thief.

Visiting the caves was a disappointment. We only saw a few and they were empty and unimpressive; Je Yang asked around and was told there were some huge statues of Buddhas and other artefacts but they were all locked up and we weren't allowed in. The only people we came across were Chinese officials and workers. One of them told us they were preparing for millions of Chinese tourists. None of them looked like they wanted to be there and it lacked the atmosphere and mystery of Tibetan monasteries; there was something sterile about the place, as if it had no heart. I started to feel bored, tired and irritated and wanted to leave. We rode back to town, ate another delicious meal and got the evening bus to Liuyuan (Lee You Anne).

The landscape we passed through that afternoon reminded me of descriptions from J.R.R.Tolkein's Lord of the Rings; wave after wave of yellow, brown and black mountains, empty of people and full of rock and mystery. The bus was small, packed and slow and I was crushed up against the engine at the front, trapped by a metal bar and baking from the engine's terrific heat. But I had a spectacular view and flirted with the pretty conductress, and the driver agreed to play Je Yang's jazz funk tape. The bus's ancient speakers distorted the sounds blasting out and it gave the journey a surreal quality. Despite the crush of people, the unbearable heat and continual bumps there was a good atmosphere, a camaraderie, and the journey passed quickly.

By dusk the rocky landscape gave way to the concrete buildings of a town, Liuyuan. Even though the bus was small there were so many people crushed inside that it took ages for us all to get off. The air was cool and breezy with a whiff of coal in the air. There was a brisk atmosphere, people were hurrying around and the buildings were dark and imposing.

We made our way to the railway station for the 22:30 to Urumqi (Oo Room Er Chee) and were grateful for the heat in the waiting room, which was crowded, old fashioned and strangely silent. I could hear the tick of the clock on the wall and a slight murmur of voices from a group of people who stood round a large iron stove. I was impressed by the cleanliness of the station, the air of efficiency and the neat, purposeful officials. As the hand of the big clock on the wall approached arrival time there was a change of gear: voices were raised, luggage and families were gathered up and a stream of railway officials emerged from the back, buttoning jackets and fitting on peaked caps.

A wild scream that seemed to come from across the desert shattered the calm of the waiting room. It was the whistle of the train and the piercing sound created a sudden panic, as if we'd been warned that a marauding army was approaching. There was a rush for the door. Hundreds were already on the platform and there was a mass jostling for position as a vast, dark green, steaming monster shuddered and hissed into the station. It ground slowly to a halt, throwing out curtains of steam and making sharp, metallic clunking noises.

The crowd was like a cast of extras in a 1920s black and white film; we shuffled and moved, en masse from one position to another as we tried to line up in front of the doors. There was barely controlled hysteria as if disaster awaited anyone who didn't get on board. Our efforts were in vain as people were spewing out of each door, like toothpaste being squeezed out of a tube, and we had to make way for them. A few minutes later everyone was on board, the crush and panic forgotten, and the officials were clucking around the platform, checking their clipboards and preparing for departure. Although many on board didn't have a seat, a sense of calm descended within. The train shuddered, whistled again then started moving. It took a few minutes to adapt; we had just been in a silent town in the desert and now we were in a completely different environment.

Je Yang pushed his way purposefully between the people who were occupying every inch of corridor space, many of whom seemed content to remain standing where they were, presumably unable to afford a seat and grateful to be on board and moving. Some were sleeping standing up, and moved to let us past without waking up. We made our way through several carriages until we found our assigned seats. Je Yang was determined to get us Hard Beds, the term for sleeper berths, and when he found the

official in charge of tickets he used every ounce of charm and persuasion
to get his way. He succeeded and we were shown two comfortable looking
bunks, far better than what I had been led to expect from the travellers'
tales of terrible Chinese trains. There was no door to the bunk space we
had been allotted but I liked the fact that we were part of a community
within the carriage.

The train looked as if it had been designed and built in the fifties,
perhaps earlier. The lighting was subdued and subtle and the colours were
tasteful – bottle green and cream. The surfaces all seemed spotlessly clean
and there was a homely feeling in our carriage. We sat down on little fold-
down seats by the window among a group of friendly people from Hunan
(Her Nan) Province.

- Where's Hunan? I asked Je Yang.

My question sparked curiosity from the group and a map of China was
found, opened up and spread out between us. They pointed to where we
were in the north-west part of the country and then to Hunan, deep in
the south-east. Je Yang said it was exotic and hot down there with some
amazing landscapes, and he got talking to our new friends who had been
on the train for almost a week. They looked relaxed and intelligent,
quite different from the Chinese people I had met in Tibet. They were
as interested in us as we were in them and Je Yang spent the evening
translating endless questions and answers.

The train thundered through the night and our group retired to the bunk
beds, stacked three high. I wasn't tired and sat on one of the fold-down
seats by the window and stared out into the black night, thinking about
the Takla Makan Desert outside, so alien to this self-contained world of
the train. Attendants walked through the carriage frequently, one carrying
a clipboard and the other a bucket and mop; one checking bed numbers
and the other mopping the floor. When I climbed into the bed I couldn't
believe how soft it was considering this was supposed to be Hard Bed class;
there was a thin layer of foam underneath a tough plastic covering, and
real cotton sheets. What luxury! What on earth had all those travellers
been complaining about? I went to sleep with a satisfied grin on my face.

We spent the next day staring out of the train's window and sometimes
chatting. Every now and then the attendants would appear with big
aluminium kettles of hot water and trolleys of steaming food. I had seen
in Tibet how people came to work with a flask of boiling water and a few
tea leaves. They would make a fresh cup of tea upon arrival and then keep

filling up the cup with more water, constantly diluting the tea, until they were drinking just hot water – which they called White Tea. We all held up our cups and the attendant filled them. I felt well looked after, almost pampered, as if I was a guest in someone's house.

I stared out of the window and wondered if this was the most lonely and deserted stretch of railway in the world. We were crossing the huge blank space that occupies the top left hand side of the map of China: the province of Xinjiang, which in Mandarin means New Frontier. When the Communists took over in 1949 and the People's Liberation Army were sent in to liberate the region there was some local resistance. Mao Tse Tung's brother was killed here. Je Yang said:

- If Xinjiang had a Dalai Lama they too would be demanding independence and getting world attention.

In colonial times the region was known as Chinese Turkestan and the majority had been ethnically Uighur (We-Gerr) with large Arab, Russian and Han Chinese minorities. Since 1949, millions of Han Chinese had been settled there and were becoming the majority. I looked at the nice people from Hunan around us and wondered if they were the latest arrivals; I presumed this was the main route that the migrants had taken.

Je Yang told me that China's settlement laws had recently been relaxed. Under the strict Mao regime everyone graduating from college was assigned a job, perhaps in a remote region, and had to stay there indefinitely. Now it was becoming more flexible and Je Yang had volunteered to come to Tibet because, he said, if you chose to come to one of the outlying regions you could go home after a few years – and get paid extra. Je Yang slightly resented the people of Tibet and Xinjiang because so many of them rejected China's civilising mission, a mission that he felt was costing the Chinese people a lot. We would argue for hours about the rights of people to self-rule and he would point to the fact that we, the British, had occupied much of the world with that same civilising mission. I tried to convince him that colonisation was really just one country exploiting another and all this talk of civilising the natives was just hot air; I didn't believe in the mission of the British Empire and I told him that when Britain lost her colonies after the Second World War, people in the UK didn't seem to mind much.

We arrived in Urumqi and what seemed like the population of a small town poured out of the train and filled up the platform, amid stacks of luggage and crowds of chattering, excited people. We entered the underground passage en masse and swept out into the street like a wave.

But the city centre was so huge that what had seemed like a massive crowd was soon absorbed, the furious wave breaking its energy and power on a sandy beach. Everything looked so big. Even the train, which had looked monstrous was now dwarfed by the station. A crowd of Chinese taxi drivers mobilised as soon as they saw us and started hustling for cab rides and hotel rooms. They had none of the charm that one finds in India; these people were pushy and devoid of humour. The big square that we found ourselves in was also without character; just a big, ugly concrete space. As we walked purposefully towards the nearest hotel I whimpered softly to Je Yang:

- Let's get back on the train.

Je Yang didn't share my grim impression of the place, at least not at first. He was delighted to have reached what he assumed to be a civilised city, although the officious attitude of the hotel clerk who scrutinised his travel documents made him think again. The view from the hotel only showed more concrete and when we walked around to explore the city all we saw was concrete. Everybody seemed unfriendly, even in the Muslim district where every other man hissed change money at us. The only good thing we found was the food.

At dawn the following morning Je Yang was at the railway station trying to get tickets to Xian. He came back with devastating news: we were stuck here for at least another two days. Time seemed to shudder to a halt. The next day, we wandered around aimlessly, each going our own ways. I crossed the railway lines, went through a slum where hundreds of families were scraping a living from mud and stone. Their shacks were made from scraps of wood, metal and plastic and plastered with mud. Some people were bent double pulling wooden hand carts that seemed to be full of junk. I followed a man who was toiling up a hill with a big wooden stick across his back; suspended from either side of the stick were two buckets, both full of water. He went towards a shack and I carried on to the top where I sat down and looked out over this grim city. Even the sun seemed to be dirty.

We spent the whole of the next day in the station, like listless tramps with nowhere to go. The ticket office was the size of the whole station back at Liuyuan and each ticket window was faced by a column of irate people. The closer we got to the ticket seller the more crushed we became. When we finally reached the counter Je Yang turned on his indignant, furious persona and started negotiating for tickets, while I tried to protect his back and stop people from pushing us out. He managed to get tickets on what they call Hard Seat, an equivalent of third class in India:

- You know what this means? Said Je Yang.

- No.

- We won't be able to sleep properly for four days.

- Why not?

- It takes four days for the train to reach Xian, and all the sleeper beds are sold out.

- I'm just glad to be getting out of here.

Our train was due at night and we spent the rest of the day wandering round the station, which seemed as big as a town. It was raining outside and the only colour, inside and out, was grey. The waiting rooms were vast, with people sitting, lying and sleeping in square formations, with corridors of spaces between them. Handsome Muslim men were swaggering up and down these spaces between the crowds, hustling the sullen Chinese to buy flick knives. As they sauntered along they talked, flicking their knives open every now and again. One of them looked at me, grinned, flicked open his knife and said in broken English:

- How much?

By the time we boarded the 23:30 to Xian (She Anne) I was resigned to sitting on a wooden bench for four long days. Having lost hope for comfort I was open to the atmosphere on the train and my sense of observation was in top form. Je Yang hadn't accepted our fate so easily and I followed him into the next carriage where we saw a scholarly looking man sitting behind a small wooden desk, hunched over his papers, lit up by a tiny desk lamp. It was the ticket reservation officer. Je Yang started gesticulating, cajoling, and trying to persuade the man to give us sleeper tickets. He was talking so fast that I couldn't understand a word he was saying. The officer stared at him blankly for what felt like hours, without saying a word, just shaking his head. Je Yang persisted and eventually the man relented and gave us two tickets for Hard Beds. This felt like a major coup.

Then disaster struck: a nasty-looking female official appeared, took one look at me and demanded that I pay three times the price. I refused. The woman then grabbed the tickets off the old gent at the desk, who didn't say a word, and told us that it's official Chinese policy to charge foreigners more. Je Yang told her that I teach English to Chinese people and get paid a local wage. She hesitated and I thought we would get away with it. There was a long pause and then she demanded to see my work permit, or some verification of this claim. I knew the game was up; I had never even heard about a work permit in Tibet and assumed there was no chance I would have been able to get one. With almost physical pain I dug into my money-belt, peeled out forty yuan, tossed it onto the table and cursed her in Scots dialect.

Because I was expecting the next four days to pass excruciatingly slowly, they didn't. I appreciated the comfort, food, atmosphere and all the characters on the train. The landscape gradually changed from spooky desert flats to black hills shimmering under a grey sky and, on the third day, traces of green. I knew that Xian would have a better atmosphere than Urumqi – how could it be worse? – although Je Yang had met some people who told him Xian is a terrible place: filthy, dangerous and expensive. By the time we reached our destination most of the passengers had already got off the train at the various places we'd stopped at, and there was a surprisingly small number who disembarked with us.

As soon as we stepped off the train at Xian station I knew that I liked the place. The station itself had an elaborate design and as we went into the street I could feel this was a proper, cosmopolitan city. After Urumqi it felt modern, welcoming and exciting. I had learned on the train that Xian was over 3,000 years old and had been the terminus for the ancient Silk Road trading route. I wondered why ancient cities tend to be so much more successful at being modern and attractive than new ones?

Je Yang didn't seem to be appreciating the wonderful place that we were in. As we walked into the city he told me that he couldn't stop worrying about the exams he had to take at one of the city's universities.

We hit the jackpot that evening regarding accommodation: a guest apartment in the teacher's wing of the university. We were speechless with awe, like a couple of peasants arriving in the big town for the first time, examining every detail of this most luxurious abode; an en-suite bathroom, hot and cold running water, huge windows with glass you could actually see through, clean sheets, wall-to-wall carpeting and perfectly plastered and painted walls. After the best shower ever and preening ourselves in the full-length mirror, we went down to eat in the canteen.

All my experience of food in canteens told me not to expect much that evening, but the food was exquisite and the prices were subsidised and absurdly low. We sat next to a dour-looking group of foreigners and I listened to their conversation to try and work out what country they were from. We hadn't seen a foreigner since leaving Tibet and I was keen to meet people and talk. When I worked out they were Russians I leaned over and tried to chat in English. Nothing. Just stares of incomprehension. They had probably come here to learn the language and when I tried talking to them in Chinese I got a blank look of incomprehension. I asked Je Yang to intervene and he said:

- Ni na li ren (where are you from?)

One of the Russians jerked his head round sharply, as if he'd been prodded in the back, with a look of disgust on his face. I thought I heard him hiss out the word Smolensk but wasn't sure. Maybe he had cursed us. They got their message through very efficiently: we don't want to talk to anyone. An American later told us that when the Russian students first arrived they had been really open and gregarious – until their Communist Party Group Leader had showed up, a guy called Boris – and then they all clammed up and cut themselves off from the other foreigners.

We had four days to kill before Je Yang's exams. I wanted to explore the city and I assumed he would be revising for the exams he'd been so worried about. To my surprise he wanted to walk around the city with me. My second impression of the city was less enthusiastic; the main problem with Xian seemed to be pollution. There was a heavy blanket of smog hanging over the city, clogging the sunlight and turning everything slightly grey. The air was muggy and sticky. It smelt bad and after walking around for a few hours I felt like collapsing.

In 1974 some peasants near Xian were digging for a well. They uncovered a head of a statue and further digs revealed the Terracotta Army: hundreds of ancient clay statues of soldiers dating back more than 2,000 years. The statues were in perfect condition and it became an international media sensation: the greatest archaeological find of the twentieth century! Visitors flooded in and Xian became one of China's top tourist destinations. Unfortunately the peasants who found the treasure trove lost their land and weren't compensated.

We didn't have the energy to wait in the massive queue to see the statues and I felt sorry for those who had travelled so far to see them. Instead we visited the huge city walls, which had been renovated with modern materials that made them look new – their ancient charm had been painted over.

The best thing about the city was being accosted by chatty people. I was intrigued by a pretty young Chinese girl who had the courage to come up and chat to me in front of her friends. Her name translated as Swallow and she said she wanted to practice her English and asked if we could we meet that evening in a nearby park. How could I refuse?

Meanwhile, Je Yang had been collared by a smarmy youth whose confidence indicated a life of privilege – it turned out his dad was a local Communist Party boss. He insisted on conversing with Je Yang in English which he spoke fluently – with an irritating American accent. Although he talked constantly he didn't say anything of note and we nicknamed him The Windbag.

My meeting with Swallow, by a lake in the park, could have been romantic if I hadn't been so wary of getting involved with Chinese women, especially ones as young as this. Everything about the scene was wrong; there was rubbish lying around the park, the ancient pagoda looked like it had just been built and our conversation was inane. Her English was bad and we switched between English and Chinese. The only thing we talked about was pop music. I quickly got bored with Swallow. With Je Yang I could talk endlessly about the meaning of Chinese words and their etymology but if I tried to talk to him in Chinese he would wince in pain at my terrible pronunciation. Those who didn't know English seemed delighted that I was trying to learn their language.

Je Yang's anxiety was increasing by the day, even though he didn't feel the need to revise for his exams. He was usually so relaxed about life and it was strange seeing him under pressure. He explained that the Chinese tend to be afraid of exams as their future prospects totally depend on them, especially in the public sector. To an extent he was protected from the intense civil service competitiveness by being located in Tibet, where few people wanted to go. I had read about ancient China where young men would have to study intensively for years, accumulating massive amounts of theoretical knowledge, before being hired as civil servants, or mandarins. Had the same work ethic been inherited by the Communists?

We met a small community of American teachers in the university; they were living in the same compound that we were staying in but for some reason their movements were restricted and they had to respect a curfew. This made them feel trapped and there was an air of frustration about them. For the first time I noticed the wall that surrounded the compound and the guards who kept an eye on people coming and going. They were amazed that I had managed to find teaching work in Lhasa without going through official channels and Molly, the most lively of the bunch, said:

- Finding unofficial teaching work here in Xian would be impossible.

The PSB [Public Security Bureau] would be breathing down your neck in ten minutes. It's awful.

While Je Yang slogged through his exams I spent a lazy day in the luxurious apartment of Shelley, another of the American teachers, listening to Bruce Springsteen (glory days they pass you by). On the one hand I appreciated the comfort, conversation, books and music in Shelley's apartment – on the other hand I felt a bit claustrophobic, enclosed and static. My urge to travel was kicking in and I was itching for momentum, for the road. When I met Je Yang later that day he had a particular grin on his face that told me he had done well. I asked if we could go and he said:

- Go? Of course we can go. Let's get out of this place, this awful tense place. Oh Rupert, if only you could have felt the tension in that exam room. It was terrible.

We said goodbye to the Americans, hurried back to our apartment, stuffed our gear into the rucksacks – and hit the road. We boarded a packed bus that was heading to the station and I relished the thought of more days on the train. But which way to go? Shanghai? Back to Lhasa where I needed to establish some order into the life I wanted to live there.

The temptations of travelling east were irresistible, especially with Je Yang urging me to come to Beijing with him:

- It's our capital city, a glorious place with famous sites.

- I will agree to come if you agree to leave again, as soon as we can.

- I do.

- What about Shanghai? Why don't we go there? I've always wanted to go to Shanghai.

- No, it's too far and I don't want to go there.

I knew that Je Yang's real reason for visiting Beijing was to find opportunities to emigrate, and to deposit his stash of US Dollars. He obviously wanted me to come along so why not? I was sure I wouldn't be coming back to China anytime soon, although I did still want to see Shanghai at some point. The train we found ourselves on that night was less comfortable than we had experienced thus far, and we'd had no problems getting tickets. We were in the Hard Seat section where the atmosphere cackled with life. The people in this class of seating were more down-to-earth than the genteel folks we had travelled with before; they had no inhibitions and I found it fascinating to watch them argue, shout, tease each other and eat.

We chugged through north east China towards Beijing, the centre of this particular universe, and I thought about the old name for China: The Middle Kingdom. In ancient times it was so much more advanced than every other country that the Chinese considered themselves above everyone else, with a special mandate from heaven. The term middle has two meanings as far as I could make out: the ancients believed they were located in the middle, between earth and heaven. The other meaning was that China was at the centre of the known world. Even the modern name of China – Gwung Joe which translates as Middle Country – relates to this concept. This concept was one of the many old things that the Chinese Communists had retained; other things were the over-complex bureaucratic system and the colonial mission to conquer and control neighbouring countries. It's ironic that the Cultural Revolution, which had challenged old ways of behaviour and destroyed ancient monasteries and monuments, didn't question Mao Tse Tung's highly personalised rule which, in many ways, was a carbon copy of how the Chinese Empires have always been run.

I dreaded the long night ahead with no prospect of stretching out on a bed, but it passed quickly as I drifted in and out of sleep. I was sitting by the window, which was wide open, and if I leaned forward I could place my head on the corner of a tiny table that was fixed under the window. I enjoyed the warm night air and whenever I woke up with a stiff neck or numb arm, I would look around and go back to sleep. Je Yang was sleeping deeply, with his head resting on the cardboard tube from a roll of toilet paper.

Beijing was cold, dirty and vast. The crowd that flooded off the train dissipated almost immediately in streets as wide as rivers. There seemed to be millions of faceless people walking by and the buildings looked grey, featureless and dead.

I had the name and address of a Cantonese couple who lived in Beijing from a friend in London who had been here. We didn't have a phone number and hadn't written so had no idea if we could stay. Fortunately the couple seemed delighted to see us and welcomed us in. Their home was in a tall block of flats and seemed very modern; it reminded me of council flats in the UK. They fed us, showed us into the spare room and the talkative husband insisted on taking us to see the city's main tourist attraction: The Forbidden City. He was an artist and his wife stayed at home looking after their baby.

Next to our room was a balcony which was stashed full of paintings and sealed off from the weather by windows. I noticed a plastic bowl with some nasty old meat in it and I asked our hostess, who was watching me as I checked out their balcony:

- What's the meat in that bowl?

- It's dog meat.

- You eat dog meat?

- I don't eat dog meat -- it's a disgusting habit. My husband is from Canton and they love dog meat. They're very uncivilised down there.

The following morning we went to the Forbidden City, the complex of temples and palaces that had been the residence of the ancient emperors and the centre of the imperial government. The architecture was impressive but all the buildings had been over-restored, as in Xian, and looked as though they had been built, or at least painted, recently. Looked at in a certain light you could say it looked like a theme park, or something in Las Vegas.

I knew that the main requirement in restoring old buildings is to use the same materials that were originally used, even though it is more of a hassle. The material that can most easily ruin the appeal of an ancient building is paint: making paint the old way is really time-consuming and difficult. Using modern paint is much quicker but it can make an ancient building look new. Je Yang and our host were enthused by the place. I felt bored and exhausted; the heavy air pollution was getting to me. As Je Yang listened to our host's diatribe against the system I carried the baby, which the Dad had gallantly offered to take out for the day. I looked into the baby's eyes and found more interest in that new life than in all the ancient structures around us.

Suddenly I was surrounded by a crowd of Japanese schoolgirls, giggling and forming up around me. I could tell they were Japanese as they were dressed in modern clothes and walked with a confidence that I rarely saw among Chinese people. The schoolgirls were taking a group photo and liked the idea of having a westerner with a baby in it. The girls squeezed closer, giggled more and a series of shots were taken. Then they came one by one, linked arms with me and smiled like the Cheshire cat, as a series of individual photos were taken. I felt like a celebrity and a hundred young girls shouted:

- Bye bye!

The next day was a Sunday and we went out – with the wife this time – to the local park. There were so many amenities constructed within it that there was almost no sense of nature; it was just a series of roads for pedestrians with some trees in the background. It was crowded and I noticed that we weren't the only family with just one child. I thought about China's notorious one-child-per-family law, with the result that parents are punished for having more than one child. There were stories of female babies being thrown in village rivers because it was important to have male offspring to carry on the farm. What I noticed in the park that day was how pampered and controlled these city kids were. In Tibet the kids were allowed to run free; here the mothers and grandparents seemed to be constantly shouting: stop climbing that tree...don't run too fast... don't get messy... and keep the noise down. The closer I looked the more grandparents I saw looking after small children; obviously they had been brought in to look after the kids while the parents worked. Was this the result of their new economic system, which was turning towards capitalism? Would children now be micro-managed from birth by grandparents, and parents be so busy working that they wouldn't have time for their kids? I wondered what the future generation of Chinese people would be like? A lot less humble than the current generation, I assumed.

My itchy feet were becoming unbearable but Je Yang had things to do at the embassies and all trains east had been booked up for weeks in advance. We were stuck in Beijing, a nightmare prospect, and we couldn't afford the price of an air ticket. Je Yang had an old friend of a friend in the main railway station; and at the local Post Office he made calls, send telegrams and did what he had to do to find this man. He was turning the wheels of Gwan She, which means useful relations, as the only means of getting out of town.

We visited the embassies of some western countries to enquire if Je Yang could use his beautiful English, and university degree, to study abroad. The response was negative and at the British Embassy they were downright rude. The embassy staff said they were tremendously busy and made it clear they had no time for a couple of provincials like us. My faith in my British passport diminished and I felt real shame at the indifference with which Je Yang was treated; none of them showed any trace of appreciating his accent, or asking what he could do, and their body language said: Please go away. We're important and busy and you're not. We've heard your pathetic story a million times.

After a week I was feeling lonely and bored and I regretted having come to Beijing. Still there was no word from Je Yang's mysterious contact at the station and I wondered how long we would be stuck in this polluted city. After many days of hanging around our friend's flat there was a knock on the door. It was Je Yang's friend with the contact in the railway station. He was about thirty, wore a blue Mao cap and had a big smile on his face. He shouted out Je Yang's name, they hugged, chatted incessantly and went out for a walk together, but not before Je Yang translated the key information that this man had brought:

- He says we must be at the station tomorrow night and everything will be alright.

- What about the tickets? Does he have tickets for us?

- Don't worry about them. We'll sort it out and by tomorrow night we will be on the train to Golmud.

The following evening we went to the main railway station and met up with Je Yang's friend again. He led us through a vast underground hangar that was being used as a parking space for a fleet of old trucks, past mountains of parcels that were being processed by hundreds of people who, at first glance, looked like ants. We went through long, dark tunnels that smelt of urine and heard the rumble and thunder of trains passing overhead. Eventually we got to a long, dark train and we were standing by the side which was facing away from the platform. All the doors were shut and I noticed that Je Yang's friend had disappeared. I felt cheated and annoyed and wondered if Je Yang had given that guy money to lead us out here. Then a door of the train cracked open and a kindly old gent waved us over.

- Who the hell is that? I asked Je Yang, who didn't answer.

Je Yang climbed aboard and I sheepishly followed, not knowing what was going on. The old gent and Je Yang seemed to be engaged in a very polite discussion about all sorts of irrelevant issues, like the weather, and I was getting increasingly frustrated. Who was this old buffer? He looked like a retired teacher-turned-railway-attendant. Fortunately I managed to keep my mouth shut. Then Je Yang turned to me with a triumphant smile on his face and held up a piece of paper with a handwritten scrawl on it.

- What's that? I asked.

- This piece of paper is going to get us everything we need.

- What do you mean? Who is that guy?

Je Yang wasn't listening, he was powering through the carriages and I had to run to keep up. When he reached the carriage he was looking for he showed the note to a sullen attendant – whose attitude immediately changed. The uniformed attendant became polite and attentive; he jumped to attention, pulled out sheets and pillows and, with a sense of consideration I had never seen in a Chinese man, showed us a couple of comfortable looking bunks. He asked Je Yang that if there was anything else we needed – anything – he could be contacted at any time. Je Yang was still smiling and while I shared his sense of exhilaration at this sudden upturn in our fortunes, I couldn't understand how it had happened.

- What the hell was all that about? I asked. Did you bribe the old man?

- Of course not.

- So how did we end up with these beds and why is the attendant being so polite?

- That old man, as you so rudely say, is the main boss of Beijing Central: this station.

- But...how...?

For the next four days we watched northern China slip by. My thoughts were already in Lhasa and I wasn't feeling very sure of myself. I'd been away for too long and I would have to start hustling for work, money and accommodation; and then there was the visa to worry about. Je Yang and I didn't talk much on that journey, partly because we didn't have much to say after so long on the road together, but mainly because he had become embroiled in an endless series of discussions with three unusual looking men.

The big man was from Manchuria, the region to the north-west of Beijing; he was broader than the others. I wondered if his features were Mongolian? Or Russian? He spoke fluent Mandarin and I didn't want to ask questions and get sucked into their endless debate. The second man looked like a typical, short Han Chinese citizen and if I concentrated hard on what he was saying I could more or less follow the essential words. The third man was wiry, thin and belonged to one of China's many ethnic minorities; he spoke incredibly fast and I couldn't understand a single word he said.

I wasn't too happy about being on the outside of this intense group, but I had picked up a book in Beijing that I couldn't put down – Money by Martin Amis, a tale of a degenerate Brit who lived in New York City, had a high flying job, consumed industrial quantities of cocaine and alcohol and behaved like a hooligan. It was hilarious and I was much happier reading this than trying to understand what this group of four were talking about.

Sometimes Je Yang would turn to me with a grin and give me a two-minute summary of a discussion they'd been having for the last four hours:

- We've been talking about government corruption.

- Oh yeah?

- We were just hearing about a big government official in Manchuria who was in charge of a region that had just built a huge hydro-electric dam. At one point he had a visiting delegation and he wanted to provide them with some drama and entertainment. So he ordered the flood gates of the dam to be opened so it created a tidal wave. Unfortunately the district down-river got completely flooded. That was his idea of fun.

- My God, that's terrible.

- The man from central China told us about what happened in his area during the Cultural Revolution. The Red Guards came to destroy a temple and next to it there was an ancient, and very sacred, statue of a frog. They dynamited the statue and when the dust had settled they saw that a snake, a real live snake, was sitting where the frog had been. All the people there agreed that this was a really bad omen.

Gradually we left the flat, green eastern part of China behind us and entered the arid flatlands of Western China. After crossing the Yellow River, which was grey, we changed trains at an anonymous station and entered the endless Tibetan Plateau. I felt better, as if I were coming home. I felt much more at home in the wilderness than in the big cities, although I couldn't explain why. The last train we travelled on, to the final station of Golmud, was ramshackle and buzzing with the atmosphere of Tibet. I couldn't wait to get back.

When leaving Tibet I remember thinking how lonely, concrete and vile Golmud had looked. But, having seen some big polluted Chinese cities, I felt a certain grudging respect for the place. There was something appealing in the spit-and-sawdust atmosphere of the place and I could see humour in the rough banter going on between the street hawkers. Above all I could see the clear blue sky and no trace of air pollution.

The Great Northern Plain, the Changtang, seemed to roll on endlessly as we trundled across it in an old Japanese bus. I stared out of the window at a gathering storm and felt my mind being emptied of all that I had experienced in China. At midnight we stopped at a place called Nag Choo, which means Black River, where we found beds in a mud-walled shack with a tin roof. I was oblivious to the cold, the smell and the filth – I was happy to be home and slept like a log. The next day we approached the mountains that mark the northern border of Lhasa and, as if by magic, the sun broke through the clouds and our entrance into the city was gloriously lit up.

By lunchtime we were in the Lhasa Bus Station and I was staring up at the sky.

- The air, I said to Je Yang. It's so clear. I can see every rock on that mountain over there.

We went to the nearby Lhasa Hotel, sat on comfortable deck chairs and wondered what was next. We had passed the Post Office and I had picked up a couple of letters from home. My friends' concerns with money and jobs seemed so alien to me out here; I didn't know what to think of my mother's proposal to visit for two weeks, so I dismissed the idea as being unlikely to actually happen. A truck appeared from Je Yang's work unit. We shook hands and he left.

I wandered slowly into town, soaking up the atmosphere and trying to adjust to being back. The letters from home had somehow unsettled me. The first place I came across was the Pemba Truck Stop and, to my surprise, they agreed to let me stay. They must have forgotten all the dramas and arguments of the previous year. I couldn't afford to stay in one of the guest houses.

In the streets people were talking about war. China was still sending thousands of troops to the Indian border and apparently they planned to seize some disputed jungle and swamp. I visited Sir Woo who told me that he was packing up his shop and returning to Shanghai, as were most of his friends. I heard that pressgangs were operating in the park behind the Potala Palace, seizing young Tibetans and forcing them to work for the army. The last thing Je Yang had said to me before being driven off to his unit was:

- I can't afford to be seen with you for a while.

- That's okay, I said, knowing that we were good friends and that it would indeed be risky for him to be seen with foreigners.

CHAPTER ELEVEN

Even though it was a filthy dive I appreciated the Pemba Truck Stop's atmosphere and the raucous crowds who inhabited it. The fact that foreigners weren't allowed to stay there – but I was – made me feel very special. On that first morning back in Lhasa I noticed the disgusting sounds of people clearing their throats, spitting and someone having a coughing fit. The place was so incredibly dirty – there was literally nothing clean – and noisy. I got out of bed and looked through the grimy glass at the majestic Potala Palace; I opened the window to see better and a nauseating aroma of fresh human shit wafted up into my nose.

I was flat broke and worried. Never had I been so penniless on this whole journey; there were always some dollars stashed away in the depths of my money belt. My internal alarm bells were ringing – I had to find work, and fast. I went to the Shata School and they seemed pleased to see me; they said there is an English class that I could start with as soon as I was ready. But I wasn't ready; I needed a bit of time to unwind from the road, and I also wanted to look for more lucrative opportunities before getting stuck with English teaching indefinitely. Sir Woo tracked me down and with difficulty I postponed his lessons for a week. He complained about the threat of war with India, a threat that had resulted in all his friends going back to Shanghai. Last time I had seen him he was about to leave for Shanghai too and I didn't understand his explanation about why he had stayed.

A letter from the Exodus Travel Agency of London was waiting for me at the Post Office. Exodus would organise expeditions on converted trucks (the truck would become part bus, part camper van) across Africa and Latin America. They would also lead people on trekking tours all over the southern part of the Himalayas, in Nepal, and in the Latin American Andes. They had a representative in Kathmandu, whom I had met, a cockney Londoner who ran a fleet of ramshackle taxi cabs on the side. He had told me that they hadn't yet got anyone in Tibet and would like to organise treks there. I told him I'd like to be their first rep in Tibet – I didn't tell him how desperate I was for a job – although I doubted they would get back to me as they didn't know me from Adam and I had no relevant experience. But here was the letter right in front of me, in black and white, saying I could charge £40 a day, per person, to take their visitors into the mountains. That meant that if I had a small group of five that was £200 a day – a small fortune. I was rich! I started thinking about logistics and had a sudden moment of panic; could I do this? Nobody had organised treks in Tibet as far as I was aware and I wasn't exactly qualified; I hadn't organised a trek for anyone and I almost died of cold last time I attempted one.

I soon convinced myself that I could do this, I could learn, I could find the right people, equipment and routes. It couldn't be that hard. I started thinking about buses – Je Yang's driver was going to be useful – and I needed to find out where I could hire yaks and who would be the guides (Tsewong, one of our best students, sprang to mind and when I raised the issue he immediately agreed). What about food? How much to bring? Who would cook it? Would they eat tsampa and yak butter tea? I spoke to Chambay, the charming cook at the Snowlands and he immediately agreed to leave his tyrannical boss and head for the hills with me. I tried to get Chambay and Tsewong involved in planning out the logistics of the operation but they couldn't get their heads round it; all they thought about was how much money they were going to make. It was a long-term business prospect; if I could get this organised I would have a good income for years to come.

I felt more alienated than usual from the foreign travellers in town and was in no mood to meet them. They tended to take themselves far too seriously and most treated Tibet with a solemnity I found inappropriate and boring – but how were they to know that the Tibetans deal with their tough life with humour and irony? My only friend at that point was Paola from Italy, whom I had first come across at the Cheese Factory. She had long black hair and an air of elusive mystery about her. She was fluent in Mandarin and completely absorbed in the Tibetan culture and religion; she was also learning Tibetan the slow way – struggling with the complex grammar and archaic religious terms. She didn't want to take the short cuts that I had taken by learning the essentials on the streets and in cafes.

Paola was the only one I invited to the Pemba Truck Stop and she was able to blend in with the scruffy locals in a way that none of the other foreigners could have done. Even Je Yang would have struggled to have fitted in at the Pemba; his finely tuned sense of hygiene would have been offended and he wouldn't have been able to tolerate the smell. Paola would climb up the steep, sticky ladders-cum-staircases, sit with me on my creaky little bed and share intimate moments. She never complained about the noise, smell or chaos and I admired her for this. Our relationship was platonic and she didn't want it to become anything else, but the more time I spent with her the harder it became to suppress feelings of passion from bubbling up. Paola was, above all, a very spiritual person, and said she wasn't interested in romance, passion and all those worldly activities. I agreed with her in theory – as long as I could spend time with her – but I was desperate to get her into bed. If I got too close she would get up, pinch my cheek and say:

- You are il pericoloso. I must go.

No sooner had I started to feel settled, and was ready to take up my teaching duties, when disaster struck: Bettina Hertzog turned up on horseback. At first I didn't recognise her. Was this the beautiful German I had hung out with in Kathmandu? Her handsome features were sunburned and windswept and her long blonde hair was now brown. I had really fancied her in Kathmandu, even though I knew I didn't have a chance. That feeling had faded now that I had become totally absorbed with Paola whom, I was sure, I could win over if I was persistent enough.

Bettina had ridden all the way from Kathmandu, a journey that had taken over a month. She had travelled with an annoying American woman called Cheryl and they were in the process of splitting up. Bettina told me she couldn't go any further with Cheryl and had decided that I would be the ideal partner to ride with all the way to Chengdu, over a month to the east. Hang on a minute, did she say she wanted me to ride with her across Eastern Tibet?

- You must be out of your mind, I said, there's absolutely no way I can come with you. First of all I am very busy, about to start teaching. And I really need to earn some money. I can't afford to go. I'm broke. Secondly, I can't ride. I've barely ridden a horse in my life and there's no way I could ride one for a month. Thirdly, the eastern part of this country is dangerous and we might get attacked, robbed, kidnapped and murdered. Who knows what will happen?

- Well I say you are coming with me, she said with a smile and a look that said the decision was already made. You've got two days to get ready and then we're off.

- I can't. I keep telling you that I can't come.

She was a determined woman and dismissed all my arguments as irrelevant nonsense. She had decided that I would come with her and that was the end of the story. For the next two days I was tortured by the dilemma. Should I take up this opportunity to see the wild east of the country with a beautiful woman? Could I put this knowledge to good use for the Exodus work? I was afraid of horses, of liberated women, of Eastern Tibet and I was afraid of the unknown. I had settled into Lhasa and wasn't ready for a change.

I needed second opinions. Isabella was enthusiastic, she offered to lend me some hard cash and kept her advice short and succinct: Just go. Paola just looked at me wistfully and suggested I do what my heart told me. Je Yang wasn't sure. He seemed to need my friendship and thought the idea of riding through eastern Tibet completely insane. When I explained that Bettina knew a lot about horses he grudgingly gave me his blessing. He then told me that we couldn't do the bus business at the moment anyway, because the vehicle had been requisitioned by the army. What really convinced me to go was when I ran into Big Jack who said:

- Hey Rupert, did you meet that hot German babe?

- Who? Bettina?

- Yeah. She's looking for someone to ride with her through Eastern Tibet, and that someone is gonna be me. Yessir.

The day of reckoning arrived and with a severe case of butterflies in my stomach I accepted Bettina's offer of riding twelve hundred miles to Chengdu. I sensed that behind her determination was a powerful courage and as soon as I accepted the challenge to go I felt I had absorbed some of this courage, and this dispelled my shadowy fears. I packed up my affairs in Lhasa. Je Yang agreed to take on the new evening class at the Shata School; he would be a great teacher and the kids would love him. I asked Roger to help with the Exodus job by mapping out some trekking routes, and he agreed to work with Tsewong and Chambay on planning the food and logistical side of the job. I doubted they would do anything, and knew I could pick it all up when I got back. With some of the money I had borrowed from Isabella I bought the scruffy-looking horse from Cheryl, the annoying American, and went to the market in search of the various bits and bobs that horses need.

On the evening of departure my nerves were in shreds and I kept asking myself if this whole idea wasn't completely crazy – but it was too late to change my mind. I spent my last evening with Paola at the Pemba Truck Stop and I was already missing her. She said she needed to understand me better so she could protect herself from me, and asked if she could read my horoscope? Of course! She pulled out her notebook, asked some questions, scribbled some notes and said that my male side is peaceful but my female side is full of fire. This didn't make any sense but it sounded mystical and made her seem more attractive than ever.

We left the city under a cloud of black rage. Bettina was furious that I hadn't turned up until 8 a.m. that morning.

- What the hell are you doing with that lump of butter in your hands? She said.

- We'll need it for our tea.

- Get rid of it. We can't take any extra baggage!

- I need it...

- Not another word. Get rid of it now.

This wasn't what I had signed up for, I wasn't used to being bossed around like this. Who did she think she was? I withdrew into a sullen, dark mood and we rode out of town in a poisonous, silent atmosphere which lasted until the sun rose high into the sky. She broke the silence:

- The horses' needs must take priority over ours. If we look after them they will look after us.

This made perfect sense but I was in too much of a bad mood to admit it. I was really annoyed about our lack of equipment and humiliated by the fact that I had got rid of that lump of butter (having given it to a passing pilgrim). Bettina had insisted that we could only take the absolute minimum in terms of luggage: no big saddlebags, no spare clothes, no camping equipment, virtually no food supplies and no books or luxuries. The only things she would allow me to take were a bowl, a jacket, a small bag of tsampa, some money, an empty grain bag for the horses and a sleeping bag. The only thing I managed to smuggle past her eagle-eyed inspection was a packet of dehydrated Knorr soup. Her plan was to scrounge food for the horses three times a day from local villagers and this was why she needed me; she knew that I had a basic grasp of the language and assumed that I would be a good scrounger.

I was prepared for the worst on that first day and, as a result, really enjoyed the ride. The weather was perfect, the road was flat and the riding was easier than I had assumed. I rode until my bum ached beyond endurance and then walked beside the horse, leading it along at a fast march. By the afternoon my black mood had lifted, we were chatting and I was feeling light and jaunty. We passed the turnoff to the Ganden Monastery, which I had visited a few months earlier, and by early evening entered a stone-built village.

It seemed that the whole population of the village was staring at us. I said in a loud voice that we needed food for the animals. Nobody reacted. A long moment passed and I told Bettina that we must be patient and just wait for as long as it takes. After a while I pulled out some money, repeated my question and a man came forward and led us into the village, followed by a mob of ragged, chattering children who were intrigued by our every move. He took us to a small yard where chickens, ducks, pigs, sheep and horses all jostled for space. The animals seemed resentful at our intrusion – did they sense we would take away some of their food? – but the children were delighted. The man turned into a kind host and he sold us some grain for the horses, gave us tsampa and butter tea for ourselves and let us sleep in one of the outhouses. I felt happy and at home with these people and couldn't take the big smile off my face for the rest of the evening.

By the middle of the second day we had left the Lhasa Valley behind and the landscape was changing. The valleys were now wider, the small, cultivated areas were greener and the mountains were a deeper, darker shade of brown. The river that flowed through the flat- bottomed valley seemed to spread out in a delta, with lots of rivulets branching out and reconnecting to the main body of water, leaving vast areas of dry gravelly riverbed between.

I felt wonderful, and hungry – in fact the only thing I thought about was food. I was obsessing about the delicious Chinese food from street vendors in Lhasa, and hoped that somewhere in this wilderness we would find a Chinese cook who would offer us delicious sweet and sour meals at a roadside shack. I tried to prepare myself for the worst; there would be no roadside restaurants in this wilderness.

At evening we stopped at a lone house by the roadside where a tragic looking man was clutching a baby goat that was, he told me, only seven days old. He willingly gave us food for the horses, tsampa and tea for ourselves, and a dry place to sleep. This was Bettina's idea of a good evening meal. I wasn't sure I could take it for the next month. My craving for Chinese food didn't subside and as we settled down to sleep that night I grew glum about the prospect of eating barley flour for the next thousand kilometres. Bettina had got into the idea of roughing it, and she was one of the few foreigners I had come across who actually enjoyed eating tsampa. I harboured an illicit desire to eat properly at the first available opportunity.

The next day we struck gold – a ramshackle roadside shack that contained a Chinese cook making meals in a filthy black wok over a fire. I savoured every drop of pig fat, greasy vegetables and MSG (Monosodium Glutamate), the food additive that travellers love to hate. I wolfed down a second helping as Bettina looked on disapprovingly. I was beyond caring what she thought and felt a new determination to eat Chinese food at every opportunity – who knew how many more of these roadside gourmet outfits we'd find.

We soon learned that trucks were the kings of the roads – they would thunder by in clouds of dust – and vicious stray dogs were a constant threat. After having my leg savaged by a mutt and being almost pushed off the road by a truck, both on the same day, I learned to be more wary. The trucks were the bigger danger; if any part of the speeding vehicle touched us it could be lethal; and the drivers just didn't seem to notice us. The dogs, on the other hand, I could handle, and I practiced my stone throwing skills at every opportunity.

Getting food was harder than I had expected. The villagers didn't have much, they were wary of outsiders and there weren't many settlements. In the village of Rinjeeling I developed a technique for getting food and shelter: we would go into a village and choose the house that seemed most likely to take us in; the inhabitants would ignore my request for fodder and we would stand patiently in the street until they relented, which they invariably did. Once the horses were fed they would always give us something to eat and somewhere to sleep, usually in the yard. We would offer them money but they usually refused it. Patience was the key; to wait around, perhaps for hours, until they relented. I learned that just standing there for long enough can create a sort of moral pressure that usually results in getting what you want.

By the end of the first week all the excitement of travel I had felt when leaving Lhasa had faded away. I had agonising saddle sores on my bum, I was always tired and hungry, the horses needed constant cajoling to go on and Bettina's temper was like an explosive device that was ready to go off at any moment. When I thought that we had over a thousand kilometres to go I just wanted to lie down in the ditch, close my eyes and never wake up again. My saddle sores were so painful that I spent a lot of time walking alongside my horse and all I thought about was the incredible luxury of stopping and eating. I became numb to all other sensations, didn't notice the views any more, didn't hear when Bettina shouted at me. It was as if I was in a dream.

Bettina set a target of riding fifty kilometres a day. I assumed she based these targets on how long it would take her to cover distances at home in Germany, where the horses were well fed, properly sheltered and healthy. Bettina was in pretty good shape herself; not only was she tall, slim and beautiful but she was incredibly strong and tough. I felt like a 90-pound weakling by comparison. The skinny Tibetan horses didn't seem too happy to be on the trot all day and I moaned constantly about being exhausted, in pain and starving.

I lost track of time and space. I had no idea how long we had been riding, where we were or what was going on. I was way beyond pleasure, pain or sensation. I was just plodding along, putting one foot in front of the other. I passed the stage of complaining and feeling sorry for myself, all I could do was stumble blindly on. Meanwhile Bettina was riding cheerfully on, seemingly not feeling any fatigue or doubt and looking forward to another month of torture. At one point I told her I couldn't do this any more and I went over to the ditch at the side of road, collapsed into it and lay there in blissful comfort, looking at the sky and enjoying every moment of rest. I was panting with exhaustion and really felt I couldn't go on another step. She should have taken Big Jack, who could have marched to the Gates of Hell and back without breaking sweat. To my surprise she joined me in the ditch and showed her tender side; we cuddled and she admitted that she too felt tired. It was an intimate moment but I was so deeply exhausted that the idea of anything erotic didn't even cross my mind. All I wanted to do was sleep forever. The only sounds were the wind and the horses clomping around looking for grass; very few trucks seemed to use this road, even though it was the main route from Lhasa to Chengdu.

During the second week I was able to ride all day without feeling continually exhausted and my saddle sores were settling down. The landscape had changed again and now consisted of big wide valleys with distant mountains climbing out of them. We were heading up to a distant pass that was taking days to reach. We came across nomads, their yaks and tents, some heather the horses liked and the occasional sheep. We passed a village and I said:

- Bettina, we should stop here. God knows when we'll next find a village.

- Not yet, let's keep pushing on, we haven't reached our quota yet.

- Damn the quota, what if we don't find anyone?

- Have faith, she said with a charming smile. However much of a slave-driver she was, she could be so charming and persuasive that I couldn't stand up to her.

Hours later darkness had fallen and my stomach was in full protest. I was sure we wouldn't find anywhere to stay that night and we'd end up huddling in a ditch. Just after I had given up hope we came across a handful of brown buildings that seemed to blend into the dark earth. The walls were made of mud, the roof was turf and if it wasn't for the boisterousness of the Khampa tribesmen who shouted as we passed, we never would have seen the place.

- Do you have any hay? Asked Bettina in English, putting on her winning smile, showing a set of perfect white Teutonic teeth. I translated.

- Hay? Just look around you, said a young Khampa, and we looked at the vast, bleak landscape.

- I think he means no, I said to Bettina. There's no grass in this landscape and they probably don't have any hay stashed away. Let's stop here as they will surely let us stay. They look friendly and fun. We dismounted and joined them. Soon enough the young Khampa turned up with an armful of roots, which the horses devoured.

Having got the animals fed and tethered – always Bettina's top priority at each stop – we went inside one of the mud hovels. A family was sitting round a yak-dung fire, although there was no sign of the young men whom we heard shouting outside. With us round the fire was an old couple, a young boy and a beautiful teenage girl with gorgeous olive-coloured skin and long, shiny black hair. She looked like a goddess and I was falling under the spell of her beauty.

She had attached herself to Bettina and was leaning lovingly towards her, like a cat that was hungry for affection. Bettina responded in kind, putting her arm round the girl, stroking her hair in a manner that was loving and natural. They settled down to sleep on the bench they'd been sitting on and, for the first time on the trip, I felt pangs of sexual excitement pushing through the layers of exhaustion. I guiltily thought of a menage a trois with this pair, a gorgeous threesome, and immediately dismissed the thought as crazy and dangerous; what would the Khampa boys outside do to me if they found me messing with their beautiful teenage sister?

I turned my attention to the cooking pot that was hanging over the fire. There was some kind of evil-looking soup boiling away and I took out my penknife and started poking around in it, not really sure what I was looking for, just trying to steer my mind away from erotic fantasies. There was something big in the pot, like a stone, and I took a stick and fished it out. It was a sheep's head.

Hmm, this was interesting; perhaps I could use it to provoke Bettina, who was cuddling up to the teenager and already half asleep. I got to work on the sheep's head with my penknife and carved off a piece of its face:

- Fancy some lip? I said to Bettina, dangling a piece of gristly meat in front of her. The Tibetan girl didn't react. Bettina shot me a look of such horror that I felt a thrill of satisfaction. I held the meat above my mouth and ate it, smacking my lips in satisfaction. Bettina recoiled. I turned my attention back to the sheep's head and said:

- How about an eye? Some brain?

- You're disgusting!

The family were impressed with my antics with the sheep's head – obviously this was what they did – and they handed me a huge dagger, pointing out the joint at the back of the sheep's jaw, indicating that I should dig the dagger in deep and prise the jaws apart. I followed their advice, opened up the skull and proceeded to pick out the bits of gristle and share them round the room. When I got as much as I could from it I tossed it back in the pot. By now Bettina's shock and horror had passed and she had managed to find her humour; she was looking at me with a warmth and affection that I hadn't seen in her eyes before.

We slept together that night, in the yard, under a cold, spitting sky. They had given us a filthy old carpet that was heavy but, with a bit of imagination, felt like a downy. I was lying close to Bettina and, with my newly aroused sense of eroticism, was tempted by her beautiful body. There had been so much bad feeling between us over the last few days – I was still smarting from her bossy style – that to indulge in a sexual relationship would make things more complicated. It was better to resist her sexual magnetism as we would be constantly together for the next few months, and the last thing we needed was the kind of bitter arguments that real couples tend to indulge in.

The next day we reached our first high pass – a bleak, windy and frozen landscape where there seemed to be no living creatures. We took short cuts up the mountain, struggling up steep slopes of scree, a difficult surface that the horses managed with aplomb. They seemed to be bred to climb up steep mountains and they could follow us wherever we went. I was oblivious to the view at the top, not wanting to stop and think. As we trotted down the other side of the pass I felt a sort of hypnotic locomotion, only aware of the endless momentum of just keeping going. I had reached the point where riding, walking and running all day were no longer exhausting. It was almost becoming enjoyable.

That evening we approached what seemed to be a big town; in reality it was only about ten houses, including a decrepit restaurant, but to us it seemed like a metropolis. As soon as I saw the Chinese restaurant I moved towards it like a sleepwalker, unable to control the direction I was going in. The aromas of Chinese cooking were pulling me in as powerfully as if I were a fish on a line. I could hear Bettina shouting something about the horses taking priority, their need for food and then we could indulge. I wasn't listening. Her words were as irrelevant as the wind. She jumped off her horse and had to stand in front of me in order to pull me out of my trance. It took hours to find fodder for the animals that evening. Night had fallen but thankfully the restaurant was still open.

The restaurant was a low shack that was dark and smoky inside. The cook's fire radiated a heat that we luxuriated in. The aromas were heavenly and when the food came – rice and vegetables – I couldn't remember ever having eaten anything so delicious. I wolfed it down as though my life depended on it, shovelling the food in with chopsticks, taking gulps of Chinese beer and having to stop now and again to take gulps of air. Bettina was a model of self control compared to me; she ate with dignity and while I lay back burping and farting she was making calculations in her note-book; distances, quantities averages and estimates. She had kept a sharp eye on the little concrete posts that are planted by the road every kilometre, each of which was painted white and marked with the distance from Lhasa. I tried to avoid thinking about how little distance we'd covered and how much more we had left to do; I didn't like to look at those mile-posts.

We heard a truck roaring along the road, getting louder and louder. It slid to a halt in the gravel outside the restaurant and the engine was killed. There was a moment of silence and then came the sound of men jumping out of the truck, shouting and moving towards us. The door burst open and a big Khampa in a belted cloak stood silhouetted in the doorway; he stood there arrogantly, as if surveying his lands, and he feasted his dark eyes on Bettina, licking his lips. Bettina stared back at him and then laughed out loud, a reaction that seemed to break the macho spell he had momentarily cast over us. He was thrust aside by the rest of the group who poured into the small room and occupied every table. They had obviously been on the road for days and finding this small eatery seemed to make them wild with joy. They were burly Khampas, the macho men from the east, and they bantered noisily with the cook and took armfuls of beer. The room was bursting with the roar of ten people all talking at the same time and it felt like a feast from ancient times. When the bill came, their leader went to each of them demanding cash. This was obviously a ritual for them; they pled poverty and refused to cough up. He had to shout, slap and wrestle with some until they would dig deep into their cloaks and pull out a few coins.

That night we had beds – the first beds since we had left Lhasa – and even though they were simply iron frames with scraps of cardboard instead of mattresses, it felt like a proper hotel. The room was a concrete block with a door that wouldn't shut properly and a window that had been smashed long ago and boarded up. It was freezing and I went to sleep thinking: We're descending and it has to get warmer! I can't take this cold anymore!

From the dark, subterranean depths of deep sleep I heard a metallic clunk. Immediately I was awake, all senses on full alert. I heard the dragging of metal on gravel and the sound of a horse moving. One of the horses had pulled up its stake, which we had driven with real difficulty into the stony ground outside, and I could hear the drumming of hooves. The horses were running away!

Instinct kicked in and before I had time to process this bad news I shot out of bed, propelled by a demonic force that reacted so fast that it didn't seem to be mine. My big black cowboy-type boots were sitting by the side of the bed and my feet landed inside them as if it was an action I did every day at the Fire Station. In less than two seconds I was outside the room, sprinting, following the horse that had disappeared into a dark field. I was following the fading sounds of drumming hooves and running as hard as I had ever run in my life. I reached the top of a river-bank, leaped over and charged down the scree. The river-bed was dry and rocky; and there was the horse, struggling to get up the bank on the other side. I rushed to it, grabbed its halter and paused. It was Pungya, Bettina's horse, and it had almost managed to get away.

As I led Pungya back I realised that I had never reacted as fast as this in my whole life. I didn't know I could run that fast and I'd certainly never seen Pungya gallop like that. It was only at that moment that I started to process what had happened, putting together the sequence of events. What puzzled me was how I had gone from deep sleep to full sprint in a couple of seconds – without any conscious decision-making process on my part. Instinct had cut through normal rational thought, the sound of the horse escaping had somehow mobilised me in a way that was completely outside my experience. It was as if my mind was asleep during the whole run, and yet I did everything perfectly; as if I was being controlled by another brain, one that did this sort of thing all the time. Do we all have some sort of emergency response system that takes over at critical moments, bypassing the need for ponderous thought? If I had thought about what was going on, if I had said to myself I'll get up in a minute, or any of the usual dialogue that goes on in my head every morning in bed, the horse would have got away. I got back to the room, tied Pungya up to the back of a truck and flopped down on my bed – panting and burned out. I must have consumed an incredible amount of energy. The next morning I was exhausted but Bettina was grateful and sympathetic and she let me linger over breakfast a bit longer than usual.

The days ground by. Although we were sometimes covering sixty kilometres a day it felt as if we were making no progress at all. The distances were so vast, the landscapes so endless that Chengdu didn't seem to getting any closer. The scenery was changing and the more we descended the more green and lush it became; the valleys were becoming narrower and steeper. We came alongside a powerful river with white water that was roaring its way down a narrow valley. We could hardly hear each other talk above the din. At one point the river split around a tall rock that had a flat area on top, with trees growing out of it. Suddenly I had an idea and shouted across to Bettina:

- Let's stop here and go and live on that rock. It looks like paradise.
- Great idea.

It was getting harder to find villages and, when we did, getting food out of them was always a struggle. The villagers had worked hard to gather their food supplies and I sympathised with them for not wanting to feed us; I felt occasional pangs of guilt about being constantly on the scrounge. In one village an angry Communist Party official approached us and demanded to see our passports and authorisation to travel in this part of the country. He was red in the face, indignant and talking in the name of the state – meaningless in this wilderness – and he reminded me of drunks I had seen in Scotland. We stood there and listened to his lecture about authorisations, and hung our heads respectfully in mock shame. The storm of his anger passed and he became curious, almost sympathetic – and let us go.

The relationship with Bettina was still difficult but we worked out a rough system whereby we could function quite well. In the mornings we would argue like an old couple, in the daytime we would ride in silence and in the evenings we would talk. She told me about her father who had been a young officer in the German Army during the war. He was captured by the Russians and sent to a prison camp in Siberia. When they found out that he knew about horses they had him lead a group of Germans to accompany herds of fresh horses all the way across Russia, from Siberia to the front line in the west of the country. At the end of the war he was about to be released when they found some manuscripts on him – he was smuggling out the writings of his colleagues – and he was kept on in this job for many more years.

It took the Germans months to move the horses across Russia, walking all day every day. When they stopped at night they formed horses into a circular corral and this would provide protection against the wind and insulation against the cold. When the temperature dropped to minus twenty centigrade, and below, they would dig a huge hole under the snow and all the men and horses would clamber inside and survive for another night. I was fascinated by these stories and it helped me to understand her motivation for this trip; she was following in her father's footsteps and I now understood where her iron discipline came from. I imagined her father getting his charges up at dawn, driving them along all day, carrying the absolute minimum, being ruthlessly tough on stragglers – and witty round the campfire at night. They must have worked out ways of getting food from the locals, which must have been tough considering they were the enemy and there was a terrible food shortage in Russia at the time.

My attitude towards Bettina changed after hearing all this. She had told me the story in a kind way without any intention of giving a moral lesson (if my father could march all day through the frozen steppe, for years on end, then you should be able to ride without constantly moaning and stopping for breaks). It was a great story and it had a profound effect on me; I realised that what we were doing was like a donkey ride on the beach compared to what her father did, and I became aware that I had been behaving like a spoilt teenager who had been forced to operate outside his comfort zone, and I was carrying a sense of righteous indignation. If anything went wrong, or if I was feeling bad, I would blame Bettina for it; after all it was she who dragged me out here.

I started to behave like an equal rather than a victim. I suddenly grew up. I also started appreciating the fact that Bettina had the drive to organise this whole trip, and keep us going every day, and I felt a twinge of pride in the fact that she had chosen me as her companion. If she had ridden with Big Jack, whose temper was as explosive as hers, the result could have been disastrous.

By this time each village seemed similar to the last one, but there was one place which really stood out – a village that was quite literally standing on a clifftop, towering above the lush valley below. The gorges we were passing through only had enough space for the river and the road, and this village was located on a narrow strip of land by the river. There was a strong wind blowing and the telegraph wires above the road were whipping back and forth, as if trying to make music with the charging river. Often we would argue about where to stop – I always wanted to stop sooner than her – but on this occasion we both knew, without a word passing between us, that this is where we would stay that night.

We led the horses through the flat bottom of the valley, an area that was strewn with massive boulders. Hundreds of sheep, goats and yaks were being herded along the flat area by a roving group of children and old men. We naturally joined this traffic and heard the joyous banter that was being shouted across the valley floor by the children; our appearance had excited them and they ran up to us, screaming with laughter. The big flock of animals was converging on a narrow path that climbed a steep rise to the village above, as if we were being poured into a funnel. The children took up key positions around this movement, using slings to hurl stones at sheep straying off the path and shouting orders at one another. A baby goat stumbled into my path and fell over. I picked it up and held it protectively in my arm, as if it were a cat, and carried on up towards the village.

A small crowd was standing at the top of the hill, at the entrance to the village. They looked at us with a mixture of friendliness and suspicion, picked up their animals from the flock and took them home. The children didn't have any reservations and they surrounded us, showering us with questions: where are you from? Where are you going? What do you want here? I lifted one of the boys onto my horse, Tashi, and walked him through the village as if he were a young emperor. The children followed and roared with delight. I told them we needed fodder for the horse and I could see them running off and passing on the word. Nobody came forward with an offer of help and time seemed to stand still. I told myself be patient, we're not in a hurry, we're lucky to have found a village, especially such a beautiful one.

Suddenly the children fell quiet and two men in threadbare blue cotton suits approached. The sight of the blue cotton sent a shudder through me as I knew it meant local Communist Party officials. They were Tibetan cadres and obviously from the village; their grasp of Mandarin wasn't good and their demand to see our passports and non-existent travel papers wasn't as officious as usual. After we had been through the formalities of examining our passports, the two cadres couldn't suppress their friendliness any longer, they laughed out loud and said:

- Welcome to our village.

The officials hurried off and I noticed that all the adults had melted away and night was falling. It was the most beautiful village we had seen yet, the most boisterous and fun group of children we'd come across, but we were no closer to getting any fodder for the horses or a place to sleep for ourselves. I still wasn't worried; I knew something would happen. I felt a good atmosphere in this village.

Something was pulling on my jacket and I looked down and saw an old woman with a hunchback and just one eye. She was indicating a nearby alley and gesturing for us to follow. I glanced at Bettina and, without speaking, we agreed. There was no other offer on the table so why not? She wore black woollen clothes and had a leathery face that was lit up by a big smile. We followed her down the narrow alley, with twenty children behind us, and the fact that nobody spoke made the clip clop of the horse's hooves, and the sound of all those feet, remarkably loud. The old lady reached a huge wooden gate with ancient double doors, three metres high, and we followed her inside. The children remained in the alley.

I was speechless. We were standing in front of a huge stone built mansion that looked as if it had been constructed hundreds of years ago. It was empty, three storeys high, had wide windows, although there was no glass in the frames, and an elaborate roof that was still intact. The doors still looked solid and my first thoughts were that this place could be renovated and turned into the most incredible house in Tibet. It had a ghostly feel to it and I understood why the children didn't want to come into the yard; there was probably a horror stories about the aristocrats being driven out by the Communists.

We heard a shout from above, looked up and saw an armful of hay come floating down. Someone had climbed up to the attic, where there was a door that overlooked the yard, and thrown down some hay. Another armful floated down and we gratefully gathered it up and fed it to the horses. The old lady then led us to an old fashioned stable and showed us well-built stalls where the horses could spend the night. We had never seen anything like this in Tibet and Bettina, who was bursting with gratitude, went over and hugged the old woman so hard I thought she might crush her.

The old lady then invited us inside. She led us past a yak that was munching hay in the hallway and saw inside the big rooms on the ground floor: the floorboards had been taken away long ago and the elaborate plasterwork on the ceiling was riddled with bullet holes. There were hens settling down for the night on windowsills, fireplaces and all over the stairs.

The old lady showed us into a smoky little room at the back of the ground floor, the only room that was lived in. It struck me that this room was the same size as a typical peasant dwelling, and I wondered if the old lady and her husband were part of the unfortunate family that had been driven out by the Communists. She stood above the fire muttering into the flames, like an old witch, and her husband behaved like the perfect host, offering us tea, tsampa and conversation. He too only had one eye. There was something very different about this couple. Their hospitality was gregarious without any sort of fear. With everyone else we had stayed with you could sense that there was a slight worry in the atmosphere; what would happen if the Communist Party officials found out they had entertained foreigners? This couple seemed beyond caring. I assumed they had lost so much, and were so old, that they just didn't give a damn if they were punished for disobeying the party line. They seemed to get a lot out of being good hosts and we reciprocated by being as communicative as possible. In each of these encounters with Tibetans I would practice new words, learn others and improve my language skills by a notch.

The following day was a Sunday and Bettina decreed that it would be our first day off. It was strange not getting up at dawn and marching all

day and initially I didn't know what to do with myself. Then I explored
the house and found some intriguing Chinese graffiti that I was unable
to decipher. This was the first moment on the trip that I regretted not
having a camera; many of the other images I had seen were recorded in
my memory.

I asked the old lady where the toilet was and she pointed up, to the top
of the house. I went upstairs and found it in the attic, located on a wooden
platform that was jutting out over the back garden. As I crouched down to
relieve myself, satisfied that my excrement would be put to immediate use
in the kitchen garden, I got a bird's-eye view of the village. When it was
time to go the old lady, who had grown very attached to Bettina, walked
with us proudly through the village and down the slope to the boulder-
strewn plain. I could tell from her eyes that she was sad to see us go.

As soon as we were out of sight of the village we went down to the
frothing river, stripped off, plunged in and washed. It was the first full body
wash we'd had since leaving Lhasa; in that environment it felt natural to
wash only rarely. It was so cold that you didn't feel the build-up of sweat
and dirt, hot water was only made for cooking and none of the locals
seemed to wash more than their hands and face (this was one of the
reasons the Chinese despised them). Getting in the icy water was terrible,
I squealed like a pig and washed as fast as I possibly could. Standing on the
river bank, I felt frozen solid. Within a few minutes my skin was glowing, as
if electrified, and it felt incredible. A truck thundered by on the road above
and a cheeky face of a young Khampa was leaning out of his window,
looking at us in delight, whistling and screaming.

It was still our day off and although we planned to take it easy, lots of
things happened: we came across a truck stop and I charged in and ate a
delicious meal; the Tibetan waitress made a pass at me but I told her I was
in love with my horse and she threw us out; we found a blacksmith and I
had to wrestle my disobedient horse to the ground, until we managed to
tie up its legs so the blacksmith could apply new shoes; the sky was filled
with dark clouds that rumbled angrily and spat drops of rain at us; we
drank chang with some villagers, slept outside by a ruined monastery and
Bettina and I enjoyed our first, and last, night of passion.

The following day we came out of the narrow gorge we had been riding
along and found ourselves in a wide valley that was lush and full of trees.
We had grown used to the background roar of the river being amplified by
gorges but here the wide valley absorbed the sound. Looking at our road

map, a tiny map which hadn't shown any of the villages we'd stayed in, I guessed we were approaching the big Chinese town of Bye Eee (which translates as Camp Eight One). After Bye Eee, the next town on the map was Tibetan – Nying Chee – which I knew was the capital of the fertile Kong Poe region that we were riding through; the last stop before the wild land of Kham.

I felt a sense of gratitude at having this opportunity to see some of eastern Tibet and started thinking that perhaps I wouldn't rush back to Lhasa as soon as possible; maybe I would keep riding with Bettina all the way to Hong Kong. I was becoming more fluent by the day, drinking chang with old men, talking incessantly, less inhibited about splurging out my thoughts in ungrammatical Tibetan – entertaining children, sleeping in barns and yards and living cheek by jowl with pigs, chickens, dogs and yaks. After staying in a village that was hidden by trees and had an ingenious network of channels, which fed water through each household.

After those idyllic Tibetan villages the shock of reaching Bye Eee was terrible; a big, modern nightmare with dusty, concrete streets in a grid format, populated by bored Chinese soldiers and delinquent Tibetans who seemed to have drunk too much. We covered our faces in the hope that we would be able to pass as Tibetan travellers – none of the soldiers gave us a second glance – and we slipped through the town like ghosts. I felt tainted by contact with the place. On the far side of town we stopped at a big Chinese restaurant and indulged in delicious steamed dumplings, served by a charming old peasant from Yunnan Province with hands the size of shovels.

By the end of the following day we had passed the town of Nying Chee, a small Tibetan town that had been swallowed up by a Chinese garrison. We ate delicious sweet and sour fish and the cheeky waiter demanded a ride on one of the horses. After indulging him we headed back into the wilderness where, for reasons I couldn't really understand, I felt more at home. We had been passing through thick forest and by late afternoon we ran into a work gang, Chinese lumberjacks, and we got chatting:

- Where are you going?
- Chengdu.
- Long way. You know there are no villages up there. High pass ahead. You can stay with us.

As always, I was keen to stop at the first opportunity while Bettina was determined to push on. I relented and we started up the long, high pass.

Fortunately we had a small bag of barley grain that would keep the horses going for a few days. By dusk it was raining and we came across a wooden shack with a tin roof, one of many we had seen that houses gangs of road workers. We had passed hundreds of these road workers over the previous weeks, all shovelling gravel from the edge to the centre of the road, but they rarely waved or showed any sign of friendliness.

At nightfall we found a small settlement by the side of the road, made up of mud huts and a road workers' shack. A friendly shepherd invited us to sit round a small fire while his son entertained us with songs and dances. The road workers joined us, drink was passed round and a party atmosphere built up. I asked about fodder and they looked at me blankly. The shepherd's son interrupted his one-man-show and said:

- You see that grass cannot grow up here?

- Yes.

- Come with me and I will show you what you can feed the horses with.

He led me up the hill to a stand of wild bamboo and said horses love bamboo leaves. I had a penknife and he had a Khampa dagger and we cut out two armfuls of the juicy leaves, carried them down and fed them to the grateful horses. Later that evening one of the road workers, dressed up in flares and high heels, started dancing and singing in the flickering firelight the latest Chinese pop song:

- Jeemy, jeemy, jeemy – aja, aja, aja.

That night we slept inside a wooden shack and the sound of rain hammering on the tin roof was deafening. Water was dripping through holes in the roof but we were grateful for the shelter and had a good sleep. It took us all of the next day to cross the high pass – where Bettina left a white silk scarf on the cairn – and we hurried down the other side as quickly as possible, spurred on by the biting cold and our lack of warm clothing.

The landscape seemed different on the other side of the pass; a strange green light, big rolling hills rather than sharp mountains, a constant drizzle and an indescribable feeling of mystery that reminded me of the west coast of Scotland. For day after day we passed through thick forest and the occasional village where the houses were made of wood. Even though it all looked very lush, getting food from the local people was always a struggle and every evening we would hang around for hours before being welcomed in. Some nights we found enough grass for the horses, growing by the side of the road, and we would sleep in the open.

By our second Sunday we were camped out under a big rock between the road and the river. We had passed through the rolling hills and were back in a steep gorge where the road had been carved into the rock. The river, much bigger now, made a constant background roar and after a while we didn't even notice it.

I had managed to scrounge a small bottle of petrol from a Chinese cook, as well as a large tin that once held pork. With a handful of dirt and a splash of petrol, I was soon boiling water for tea and the remnants of the horses' barley – which we ate. Getting water involved leaning over the frothing river and trying to avoid getting soaked. The water itself was so churned up that it was white; full of tiny bubbles, sand and fine grit. The idea that it may not be safe for drinking flashed across my mind but there was no choice.

As we were eating our delicious boiled barley dinner we saw a line of Tibetan pilgrims standing on the road above, looking down on us curiously. They all had smiles on their faces and had probably been walking for weeks. They had no bags and looked even hungrier than us. We took pity on them, invited them to come and join us and gave them the rest of our cooked barley. I boiled several tins of water, made tea and experienced the warm glow of satisfaction that comes from being the host and sharing everything that you have.

As the landscape grew harsher Bettina and I became closer. We understood each other better, argued less and were able to make decisions more smoothly, often without even talking. As the road became steeper my own confidence grew, and Bettina seemed to become less bossy. Perhaps I was starting to fulfil the role that she had assumed I would take from the start – as an equal – and I was settling into it, feeling I could go on and on. I felt happy about riding with her across Tibet. I wondered what Sichuan would be like. Maybe we could make it all the way to Hong Kong? The few people I had met who had travelled this route said it was incredible.

A few days later we came to a confluence of rivers, where the torrent we had been riding alongside now joined an even bigger river, forming an unbelievably huge body of water that made so much noise it was almost impossible to speak to one another. The only familiar feature was the telegraph wire, which had doggedly followed the road and river every step of the way. The gorge we had been travelling along for days suddenly opened up into a narrow plain, where the river had spread out over a wide area and left a chaos of massive rocks lying everywhere. We approached the remains of a bridge that the torrent had swept away. A big gang of Khampa road-workers beckoned us to cross over the newly constructed pontoon bridge and we crossed it carefully, leading the horses. The bridge wobbled and shook from the elemental force of the water below. The horses became jittery; we had to hold them tight and pull them hard to get across.

The Khampa road workers were perhaps the friendliest people we had yet come across. They were lounging around like English gentlemen, spreading themselves lazily over the side of the road. They offered us strong black tea, flavoured with salt but not butter, and served it in crudely carved wooden bowls. We relaxed, chatted and joked and they didn't think it at all odd that we were heading all the way to Sichuan. The map was brought out and they worked out where we were and we realised that we were almost half way to our destination of Chengdu, the capital of Sichuan.

The next ten kilometres of road were among the toughest we had yet encountered – the gorge more like a ravine, the road narrow and the drop down to the river below quite terrifying. Its intimidating roar, the constant rain and the slipperiness of the gravel road made us feel very unsafe. The edge of the road plunged directly down into the ravine and it felt like gravity was pulling at the road, biting chunks out of it, about to dash us all on the rocks below.

We hadn't seen a vehicle all day. Late that afternoon we came across a convoy of Chinese military trucks that were parked in a line pointing to the east, towards Lhasa. Hundreds of soldiers in green uniform hung around listlessly, staring at us blankly. A section of the road ahead had collapsed and a gang of Khampas, supervised by Chinese men in white helmets, were cutting trees, shovelling rock over the edge and placing explosives. The shattering sound of an explosion swept over us, barely attracting the attention of the soldiers, but making the horses nervous and jumpy. We waited for about three hours before we were allowed through, picking a route through mud, rock and broken bits of timber. It looked like a war zone.

Tang My is the main town in these parts, at least on the map. In reality it was nothing more than a few shacks, a truck stop and a grotty looking Chinese restaurant that perched on the edge of the precipice. I saw the Chinese cook standing in the doorway of his shack, wiping his bloody hands on his apron and looking at us. We went inside to eat fried vegetables and let the horses graze freely; we were surrounded by lush-looking greenery and we could see them from the restaurant. An hour later we came for them and the horses seemed rather bloated and also asleep, while standing. Very strange. We had never seen the horses fall asleep in the daytime and had to scream at them in order to wake them up.

Everything seemed to go into slow motion that evening. The horses were so tired that we had to drag them and every step was an effort. We made pitifully slow progress and decided to camp early, by the side of the road. I lit a fire and started boiling some water while Bettina talked sweetly to her horse, Pungya, in German. I could see that she was actually a very affectionate person, perhaps like the stereotypical English gentleman who shows more affection towards his dog than to his wife. The horses were really sick and we reckoned that while we were having lunch they must have eaten something poisonous. The horses couldn't eat or drink and they had glazed expressions. I started feeling twinges of panic and wondered what we would do if they died.

As night settled five lively pilgrims walked along the road, greeted us with great warmth and joined us round the campfire. They hurried off and collected more wood, built up the fire and boiled up a big pot of tea. Their only possession was a big blanket and all of them slept under it. The following morning the horses seemed better, especially Pungya, Bettina's mount. I asked the leader of the pilgrims, a boy, for advice and he thrust his fingers deep up Tashi's nose. He looked at the slime he'd gathered and said:

- It has been poisoned. You must give it arak.

I discussed this with Bettina. Arak is Chinese fire water, a liquor that is so strong that one taste of it burns the mouth horribly. We agreed that we shouldn't follow this strange advice and we'd hope for the best. The pilgrims said goodbye and started walking towards Lhasa and we carried on towards the east. I felt a sense of unease growing within me. After a few kilometres I realised that my horse, Tashi, had not recovered at all. A big artery in his neck was thumping, he was wheezing heavily and his eyes were swivelling madly; he seemed unable to focus. Bettina, whose horse had made a full recovery, rode off to find help while I kept slowly urging Tashi to make one step after another. The hours slipped by, nobody appeared and he lay down at the side of the road, breathing heavily. I withdrew into some bushes and stared into space, unsure of what to do or feel. I tried to lighten the load for Tashi by taking off his saddle, which I hid in the bushes, hauled him to his feet and pulled him step by step along the road.

At dusk I could see a rider in the distance and then realised it was Bettina. Her face was grim and she asked me if Tashi was bad; I nodded and she went over to him. As soon as Bettina saw the state of my horse she burst into tears. I didn't join her or hug her as I had withdrawn into a cold space where there were no thoughts, a sort of inner wilderness.

We cajoled and bullied Tashi another two kilometres, to a road workers compound that Bettina had spotted on her scouting mission. Unusually, there were no Chinese workers staying there – just an old Tibetan couple. The old man welcomed us in and seemed to understand what was going on with the horse. Tashi had got worse and he was staggering, blindly, in circles, making strange whinnying noises and eventually collapsed and lay on the dirt floor, shuddering. The old man, who had been studying the behaviour of the horse, gave me a look that seemed to accept the fact that Tashi would die and there was nothing to be done. He showed us into a big empty room with a wooden floor and then retired for the night. Bettina wasn't ready for bed, and how could we sleep with such suffering going on outside?

- We have to kill it, she said.
- What was that?
- Tashi is going to die. We need to kill it. To put it out of its misery. I normally carry a lethal injection in case of situations like this arise but I don't have it here. I do have a syringe and needle.
- What good is that going to do?
- You can inject air into his bloodstream and that will kill it.
- You want me to do that?
- Yes.

I injected air into one of Tashi's throbbing veins and waited. It had no effect. Bettina found a thick piece of wood, a pick axe handle, and asked me to bash it on the head, in a special place she said would kill it. I wielded the club and wondered if I could do it, and then saw the old man watching us:

- Yo bo min do, he said, which means no good.

I agreed with him, put the pick axe handle down and went into the room. I wasn't able to kill Tashi. I was going to lie down and try to sleep. Under normal circumstances I would have appreciated the comfort of a wooden floor, but nothing could offer us comfort that night. Eventually

Bettina joined me and we both stared up into the pitch-black sky. I could feel a sense of guilt radiating from Bettina – was she blaming herself for the situation? A powerful sadness descended over us. The silence of the night was broken by Tashi who was thumping the ground with his hooves, flailing with death and making a heart-rending wheezing sound.

At daybreak Tashi was stiff with rigor mortis. His eyes were wide open and staring blankly into space, his teeth bared in a final grimace of panic and agony. There was nothing to say. The old man offered us tsampa and eggs but we couldn't eat, both of us felt nauseous and sick at heart. The old man gave us a small bowl of tea each and indicated to me that I should follow him. He was the only one among us who had a sense of purpose.

He went and got his hand-tractor started. These are small engines, mounted on two wheels, that connects to a trailer. The driver sits on the trailer and steers with two long handlebars that are attached to the engine. They are simple, ingenious and the foundation stone of Chinese agriculture. He reversed the contraption into the yard, produced a rope and tied the dead body of Tashi to the back of the trailer. Without saying a word, he indicated that I should jump on. Bettina looked on with red eyes, saying nothing, and didn't join us.

The engine roared, protesting at the extra weight, and with a shudder we drove slowly down the road – dragging the corpse behind us, leaving a wake of ruffled stones. We drove down the road for less than a mile until we reached a part where the gorge came right up to the edge of the road. In a few months it would, surely, swallow up the road completely. The old man hopped out, untied the horse and between us we dragged it to the precipice. I took one last look at the horse, focusing on the metal horse-shoes that were such a struggle to fit and wondered if I should take them off.

With great difficulty we got Tashi to the edge of the cliff. We sat down and pushed him towards the edge with our feet, inch by inch. We seemed to be making no progress. Suddenly there was a loud whooshing sound and he was gone. Plucked into the abyss. I jumped up, looked down and saw him crash into the rocks below. There was a long moment of silence followed by a sickening thumping sound being echoed from across the gorge. I could see Tashi lying on the rocks below, like a small toy horse, and I thought I heard a voice drift up and say: Why did you let me die?

Bettina had everything packed up when I got back and, without a word, we resumed our journey eastwards. We ambled along listlessly and I felt the heart had been ripped out of our journey. I was adapting to the new situation quickly and had decided to go on with the journey; I was feeling strong, fit and able to walk to the ends of the earth. My luggage was minimal, just a couple of small bags, and I had left the only heavy item – Tashi's saddle – back in the road workers' house with the old man. I had told him to sell it if he could, and I would visit him on my way back. Losing Tashi was a tragedy but it didn't end my capacity to carry on; I had walked and jogged a lot of the way and would keep doing so, alongside Bettina, all the way through Sichuan province to the east. Just as this new sense of determination was building in my mind, Bettina came to another conclusion:

- You know Pungya is from Western Tibet? She asked,
- Yes.
- Well, there isn't much grass in that part of Tibet.
- I know, it's like a desert really.
- Exactly, and the problem is that this part of Tibet is full of strange plants that grow at the side of the road. The horses aren't used to them; they don't know what's safe to eat and what's not. That's why Tashi died.
- I see what you mean. We need to take more care...
- What I mean is this: you must take Pungya back to Lhasa. Return him to his homeland or he too will be poisoned.
- I can't go back without you...I won't leave you out here on your own.
- I'll be fine. I can hitchhike to Chengdu and then get to Hong Kong. Soon I will be back in Germany, at college. You belong in Lhasa.
- I want to come with you. I don't want to go back alone.

Her mind was made up. She was going to hitchhike eastwards and I was going back to Lhasa with Pungya. End of discussion. Even though I prefer to travel alone, after two weeks in the saddle with Bettina I wanted to go on with her. We had worked out something quite unique between us and I was only just starting to appreciate it. I spent the rest of the day trying to persuade her out of the decision but she was determined and nothing would change her mind. By the end of the day I accepted the fact that this would be the best course of action for the horse, even if it wasn't what I wanted to do.

We found a beautiful wooden house by the side of the road and the old couple inside reluctantly let us stay. There was a man in one of the rooms who was chanting so loudly that his deep bass filled the whole building. They gave us glasses of Arak, the local firewater then left us in peace. We spent our last night together chatting, in fact we talked more that night than we had during the whole trip. We slept in a long, thin hayloft and we lay down in soft, warm hay and listened to the old man's chanting long into the night.

There was no time for sentimental goodbyes the following morning. Bettina was tacking up Pungya, whispering goodbyes and briskly getting her stuff together. I lingered in the warm hay for a moment longer. We got some bowls of tea, mixed it with some tsampa and I got my stuff ready. It was time to part and she made me promise that I would get Pungya back to Lhasa safely. I agreed with more confidence than I felt; I really wasn't sure if I could get back to Lhasa on my own. She was my leader and I had no idea how I would cope alone. We walked down to the road and stood looking awkwardly at each other, searching for appropriate words. She said something about feeding the horse at the right time, we briefly embraced and I jumped onto Pungya and started riding towards the west. After a few minutes I looked back and saw a beautiful, slim figure, dressed in black, standing in the middle of the road, watching me.

I rode all that day with a sense of mental numbness. My mind was empty and my only thought was to just keep going. Later in the day the numbness faded and I felt a deep wound of sadness open up within me. It was overpowering. I stopped and tried to think, tried to understand the powerful feelings of regret that were running through me: What am I doing here? I said to myself. On Bettina's horse! How could I have left her alone? Who knows what will happen to her? I must join her.

Impulsively, I swung the horse round and started cantering back towards the way I had come. After a few minutes I stopped and realised this was ridiculous. She was gone. It was too late and she was probably inside a truck by now. I saw Bettina in a new light, admiring the qualities that I deliberately ignored: bravery, determination, compassion and such generosity in giving me everything that she had cared for. Her goodness contrasted with my own selfishness, insensitivity and laziness. I also felt an overpowering sense of guilt for leaving Bettina on her own, in the middle of nowhere. The only thing that kept me from hurling myself into the gorge was the promise I'd made to get the horse back safely. That promise became my mantra, my mission and it helped to keep me going.

All that day I rode on with an extra burden of misery, like a heavy rucksack, on my back. It began to pour with rain, which felt like divine punishment for my sins. I deserved it. I wondered if I would be able to

maintain Bettina's discipline of travelling at least fifty kilometres a day.
I doubted it. The rain and my mood seemed to have changed the road:
when we rode along together it was exciting and beautiful. Now it was
treacherous and vile. Evening approached. I came across a roadside village
and was about to approach a house when an old hag appeared and, before
I could say a word, she shooed me away as if I was an evil spirit and then
set her dogs on me. I couldn't feel any anger or blame towards her; perhaps
she saw me for what I was. I rode on until the next village where everyone
seemed either drunk or mad. I found a place to stay and shared a grimy
floor space with a baby who was being looked after by two young girls
who also slept on the floor. Pungya was standing outside, in the rain,
munching on wet hay.

The next day I descended back into the gorge we had traversed just
a few days earlier and could hear the thunderous roar of the river long
before I saw it. I rode and jogged as hard as I could all day, trying to blot out
my feelings and by evening had left the gorge, entered the lush plain I had
so appreciated with Bettina and started the long climb up to the pass. That
evening I stayed in a village of wooden houses where some boys took pity
on me and helped me find some hay. We had been in this village before and
some of the men recognised me. One of them said:

- Aja kaba do? (Where's the lady?) I found it really hard to answer. I
hadn't thought about how I would explain her absence. My answer seemed
to satisfy them:

- Chamdo, Shang Gang dro gee yin (She's gone to Chamdo and Hong
Kong).

The rain continued for all the next day as I plodded up the high pass,
wallowing in misery. Although my eyes were dry and I hadn't actually
cried during this time, my heart seemed to be sobbing. As I crossed the
high pass I could see that the weather was better on the other side; I looked
to the east and waved goodbye to it. As I started to descend I realised that I
couldn't go on wallowing in self pity: You've got to get a grip, I told myself.
Feeling miserable about Bettina isn't going to help anyone. Get over it.

On the way down from the pass I left the winding road and cut across
open country, walking over heather-type plants and jumping across
streams. I started to develop a working relationship with Pungya. He was
a bad-tempered beast and we didn't like each other much, but he had one
quality that I found rather remarkable: he could trot really fast. If I ran
alongside him, pulling him along, he would trot in a way that I've never

seen before in a horse. It was half-trot, half-canter and with each step he seemed to lift up into the air and float along for a half second. In this way he seemed to glide along, to move effortlessly, and as I jogged beside him we would eat up the miles. He could cover great distances without seeming to make much effort.

Days later I staggered into Nying Chee, the capital of the lush Kong Poe region. My only impression of this town was that it was the Chinese garrison, the old Tibetan centre and, most importantly, the Chinese restaurant where Bettina and I had eaten delicious sweet and sour fish only a few days ago. I found myself outside the restaurant, licking my lips in anticipation and noticing how big the actual building was compared to the usual roadside eating shacks we had come across. This one was almost as big as a modern American house, built entirely from scraps of wood and had the steep pitched roof of an alpine building, presumably to deal with large amounts of snow in the winter. What was unusual was that the whole rickety structure was standing on top of a steep cliff, held up by hundreds of spindly looking bamboo poles. A stream of evil-looking rubbish flowed from under the building into the gorge, like a black diarrhoea stain on the inside of a toilet bowl. Surely the whole establishment would go plunging into the depths at the first hint of an earthquake? And wasn't Tibet in an earthquake zone? The idea of hundreds of diners gorging on sweet and sour fish as they plunged to their doom seemed quite funny. The image made me laugh for the first time in days.

I tied Pungya up to a tree outside the restaurant. The Chinese waiter was standing in the doorway, looking at me with interest. I looked back and tried to cover up my feelings of suspicion; this was the only person on the whole trip who I really didn't trust at all. We had met him before and he had asked for a ride on the horse. He was what the Scots call a chancer and I knew he would gut me and sling me down the gorge if he could make a quick buck and get away with it. This thought didn't bother me as the restaurant was full and if I kept my wits about me he wouldn't get a chance to do anything.

I was so focused on the waiter that I barely noticed a figure who was striding past in the opposite direction. Suddenly a voiced boomed out in native English:

- Hello there! Isn't it Rupert under that hat? I froze. Rooted to the spot. I glanced up and looked at the big bearded figure who was standing in front of me. He looked a bit like Big Jack but was better dressed and spoke in a well-educated English accent. Who the hell was he? I hadn't spoken English for days and felt tongue-tied, as if I had forgotten my own language.

- I...er...um...

- Don't you remember me?

- Um...

- Charles! Charles Ramble, remember? We met in Kathmandu.

- Of course, at the Canadians' house.

I remembered. He was one of the most impressive people I had met. He was the only genuine Tibetan scholar I had come across, he knew Tibetan fluently, could navigate his way through several of their dialects, wrote books and was a serious anthropologist. I remembered him as an Oxford-educated slightly weedy intellectual but the man standing in front of me was big, strong and impressive. He had the physical presence of Indiana Jones as well as the same hat.

- Look, I've got to catch a bus to Bye Eee in half an hour. Why don't you join me there this evening for dinner? We can talk.

I forgot all about the Chinese restaurant and walked with him towards the bus station. This was my first chance to have an interesting conversation with a fellow countryman in ages, and I was enthused by the prospect. I had so much to tell him; a flood of experiences and questions were bubbling to the surface. But where to begin? I decided to steer the conversation away from me as it would be frustrating to start opening up and then be interrupted by his departure.

- What are you doing in these parts? I asked, looking at his lethal sheath knife which must have been a foot long. I also noticed with a slight twinge of jealousy his pots, pans and high quality trekking gear hanging from the side of his rucksack.

- I've been exploring the Bon Mountain. You know it? The one over there? He pointed at a distant peak and I shook my head in ignorance.

- Is that a sacred mountain? It looks pretty ordinary to me.

- That's the Bon religion's most sacred spot in Tibet. I've just spent three days walking round it, staying in their secret meditation caves. My legs are aching.

- Isn't Bon the religion that was in Tibet before Buddhism took over? I'm afraid I don't know anything about it. I'm very ignorant.

- Don't worry. You're in good company. Most Tibetans know nothing about Bon. Less than two percent of Tibetans practice it and most of them live around here.

We had reached a windswept yard where a scruffy old bus was parked. A group of bored looking Tibetans sat on low stools outside a teahouse, drinking chang. They stared at us blankly. An attractive, harassed looking Tibetan woman with a leather satchel stood by the bus and Charles bought a ticket from her. I was stunned by his fluency; I had never heard a foreigner speak Tibetan so well, in fact I could hardly think of any foreigners who spoke much of the language. My grasp of it was appalling compared to Charles', although I could make myself understood. The bus roared to life and released a huge cloud of diesel fumes. Charles loaded his rucksack into the hold and prepared to board. He signalled me to join him at the door and said:

- Before I go I must say one thing.

- What's that?

- If an old lady gives you an egg – refuse it.

- Eh! Why's that?

- You see, some of the Bon practitioners like to poison people so they can take the dead person's spirit.

- What?

- It's part of the ancient animistic tradition. They usually do it through liquids or eggs. So don't accept any eggs or unusual looking liquids or foods.

- I'll keep that in mind.

- The poison can take up to six years to take effect. Just take care.

- You know my horse just got poisoned near here?

- I shouldn't imagine anyone would want to poison a horse, he said, laughing. Meet me at the Bus Station Hotel at Bye Eee. Ask for the New Sue Drang.

- Bye.

The door of the bus snapped shut angrily and it jolted forward. The other passengers were staring vacantly ahead and the bus climbed a small hill, spewing more grey fumes, joined the main road and headed east towards Bye Eee and Lhasa. The sun came out and this spurred me into action. I gave two handfuls of barley to Pungya, still tied up under a tree, and he whinnied with appreciation. I watched him devour the barley grains and swallow them whole; I wondered if he would get any nutritional value from the grains if he didn't chew them. I entered the Bus Station Cafe, a barn-like wooden structure where lots of Tibetans were sitting around doing nothing, and ordered a big bowl of Bow Dze (dumplings) from the

Chinese chef. I sat down, dipped the dumplings in chilli sauce that was in a tiny plate and noticed that a community of chickens was living above the tables, among the rafters, shedding feathers and other droppings. It was time to go. I rode as hard as I could for the next few hours so that I wouldn't miss Charles and I could feel the dumplings sloshing around in my stomach. Eventually I reached Bye Eee with its grey concrete buildings receding into the distance. What a dump!

I found Charles in a seedy truck-stop by the Bus Station. The staff were unfriendly and rather shocked to see another foreigner show up. They told me that my horse was not allowed. I ignored their protests, tied up the horse across the road followed Charles up to his room where I flopped down gratefully on the spare bed. The sour-faced Tibetan woman who ran the joint followed me to the room, muttering darkly. We both ignored her and she went away. The door stayed open.

- Nice place you've got here, I said.

- Very funny. I'm leaving tomorrow, back to Lhasa for some real comfort. Let's go and eat something. You know anywhere?

- Yes, I know a Yunnanese restaurant that does great dumplings.

- Sounds good, let's go.

The walls and ceiling of the restaurant were black with a sticky gunge that, I assumed, was congealed cooking fat from the woks, mixed up with smoke and soot from the fire. The only reason I noticed the filth was because Charles seemed rather shocked by it, but he quickly recovered and didn't complain. He probably cooked all his meals with his fancy cooking gear or ate with local families. Charles was a vegetarian, which was very unusual in this part of the world.

- Gee dan, dofu bow dzer (boiled eggs and tofu dumplings), I said to the Chinese waiter, the friendly peasant with shovel-like hands whom I had met before.

- Where did you learn to speak Chinese? Asked Charles.

- I don't know how to speak Chinese.

- What? You just spoke it.

- I just know how to order food, ask for directions and how to buy stuff in shops.

- Where did you learn it?

- I'm not sure. I never really studied it, apart from the first chapter of a Learn Chinese book from the 1930s. I just listen to people, keep my ears open, write down words that I hear. I'm surprised you didn't learn any

Chinese, it's easy.

- I know, I should. I feel guilty about it.

Back at the hotel, where I installed myself in the spare bed, the conversation was invigorating. We talked about life in the various regions of Tibet, the long history of the country, folk tales, how he learned Tibetan, and life in modern Britain. A single light-bulb shed a dim glow and made the room, which had metal bars on the window, seem stark and bare. It was colder than outside and I assumed the concrete walls had turned the room into a big fridge. I was wearing all the clothes I had with me and realised that sleeping outside was better than this. The only sounds were distant trucks and the sound of Pungya munching the hay that I had found for him.

Charles told me that he came to this region with two journalists, one from Finland and one from Canada. They were hoping to get an exclusive about the Chinese preparations for war on the Indian border.

- And where are these journalists? I asked.

- I have no idea.

- What do you mean?

- Sean, the Canadian one, was walking with me round the Bon mountain but we lost each other and I've no idea where he is. The Finnish one was last seen trying to cross the Tsangpo in a coracle.

- A coracle? What's that?

- It's a traditional Tibetan leather boat, shaped like a soup bowl.

- And what happened to him?

- I'm not sure. I heard he got arrested.

- Aren't you worried?

- Not in the least. They'll be fine.

We carried on chatting late into the night and just as I was drifting off comfortably to sleep the door opened quietly and two men, like shadows, slipped into the room. An electric bolt of fear shot through me and I sat up. One of the men was a Chinese policeman – young, thin and nervous looking. Although he had a pistol attached to his belt he didn't seem to be a threat. The other man, a slim Tibetan in his mid-thirties, wore a blue civilian suit with a tie and had cold, dark, expressionless eyes that seemed to take in every detail. He had an air of quiet, understated confidence, and a sinister sense of calm that suggested great power. He gave me the feeling that he was familiar with death and wasn't afraid of it. He was quite different from anyone I had ever met in Tibet or China and I was terrified. The Tibetan approached my bed and carefully arranged a small patch by my feet and gently sat down. He didn't say a word. The Chinese policeman, obviously the junior partner, sat down gingerly on the end of Charles' bed. I was frozen in terror and the silence was prolonged and agonizing.

- Wo shi gong anne jew (I am the police) said the sinister Tibetan. He spoke in rapid Mandarin and soon lost me.

- Ting boo dung (I don't understand) I said.

I was unable to suppress surging feelings of despair and helplessness. A flicker of irritation crossed the Tibetan's face and I wondered if that was his expression just before the start of the torture session. His look of sinister calm soon returned. A long moment of silence followed, I looked at Charles for help and he began to talk in fluent Tibetan. I breathed a sigh of relief and Charles answered a whole series of questions. The Tibetan translated into Chinese and the uniformed policeman noted everything down in what looked like a school kid's jotter. Charles turned to me with an expression of innocence and said:

- Did you know this was a forbidden area?

- Really? I had no idea. Nobody told me this.

- He wants to know everything: where you're going? Where you have come from? Who you were with? And why you have come here?

Charles translated, everything was noted down and it took hours. The Tibetan's level of professional interrogation technique never slipped, and neither did he show any trace of humanity or warmth. While I was melting with fear, Charles seemed equal to the evil presence in the room and I added courage to his list of qualities.

- Give him your passport, Charles said calmly.

- My passport? I said weakly.

- Yes, he says he will return it tomorrow with a decision. He says we mustn't leave the hotel until he returns. I groped into my crotch and searched for my hidden money-belt, not having looked at it for weeks.

- What have we done wrong? I asked, trying to sum up a note of indignation.

- We're in a forbidden military area and you've got a horse. We're not allowed here and you're not allowed to use a horse without special authorisation.

I meekly handed over my passport and felt more vulnerable than ever. The man in blue was watching our every move, like a snake that's about to strike. They stood up stiffly, moved towards the door, didn't look back and were gone. We heard an engine start in the yard and a vehicle drove off. There was a long moment of silence and tension, until Charles blurted out:

- Fucking hell! I was terrified.

- Thank God Doctor Death has gone, I replied. The atmosphere soon relaxed and we started joking about our fate.

- He's obviously going to report us to Lhasa or Peking and ask them for advice. He's probably never had to deal with customers like us. He'll be used to dealing with Tibetans, whom I'm sure he doesn't treat so politely.

The following day crawled by. Although there was a chatty atmosphere between us there was an unbearable tension in the air – what was going to happen to us? We talked and talked, mainly about the war that was building up in the south and we saw military convoys trundling by constantly. Charles seemed to know a lot about it and I was fascinated. He said the Chinese have a large quantity of American artillery, and an endless supply of troops, while the Indian Army was an equally powerful force with the advantage of having modern command and control systems. What this meant in practice was that Indian commanders could use their initiative whereas in Communist armies all decisions have to come from the top – resulting in confusion on the ground and a much larger loss of life.

- Have you heard how the Chinese military logistics are organised in this area? Asked Charles.

- No.

- There are thousands of Chinese troops camped up in the most inhospitable mountains in the world. They need a lot of supplies and so they have press-ganged the local population into supplying them.

- What do you mean?

- The main supplies come down this road by truck but these roads don't go right down to the frontier, which is high in the mountains. They need thousands of people, horses, mules, yaks and donkeys to move the supplies up to the front line. And who do you think has the honour of doing this?

- Er, I'm not sure.

- The local people of course.

- I wonder if that's where my horse will end up?

- If they just take it we'll never know what happens to it. Frankly, I'm surprised that they didn't confiscate it last night.

- Maybe because they couldn't fit it into their car.

- Good point.

By midday our stomachs were rumbling and there was no sign of anyone from the police force. The hotel staff were icily ignoring us. I resented the boss even more as I was sure it was her who had informed on us. Feeling like conspirators, we snuck out to the local noodle house and relished each mouthful as if it were our last.

By late afternoon the room had become claustrophobic and it felt like a prison cell. We even had bars on the window. In a spirit of defiance we walked into the back yard and stomped around the dust, not quite knowing what to do with ourselves. We were like prisoners who had been allowed out for a walk in the prison yard. I walked over to a pile of rubbish that was stacked to one side of the yard, against a wall, and looked aimlessly at the trash. I spotted a glass bottle and had an idea. I grabbed the bottle and started searching for others, eventually finding six of them. Charles looked on with curiosity, asked me what I was doing and I said:

- We're going to have some fun.

I lined up the bottles on the wall above the rubbish heap and started searching the yard for stones, telling Charles to do the same. When we each had a pile of stones we started throwing them as hard as we could towards the bottles. I smashed the first one, let out a cry of triumph, and this brought out the competitive spirit in Charles. Glancing over at him hurling rocks at bottles I wondered what his colleagues at Oxford University would think of this unseemly behaviour. When all the bottles were smashed we rushed back to the rubbish heap and rummaged around for more. We had found our vocation. Nobody from the hotel had come out to tell us to stop but a small crowd of children had gathered and were watching us, in silence.

We threw stones until our arms started to ache and there were no more bottles to find. The day slowly passed into evening and the police still didn't come. We felt disturbed and hungry. Was this endless waiting a tactic to soften us up before the real interrogation begun? The worst thing about this was the waiting, the uncertainty and the tension this caused. Would they swoop in during the night, catch us asleep and then haul us off? I decided to sleep with my clothes on, ready for anything. We talked late into the night.

- Why are they going to war? What's it all about? I asked.

- It all goes back to the British Empire, the Raj. Have you heard of the McMahon line?

- No.

- It was the frontier that the British drew between India and Tibet, a border that the Communist Chinese never accepted.

- Was Tibet part of China when they drew the line?

- No, and that's the problem. The Raj recognised Tibet as a suzerain territory of China, in other words as an independent country that paid tribute to Peking. The Communist Chinese can't accept this and their version of history is that Tibet has always been part of China.

- Was it always part of China?

- No. Tibet was conquered by China at various points in its history, when the Chinese dynasty was youthful and strong, but their control would always lapse as it was too remote to control and too inhospitable to populate.

- All this happened so long ago.

- The Chinese have a very long memory, especially when their honour is involved and they feel they've been insulted.

- Insulted?

- Well yes, think about it. The Tibetan exiles claim they were an independent country until the Chinese invaded in 1951. Lots of people support this view and the Chinese probably suspect the Indians do too. For that reason the Chinese feel that the Indians need to be punished, hence the military build-up in this area. Apparently they are planning to invade North East India and occupy some territory.

- What is this territory they're planning to take? Is it valuable in some way?

- Not at all. It's just hilly tribal land, forested, where it rains all the time.

The next day at three in the afternoon they came. A van swung into the yard, parked by our window and four people jumped out. We were in the bedroom and we braced ourselves for the encounter with Doctor Death. As they piled into our room we realised with a sense of delight that he wasn't with them. A big Chinese policewoman was in charge and she was trying hard to keep the others under control, to stop them being so cheerful. The two uniformed policemen were Tibetans and they looked just like the kind of people we had met in the villages. One of them was a Han Chinese in civilian clothes, with a round face and a huge smile across it. He looked confident and spoke in English:

- Herro. My name is Lee Fang. I am English teacher. Police ask me to interpreter. I here to help you.

The room filled up with conversation: I started talking to the teacher in English; Charles chatted with the policemen in Tibetan and the policewoman, who was getting increasingly frustrated started shouting over the top of all the babble with orders that nobody listened to. If Doctor Death had been present there would have been instant silence. The woman pulled out a school jotter and announced that she was going to read out our sentence, and the teacher signalled for us to be quiet. He then translated her words:

- You both must pay fine of seventy yuan (£10). For be in forbidden area. He then looked at Charles and said:

- Mistah Rambo can go today. You free to go. The lady handed Charles his passport.

- Mistah Mullee must sell horse. Silence descended and everyone looked at me for a response. I broke the silence:

- I can't sell the horse. It belongs to someone else. I have to get it back to Lhasa. This pathetic show of resistance made the whole group laugh. They knew I didn't have any choice.

- You see Mistah Mullee you must sell horse in two days or police they will take horse and use it for themselves. You sell horse or you have big trouble. For you, passport in two days, after you sell horse.

- Don't you see! I can't sell the horse.

They weren't letting my useless protests interfere with their fun day out. I couldn't understand why they were so cheerful and their attitude became annoying. Charles was already packing his rucksack and I followed them out to their van. The English teacher leant out of the passenger window, pointed at Pungya, laughed and said:

- Maybe you get lots money.

- Bastards, I shouted, waving my fist at the departing van.

I can't sell the horse, I said to myself. Bettina would kill me and I promised her to get Pungya back to Lhasa. I went inside and saw Charles finishing his packing. I was shocked:

- What are you doing? You can't leave me here.

- If you don't sell it they'll have you, Charles said with a laugh. I pointed up the hill and said:

- Will you come with me to that village up the hill, before you get the bus?

- Okay.

We led Pungya up the hill, following a narrow muddy path through puddles and past walls. A dog rushed out and yapped hysterically at our heels and Charles picked up a rock, fondled it and kept his eye on the dog, waiting for the right moment to throw it. We soon reached the village and it was small, lovely and surrounded by so many trees that it was invisible from Bye Eee. The villagers came out to look at us and Charles took up position in the middle of the village square and shouted out:

- Who wants to buy this horse? This fine horse. Only a thousand yuan (£110). A flurry of shock, then laughter rippled through the crowd.

- A thousand for that nag? shouted a dark skinned old man. You must be mad, he said. Everyone laughed again. Another man stepped forward and said:

- I'll give you two hundred for it. I pulled a face and waved him away. Despite their laughter they were interested as Pungya was a good horse with a great figure. A third man came up to him, stroked him and said:

- Nice horse, but he's a stallion and his cock is too big – look! Look!

Everyone crowded round to look as Pungya dropped his elephantine penis which started to become erect, growing to over a metre long. Pungya slapped his stomach with it and looked at the crowd with defiance. The children roared with laughter and danced around the horse, pointing and screaming. When the men realised that I wasn't going to bargain they lost interest and wandered off. I turned to Charles with an innocent expression and said:

- At least I tried to sell it. I can honestly say that I did.

- I really have to go. Come on, let's get out of here.

A kind family agreed to stable the horse for the night and as we walked back into town my mind started racing through various scenarios; maybe I could pretend to sell the horse? The police had told me to sell the horse but how would they verify it? Charles got on the early evening bus and promised to keep in touch and that evening I decided that I wouldn't sell the horse unless they somehow managed to force me.

The next morning after visiting Pungya and buying him some hay I entered the police station, a grim compound of low concrete structures with tin roofs, clutching the scrap of paper they had given me in exchange for my valuable passport. The police station was right next to the main road and there was continual rumbling and dust as military convoys passed by. How was I going to find my passport?

After asking around I found a buck-toothed policeman who had my passport and knew a few words of English. I was in luck. He beckoned me into his room which was big, concrete and bare. The only furniture was his desk and a chair and the only thing on the walls was a mirror. I knew his English was terrible so I spoke slowly:

- Tomorrow I sell horse. I will get seven hundred yuan. I emphasise the seven hundred by repeating it in Mandarin and holding up seven fingers.

- Can I have my passport back please? His expression was full of doubt and suspicion and he seemed torn between returning my passport, which was now lying on the table between us, provocatively, and mistrusting me. An idea lit up his face:

- You show me money. Horse money. Tomollow. I see seven hundred yuan then tomollow – passport.

I left his office cursing myself. I was the most incredible idiot. Where on earth was I going to find seven hundred yuan? I counted out all my money and realised I only had a hundred yuan –nowhere near enough to show the policeman. Why on earth did I state such a high price?

That evening I was out of ideas. If I changed the rest of my US dollar stash I could maybe get five hundred yuan. The problem was you couldn't change money legally in a place like this and the dodgy street hustlers who hissed change money in the centre would rip me off. I didn't even want them to know that I had any dollars.

I was in the restaurant writing up my daily diary when I saw a sight that I had been praying for: foreign travellers. Two dishevelled and exhausted looking westerners walked in; they looked like they hadn't washed or eaten in ages and they flopped down at a table. They didn't even notice me, perhaps assuming I was a local. I went over and used every ounce of charm to ingratiate myself with them with one goal in mind, to get them to take some of my US dollars and give me some yuan. Surely they had more money than me? Didn't everyone? The travellers were American and friendly, they were glad to meet a fellow westerner and exchange information. I gushed with helpful advice.

They had hitched from Lhasa to Bye Eee, had been stopped by the police on the road and sent back. They tried again at night, managed to evade the police and got through. I advised them to get out of town and watch out for Doctor Death. I asked if they had seen any fighting and one of them replied:

- We saw a large military parade in the town back there. Thousands of Chinese soldiers were in formation, chanting military songs and waving their machine guns around. Man, was it freaky.

Eventually I popped the key question and asked if they could change twenty dollars into yuan. They wanted to help, checked their stash and said they could only change ten of my dollars. I gratefully accepted their offer and we exchanged notes and then retired for the evening. I needed a new plan of action. I had painted myself into a corner with this absurd claim that I was going to sell the horse for seven hundred yuan. Then I had an idea that I was sure would work.

The next morning at dawn I snuck out of the hostel, crossed the yard, jumped the wall and shot up the hill. I found Pungya and saw he had pulled up his stake and was stomping around the yard in an annoyed way. I grabbed his harness, hammered it into the ground with a stone, found the boy and wheedled some hay from him. When the boy opened the back gate the guard dog saw me and exploded in rage; it threw itself at me like a barking missile. Fortunately the dog was tied to a wooden fence with a thick chain, which caught it by the neck and choked it. When the dog recovered its breath it barked savagely and strained hard against its chain. I threw the hay at Pungya's feet and talked to him: Hurry up and eat you old nag! We've got to get out of here. I've got to get you to a safe house.

The horse was taking ages to eat its breakfast so I wandered over to the house, knocked on the door and asked the boy, as nicely as I could:

- Cha doo gay? do you have any tea?

The boy looked at me inquisitively and he signalled that I should follow him. He led me out into the yard, towards the back fence where the dog was still barking. As I passed close to the dog it leaped at me with Herculean force and almost got its teeth into me. I jumped back and noticed with horror that the dog had broken its chain. I managed to get behind a door but the dog crashed through it like a bull and sank its teeth into my knee.

Instinct and anger took over. I grabbed the dog's chain – with the dog at the end of it – and started to swing it round and round. Within seconds the boy had appeared and I hurled the beast at his feet, noticed his apologetic expression, grabbed my horse and walked out cursing. I looked at my knee and, to my surprise, saw that it was fine. The dog had only got its teeth into my trousers, which were shredded at the knee.

My new plan consisted of walking with Pungya for about three hours, in the direction of Lhasa, where I remembered a friendly old man I thought could be trusted to look after Pungya. I reached the village, which was full of fresh young trees and little streams gurgling in the background, found the old man and left Pungya with him. I hurried back to Bye Eee with a growing sense of dread.

I got back to town and was hot and hungry. There was no time to eat; I needed to change dollars, go to the Police Station, get my passport back and then get out before nightfall. How the hell was I going to change money without being ripped off? I asked a dodgy-looking Khampa who offered me one yuan for one dollar, rather than the usual five, and I told him he was mad and walked off in a darkening mood. What the hell was I going to do? How was I going to show the policemen the money? I started to panic and have cold sweats. I realised that I could just tell them the truth, but I was so tied up in my pathetic deception that there seemed no way out.

Suddenly I saw the one money changer that I thought I could maybe trust, a big Khampa who I had heard was honest. I followed him into a fancy looking Chinese shop. It only had tins of fish and stacks of boiled sweets. I saw the Khampa man, went over to speak to him and was just about to pull out my precious US dollars – when three policemen came in through one door and three in the other. When I saw that Doctor Death was with them my insides turned to ice. I knew I was going to be busted and this whole shambolic farce was about to come crashing down. I managed to hold back my sense of panic and I recognised some of the faces, thanking my lucky stars that I hadn't done the deal with the Khampa – who had already disappeared from the shop.

Most of the policemen took up positions at either door, keeping one eye on the street and one eye on me. Doctor Death and one other moved in for the kill. This was it – the moment of truth. He called over the buck-toothed policeman, the one who knew a little English, and they approached me, muttering to each other. My passport was produced from the pocket of a trenchcoat and the English speaking cop said:

- You smell horse? I looked at him blankly, not understanding his question for a long moment.

- Oh yes. I smell horse. To man over there, pointing in the opposite direction to where Pungya was hidden. I tried to look calm and confident.

The game was up. If they asked to see the money all I could show them was US dollars and everyone knew that Tibetans were strictly forbidden from handling foreign currency. It would be totally unconvincing. Time seemed to crawl by and they didn't ask the dreaded question. They started to mutter furiously between themselves and the buck-toothed character stepped forward and said:

- Okay Mistah Mullee. Here is your passport.

I stepped out of the shop carefully, not really knowing what to think. I'd got my passport back, I had tricked them. I could go and get Pungya and return to Lhasa. Perhaps it was an elaborate ruse, perhaps they had been monitoring my every move and were going to arrest me. I looked round and saw the policemen heading off in the other direction; one of them waved at me. I got round the corner and jumped for joy. Yipee! I had done it, I was relishing every moment of my new found freedom. I went to the hostel, grabbed my luggage – two small saddle bags and a sleeping bag – and started walking towards Lhasa. I passed the restaurant and the friendly Yunnanese chef looked at me sympathetically and asked if I'd like to eat something. I couldn't resist.

- Shir bow dzer han kwai: (ten dumplings, very quick). I said

I sat down but was unable to relax. I was too close to the police and the shadow of Doctor Death. I needed to disappear, to get into the hills, out of sight and wouldn't feel safe until I was a long way from here. I went through my passport carefully, page by page, checking for anything that would incriminate me as a wanted criminal. Nothing.

As I was tucking into the dumplings I felt a finger tapping my shoulder and instantly all my fears returned. With a sense of terror I turned round and there was Doctor Death, looking at me with his neutral expression and dead eyes. Men in green stood behind him, one of whom had a machine gun. This was it, they had given me a moment of freedom – now I was going to jail. The policeman with the buck-teeth stepped forward and said:

- We want piece paper.

- Sorry, what do you want?

- Piece paper. Receipt for passport.

I sighed with relief. They just wanted to pick up the receipt they had given me for my passport. They didn't want to see my money stash, to verify my story of selling the horse. I stood up, found the receipt, handed it over cheerfully and sat down to finish my dumplings.

That night was spent in the village with the old man and the following day I was heading back to Lhasa, with Pungya, avoiding the roads. I started to appreciate how convenient it had been to stick to a road. Now I was having to negotiate river beds, hills, rocks and spiky vegetation. It was five hundred miles to Lhasa and I doubted my ability to keep going every day without the Teutonic discipline of Bettina.

The villagers were friendly and every evening I was able to scrounge some hay and barley for Pungya, and tea and tsampa for myself. I was eating up the miles, getting into a good routine – and then disaster struck: I caught a pig eating some precious barley that I had scrounged for Pungya and in a fury I ran over and kicked it in the butt as hard as I could. The pig hardly noticed my exertions, although it did wander off. I was in excruciating agony. I had kicked its hard tail bone and felt like I'd broken my toe, which I was clutching as I hopped around the yard. The swelling didn't go down for days, I couldn't walk properly and just to make things worse I found a raw saddle sore on Pungya's back, just where the saddle was placed, which meant I couldn't ride him. I cut my daily target from fifty kilometres to twenty.

The villages started to look like one another although one of them really stood out, a tiny place that was built around a series of ancient watch towers – small, round, defensive forts that were built of rock centuries ago and abandoned in modern times, surrounded by mature trees. The family who took me in were friendly and we talked about our injuries: I showed them my swollen toe and the old man told me that his horse had stepped on his foot that morning and he too was in agony. I slept inside, on the comparative luxury of a carpet.

The following morning I awoke at dawn and watched the woman of the house clean the fireplace, light a smoky fire using dried yak dung as fuel, waking her daughter and making tea. Why is it that Tibetan women always seem to be working while the guys tend to just sit around? After a fresh tea I stepped outside to feed Pungya and prepare him to leave. The daughter released a small flock of sheep from the back and they rushed through the yard. There was a small piglet among them, small enough to be seriously cute, and I looked at it fondly. I harboured no hard feelings towards the species. I noticed it run towards me and I made no move to avoid it, and then it stepped momentarily on my bad toe and shooting pains electrified me. I squealed in pain.

After a few days I reckoned it was safe to use the road again. As I plodded towards Lhasa the pain in my toe, as well as my fear of the police, subsided. Every day military vehicles passed by and I was convinced the drivers would tell the police who would come and arrest me. I gradually realised the drivers probably saw me as just another dirty peasant. I kept my face well covered by a scarf and a wide-brimmed hat and my clothes hadn't been washed in weeks. I started to use the road a bit more and

would stop at truck stops for refuelling with Chinese food. I even slept one
night in a roadside army camp, where a drunken Tibetan porter waved me
in cheerfully.

I approached the last high pass before Lhasa. It's called Baa La – the
word La means Mountain Pass in Tibetan. It seemed higher and more
intimidating this time round as I was alone. I needed to answer some
difficult questions: did I have the energy to get over this seventeen thousand
feet monster in a day? Could I rely on the Khampa family who fed us
sheep's head soup the last time we crossed over? Would they still be there?
The only way to find out was to head out at dawn and hope for the best.

As I left the army camp I got chatting with a group of Chinese truck
drivers and they told me there was not going to be a war with India.
They claimed to have friends in the army, other drivers, and they seemed
convinced that the whole thing was just a rumour. Wasn't it also a huge
waste of money? I wondered how much money they had spent on fuel
in trucking all those soldiers around, not to mention all the supplies that
were needed.

It was a perfect day: dry cold, hot sun in a cloudless azure sky. The
landscape was rocky, bleak and spacious. I felt delighted to be outside and,
for the first time since Bettina had left, felt as if I was shaking off the blues.
About six hours later I caught a glimpse of the top of the pass – still hours
away – and hunger was starting to kick in. Fortunately my energy levels
were high and I could keep going for the rest of the day.

Then two big dogs appeared, about fifty yards down the road and
knew they meant business. They were watching me suspiciously, trotting
towards me with a malevolent calm. I reacted instantly, threw myself off
the horse, jumped into the verge and selected a suitable rock. With one
short glance in their direction I did the most impressive throw ever done
in my life, and I wished Bettina had been there to see it. The rock arched
high into the blue sky, cracked down in front of the first dog, smacking it
in the face, and had enough momentum to reach the second dog, which
it punched in the guts. Both hounds yelped in pain, stopped in their tracks
and then withdrew from the road. In my daily battle against dogs, this felt
like a real triumph.

Then I noticed a nomad's tent at the bottom of a scree run. Since this
might be my only chance to get some nourishment I charged down the
loose rock, which Pungya negotiated brilliantly. I wondered if this ability
to handle rocky terrain was a characteristic of Tibetan horses? I reached

the black woollen tent in record time and stood before a huge Khampa man who was looking at me suspiciously. Did those dogs belong to him? He was standing proudly, with one hand on his dagger, saying nothing, the red plaits in his hair being blown by a strong wind.

I kept my distance so he could sniff me out before we spoke. I took out Pungya's metal stake and hammered it into the ground. I could feel his intense black eyes scrutinising me and I knew he was weighing up the risk of offering help. From one of the saddlebags I took out a small pile of compressed hay and Pungya whinnied angrily; he hadn't eaten all day. I watched Pungya gobble the hay like a hungry dog and look at me accusingly. I let as much time as possible pass, perhaps ten minutes, before approaching the Khampa who was still standing by his tent with his hand on his dagger. Eventually I summed up the courage to state my business:

- Troo tsong your bay? Can you sell me some barley?

He didn't reply, or react, but he did gruffly accept my presence and invite me inside the tent. It was warm inside and felt wonderful. He still wasn't talking. He gestured for me to sit on a rough carpet and told his wife to make tea. The tea was incredible because it contained fresh yak's butter, not the usual rancid variety. He had quietly given Pungya a double handful of grain and some hay and didn't seem to want any money. I discreetly took out a few notes and hid them under a pot, something I always did when payment was refused. An hour later I was rested, energised and ready to get to the people with the sheep's head soup on the other side of the pass.

We left the road on the last approach to the pass, as there wasn't time to make it over the top without taking a short cut. We cut across wild country – steep little river-beds, cut into the heather by long-gone storm waters, and marshes. When we reached the top of the pass the landscape flattened out and I noticed the view, waves of blue and brown ridges stretching out into the horizon. For the first time I really felt like I was on the roof of the world and I wanted to share the moment with someone. I wondered where Bettina was?

The short cut down from the pass led through more scree – millions of tons of loose rock had cascaded down the mountain. Again I was impressed at how deftly Pungya managed to follow me down and I wondered if a western European horse could have done it. We rejoined the main road and pushed hard into the evening, aiming to reach the Khampa settlement and their sheep's head soup before the sun went down. We kept up a jogging pace for hours on end, entering a sort of auto-pilot phase, as the sun dropped down behind the purple mountains.

At last I caught sight of the Khampa settlement and immediately my body started to give up, in anticipation of a rest. Each step became laboured and difficult; I staggered into their little compound like an old man on his last legs, stepping on a soft surface made of yak dung. A crushing wave of disappointment hit me as I realised there was nobody in; the place was deserted. I sat down on the soft dung, unable to comprehend the bad news, feeling bitterly let down by the Khampas who I was relying on to be here. A few minutes later I became aware of a terrible hunger gnawing at my insides and I had to get up and do something. As I wandered around looking for scraps of edible plants among the heather, I laughed at my own stupidity: why would they wait for me? They had no idea I was coming. They didn't even know my name. And they're nomads, of course they've moved on. Why would they hang around at the top of a pass? After feeding Pungya what scraps I could gather, as well as the scrapings of barley seeds from my saddlebags, I ate a small bowl of tsampa and cold water – a disgusting combination that not even the Tibetans eat. I slept on a soft pile of sheep dung.

The following morning I got up and left without having anything to eat. There wasn't anything to eat. I set off in a reasonable mood, confident I would find some nomads that I could buy some food from. Initially the walking was easy and I set out jauntily. After a few miles I felt completely exhausted and had to lie down in the soft welcoming ditch. I lay my head against a rock and instantly fell into a dream. I was transported to the Highlands of Scotland where my family used to live when I was very young. The mountains were different from the ones in Tibet, they were softer and more rounded. The sky was cloudy, the air felt damp and there was a slight whiff of the sea. The shattering sound of a helicopter broke the silence and it was heading directly towards me; I looked round and saw a small shed and a large H painted onto a patch of tarmac. I was on a helipad. The helicopter landed, turned off its mighty engine and the deafening roar slowly decreased in volume. A man jumped out, ran over to me and said:

- Thanks for coming Mister Murray. We'd like to offer you the job. You'll be in charge of this helipad from Monday! I awoke with a start, and blurted out:

- No! Sorry, I can't do it. I have to get Pungya to Lhasa.

I looked around at the unfamiliar mountains wondering where I was.

Where was the helicopter, the man, the Highlands? Shocked by the clarity of the dream I wandered on slowly, thoughtfully, knowing that I was reaching the end of my reserves. I couldn't go on much longer, but I couldn't stop either. I felt like one of those characters from an adventure story – lost and thirsty and staggering through the desert. Eventually I got used to the hunger and exhaustion and I entered a trance-like state where thoughts of life and death merged into one. All I knew was that I had to keep putting one foot in front of the other. Pungya became listless and he followed me obediently, as if he knew I was his only chance of survival. I would pull him and he would step forward jerkily, as if he too had retreated into a trance state.

Time lost all meaning and we wandered on blindly, one step at a time. My mind was empty and I wasn't even thinking about food or rest anymore, just keeping going. We rounded a low hill and there – resplendent and glorious in front of us – was the most perfect village I had ever seen. There was a nomad encampment arranged nicely on the left, above the road and on the right hand side of the valley, perched on a rock, was the most exquisite little monastery. Houses and their yards were spread out in the middle. It seemed too perfect to be true and my dulled senses told me it was a dream, or a mirage. Had we passed this place when we came through the first time? It looked vaguely familiar but I wasn't sure.

I staggered up to the first house and stopped by the gate, not sure if I could speak or not. A cheerful old woman came out, took one look at me and told me to come inside the yard. I staggered in with Pungya without saying a word. She seemed to know that we were hungry and beckoned me into the house. There was a small fire blazing and hanging above the fire were white squares of cheese on string, like bizarre necklaces. I touched one of the pieces of cheese and it was hard as rock; it had been hanging over the fire for so long that it had solidified completely. I wondered how people ate such cheese. Maybe it's like sucking a really hard-boiled sweet.

The brisk old woman handed me a plate of soft white cheese and I sat down to indulge. I had never had soft cheese in Tibet and it was indescribably delicious. Soft cheese was the one western food that I sometimes craved and I remember being enchanted by the sight of Australia canned cheese, which I had seen in a Kathmandu shop window. The woman served me more cheese after I had wolfed down the first plate, and then gave me tea and let me rest for a few minutes. As I dozed off by the fire she banged a pot loudly and shouted at me:

- Get out! Go and feed that poor horse of yours.

The old woman shooed me out of the yard and wouldn't take any money. I threw some notes on the ground but she picked them up and stuffed them in my saddlebag. She didn't have any fodder for Pungya, and said:

- Go to the road workers compound. They have plenty of fodder.

I walked down to where the road workers lived and entered the most impressive settlement I had yet seen for this type of worker. We had passed scores of road workers' shacks – all of which seemed sad places with as little food as we had. Every day we saw the listless and unfriendly workers, usually from central China, shovelling gravel from the side of the road into the centre. This place was extraordinary by their standards: there were several cottages, each with its own little garden, and a large stable for horses. There was no waiting, no negotiations, no begging or bargaining – the road workers took one look at me and Pungya and pointed to the stable. They had more hay inside than I had seen in years and Pungya was allowed to eat as much as he could. I lay down in a wide, empty, dry and comfortable horse trough and fell into a deep, dreamless sleep. Just before dropping off I felt an insect walking across my face but was too tired to do anything about it.

CHAPTER TWELVE

I was suffering from culture shock. After a month on horseback Lhasa felt like a vast and sophisticated metropolis. I hadn't seen an asphalted road since I had left and I was fascinated by the smooth, clean blacktop. I couldn't get used to the huge number of restaurants and cafes, all of which seemed to be full. I had grown used to one restaurant per settlement – even big places like Bye Eee only seemed to have just one restaurant. As I sneaked towards the centre of town like a criminal, fearful of being spotted, I couldn't get used to the number of people who were walking around. I felt like a wild man, a tramp, an outsider and I didn't want anyone to recognise me. I went around with my wide-brimmed hat pulled down low over my brow and a thin scarf over my mouth – the same disguise I'd been using to avoid the police.

It was August and Lhasa was hotter than I had ever known it. Someone had told me that Lhasa was on the same latitude as Cairo, and at the time this fact that had seemed meaningless as Lhasa was so high and usually so cold. Now it made sense. It also made sense that there were no pilgrims in town; it was too hot, and it was also the busiest time of the year in the fields. It was harvest time.

Having reached the centre of town I didn't know what to do with myself, and my instinct was to turn around and go back into the countryside. I had left Pungya, who was exhausted, with an old couple in a village about five miles away and I had slept there the previous night. I told them I would go out there every day to feed him. This was my only connection with the life that I had grown used to.

I was broke, had to find work and assumed my job at the Shata School was gone. Angri La, our contact at the Political Consultative Conference, must have been furious with me for taking off in such a cavalier fashion after asking me to take on the evening class. In fact, it was worse than this: he had set up the evening class with me in mind; I was to be its main teacher. He had trusted me with an important responsibility and I had disappeared. They must have a replacement by now.

I knew I should go and see Roger and Isabella, Sir Woo and Je Yang, but couldn't face any of them. I was sure my name was dirt and my chances of teaching again were non-existent. I didn't want to think about it. I should have stuck with Bettina. I went into a Chinese barber shop, sat in the big chair and looked at myself in the mirror for the first time in a month; a filthy, hairy tramp. A surly hag approached and looked at me with horror. She seized a fistful of my long hair, brandished her shears in the other hand and cut it all off. Later that day I ran into Je Yang, who said:

- You're not dead?
- Not yet. How are you?
- Teaching the Shata evening class is exhausting.
- I can imagine. Teaching is one of the most tiring things I've ever done.

I was homeless and landed with a knackered nag that had to be fed twice a day. Having got the horse to Lhasa I wasn't sure what to do with it. It would save a lot of hassle if the family who were now housing him agreed to keep him indefinitely. The idea of selling Pungya brought up traumatic images of Doctor Death. For two days I let depression and feelings of failure drag me down; I was daunted by the future, unable to face up to getting a job, missing the freedom of the open road and the camaraderie of everyone I had met over the last month. I went to the Post Office, hungry for word from the two Bettinas, but neither had written. I assumed Bettina Tucholsky, my girlfriend from Austria, had dumped me and this added to my feelings of misery.

The only person I felt able to visit was Joga, the short hunchbacked lady who had let me stay in her hovel so long ago. She seemed pleased to see me and, having sat me down amidst her Khampa friends and given me a cup of chang, insisted that I come and stay. I accepted without hesitation as her place seemed palatial compared to where I had been sleeping for the last month. I went straight back to the village where Pungya was located, bought some more fodder for him, grabbed my saddlebags and re-located to Joga's place and claimed the wooden bench I had slept on before. I told the family in the village that I'd like to leave the horse with them but they seemed reluctant. When I said I'd try and find a foreigner to buy it, and they could keep the proceeds, they cheered up considerably.

The atmosphere of drunken bonhomie at Joga's suited my mood perfectly. Every evening the room was full of rough Khampa men from the east, all dressed in thick cloaks and with their daggers on display, and big middle-aged women in floor-length woollen dresses who would constantly fill up our bowls with cloudy, alcoholic chang. The women were all resident in Lhasa and they would talk endlessly, sing sometimes, tease the arrogant Khampa men and act outraged when dirty stories were told. When I wanted to sleep, a small crowd would have to be cleared from my bed and if they refused to move, Joga would come over and shout at them, sometimes even hitting them with her wooden spoon. The Khampas loved it when she got rough with them and the more she slapped them the more they would laugh. I was able to fall asleep immediately in this environment. Joga appreciated my company because I wasn't as rowdy as the others and I promised to pay her rent. I also suspected I was something of a tourist attraction for her friends; an exotic foreigner who spoke a bit of Tibetan.

Je Yang soon heard that I was living in Joga's place. He made his way down the smelly alley, was welcomed inside and said to me in English:

- So, you've moved back into the slums?

I hoped Je Yang would ask me to help with the buses as I really needed to pay back Isabella. He didn't mention it and I assumed the illegal operation had ground to a halt. I could feel my self-confidence slowly returning and I knew if I just had faith, everything would work out.

- This teaching is killing me, said Je Yang. You just don't understand how exhausting it is. I only have to do it three times a week. Preparing for it is so stressful. I'm so feeble.

I felt sorry for him. He was a sensitive soul with a delicate constitution and I realised that teaching, or Tibet for that matter, just wasn't right for him. I could imagine that some of the characters in that evening class could give him a hard time and he was the kind of person who would take any form of mockery very personally. Je Yang needed to go abroad, if only for his peace of mind.

- How can I help you? I asked. He looked at me with a smile. He had obviously been waiting for this moment. He pulled out a slim booklet from his inside jacket pocket and said:

- Lesson Twenty-one. Tonight at eight thirty. Shata School. Please.

I had been feeling an increasing sense of guilt about Angri La's evening class, especially now that I knew that it was causing Je Yang such stress. It seemed I was leaving a trail of disappointed people behind me – and here was a chance to redeem myself. My first instinct was to wallow in self pity and complain that I wasn't ready to mingle with people yet – I was suffering from culture shock, dammit! One look at Je Yang told me that his anxiety was worse than mine and I had to just bite the bullet and get on with it.

The evening class had been set up for professional Tibetans who knew a bit of English. The big idea with the Political Consultative Conference, of which Angri La was a member, was to train up more English speakers to deal with the influx of tourists. Thanks to me, this teaching project was moving at a snail's pace. They couldn't solve the problem by importing lots of Han Chinese teachers as there was a shortage of English speakers in main-land China too. Looking on the bright side of things, if I kept my nose clean I could end up teaching English indefinitely in Tibet.

Most of the evening students had jobs. None had cars. They were almost all Tibetans. Every Monday, Wednesday and Friday the twenty students would leave their bicycles in the yard and come into the big classroom, a former chapel in the Shata Palace. It felt like I had a cross-section of Tibetan society in my classroom.

In the centre of the room sat the round faced and sharp-witted Tenzing, shouting out the answers with a speed and accuracy that annoyed the others. He worked at the Potala Palace as an official guide and translator and he would cycle back as fast as he could after the class so he wouldn't be locked out. Jigme – pronounced Jimmy – Taring was from Lhasa, a city his ancestors had once ruled. He told me proudly one day that his grandfather had been the Prime Minister (the Great Tsarong). Most of his family had been imprisoned by the Chinese for being Enemies of the People – the charge that Communists used against anyone they disapproved of. Jigme was in his thirties and his handsome looks suggested that he had escaped imprisonment. I assumed he had done this by becoming an avid Communist – but if he was a Communist why was he telling me about his glorious aristocratic family?

The other students were from more humble backgrounds and there was a good buzz in the air. By this stage my Tibetan was good enough to pick up swear words and terms of ridicule. I found it easy to get into banter with Tibetans but, for reasons I couldn't understand, I couldn't get into this kind of humorous small talk in my own language, in English.

Pert See, the dilettante of the group always arrived late. He sauntered to the back of the class, sprawled out on his chair and tried to impress the girls with his much-coveted Yamaha 125 motorbike. He was a mechanic working in a garage by the Potala and he became quite good at English. In front of him sat a truck driver, a beautiful schoolgirl, a businessman and a geologist who had been sacked from his government job for going to India.

In the front row sat university lecturers (geography and public administration), office workers from the big hotels, an editor from the Norbu Linka Publishing House, a Tibetan doctor who worked for the police and always turned up in uniform, an engineer of thermodynamics, a chef, and a lone Chinaman who didn't know a word of English, or Tibetan, but was treated with respect even though the others suspected him of being a plant from the People's Liberation Army.

I taught them three times a week for the rest of the summer, through the monsoon season and into autumn. At first it was difficult. Two hours of teaching was more exhausting than riding a horse all day or humping furniture up and down stairs in Edinburgh. I had to be on form to teach – if I was out of energy on a particular evening the class would just go to pieces. I could see what Je Yang's problem was now; he would have been unable to inspire them, or control them and they would have ended up intimidating him.

When I first walked in I was struck by terror – stage fright – at the prospect of speaking to so many people, row upon row of eager, silent, interested faces. I soon got over this and tried all sorts of tricks to break the stiff and formal attitude of the Chinese classroom. Eventually I managed to work out their sense of humour and they started to realise that their teacher wasn't interested in the formal rules of their educational system. In the Chinese culture the teacher is revered as a leader and there would be a permanent distance between teacher and students. It took them a long time to understand that this particular teacher actually wanted to accompany them to the teahouse and get to know them. Every week someone new would join the class and it kept growing.

I would spend at least an hour preparing each class, writing down lists of words that they should have learned and thinking up interesting ways of practising them; useful phrases that they might use in daily life. I didn't like the way that English was taught in Chinese schools – students would study from books for years before saying a word. I kept meeting people who had studied English in school who were tongue-tied; unable to construct

a sentence without the crushing feeling of shame they felt when making
a mistake. My way of learning a new language was built round making
mistakes; when I learned a new Tibetan or Chinese word I would repeat
it to anyone I would meet in the street; if they laughed at my ridiculous
pronunciation they would correct me and I would be more likely to
remember it. I didn't speak any Tibetan in the class but, by knowing it, I
could keep track of what they were talking about. It took about a month
before the students had the courage to address me in English. We would
have conversations like this:

- How are you teacher?
- I'm fine.
- Where are you going today?
- I'm going to the teahouse.

The classroom was large, unheated and badly lit. Clumsily inserted
wires thrust through the narrow windows and stretched messily across
the room to one bare light bulb above the students, and two above me.
The bulbs were so bright that I couldn't see the walls and I felt as if I was
on a stage. This encouraged me to project my voice across the room and I
would address the people in the back row. I tried to crack the odd joke but
it took months before they could get them, and it took me equally long to
work out their humour.

Power cuts were a constant occurrence in Lhasa. At least two hours a
night were spent in darkness, or candle light, and it was routine for the class
to be suddenly plunged into blackness. It became so normal that when the
lights went out I would just carry on talking as if nothing had happened.
Most of the students would just sit there calmly while the cheeky mechanic
at the back would leap to his feet, find the hurricane lamps and get them
going. I would use these moments to practice conversation skills:

- Oh dear, the lights have gone out. Now it is dark. All of you now say
the word dark.
- Duck, they would say.
- Not duck – dark.
- Aha, now we have light. Thank you Pert See.

I was so pleased to be back at work, and so focused on making the classes
enjoyable for everyone, that it took a while to realise that I was being paid
a pittance. Seven yuan, about one US dollar, was the going rate for an
hour of teaching in Lhasa, and this was barely enough to live on. Living
on pennies made life in Tibet a daily challenge because the Chinese had

imposed a two price-system whereby foreigners were charged double for hotel and transport services, and market traders and shopkeepers would treble their prices as soon as they saw a foreigner walk in the door. There was a good reason for this – foreigners got paid way more than Chinese – but it wasn't fair on those of us who lived locally. The upshot was that I had learned to bargain hard for everything and I enjoyed the hustle that went with it.

The real problem was that I owed both Isabella and Je Yang a thousand yuan each.

I made forty-two yuan a week from the teaching job and if I used all of this income it would take about a year to pay them off. What could I do to earn more money? Turn to crime? No, nothing worth stealing. Appeal to the folks back home? No, that's only for the last resort. Go to Taiwan?

Some time later I ran into Je Yang and we went to a teahouse. He thanked me for taking the evening class off his shoulders and asked me if I could help him with something else. My heart stopped in my throat: Please let it be the buses. He hadn't mentioned the buses since I had got back and I assumed he wasn't doing the business any more, after all it was illegal and risky. I had been so convinced that the bus business wasn't working, or that I wouldn't be needed for it, that I forced myself to not think about it. It just wasn't an option. Then I realised that maybe it was back on the cards and my mind was filled with optimism.

- Will you help me with the buses, Je Yang said glumly. I wanted to scream YES and hug him. It was hard to keep my cool.

- Sure, what's the situation?

- The problem is that the bus has really deteriorated. All those long drives to the border have ruined it. The foreigners all complain to the driver that it's too slow and they hassle him all the way to the border. I don't know what we can do.

- Just leave it to me, Je Yang, I said with a sudden rush of confidence. Let me deal with the problem. I'll think of something.

Life became busy. Between standing in for Roger, who was continuing his explorations of the wilderness, teaching the evening class and feeding the horse twice a day I had to find time to deal with the foreign travellers. I grew to dread the meetings I would arrange to sell tickets and answer questions – especially the Americans who tended to be pushy and suspicious. A typical conversation would go something like this:

- Hey, how do we know you're not going to rip us off?

- Do I look like a crook? Everyone knows me round here.

- You could just run off with all our money.

- Do you really think it's worth my while to do that?

I would leave these meetings with thousands of yuan stuffed down my trousers. I thought about running off with this money and realised it would be absurd; the money would soon run out and my reputation would be destroyed – and reputation is all you really have at the end of the day. This thought must have occurred to people in business throughout the ages and the vast majority of them would have worked out that it's so much safer and more profitable to stay honest.

After I had organised the second bus trip since getting back I had a brainwave:

- I've got it, I shouted in English to a bewildered old Tibetan who was sitting opposite me in a dingy teahouse by the Kirey Hotel. He smiled kindly at me.

I dashed into the empty hotel room that I was temporarily using as an office, pulled out a large piece of paper that I usually made the bus posters with, and began to write in large capital letters: SLOW BUS TO NEPAL. Under this heading I wrote some smaller text:

Don't miss this bus trip! Four fascinating days on the road. See the monasteries in Gyantse, Shigatse and Sakyapa. Only 120 Yuan. Leaving Monday July 25th from the Kirey Hotel gates. Sign your name here and get your ticket on Saturday.

It was a masterpiece and they loved it. We filled every bus from then on and I felt good about being honest and providing the cheapest tour bus on the road. By telling the travellers that the bus is slow, that it will be a hard journey and asking each of them if they were prepared for it – it turned the whole trip into a challenge and the complaints stopped. The trips became more popular, they stopped whinging and moaning at the driver and we started making serious money. When I met the driver he handed me a wad of cash, over two thousand yuan, and I was able to pay off Isabella and Je Yang. By late summer my money-belt was no longer empty and, for the first time in years, I was able to start saving.

I wasn't satisfied. I was yearning for something else but wasn't sure what. Where the hell was Bettina Tucholsky? She had said she might visit me here, an idea I dismissed at the time. If only it were true, but she hadn't even written to me. There was a postcard from Bettina Hertzog saying that she had reached Hong Kong safely and she hoped that Pungya was safe. I hoped she would be pleased that I had managed to get the horse back to Lhasa.

Although I wanted a woman my experience of relationships hadn't been successful. I didn't feel attracted to the foreign women who came to Lhasa and while there were many beautiful Tibetan women around I was afraid of getting tangled up with them. I still fancied Italian Paola with her long black hair and mysterious behaviour, but she was too religious and had been avoiding me ever since I had got back from the horse ride.

My mind often wandered back to Vienna where I had been a mural painter and where I believed my heart lay. I wanted to do some painting, some creative work, alone, without people or money – although I still didn't know how to paint a picture. All I had learned in Vienna was to draw straight lines and colour-in shapes. Then I remembered the furniture painters in the yard at the Cheese Factory hostel and I wondered if they would let me work with them as a volunteer.

The old man in charge of the furniture-painting workshop shrugged when I offered him my services. He didn't say yes or no but he waved a hand towards the lads who were sitting cross-legged on the floor and I took this as a sign that I could work, or at least hang out with them for a bit. I spent some days with them, painting a swirly dragon onto a piece of wood and watching everything they did.

The boss was thin and had a bright, wrinkly face. His manner was quiet, slow, patient and exact and he was the only one who worked on thangkas – Tibetan icons – all of which were based round the same layout; a central deity, frozen in mid-dance, arms akimbo, surrounded by hills, clouds and smaller, lesser deities in the background. They were simple, beautiful and had a fun, cartoon-like feeling about them. The actual painting was done on pieces of very thin leather which had small holes punched all round its edge. They would put string through these holes and stretch it tight by tying it to a small wooden frame – leaving a gap between the frame and the parchment. This gave the thangkas a robust, drum-like feel and it was surprising how manoeuvrable it became; the old man could hold it in an infinite variety of positions as he sat cross-legged on the concrete floor, or prop it up against a piece of furniture.

The old man was a gentleman and artist of the Old School. His three young apparatchiks were thugs by comparison. They wore nylon Chinese clothes, spoke guttural Tibetan and didn't seem to care about the interesting cultural experience they were exposed to. Their job was to paint the furniture, which was badly built wooden reproductions of ancient Tibetan designs. Although they applied paint in a slapdash manner I couldn't fault their work – the end result looked pretty good. Their main interest was having a good time and telling jokes, a dialogue I soon picked up on and joined in. I used my time with them to practice telling jokes in Tibetan, confident that they wouldn't judge me for poor grammar or inability to get the timing right, and they loved the distraction. They were keen to learn English and I would teach them phrases that I had heard in Indian stations:

- Gub dee, gup dee! You like gup dee! This was the cry of the Chai Wallah in every Indian station, selling cups of tea. I felt the phrase suited these lads.

My daily routine became fuller – the teaching, the buses and now the painting. I was busy and it felt good. I had also persuaded Isabella to take on Pungya. A week with the furniture boys was enough; I had progressed from jittery beginner to the stage where I felt confident with a brush. Although I couldn't paint a full scene onto a piece of furniture I could fill in shapes that had been sketched out by the lads and the one thing that I took away with me was the ability to draw Tibetan-style clouds – a short straight line with three half bubble shapes above it. It was surprisingly easy to do and I started using the symbol as a kind of signature from then on.

Having had a very basic grounding in Tibetan art I started looking at the murals in the temples with an eye for the detail, brushstrokes and techniques. Every temple and monastery in Tibet was filled with painted walls and nothing was left bare. The entrance halls had four guardian kings that looked like huge demons, and the idea was that they were keeping the evil spirits out and protecting the faithful. Each of these kings was fat and huge: one of them has a string of human skulls slung round his neck as he goes on the rampage, killing sinners and demons; one strummed a long necked guitar and seemed quite peaceful (perhaps luring his victims into a false sense of security); and the other two rode yaks as they rampaged through the underworld, crushing, burning and destroying the wretched demons. The images inside the temples were serene portrayals of Gods, saints, hermits and reincarnated lamas.

One afternoon I was sitting in the improvised staff room at the Shata School, a tall thin room with a window. I was idly passing the time with Angri La, the closest thing we had to a boss. The sun was piercing through the murky window and the air was hot.

- It's a nice day, I said.

- I disagree. Look there's a cloud. I looked up into the sky and only saw a deep blue azure colour stretching out into infinity. Was he mad? Better change the subject.

- Can you tell me about that mural on the wall above your head? I said, pointing to some faded remains of an image. He took a deep draw on his cigarette, looked at me wearily and said:

- I can indeed. This room was once an entrance hall to the chapel in there (pointing into the classroom). The guardian deities were portrayed in here and the remains that you can see over there – look – are still good. The Shata family were very rich and they only used the best artists.

- What happened here?

- The Cultural Revolution happened. Young soldiers destroyed anything that was old or cultural or religious.

- Were these murals destroyed?

- No, someone came in here and plastered over all the paintings. They were quick-thinking as they managed to save them, even though they are still hidden from view.

I stood up and started examining the wall with renewed interest. I placed my palm against it, feeling it and then started to move my arm in a big sweeping arc. Little bits of paint fell to the floor. I could see rich colours underneath the spaces where the paint had peeled and I started to pick at them with my thumb, as if it were a scab. With a growing sense of excitement I pulled out my penknife, opened the blade and used it to get under the thin layer of plaster and paint. More and more small bits were falling away and within minutes I had uncovered a patch of ancient, glossy gold paint. It glowed brilliantly, even though it had been covered up for so long. Angri La watched me through his dark glasses with a detached sense of amusement, sitting by my desk, feet up, smoking lazily on his cigarette.

- It comes off easily, I said with an enthusiastic grin. Could I restore it?

- Of course you can. I really don't understand where you find the time to do all the things that you do. It will take you about three years.

I wasn't remotely bothered by the amount of time it would take, in fact this would give me another reason to stay in Tibet. The more I scraped the more I got drawn into it, the more exciting and compelling it became and I gradually forgot about the presence of Angri La in the room. An hour later I stood back to examine what was uncovered and saw a swirling orange shape. I had no idea what it was but Angri La stood up, looked at it carefully, hummed and said:

- Oh yes, it's the outer edge of a great cloak.

The following weeks I became obsessive. I spent every spare moment scraping the thin layer of plaster from the mural – between classes, after meetings, first thing in the morning, late at night. It became a channel for my emotional energy and the more I got into it the more complex the task became. I felt real passion for the work. The image I was uncovering was one of the four Guardian Deities that guard monasteries and temples. It became my own secret project and I developed a sense of protectiveness about it and knew that if I told someone, if I shared my enthusiasm with even one person, they would almost certainly tell someone else, who would then tell someone else, and before I knew it there would be crowds visiting, gawping, taking photos and obliging me to explain the project in an intellectual way.

I was revealing a deity with a long-necked guitar type instrument, an enigmatic smile and a big tummy and I could feel that his presence was fun-loving and good. The more I worked the more I grew to admire the mural; it was a work of infinite talent, far superior to other murals I had seen in Tibet. I didn't let myself really indulge this opinion, after all who was I to judge? I hardly knew anything about art in general, let alone Tibetan art. Surely my view of it was biased by my close proximity to it. Could I really make an evaluation, a comparison? Of course not. Did I want to call in an outside opinion? No.

Every detail was perfect, every intricate design brilliantly executed, the colours seemed to blend in with each other naturally and it had a unique sense of rhythm and fun that I hadn't seen in other murals. The small figures seemed to be dancing around the fat deity and their sense of movement had been captured so vividly that they seemed alive.

Sometimes the students helped me for brief moments between classes, although they lacked patience and tended to be more trouble than they were worth. I didn't encourage them to come in after the first few times and never found one who was particularly interested. I realised there were two possible approaches to a task like this: a quick, rough uncovering of the whole space; this would allow a good look at the whole mural which was arrayed along a wall that was six metres long and three metres high, and I could finish off the partially uncovered bits at my leisure. The second approach was to work slowly and with infinite care on a small area – and I preferred this approach as it meant the rest of the mural would remain a mystery until long into the future. The tiny area I was working on was revealing a multi-coloured robe that seemed to be moving.

The most satisfying moment was uncovering a particularly detailed piece of the mural. I couldn't understand why so much detail was concentrated in the bottom left-hand corner of the room. With my penknife I uncovered a vein of deep, dark blue, which swirled downwards and was inset with floral designs in gold leaf. Circular gold shapes followed this river-like descent of dark blue and gradually I revealed a gold necklace, which was intertwined with other necklaces. Above this intoxicating mix of rich colours, was a big, bland splash of off-white paint and I couldn't work out why they had ruined such artistry in this way. It was only when I stepped back from the mural, after a few days, that I realised, with a sense of shock, what the artist was trying to represent:

- Of course, I said, laughing at my own blindness. It's a woman! The white splash of colour is her face.

Suddenly it all fell into place. All the detail, all the rich colours began to make sense. It was a woman, a beautiful one and she was dancing for the fat-bellied deity. Her torso was semi-naked, divided by strips of orange and yellow cloth, and she seemed to be in mid-motion. She held four green leaves and a billowy pink rose. Her hips were swinging, heavily laden with necklaces, and what I had assumed to be some sort of surrealistic tree trunks turned out to be her legs. The strange white frogs that had so intrigued me a few days before were – of course, how obvious – her feet. As I uncovered the surrounding area a sense of discovery grew within me and I felt pride in finding her. At last I have a beautiful girlfriend, I said to myself with a smirk.

The wall of the little room had been punctured with small holes, probably bullets from a machine gun. Then I noticed something that I had overlooked up to that point; this beautiful woman had a small bullet hole directly between her eyes. I felt an ominous shiver of cold ice run through me as I realised that she had been shot, killed, murdered. For a moment I was in a state of shock and my thoughts stood still.

After this discovery my heart seemed to go out of the project and I started to lose the passionate energy that I had put into it over the previous month. As if on cue, other things became more important and I didn't seem to have any spare time for the restoration project. I had become withdrawn from the outside world and there was nobody to share my discovery with. Now it was time to re-connect with society and see what was going on. Lhasa was full of foreign travellers.

Avoiding travellers was easy as they all hung around certain places and very few of them made it into the backstreets. I had never seen a foreigner walking down the stone paved lane where the Shata School was located, even though it was literally round the corner from the Barkhor, the ancient heart of the city. One evening I was in a teahouse listening to two Americans:

- Yeah man. All these tourists are ruining Lhasa. They're everywhere.

- Hey man, said the other one.

- You gotta light? My Goddamn joint's gone out.

- You know what I would do if I was a millionaire?

- Hmm?

- I would buy that big Potala Palace over there and turn it into a Holiday Inn.

- Good idea man. Do it.

- Sure thing man, just need to make a few bucks first.

I felt privileged to be living among the Tibetans and also be able to interact with the travellers whenever I felt the urge. All this changed when Roger and Isabella decided to take a break, their first break together since I had known them. As far as my quiet life was concerned all hell now broke loose.

Isabella had set up the Travellers' Co-op long before I had arrived. Her aim was to help foreigners find their way around a land where almost nobody knew English, where there were no tourist information offices, no bookshops and no maps. Every evening from five thirty to seven thirty, when she opened up the room in the Kirey Hotel, Isabella would sit by her bookshelves, give out information and answer questions. I had avoided the place since I'd got back from the east as I knew, sooner or later, that I would get dragged into this exhausting operation – a prospect I wanted to delay for as long as possible. Now the time had come to face up to it; I had to deal with the travellers and there was no way I could refuse Isabella as she had been so good to me over the previous year.

- It's midsummer, she had said to me.

- Hmm...I groaned inwardly at what was to come.

- I want to take the horse round the valleys. Rupert dear, we need someone responsible to look after our students, the flat, the Co-op and the cats.

The cats and the flat I could handle but the Co-op? And her classes? I accepted the task without complaint and she went into the hills with a bag of tsampa, a raincoat and Pungya the horse.

What had felt like a full routine now became insane. I was constantly rushing from one responsibility to the other. The main benefit of all this was that I could move into their spacious flat, although I didn't have time to enjoy the space. Summer was turning into autumn and the weather was changing; clouds were gathering above town and the rainy season was coming. The clouds didn't break for another two weeks, there was a build-up of atmospheric tension in the air and people would look up questioningly at the dark, moody, brewing clouds. One evening I raced from a bus trip meeting to teach Isabella's afternoon class and some people threw a bucket of water on me as I rode past; I looked back and they were laughing and pointing at me. I couldn't understand it? Was I about to be hounded out of town? I arrived in the Shata yard dripping with water, feeling rather silly and the students, who were laying around the yard languidly, started laughing at me.

- Why do they do this? I asked. The students giggled and conferred with each other. They weren't quite sure what to say.

- Before big rain come all people they waiting. We throw water until the rain he come. Then we no need throw water. Sky throw water.

My old bicycle became the mainstay of this speedy lifestyle. Moments after finishing Isabella's afternoon class, which I now found easy to do, I would jump on it and speed through the crowded Barkhor circuit, the streets that wrap round the Jokhang Temple, get to the Kirey Hotel and open up the Travellers' Co-op. For two hours I would answer their questions, which they would invariably put to me in a pushy and impertinent way:

- Are you getting paid for this?
- No.
- Why do you do it?
- Good question.
- How do you say goodbye in Tibetan?
- Tashy Delay.
- Do you know where I can buy some dope?
- No.
- How long have you been here?
- Not sure.

- Where are you from?
- Scotland.
- Is the road to Shigatse open?
- Yes.
- Have you been to Mount Kailash?
- No.
- How do I get to the Nepalese border?
- Get the bus. Look at that sign outside and come to the next meeting.
- Can I hire a car in Lhasa?
- No.
- How much does it cost to buy a motorbike?
- No idea.
- Can I borrow this book?
- Of course. All the books are for borrowing. Bring them back and leave us any books that you don't want.
- How do you say egg fried rice in Chinese?
- Gee Dan Jow Fan.

I persuaded some of Isabella's young students to join me in the operation and said it would be a good opportunity to practice their English. Initially they were very shy and didn't know how to stand up to the travellers' bullying way of talking to local people. I explained that these people are basically lost and frightened and they cover this up by behaving in a pushy manner towards local people. Within a few days the students were more comfortable and it was a useful distraction as it would get the travellers' attention off me, and I smirked at the long-winded way in which the students would answer simple questions. The travellers' warmed to the students as they generally never met a Tibetan who spoke more than a few words of English.

The Co-op was supposed to close at seven thirty, which was exactly when my evening classes – on Mondays, Wednesdays and Fridays – were scheduled to start. Getting the travellers out of the little room was hard as they found it comfortable and I had to shout and bang the chair on the floor in order to clear the room. I would race over to the Shata, arrive breathless, see the students lounging around in the yard, pull out the key and let them into the classroom. Sometimes I would take a few minutes to pace round the yard and gather my thoughts. The students always seemed to be pleased to see me and this was rewarding; it made the whole thing worthwhile.

One evening I was teaching the evening class when the rains broke. A deep and long roll of thunder, cracking violently overhead, rolled through the town like a tidal wave, shaking the buildings. The thunder in Tibet was far louder, and lasted much longer, than its equivalent in Scotland. Although Britain is well known for its rainy weather I had never experienced anything like the torrential downpours of Tibet.

As I got to know and like the students my confidence grew and my voice found new dimensions that I never thought I possessed. I could now project my voice to any part of the room as easily as breathing. With this new confidence came humour; I was able to make the classes witty and more enjoyable in a way that I hadn't been able to do before. As the rainy season rumbled by more and more people joined the class, until they were crammed up against the back wall. When Sir Woo, my first English language student in Tibet, showed up, I greeted him warmly. I also thought to myself: I wonder if he really does know the Chief of Police and, if so, could he get me a work permit? I'm not going to ask him as it was a nightmare last time.

My daily routine consisted of organising, planning, teaching, listening and discussing. Now that Roger and Isabella were away, and Angri La seemed to have disappeared into the woodwork, I felt a new sense of responsibility as if I was running the Shata School single handedly. I had long since passed that moment when I had doubted that anyone would ever give me a job and was now at the stage where I thought I should be better paid for my efforts. I was encouraged in this by the appearance of scores of English teachers who worked in main land China and were taking their holidays in Tibet. These teachers were amazed at the miniscule size of my pay, and I knew that they also had spacious apartments provided by the state. I didn't grow resentful as I had something far more valuable than any of them – freedom of movement. Their jobs obliged them to remain in the same place for a minimum of six months, and often two years, and I couldn't imagine them being allowed a month off. The one thing they had that I really needed was a resident's permit.

I had a new plan for getting a visa renewal. I would wait until the very last moment, a day before it ran out, and then go to Angri La and the other old leaders and demand their assistance. I had tried this before but Angri La had insisted that the Political Consultative Conference, the Deng She, had no power. I didn't believe it – it was, in theory at least, supposed to advise the government and the Communist Party about how best to rule Tibet. Surely they could at least speak to the police on my behalf?

I went to Sir Woo's workshop and asked him to write me a letter of recommendation, which he did immediately, on top of a big old Hitachi TV. The monitor, or group leader, of the evening class did the same and he asked everyone in the class to sign it. I then wrote out, and had translated into Tibetan and Chinese, a letter to the passport office at the police headquarters, requesting a visa. Then I found Angri La and his colleagues in their quiet office. He squirmed with unease when I handed over my passport and all the supporting letters. When I saw their faces and their total lack of enthusiasm I realised they weren't going to make much effort with this and it was likely that I would end up with an expired visa and would have to scurry to the Nepalese border where I would get a heavy fine – and may even be denied the right to come back. I put these negative thoughts to one side, carried on with my busy routine and started to appreciate what may well be my last moments in Tibet.

Two mornings later Tenzing La appeared in the Shata School yard on a bicycle. Tenzing was a member of the Deng She, the Political Consultative Conference, and was the official leader of the Shata School, even though he had only visited the place once, as far as I could recall. His cheeks were so saggy that they looked as if they were melting, but he had a friendly smile and his black eyes twinkled. He was so old that he made Angri La seem almost youthful. He carefully placed his old bicycle against the whitewashed wall, walked towards the school door where I was standing and I knew from his satisfied grin that he had good news. I didn't connect his visit to my passport request, as Angri La had been dealing with it.

He came up to me, opened his briefcase, pulled out my passport and handed it over. I noticed a small slip of paper fall out of his bag but I was so desperate to see if they had got me a visa that I didn't look twice at it sitting there in the mud. I quickly flicked through the pages and, to my horror, noticed that there was no visa. I was in deep shit. I looked at Tenzing La, who was still grinning, and he handed me the small slip of paper that now had traces of mud on it. I opened it and read out aloud:

- Temporary Resident's Permit for Foreign Workers Staying in the Peoples Republic of China. It was stamped and signed and gave me another six months. I couldn't believe it. I spoke to him in Tibetan:

- How did you manage it? Nobody gets these without a contract. I've never heard of it happening before in Tibet. He just smiled some more, shrugged and went to get his bike.

I felt a surge of happiness and gratitude. I thanked Tenzing La profusely, accompanied him back out into the street and he behaved in a way that suggested he didn't want any reward, not even gratitude, and this was the sort of thing he did every day. I could tell he was happy, and pleased to have been instrumental in keeping their main teacher.

For the first time in almost a year I felt a real sense of belonging, of permanence in Tibet and thought that perhaps I really could make this my home for the rest of my life. It was what I wanted although there were so many bureaucratic blockages to be overcome. My growing sense of confidence told me that I could deal with these, one at a time. I just had to be patient and everything would work out fine. I felt like the captain of a ship who has an endless series of challenges but is steadily heading towards his destination.

I started to see the Shata School from a different perspective. I had worked in it, grown to understand it and realised its shortcomings and potential. Now I had the confidence to do something about it. Isabella's class was coming to an end and the China Travel Service wanted to employ all her students as guides. The closer they came to the end of the course, the more her group started to lose momentum – students would turn up late, some wouldn't show up at all and there was a listlessness among them. I was looking ahead to a new intake of students, thinking about how the syllabus could be improved, what could be done to the rooms and what kind of new teachers we needed. I spent days writing a report about what had been done in the school's first year. I suggested that the school be modernised and made some suggestions as to how. The report became a proposal.

Finance was obviously the stumbling block and I suggested three possible sources: the various agencies of the Tibetan government, all of whom were apparently hell bent on economic development; the agencies of central government like the Ministry for Minorities and, thirdly, the foreign embassies in Beijing. The embassies would have been the easiest way to get some investment money, although the least acceptable to the diehard bureaucrats I imagined were pulling the strings in Lhasa. Je Yang translated the eight-page document into Chinese, I proudly handed it over to Tenzing La and I waited and waited for a response. Surely somebody would read it? Nothing.

I asked Angri La who shrugged, pretended he didn't know anything about it and promised to investigate. I was sure he'd read it and when I next cornered him he continued his story of not knowing anything about the report. I persisted and he eventually admitted that the Deng She leaders had been afraid of my proposal and were not going to do anything with it. I realised that I had stirred something up that I didn't really understand and left it at that. I remembered how long it had taken for them to hire me in the first place and perhaps I'd been a bit impulsive with this proposal. It was almost certainly a mistake to mention foreign sources of funding and perhaps I should have waited for Isabella before submitting it.

By this stage I had given up on Bettina Tucholsky from Vienna. She hadn't written to me in months and this convinced me that her spring time suggestion of visiting Tibet was just a passing whim. I had clung to the hope that perhaps she would show up out of the blue. Whenever I thought about it I assumed she was going out with someone else. I hadn't quite moved on; I was in a neutral zone, and was so busy with all my various commitments that there was just no time for thoughts about relationships and love.

Then there was Italian Paola, who had a gorgeous, sultry look and incredible long black hair. I had always had a soft spot for her. She was holed up in the Tibetan Hospital and I never saw her on the Barkhor anymore. I had no idea what she did, who she hung out with or where she was from in Italy, and all this made her seem more mysterious and attractive. Then she started showing an interest in me. One day she turned up at the Shata School and was directed into the little room where I was doing some hurried mural restoration. This was an ideal setting for our reunion as she was deeply interested in Tibetan religion, culture and art and it impressed her that I could talk so passionately about my work on the murals. Paola was the only person in the country that I was happy to discuss the painting with, and she appreciated it without saying anything.

One beautiful day Paola visited me in Roger and Isabella's sunlit apartment in the Shata yard. She said she could only visit me for a meenit. Half an hour later she made her move – she put both arms round my neck and gave me a slow kiss on the lips. It felt as soft as velvet and more perfect than anything I had ever experienced. I hadn't had this kind of contact with a woman all year and within a millisecond I was smitten. I couldn't believe it, she had spent months avoiding me and telling me she couldn't possibly come out and meet me for an innocent cup of tea:

- What the hell are you doing Paola? I said with a grin that I couldn't take off my face. She didn't reply.

I felt as if all my emotional energy had been piling up like a huge mound of bricks hanging over me. Each month more bricks would be added to the pile. I was unaware of this weight hanging over me until that moment, and then it all came crashing down like an avalanche – terrible, destructive, powerful but also wonderfully exhilirating . I was in heaven.

It never went any further than that one incredible moment, which was preserved in my mind as the most perfect kiss of all time. From that moment on she kept her distance and called me pericoloso, which means dangerous in Italian. Maybe my enthusiasm for her was putting her off. I became obsessed with her, all I wanted in life was Paola, she had unleashed a monster within me, and any spare moment I would try and find her. Every night I would be under her window at the Tibetan Hospital, leaning on the railings like a drunk, shouting up messages of love. When I realised that she really didn't want me I felt like I was in hell, and my commitment to my various jobs began to waver.

One evening I was leaving the Kirey Hotel after closing up the Co-op, later than usual, and the girls in the reception called out. I popped my head in and a Tibetan girl in a pink hat said there was a letter for me. She looked like she was about to burst out in a fit of giggles but I couldn't work out why. I opened the big wooden trunk that stored all the incoming letters and fished one out with a postmark from Hong Kong. I ripped open the letter and assumed it was from one of the many people who had promised to write. Oh shit, I said to myself, with a horrible sinking feeling. It's from Bettina Tucholsky, and she's coming here!

Despair flooded my mind. What incredibly bad timing. I had been nurturing my warm and friendly feelings for her all this time, I had managed to avoid getting too entangled with Bettina Hertzog in Eastern Tibet – and now, just a few days ago, I had fallen hook, line and sinker for Paola. What a disaster. And this poor girl was travelling half way round the world to see me. Oh my God, what am I to do? I said out loud to the bewildered receptionist, who seemed afraid of my dark expression.

At least I have some time, I thought, with a flush of relief. It takes about a month to travel to Lhasa from Hong Kong, overland. I then checked the date on the postmark: Oh no, it was sent a month ago. That means she will be arriving any day now! What am I going to do? My mind went blank. My guts were gripped by terror, as I had loved Bettina and didn't want to be cold and distant towards her. What else could I do? My heart was full of Paola, obsessed with her, and there was no room for anyone else. I rummaged around desperately in the wooden trunk for any other messages and found a handwritten note that had been written in capital letters:

- TO RUPERT. I'M HERE, KIREY HOTEL. BETTINA. I was dead and had gone to hell. I stepped out onto the street, looked up at the sky hoping that the Gods would put me out of my misery.

CHAPTER THIRTEEN

I wandered down the street towards the Muslim teahouse, one of my favourite haunts, and the owner spotted me and shouted a greeting, inviting me in. Normally I would have been in there like a shot and we would have been sitting down chatting. That evening I barely heard him, didn't reply and was lost in a nightmarish world of my own. I was trying to explain things in my head, going round and round in circles. I was staring vacantly towards the crowd that was gathering outside the cinema, seeing nothing.

How could we expect a relationship to work out if we had only been together for a weekend, if we hadn't seen each other in a year and if we were separated by thousands of miles? I was trying to justify things in my head. I felt a sudden burst of anger and I shouted out: Why the hell didn't she write? Why didn't she tell me she was coming?

My anger passed as quickly as it had come. How could I be angry with her? She was such a good person. She had a round face, a bright smile and was warm and cuddly. She had been my best friend in Vienna and we had spent many happy evenings together, drinking beer and talking late into the night. Our friendship was similar to the friendships I had had with men over the years, where talk was the glue that held it together. And for my first few months in Vienna I didn't fancy her physically, didn't even think about going out with her or sleeping with her. I was just enjoying her personality – she was one of the nicest, funniest, most interesting friends I had ever had.

On my last night in Vienna, when both of us were blind drunk we did the deed that changed the status of our relationship totally – we became lovers. The next day I left Vienna and hitch-hiked to Budapest and, on the spur of the moment, she decided to join me there. That weekend we wandered around that beautiful city, hand in hand, visiting Roman catacombs, ancient spas and Victorian pools, art galleries and parks – in a dream of love, intimacy and humour. Although I told her that it couldn't last, that I didn't trust myself emotionally, we got so close, and I felt so strongly for her, that it seemed like our bond was unbreakable and our feelings would last forever.

I felt myself being drawn back towards the Kirey Hotel which I had left only a few minutes before. I noticed, for the first time, that the sign of the hotel was written in English, Chinese, Tibetan and Mongolian. Why Mongolian? I was being drawn back towards Bettina and I couldn't stop myself. I still had no idea what to do. Should I run? Where to? Should I tell her about Paola? I couldn't. Should I just act as if everything was as before? I realised this was the easiest course of action, even if it was also the most cowardly. The fact that it was the least honest approach made me feel even worse. When dealing with women and emotional issues I was weak and helpless, like a child. I was a leaf, being blown about by the wind and totally unable to control the direction in which I was going.

- Where is she then? I said to the receptionist in the pink hat. She glanced at me with a look of faux innocence, as if she had no idea what I meant.

- Sue? (which means who in Tibetan) she said, returning to her pile of forms for the Public Security Bureau. She pretended I wasn't there.

- My friend, I said quietly, appreciating these last moments, the quiet before the storm.

- Her name is Bettina Tucholsky. From Ow Da Lee (Austria). She's just arrived. I went into the receptionists' room and stood there waiting for the information. The receptionist suppressed a smile and then put on her angry face:

- Kyo! (get out) she cried, using the word that Tibetans shout at dogs. She pushed me but I didn't move. We both laughed. Then she relented and said:

- Room S24.

Something inside me said that I should be running up the stairs like an infatuated lover with a bunch of flowers in my hand. There was no way I could do that, even if there was somewhere in town where cut flowers could be bought. Instead I stood in the inner courtyard and looked up at the balconies, four levels of them on three sides, and waited until I saw her. After a while she appeared, we waved and I went up. She greeted me with a warmth and affection that immediately made me feel guilty because I knew

I couldn't return it, even though I did hug her. Although she was wearing a scruffy old jumper, dirty jeans and clomping great climbing boots she was looking great, more attractive than her image in my memory. Was my mind playing tricks on me? Had I deliberately distorted the memory of her to justify my sudden loss of interest? I didn't know what to say and everything that came out of my mouth seemed wooden, stiff and inappropriate:

- Come and stay in my flat! I blurted out, without thinking. I said it because I wanted to act the good host and didn't know what else to say. What I had done was given away the one thing – privacy – that could have given me the space to work something out. She agreed, packed her rucksack, which I carried and she followed me down the backstreets. The only thing I could think of to talk about was the weather:

- Rotten time of year to visit, I said blandly, this is the rainy season, the Monsoon time. Should be over soon. Usually the sky is so blue it's ridiculous. Sometimes we don't see a cloud for a month.

I had no experience of suddenly sharing a flat with someone who was once close but now was in this hazy no-man's-land. I knew that an awkward and difficult atmosphere would descend as soon as her initial fascination with Roger and Isabella's flat passed:

- Do you really live here? You're lying!

- Actually I'm looking after it for an English couple who are on holiday

- It's amazing. Who painted those wooden pillars? Whose is that huge music machine?

- Er, that belongs to Roger. He's English.

I should have faced up to my fears and told her everything that had happened with Paola. But I couldn't. We went back to the hotel and met with Uli, a beautiful Austrian who Bettina had travelled with from Vienna. For the next couple of days they walked around the city, visited the obvious places, while I worked and desperately tried to figure out how to tell the truth.

- Hey Paola, I said in a manic voice. I had burst into her tiny bedroom on the top floor of the Tibetan Hospital, something I had never dared do until now. She looked up slowly from her pile of books but said nothing. I tried to embrace her. She pushed me away sharply.

- Guess what! It's unbelievable. My girlfriend from Vienna has just turned up, just like that, out of the blue. What shall I do?

- What do you mean?

- What shall I do about you?

- Ees good for you. Today you are a lucky boy.

- Paola, you don't understand. It's you I'm crazy about. She glanced at me swiftly and I detected a momentary look of warmth that was quickly suppressed.

- No! You can't have me! You are pericoloso! She got up and pushed me towards the door, shoved me out and slammed it. All this made me even more infatuated with her and I picked up a suggestion she had made long ago to help her translate medical texts, my role being to edit her poorly written English, and it gave me an excuse to spend time with her. Soon enough they both met and Paola later said:

- Bettina is very nice girl. You are a lucky boy. I leave you now, and she went off to a religious festival up a mountain. I was consumed with guilt about Bettina.

With Paola out of the way I hoped that things would click with Bettina. Of course they didn't. It was all wrong and she started to feel it; she had probably felt it since her arrival. My burden of guilt increased with every day that passed and by the end of the week I felt the overwhelming need to come clean, but until I blurted it out I still wasn't sure what to say and, of course, it all came out wrong:

- Hey Bettina, I said one night, as I was about to climb into Roger and Isabella's big double bed with her.

- Yes, what is it?

- I need to tell you something. I don't find you physically attractive. That's just the way it is. I then explained that this wouldn't change anything between us, after all we are good friends and I hoped we always would be. I had hoped to tell her the truth and start from scratch but I was too cowardly to tell her about Paola. I could see that she felt wounded.

- How do you think it feels to travel half way across the world, visit someone you think is special only to discover he doesn't find you physically attractive? She turned towards the wall, curled up into a ball and didn't say another word. I sat down at the table, opened my page-a-day diary and stared at the blank page.

Bettina soon bounced back from this low point and we found something of mutual interest: the mural in my little room. She wanted to work on it and I agreed immediately as I had been neglecting it. She spent a lot of time on her own, in the little room, and the painting took on a new life under her guidance. The deity's vast stomach was divided into sections where different experiments were tried out; some pure alcohol there, cotton wool and water on that bit, and she had found some soft paintbrushes which she used like a make-up brush on a woman's face.

- You're so professional, I said with a sense of awe when I saw what she had done with the stomach.

- I feel like a butcher, she said. Kind soothing words fell from Bettina's lips: Without you there would have been nothing.

I was losing my grip, I could feel it as I cycled blindly through crowded alleys, not seeing, steering by instinct, consumed by confused thoughts and feelings. Until recently the juggling act of my various responsibilities had been invigorating, exciting, motivating – it reminded me of dancing. Now I felt rudderless and no longer in control. I was like a weak captain who had been overthrown by his own crew, locked up in the hold for a while, and then released and allowed to wander around as a harmless buffoon. Sometimes I felt as if my life had been a shipwreck and I was the stranded sailor, in the sea, clinging to a piece of wood. This feeling had come about since Bettina's arrival although I couldn't blame her for any of this, she had been a model of charm and consideration. The problem was me. I was cracking up and had no idea what to do.

Roger had just got back from his latest expedition and he took over the running of the Co-op on alternate days. When it was his turn he would turn up late, face a crowd of angry travellers and struggle to deal with their questions. I felt obliged to help him out by opening up on time, holding the fort until he came and then, each time, being unable to leave.

When Isabella got back from her horse trip she soon took over the Co-op, getting Roger to do what he liked best – riding around town on his big trike, acting as a sort of courier. She was the lynchpin of the foreign community in Lhasa and I breathed a sigh of relief when she returned as it took some of the pressure off me. I had to vacate their apartment and that made me homeless, a minor problem that could be dealt with later. I wanted to get out of town, I was suffocating, and so I proposed to Bettina that we go to Gyantse. She wanted to bring Uli, her Austrian travelling companion, which was fine by me as the three of us got on well together.

Gyantse was an antidote to all the bad feelings and high pressure that I had felt in Lhasa. I'd forgotten how amusing Bettina was and Gyantse revealed her perceptive and unusual sense of humour. We stayed in a cheap hotel run by an attractive Tibetan woman who was charming with us but cruel and depraved with her hunchbacked sidekick whom we called

Igor. We did things I never would have bothered doing on my own, like walking round the ancient walls that wrap round the town centre and carefully examining the skulls and images of death in the hallway of the main monastery. The townspeople were friendly, they would invite us in for tea and ask where we were from, and in the market there was loud banter between the peasants and the market traders.

Back in Lhasa, Bettina and Uli checked back into the Kirey Hotel. I said I couldn't afford to stay there, which was partly true. I had two other reasons for not joining them: I wanted to be on my own for a while and felt like protesting about my accommodation situation. The Deng She, the Political Consultative Conference, had promised to resolve this problem but had done nothing about it. I was fed up, thought I was doing a good job, for a paltry reward and went on strike. My form of protest was to sleep in the park, the Norbu Linka, next to the Dalai Lama's former summer residence, and tell everyone that I was sleeping rough because the Deng She wouldn't give me any accommodation.

Most people I told thought the idea of me camping out was quite amusing, and I probably made it sound like fun. I had a small Muslim student called Amala, a petite girl who hardly ever spoke but who took action when she heard about my sleeping arrangements. Amala took me round to her house, located in a small and spotlessly clean courtyard, right next to the Shata School, and introduced me to her Granny. The courtyard was tiled all round, shaded with exquisite plants and was quite unlike anything I had seen in Tibet. I felt I had been plunged into a tropical paradise. The family knew all about me and were infuriated that the Deng She hadn't provided me with a room – and gave me one of the most delicious meals I ever ate in Tibet, They insisted I come round three times a day for meals.

Amala's father owned a huge bottle-green motorbike, a German design from the 1930s, with a sidecar that had two seats – one for me and one for the Granny . We set off in a cloud of fumes, roaring through the backstreets, scattering people left and right, heading for the Deng She. The Granny marched in to Angri La's office and berated him for not providing the English teacher with a place to live. Angri La squirmed with embarrassment, made some excuses and within a few minutes agreed to provide me with a flat. I couldn't believe it. We all marched outside again, Angri La got on his bike and we agreed to meet back at the Shata courtyard. Twenty minutes later we walked into the staff room, exactly where I had been working on the murals for the last few months and Angri La told me I could use it as a bedroom. This made sense as they had some authority over the building – they had given Roger and Isabella the upstairs flat.

I installed an old camp bed and a little petrol stove and felt like I was sharing a room with the fat-bellied deity and his beautiful consort. The only problem was that at midnight they would lock the gate and, at some point during the night, Roger would turn up and bang on the door, demanding entry. I would get up, find the keeper of the key, and let him in.

My routines continued and Bettina, Uli and I decided to travel to Ganden Monastery, a few hours to the west of Lhasa, to watch a big religious ceremony. We hitched there in a truck and joined a massive crowd of Tibetans who were making their way up the hill. It felt like being part of an elemental force, like a river, and when we reached the monastery, which was once a small town, we flooded into the old streets, made up of destroyed buildings, and I saw the place fully populated as it used to be before its destruction during the Cultural Revolution. The sky was overcast, black clouds were visible on the horizon and we could hear a distant rumble of thunder. A cold fog descended and made visibility difficult. Every abandoned building seemed to be full of people from Lhasa having picnic lunches. The sound of wind and people talking was interrupted by a haunting, booming, bass note of huge Tibetan horns. Dense crowds surrounded the main buildings and I could hear people weeping loudly. On the rooftop were monks in maroon robes blowing long horns. Then the big, wooden double doors opened and a line of monks in tall yellow hats appeared. The crowd parted, as if by magic, and made a corridor-shaped space, just wide enough to let them walk through in single file.

The monks were carrying what seemed like a huge carpet; an object so long that it kept trailing out of the main gate as if it had no end. There was a shortage of monks at the tail-end of the fabric and eager citizens jumped in to help carry it. Slowly the monks led this snake-like procession up to the highest point of the monastery where the fabric, which must have been three hundred metres long, was arranged in a straight line. The tension in the crowd was increasing as the material was prepared and an endless series of instructions were being shouted.

The monks started to unravel the fabric and it quickly unrolled down the building, revealing a massive portrait of Buddha's face. The main colours of the image were yellow and gold. A momentary silence fell over the crowd, followed by a loud ooh sound, reflecting the awe that we all felt. The Buddha image on the carpet seemed to be smiling down on us and then, as if on cue, the clouds parted and the sun came out, bathing everything in rich, warm sunlight. All was perfect for a few minutes and then the sun went behind a cloud and the vast image of Buddha started to be rolled up.

The ceremony was over and my thoughts were on food. We found a makeshift teahouse where we filled up with cup after cup of sweet tea and chunks of bread. Then the crowd was flooding back down the mountain and we hurried ahead, taking short cuts between the winding road, made it to the bottom before the horde and soon got a lift to Lhasa in the back of an open truck. I could feel the wind stroking my hair.

A few days later something strange happened. I had been working hard and was feeling guilty about not seeing enough of Bettina, so I went to look for her. She wasn't at the Kirey so I scoured the teashops and ended up in the Snowlands Hotel where I saw her with a big fellow with a black moustache. Hang on a minute, I said to myself, isn't that Big Paul? The guy from Vienna that we used to work with together in the City Art Gallery, the Künstlerhaus, where he had worked as a watchman. Was this really him? I had last seen him at my flat, at my going-away party, where he got blind drunk, chatted endlessly and fell asleep in the corner. Paul? Here in Lhasa? Impossible. A big smile spread across my face and I went up to him and said:

- Hey Paul. What the hell are you doing here?

He looked at me through sad eyes and mumbled something indistinct. He had traces of white dust in his hair and a dishevelled appearance that suggested he'd been travelling on the open road. The three of us went to a nearby Chinese restaurant where we ate dumplings and drank Chinese beer. I was stunned by his arrival and wanted to celebrate by getting drunk, his favourite pastime as far as I could recall. He was Austrian but his English was good and he told us his story, his sudden decision to get a cheap Aeroflot flight from Vienna to India, via Moscow. He produced a half bottle of Black and White Scotch Whisky and told us he had bought it in Moscow, inviting us to look at the customs stamp to prove it. He had ridden buses through India and Nepal, walked through the chaotic Tibetan border and onwards for three days until he got a lift to Lhasa. His luggage consisted of a guitar and a rucksack full of home-made Austrian wine. I was so intrigued by his appearance that it was only later that I noticed that Bettina was in a black mood.

- What's wrong? I asked. Don't you like him? She gave me a strange glance and said:

- We had an affair in Vienna. It was a disaster and I clearly told him to fuck off, and the great oaf comes all the way here to say that he loves me. The great big-footed moron.

I felt no trace of jealousy and found it hard to take their relationship seriously; he was twice her size, had half her intelligence and was much older. The most striking thing about Paul was his massive black moustache, but there was also something warm, appealing and tragic about him. I wondered if he was an alcoholic.

The next evening I invited them both round to Isabella's place and made dinner. There was still a bad atmosphere between them; Bettina was still simmering with resentment, had told Paul that he had to leave Lhasa within a week and then refused to speak with him. He turned up at Isabella's with a bottle of red Austrian wine, in a two litre bottle and I realised that I hadn't tasted wine, apart from the sickly sweet Chinese variety, in over a year. My taste buds went haywire as I felt the most amazing sensation, warm and wonderful, sweep through my body, from my toes to my face. The next day Paul was nowhere to be seen, he had packed his bags and left the Snowlands Hotel without a word. It felt strange. A month later I received a postcard from Taiwan which said: Anytime you wanna job, come to Taipei. Paul.

As Bettina's departure date got nearer we became closer and friendlier. The appearance of Paul had put our own relationship into perspective and the feelings of guilt that had tormented me were fading. She had come to Lhasa via Hong Kong but was leaving via Beijing, Moscow and the Trans-Siberian Express. She had bought the return part of the ticket from Budapest at the absurd price of $40, a quarter of what you would pay in China – where ticket prices were hugely inflated for the foreign tourists. I gave Bettina $160 in cash, with the request that she send me by post four tickets from Beijing to Budapest. I planned to sell them at a huge profit and congratulated myself on my business acumen.

The day she left was a sad one. I plodded along the dark streets before dawn, accompanying her and Uli to the Golmud bus, having nothing much to say. As Uli fought for seats on the bus I briefly kissed Bettina goodbye, felt a pang of affection for her and wandered back to my place, feeling empty. I had really enjoyed her company, she was a good travelling companion and I would miss her. I wasn't going to dwell on it, I felt motivated to throw myself into the teaching, work on the mural and improve my grasp of the Tibetan language. That night I had an evening class and one of my students, a worker at the Post Office, pulled out a telegram from his pocket and gave it to me. I thanked him, opened it and read: Coming Sunday. Flight CA 4142. Lots of love Mummy and Stewart.

I couldn't believe it: another surprise visit. I had three days to prepare, to put work-related things on hold once again and make sure that I would have some time available when they came.

I couldn't remember when I had last seen a plane. I was standing at the airport, which was quite a way from Lhasa, over an hour to the south, across a huge river. With a small crowd of people we were all staring into the sky, awaiting the arrival of the plane from Beijing, hoping to see it appear over the mountains. Suddenly, I saw a long silver tube racing down the runway and I almost jumped out of my skin with shock.

A group of people filed off the plane and I saw Stewart, and then my Mother. They passed the armed guards who had kept us off the runway, hugged me and said hello. I couldn't get over the feeling of how strange it was to see them here. They looked pale and different from how I remembered them. Stewart kept looking round at the scenery and then said in a dazed voice:

- Where's the airport building? I looked around at the grazing yaks, the empty Tibetan landscape, and said:

- I see your point. I've never been here before and assumed it was one of the most modern parts of Tibet. I suppose my standards are different from yours. On the way into town I appreciated the tarmac road, one of the only smooth roads in Tibet, and we glided along in a Japanese bus. When we got to Lhasa Stewart said:

- That's the worst bit of road I've ever been on.

As soon as they settled into their luxurious room at the Lhasa Hotel they unpacked whisky, chocolate, shortbread, new shoes for me, books and all sorts of things I had grown used to not having. I thought they would need time to acclimatise but all they wanted was to change their clothes and see the city. They were bursting with energy. We went to the Norbu Linka Summer Palace, located right next to the Lhasa Hotel, where we met with Mimi, one of my students, who took us inside a nearby building where her family lived and plied us with chang, the white alcoholic drink, questions and hard biscuits made with butter that had taken me months to get used to.

At the hotel they had hired a room with three beds in it, one of which was for me. I couldn't get used to the softness of the mattress, the sensation of real white cotton – it just didn't feel natural – and I felt better on the floor where the thick pile carpet was more comfortable than most Tibetan beds. We ate yak burgers in the restaurant and I was overwhelmed by their generosity. I had assumed that they would be exhausted by the altitude, as I had been, but they never seemed to tire and we walked around the city, visited my friends, were treated like royalty by the Tibetans and went everywhere by bike. After a few days I realised they weren't going to collapse with exhaustion so I organised a trek.

I took them on the walk I had done from Ganden Monastery over the mountains to the south, to Samye Monastery. This time I got properly organised and borrowed all the camping equipment and food supplies that we would need for a few days in the wilds. We gathered a big mound of gear, got a lift in a truck to the starting point where I hired three yaks from a dodgy looking nomad. It was becoming a proper expedition and this was useful experience that I could offer to foreign tourists in the future. We spent the first night in a village, being plied with chang and butter tea – which they hated, as most foreigners do – and then walked up a high pass the following day.

The energy that Stewart and Stephanie had brought with them soon dissipated on the endless climb. The altitude finally got to them. My Mother rode a yak almost to the top of the pass while Stewart wasted his energy by running around and by the end of the day he collapsed with altitude sickness and we had to sling him onto the luggage yak in order to make it over the top. We slept that night in the yak driver's big woollen tent and walked for all of the next day. As we approached Samye Monastery we reached a river that was so swollen and raging that it was impassable, and we had to come all the way back. I was furious but they didn't seem to mind. On the third morning Stewart told me about his dreams:

- I dreamt of terrifying demons, like those ones we saw in the temple in Lhasa. They were torturing people with fire. Then we were in a house that was surrounded by the devil and the People's Liberation Army. They sealed up the house, set it on fire and kept patrolling the outside so that nobody could escape.

- I wonder if it means anything, I said.

Back in Lhasa, Stewart had noticed how poor the city's hygiene was. It was the time of the year when the cesspits within the houses, all of which were on ground floor or basement rooms, were shovelled into the streets from where the stinking black mass would be collected by men with a handcart. I had got completely used to the smell and knew that if my bike tyre touched even a spot of the gooey mess the stink would get onto my clothes and remain there for days. Stewart had studied civil engineering at Glasgow University and he couldn't accept it:

- Rupert, why does all the sewage get shovelled into the street like this?

- That's the way they do it here. It gets transported to the fields where it's used as compost.

- Do you have any idea how unhygienic this all is?

- Er... it freezes every night in Lhasa and surely that helps to stop the spread of germs.

- They should invest in a decent sewage system. It would prevent a lot of people getting sick. It would be the first thing I would do if I was in charge.

- Yeah?

- What they need to do is dig trenches down all the main streets and lay a sewage system for the whole city. I can't believe that nobody has done it yet.

- I've never thought about that stuff. I suppose I've got use to the way they do things around here.

Just before they left there was a big thunderstorm and Stewart was fascinated by the power of the storm and spent most of it out in the rain, protected by the waterproof clothing he had brought from Scotland. I was busy teaching that day, doing the Co-op and trying to avoid getting soaked. When I met up with them later that evening they were excited by having seen a double rainbow above Lhasa, but infuriated by the fact that Stewart had left his camera in the hotel. Later I was told that a double rainbow is a bad omen in Tibetan culture; it means that bad times are coming.

Roger and Isabella had returned from their travels and were taking back most of their responsibilities, which was a relief. We had a dinner with them both, Je Yang joined us too and everybody got on famously. Je Yang was about to leave Tibet as he had been offered a better job in Beijing, and said I could carry on the bus ticket business with the driver directly. It turned out that Je Yang was booked on the same plane as Stewart and Stephanie and I accompanied them all down to the airport and saw them vanish into the long silver tube, which took off into the sky. I still couldn't get used to the sight of planes; they seemed so out of place and so remote from my own experience.

Stephanie and Stewart wrote from Beijing and said that Je Yang had been fascinated by the escalators at the airport. Je Yang wrote to say he was missing me and he hoped we would stay friends. If there was anyone in Tibet who had made my life there feasible it was him: without the frustrating, annoying, nerve wracking bus business I never would have earned enough to make Lhasa my home. For the following week I felt rather sad – all my friends had gone – and I had the urge to drink too much. I found two new drinking buddies, a Tibetan exile from the USA and a teacher from Canada who had ridden his mountain bike all the way from Kashgar, thousands of miles to the west.

My birthday was approaching and I was reminded that Roger's was only two days after mine. I would be twenty-four years old and he was hitting forty. I proposed a joint birthday party, he agreed, and I threw myself into organising it. The event was going to take place in the Shata classrooms and a neighbour helped to push the tables and chairs to the sides of the room so we could make a big space. Then we took my bike to the shop and managed to strap three cases of beer onto the back rack and went back to fetch another three. We then went into Roger and Isabella's flat, dismantled his hi-fi system and re-wired it in the classroom. I asked two restaurants to prepare big meals for delivery to the Shata School.

I wrote out invitations by hand – in English, Chinese and Tibetan – and handed them to all my students and every other local I had got to know. The students had organised a whip-round for the beer and gave me a handful of crumpled notes, a gesture that I really appreciated. They were furious with Pert See, the tall, scarred mechanic with the motorbike, for not contributing to the beer fund. This feeling was compounded by his reputation for stealing people's girlfriends and the class monitor said he would not be allowed to come to the party. On the night Pert See was the first one to show up. He greeted me warmly and made a bee-line for the booze. I stood there with him, worrying:

- Do you think anyone will come? I asked Pert See dismally, expecting the worst. He took another swig of beer, smiled but didn't answer my question.

The classroom looked like a big empty, ghostlike shell now that the furniture had been moved aside and I looked at the bare white walls and thought of all the things we could hang on them to cheer the place up. I prepared myself for the humiliating scenario of nobody turning up.

After what seemed like an eternity, people started appearing: my evening students, Sir Woo, Tibetans from all walks of life (including Angri La and some of his Deng She colleagues) and a smattering of foreign travellers that Roger had invited.

Tibetan parties follow a set of traditional rules, none of which I knew about. All the Tibetan guests had come up to me and placed a soft white scarf, a Kata, round my neck. Most of these were made of thin starched cotton, like the material used for making bandages, while some were made from beautiful silk. When the room was full of chattering people my neck had become a foot thicker with all the white scarves and I asked one of the students if it was okay to take them off yet. He laughed, said of course and I left them in my room. I had been given these scarves before, in monasteries, but to receive so many at once felt like a real blessing. By now the beer was flowing, the atmosphere was loosening up, people were slapping me on the back and a pile of presents – all of which were edible – was building up on one of the tables.

Then I learned, to my horror, that the host has to double up as Master of Ceremonies. I had always shied away from this kind of grandstanding and when I asked Roger for help he became busy with his hi-fi system which he said had a fault. One of the guests was a Buddhist scholar and he was whispering instructions into my ear about what I should be doing:

- You must propose a toast to the school, he said. I banged a glass, got everyone's attention and said in English:

- To the School. A small cheer went up and everyone drank their beer and chang. The scholar had briefed me about the other toasts that were required and I started getting into the spirit of it:

- To the Tibetans! A louder cheer went up and more beer was gulped down.

- To Roger! I yelled to cheering and clapping.

- To the Dalai Lama, I shouted, and the loudest cheer of all went up. This had really broken the ice but people were still standing around rather stiffly. Good dance music was playing. Why weren't people dancing?

- Mister Teacher, hissed the Buddhist scholar at me,

- Yes, what is it.

- You must to start dancing. Then all people follow.

Under normal circumstances I would have run a mile from such a responsibility but the beer had given me courage and without further ado I offered my hand to my pretty Muslim neighbour, drew her into the middle of the floor, a space that seemed to have grown bigger, and danced in front of the delighted crowd. I continued into the second song and Pert See the cheeky mechanic sauntered up to Jill Kluge, one of the foreigners who worked at the Lhasa Hotel, and pulled her onto the dance floor. Minutes later it was full of swinging, whooping bodies and I wondered where they had learned to dance so well. Not long after I banged a glass and shouted out in three languages:

- The food. Please eat!

The crowd seemed to react as one and there was a rush of bodies towards the tables. As they were tucking into the Chinese food I went next door where I had asked Roger to set up his slide projector so that Jurgen, a silent bearded German, could show his exquisite slides of the Tibetan landscape on the big white wall. The problem was that Roger, who had agreed to project Jurgen's pictures, had loaded the projector with his own slides. I had no idea about this as I hustled everyone through to see photos of their country; but then the lights went out and an endless series of Roger's shots came up. To make matters worse, Roger started talking about his pictures and we had to endure a long presentation. I felt a surge of real anger towards Roger, and a sense of humiliation, but the crowd seemed happy enough about it and I couldn't say anything.

The next morning I was awoken by a deep shaking which began in the floor and worked its way up the walls until small bits of rubble started to fall from the ceiling. I lay there with my eyes closed, not wanting to wake up, assuming one of the neighbours was jumping up and down in rage, on my doorstep, because I hadn't opened the door for him. Was this a new type of hangover? As the shaking grew more intense and the whole building started to move, I realised it was an earthquake. I had to get out of the room. It would take me about a second to reach the window, another second to get out where it would be safer in the yard. I was stark naked under the bedclothes and I didn't want the neighbours to see me like this so I hesitated, and as this internal debate continued the earthquake stopped. Within minutes I was fast asleep again.

When I went out later that day I noticed that everyone was talking about the earthquake. There seemed to be general agreement that it meant something and there were various interpretations afoot; the monks at the Jokhang Temple said that the statues had been awoken by the event, people in the market said it symbolised a time of strife and a student I chatted with said the earthquake represented a decline in moral standards. Later that day it happened again, just when I was having a crap through a slit in the floor on the upper storey at the Shata building. As the roof above me shook violently and the town made a roaring sound, my only concern was that the slit I was crouching over would hold up and I wouldn't end up being plunged into the stinking cesspit below. I had heard about an English teacher in Lhasa to whom this had happened; she was plunged into a pool of excrement, had to swim out and subsequently went mad. Earthquakes were a new experience for me and I found it exciting although I didn't want to imagine what it would be like to be trapped under a building. Fortunately there were few casualties that day and the only buildings that were seriously damaged were the newly-built Chinese ones; the old Tibetan structures had resisted well.

A few days later Roger said he was leaving town again. This was fine by me as I really liked his class and would be with them for a month. He was going to Mount Kailash, the fabled Holy Mountain in Western Tibet, which is over a week away by road. Mount Kailash is the ultimate location for western travellers in Tibet and only the most hardened of them attempted the journey. I had never even considered going there.

For Tibetan Buddhists, Kailash is the centre of their spiritual universe. Many pilgrims walk round Kailash three times and they say you can achieve enlightenment if you walk round it a hundred and eight times. Two of the great rivers of the subcontinent – the Indus and the Brahmaputra – rise in the vicinity of Mount Kailash and it has an important place in Hindu myths and legends. What's odd about this is that the whole region around Kailash is a high altitude desert, and I had always assumed that deserts are dry.

Charles Ramble had told me that the landscape around Mount Kailash was the most impressive in Tibet, but also the most harsh and inhospitable, and you need to be really well-equipped – or as tough as a Tibetan villager – in order to survive the climate there. An English school teacher had chartered a bus, and a truck for the baggage, and he had put notices up around the hotels in Lhasa looking for people to join him for the month long journey. I hated the idea of travelling for a month with thirty unknown people but Roger was keen to join them and offered himself as their guide. I helped him pack camera gear, tools and spare cookers and hoped it would work out fine.

The third unusual thing that happened during that period was that

Tibetans started confiding in me and sharing their concerns. This was a sign that people trusted me, and it was touching, but I couldn't understand why it had happened all of a sudden. I couldn't help feeling it was something to do with my Mother's visit. Never before had I been invited to so many Tibetan homes and many of my new friends wanted to talk about the Dalai Lama's visit to Washington DC where he was scheduled to talk to Congress about human rights.

What seemed to particularly irritate the Tibetans was that the Chinese media was highly critical of the Dalai Lama whom, it claimed, was trying to Split the Motherland. The media said he was a monk meddling in politics and they described the US Congress as an accomplice in the Dalai Lama's attempt to destabilise China. These comments stung deeply as most Tibetans regard the Dalai Lama as their spiritual leader. If the Chinese leadership had been wiser it surely would have ignored the Dalai Lama; this wouldn't have upset the Tibetan people, it would have deprived him of global publicity and sent out a message that they don't consider him to be a threat – which he isn't.

The Panchen Lama, on the other hand, was regarded with suspicion by most of those to whom I spoke. He was the number two in the Tibetan Buddhist pecking order and it was well-known that he was under the thumb of the Chinese Communist Party. I heard him being referred to as a Chinese Chopstick. He lived in Beijing, not Shigatse which is the traditional residence of the Panchen Lamas. Not everyone hated the Panchen Lama; some said he was strong-minded and had stood up for the Tibetans' rights whenever he could and it was said that he had persuaded the Chinese to introduce the Tibetan language into the school system. The Panchen Lama had a huge belly and he looked like a formidable character. He reminded me of the fork-wielding demons I had seen painted in the hallways of the Tibetan temples.

Word seemed to spread around that I was someone who could be confided in and more and more people came to see me. The main complaint was that China was flooding Tibet with immigrants and they were taking all the best jobs. Apparently there were very few jobs available for Tibetans and it seemed that Chinese immigrants got all the government jobs as well as support in the setting up of small private businesses. Another complaint was that schools were segregated and English language classes were not available in the Tibetan schools.

The overall impression I was getting was that the Tibetans didn't like having the Chinese in their country, a view I had heard many times from the foreign travellers but never, until that moment, from Tibetans themselves. I wasn't sure if this upsurge of criticism that I was hearing was connected to my status as a trusted insider or if it was a sign of the times. I had no idea that a political storm was brewing, a storm that would blow away all the resident foreigners in Tibet.

CHAPTER FOURTEEN

October the 1st 1987 seemed like just another day in Lhasa, but it took me several weeks of talking to eyewitnesses to work out what actually happened that day. It started normally enough: pilgrims walked round the Jokhang Temple and people from the countryside prostrated themselves on flagstones that were brightly polished from all the bodies that constantly rubbed up and down on them.

Just after ten in the morning twenty-three young monks from Sera Monastery gathered in the plaza in front of the Jokhang. One of them was carrying a large bag and when he opened it the others helped him to unfurl a big flag that showed two snow lions against a Japanese-style rising sun backdrop. It was the old flag of pre-Communist Tibet and was strictly banned in China where it is considered a symbol of separatism and rebellion. In India and the western world it has become the symbol of Free Tibet. I had never seen it on display anywhere in Tibet; many people had photos of the Dalai Lama in their homes but nobody dared to display this flag.

The monks had presumably made the flag themselves as it was long and thin and it fitted exactly into the line that they formed across the plaza. Then they started to walk round the Kora, the mile-long holy circuit that wraps round the Jokhang Temple, and a growing number of Tibetans looked on in astonishment. What they were doing was so reckless that very few people joined in their march, but after they completed two circuits of the Kora eight monks from the Jokhang had joined them. They were chanting:

- Poe Rang Zen, which means Tibetan Independence.

The Kora and the Jokhang lie at the heart of Lhasa and are surrounded by old, stone built buildings – many of which were painted white. Many were small shops, selling trinkets and useful items for pilgrims; some were homes, one was a school and the building nearest to the front entrance

to the Jokhang was a police station, an old fashioned stone building that
fitted in so well with its surroundings that I had never noticed it before.
According to what I heard later, the police inside the station had no idea
how to react to this outrageous display, an act of defiance against the
Chinese State that had not been seen since the 1960s.

In the past the Chinese had dealt with demonstrations like this by calling
in the army and mowing them down with machine guns, but Tibet had
opened up, there were between fifty and a hundred foreign witnesses and
the police had had no training in how to deal with civil disobedience in a
non-violent way. The police waited until the monks had completed a third
circuit before taking action.

As the monks started on their fourth circuit round the Kora they were
blocked by a line of Chinese and Tibetan policemen. A large and excited
crowd quickly formed. The policemen were armed and several of them
were wielding their big leather belts. The monks walked towards the
police line confidently and without slowing down, looked at the Tibetan
policemen, who were in the majority, and chanted:

- We are brothers!

The police attempted to arrest the monks and take them towards
the police station, which was about thirty yards away. They resisted and
fighting broke out. The monks were heavily outnumbered and one by
one they were beaten to the ground and dragged through the big wooden
doors of the police station. The crowd soon grew to one or two thousand
strong and bystanders started to help the monks in their struggle, but too
late to save them from arrest.

Although they managed to arrest the monks the police station was now
faced by an angry mob that was calling for their immediate release. A line
of policemen formed in front of the station's big wooden double doors;
they had their backs to the wall and were being screamed at from all sides.
This was a rare moment for the Tibetans to vent their pent up fury and as
the impotence of the police became apparent the confidence of the mob
grew. Stones started to fly and the police retreated into the station. One
of the last policemen to get off the street was hit on the back of the head
by a stone and he dropped his gun, an AK47 assault rifle, a Kalashnikov. A
small boy rushed up, grabbed the machine gun but it was taken off him by
a group of older boys who smashed it to pieces on the cobbles. Meanwhile
the police station was being pelted with volley after volley of stones and
the police soon withdrew from the roof and went inside.

Inside the police station the group of thirty-one monks were in a corner of the main interior courtyard, being guarded by a ring of heavily armed policemen. The monks alternated between chanting Tibetan Independence and trying to persuade the Tibetan policemen to stop collaborating with the Chinese. The police were unsure of what to do and treated their prisoners violently – at least one monk was beaten with a spade!

Then four shots were fired from one of the upper windows that looked over the courtyard; three of the bullets thumped into the plasterwork above the monks' heads but one of them hit a young monk in the top of his skull. A small fountain of blood poured over several other monks and he fell to the ground, stone dead. The monks started chanting as loudly as possible and, according to my sources, the police guards didn't seem to know why the shots had been fired, or by whom.

Outside, over a thousand people were shouting Free the Monks while several foreigners were taking photos of everything that was happening. More than an hour passed and the police showed no sign of releasing the monks – or being reinforced. The mob grew in confidence and a small group of Tibetan men approached the police cars, vans and motorbikes that were parked in the narrow street alongside the station. One by one these were ignited, and huge plumes of smoke covered the area. The vehicle nearest the police station was an old fashioned motorbike with a large sidecar attachment; a group of children had managed to set it on fire and they pushed the blazing vehicle towards the big wooden door of the police station. Soon the door was on fire and the flames quickly spread through the wooden floors and beams inside the building.

The blaze spread quickly and a senior policeman ordered the monks in the courtyard to be moved upstairs and locked into two adjoining rooms on the top floor. Armed Tibetan guards were assigned to each room and locked in with the monks. By now the fire had reached the top floor and, one by one, the doors to the monks' rooms burst into flames. The Tibetan police guards then ordered the monks to jump out of the windows. This involved smashing the glass and twisting the bars out of their frames.

As the monks began to jump out of the window into the arms of the welcoming crowd below, a police jeep suddenly roared up the alleyway, scattering people in all directions. Policemen jumped out, fired a machine gun above the head of the crowd and managed to capture three monks before retreating under a shower of stones. The last monk to escape from the station had a smile on his face despite the fact that he had been badly burned; big welts of blackened flesh hung off his body. He jumped into the crowd, was held up shoulder high by the people and then rushed back into the police station to save his colleagues.

With most of the monks free, the anger of the mob subsided and soon afterwards the police gained control of the area around the police station. The police had been getting out of the burning building by a discreet back door that the mob wasn't watching. They re-formed in the side alley by the front door of their station, were joined by a few reinforcements and took control of the alley. Although they didn't have enough force, or confidence, to clear the crowd from the main square they were shooting randomly into the crowd and one American told me he was hiding in a doorway, holding a tin bowl over his head, as bullets whizzed by. The main square, and part of the Kora, were still packed full of restive Tibetans.

Meanwhile in the Shata building, a few hundred yards away, things were pretty normal for a Thursday morning as far as I was concerned. I had not been out of the yard that morning to buy supplies and I was sitting in my narrow room teaching English to Lakdrun, a beautiful 14 year old neighbour who had been thrown out of school because she didn't want to go to China along with the brightest kids from her class. I was really enjoying being in the presence of such beauty and wanted my teaching relationship to go on for at least another four years and then....when she was old enough...

It was my first lesson with Lakdrun and we were working on the present tense of the verb to have. I was so focused on the lesson that I didn't pay any attention to the strange noises coming from outside, or her nervousness. Suddenly the door burst open and Sean, a phlegmatic Englishman, was standing there. He looked flushed and excited and I wondered what had happened to his well-known reserve. Lakdrun jumped up in embarrassment and tried to hurry off but I grabbed her wrist, sat her down and told her we'd get back to work as soon as I got rid of this visitor.

- What the hell are you doing here? said Sean.
- Teaching English to Lakdrun here.
- Don't you know what's happening out there?
- Er, no...I leaned back in my chair, feeling quite satisfied after an intensive teaching session, ready to listen to Sean tell me about some

minor problem.

- There's a bloody great protest happening just round the corner.
- What? You're joking aren't you?
- Lhasa's on fire, there's dead people on the streets.

For a few long seconds I thought he was joking, after all these things just don't happen in Lhasa, a Buddhist city where violence is abhorred. His eyes didn't share my rapidly evaporating sense of fun. Suddenly I realised that he was serious and I simply had to go and see what was going on.

I jumped up out of my chair, hustled Lakdrun out of the room, grabbed the padlock, locked the door, hurried into the yard where I saw my neighbours standing round the pump looking nervous, with none of the humour and vitality that they usually display, and went into the alley at the back. It was deserted but I could hear a roar from the direction of the Jokhang and we hurried off towards it.

The alleyway in front of the Shata leads round the side of the building and connects to the Kora, where a small crowd of old women, children and teenagers were gathered. They were shouting at some Tibetan policemen who were standing nearby. We passed the crowd and into the Kora, which was quite narrow at that point. Our route was blocked by two policemen who hadn't seen us and we walked slowly towards them, ready to dive into the gutter in case of trouble. There was an inert body at their feet and they loaded it onto a plank and moved off. I crept up the Kora and saw a blackened, burning building and Sean hissed into my ear:

- That's the police station.
- I went past here every day for almost a year, I replied, puzzled. And I never knew it was a police station.

The plaza in front of the Jokhang was full of stones, wood and debris and I wondered where it had all come from. There was a constant sound of single shots being fired. Sean was explaining what had happened when a group of policemen, who seemed to be in a state of panic, rushed by. Then a policeman spotted us and ran towards us while shooting his pistol into the air. We raced back down the alley towards the Shata, got round the first corner and hid in a doorway. He didn't follow. I felt a surge of strong anger towards the police welling up inside me, and this drove out any elements of fear. We made our way back up the alley towards the Kora when Isabella appeared with a thin blond man in glasses – who, I later found out, was the US Consul from Chengdu. Isabella was in tears and was obviously heading home.

- How did you manage to get through the police lines, I asked her.

- It's terrible what's happening out there, she said. Please come home with me. People are being shot out there. There's nothing we can do.

- You go home, I said. I have to see this for myself.

Sean and I made our way back up the alleyway and were able to get past the police by creeping round a big fire engine, that was sitting there uselessly, full of heavily armed firemen who seemed to be frozen in terror. The vehicle had been pounded with stones and every window was broken, every panel dented. We headed for the south side of the plaza, where the main crowd was gathered round a burning jeep. I joined the crowd and although nobody said a word to me, or to each other, during the next few hours, I could feel a powerful sense of anger towards the police force.

A jeep slowly approached the crowd. It nudged its way through and the Chinese driver seemed oblivious to the furious anger that was simmering all around. Immediately big Tibetan men surrounded the jeep, trying to work out if he was a policeman or a civilian. He was allowed to pass and I could feel the crowd growling in anger. Then a young man in a green cap hurled a stone at the windscreen and it smashed a neat hole through the glass, narrowly missing the driver. Nothing else was done to the jeep and it was allowed to pass unscathed.

Sean and I made our way towards the Jokhang temple where there was a huge pile of rubble and debris lying about. We looked at the group of green-clad policemen who were standing in front of the police station; they were waving pistols and automatic weapons in our direction and shots buzzed overhead. The only people between us and the police was a small group of village children who had formed a front line of stone throwers. Immediately to my right stood a young nomad boy, clad in a one-piece grey coat made of rough leather. It was furry on the inside and belted at the waist. He looked at me with a happy, relaxed smile as if was really enjoying himself. In his hands was one of the long slings that I had seen the shepherd boys use to great effect; two metres of woollen rope, connected by a small leather patch that holds the stone. He would pick up an egg-sized stone, fit it into the leather patch, swing it round his head in a long slow movement and when he released it there would be a loud cracking noise and the stone would fly across the plaza at impressive speed. Others were doing the same and the policemen, several hundred yards away, were having to jump and dive in order to avoid these missiles. I heard several of them hit the wall of the police station with a satisfying thumping sound.

The sound of a high velocity bullet, quite different and much more frightening than the light popping sound of the pistols, had an immediate effect on the crowd. Everyone bent down at the same time and tried to find cover. I had instinctively jumped behind a prayer flag holder that was embedded in a little pyramid of concrete and provided some cover, and Sean followed. We huddled there for a few minutes and guessed it was a police sniper using a high-powered rifle. After a few minutes we stood up and headed for the shelter of the main entrance to the Jokhang, joining hundreds of other Tibetans. All eyes were trained on the police and I'm sure everyone was thinking the same thing:

- What will they do next?

A skinny young boy aged about thirteen then ran towards us from the direction of the police station. He was dragging what looked like a sack. He came directly towards me and dropped his load by my feet. I looked down and realised that it was the body of a small boy. I bent down and looked into the face of a nine or ten-year-old village kid. I slapped him lightly, felt for a pulse and looked for a bullet hole. Nothing. His eyes were open and he was gazing without seeing towards the sky. His body convulsed, a small quantity of foamy blood spumed out of his mouth and I put my ear to his mouth to listen for a sound. Nothing. I ripped open his buttons and searched his torso for bullet holes but couldn't find any. Had he been dropped out of a high window? I looked up to the crowd that had formed a tight ring around us and gestured upwards with my palms. They understood my meaning at once: the boy was dead.

I looked up at the faces around me and saw expressions of horror and disgust at what had happened to this young boy, and people started to wail as if they were at a funeral. I stood up and saw some very ordinary Tibetans, perhaps students or young bureaucrats, breaking off some wood from a nearby water container to make a rough platform. They pushed their way back through the tight crowd around me and then placed the small boy onto it. They lifted the boards head-high, other hands joined in, and started to walk round the plaza, chanting as they went. This seemed to galvanize the crowd, to give it courage and they moved as a mob towards the police lines. The police fired bullets into the air and then retreated. I looked round to see where Sean had gone but couldn't see him anywhere; I was sure he'd be okay and had no intention of looking for him; I felt like I had become part of the crowd wanted to see what would happen next.

The small group who were carrying the dead boy then moved away from the main square, towards People's Road – an asphalted modern street that leads towards the Chinese shopping area and up to the gates of the Regional Government of Tibet. Although the crowd had lost its elemental fury there were still hundreds of people milling around, perhaps thousands, and we all seemed to get sucked into this group marching up the Peoples' Road.

A small beggar boy, whom I recognised from the market, led the crowd up Peoples' Road. He carried two lumps of concrete, shouted at the crowd to follow and I could see he was having the time of his life. The boy saw a Chinese man, a scruffy looking worker in a blue jacket, cross his path and screamed Chinese, rushed at him and threw his rocks. A few other boys joined in this charge but the man in blue was too fast for them and he got away. A gang of boys soon formed and they started to smash the windows of the Chinese owned shops that we passed.

A line of military jeeps and trucks parked across the road blocked the route up People's Road. At the front of these vehicles was a line of Chinese paramilitary soldiers in green uniforms. They all wore steel helmets and carried large automatic rifles. They looked young, inexperienced and nervous – and as the mob got closer they started to melt away and the vehicles, one by one, drove off in the direction of the regional government. Soon there was only one young soldier left and the beggar boy charged at him, throwing stones and hurling abuse, and he turned and ran.

The way was clear and we soon reached the end of People's Road, where the road is cut across by another one. There was a concrete traffic podium in the middle of the road, a cylindrical shaped object with a flat top. They placed the boards holding the dead boy on top of the podium. The front line of the crowd was made up of four women and a man and they shook their fists and shouted at the Chinese paramilitary soldiers who were gathered on the other side of the road, in the entrance-way to the Autonomous Government of Tibet. This group of soldiers looked like they were unarmed, but behind them was a line of trucks and hundreds of reinforcements.

The crowd kept growing but was leaderless and didn't seem to know what to do. Whenever a Chinese person appeared on the street they would be met with a hail of stones, although they all seemed to escape unhurt. At one point they attacked an old Chinese man and I rushed over to try and help him; I was joined by several other Tibetans who stopped the attack and escorted him to safety.

A blue delivery van drove round the corner, into People's Road, and skidded to a halt as soon as they saw the size of the mob. Both doors were flung open, the Chinese driver and his mate jumped out and ran into the gates of the government building. Several Tibetan teenagers approached the vehicle and tried to set light to it. They couldn't get more than a small flame going. A second group of Tibetans approached the van and one of them lay on the street underneath the vehicle and carefully unscrewed the bolt at the base of the petrol tank. Fuel poured into the street, a match was thrown and soon the van had become an inferno. The Chinese looked on impassively but didn't react.

The crowd then turned its attention to the Chinese paramilitary soldiers who were gathered in the gates of the regional government. A volley of stones were thrown in their direction and a group of about thirty unarmed soldiers rushed out towards us. The effect on the crowd was immediate; we retreated about twenty or thirty yards. The young soldiers then stopped and ran back to their side of the road. This tactic was repeated a couple of times and it succeeded in keeping the mob out of stone-throwing range. It also seemed to break the determination of the crowd, which quickly lost its appetite for further confrontation. People started to drift off. I looked at the crowd and noticed the large number of ordinary Tibetans – especially women – and the complete absence of the Khampas, the warrior clans from the east who like to strut around town showing off their large daggers.

For the next few days Lhasa became quiet, too quiet. The police retreated to distant bases and consulted with leaders who flew down from Beijing. The streets were under the control of the Tibetans and there was no protest or agitation of any kind, as if people were sick of it. There was silent horror at the damage caused and dread of the retribution to come.

For three days the charred remains of the police station continued to smoulder and the walls were falling in on themselves. The smoking ruins were full of Tibetans scavenging through the burnt debris. Pieces of intact furniture and filing cabinets were thrown into the alleyway and their contents scattered about. The Kora was littered with police records -- small cards with a passport photo at the top and some notes alongside the name and address. Children were ripping the photos off these cards and one boy had hundreds of them in a plastic bag. I didn't see a policeman for two days and the tension was becoming oppressive.

Meanwhile, in the western world, Tibet was headline news and the media described it as an uprising rather than a protest. The presence of foreigners in Lhasa had completely disrupted the Chinese response to the protest. The usual Chinese response to a disturbance like this was brutally simple and at the last comparable event, the Lhasa uprising of 1959, it is estimated that about 81,000 Tibetans had been killed. Since the death of Mao Tse Tung in 1976, Tibet was being governed with less brutality and the military had taken a back seat. Their problem was that the police had had no training in crowd control and had no experience of containing what started out as a non-violent protest. The ten or so civilians who had been killed by the police were nothing by Chinese standards, but I sensed that the Chinese felt humiliated.

Tibet had been open to foreigners until that day. About two dozen foreign journalists had arrived in Lhasa on the afternoon of the protest – they had heard about a disturbance on the 27th of September – and the authorities had no idea that they worked for the media until it was too late. The Chinese deeply resented western news coverage of the protest and they considered it an imperialist plot to break up China. Because I wasn't involved in anything political, and I considered myself neutral regarding the Chinese and Tibetans, I assumed I would be safe from Chinese suspicion.

Although the telex lines were closed after the protest, the air link to Beijing remained open and the first flight out of town was full of journalists with valuable notes from eyewitnesses, police documents and photographs. They couldn't believe their luck. Although the journalists had missed the actual protest there were plenty of foreigners who were keen to share their experiences.

Some travellers made small fortunes by selling their photos to the media and a few journalists stayed behind to trawl the town in search of background information. The Barkhor Cafe, which overlooks the main plaza was always jam packed with local people who seemed more than willing to explain why they resented the Chinese. I avoided contact with the journalists as I assumed that if my name made it into print I would risk becoming a Persona Non Grata, in other words I would be kicked out, and I had no intention of leaving the city that I had planned to make my home.

A week passed before the crackdown began. Big white posters appeared on walls all over the city, with a paragraph of text written in Chinese, Tibetan and English. Foreigners were welcomed to the region in the first sentence then warned that anyone supporting the small minority who were Seeking to Split the Motherland would be severely punished. Radio,

television and public address speakers on rooftops blared out similar
warnings, also in three languages. I recognised the voice that was reading
out the English version – one of my contacts from the Deng She, the
Political Consultative Conference of Tibet.

A new word in the English language appeared at that moment: splittist,
someone who is trying to Split the Motherland. The usual word for this
would be separatist but I hadn't met anyone, Tibetan or foreign, who
had talked about separating Tibet from China. There was no separatist
movement in Tibet as far as I could see, in terms of people spreading
rumour or talking about it. Everyone I met probably would have voted
back the Dalai Lama if they had been able to vote, but such an idea was
unthinkable and everyone knew it.

For the first time since I had been in Tibet heavily armed soldiers started
appearing. Trucks with sirens blaring drove through the streets. They
would roar along, the soldiers in the back glaring at passers-by. Foot patrols
of ten heavily armed men would walk round the Kora holy circuit. They
would walk round it in the opposite direction as if they wanted to provoke
the Tibetans. At dusk motorbike patrols would roar about the town centre
with a soldier in the sidecar handling a huge machine gun that was bolted
on. A police witness appeared in all Chinese media, explaining how he had
managed to hold off fifty foreigners who were attacking him. I suspected
that the Chinese were unable to question their legitimacy in Tibet, or their
treatment of Tibetans, so they were desperate for a scapegoat and the
foreign travellers fitted the bill nicely.

The line of the official media was that the protesters were local
vagabonds and out of town troublemakers who had been stirred up by
foreign agents. Those involved, the media declared, had until October the
16th 1987 to give themselves up and receive a pardon. Nobody believed
the sincerity of this amnesty and I didn't hear about anyone who turned
themselves in. But the feeling of mistrust between people grew rapidly
and my Tibetan friends started warning me that so-and-so couldn't be
trusted as he had become a police informer.

Dorje Tsering, China's puppet leader of Tibet, held a press conference
in Beijing at which he announced to the world that Tibet was still open
to foreign visitors. On the ground, the exact opposite was happening
and tourists, both foreign and Chinese, were denied access to Tibet at all
frontier crossings. The American Vice Consul was denied access to a flight
from Beijing to Lhasa for over two weeks, and was told that all planes are

full of Chinese tourists. The fourteen international journalists who had remained in Lhasa were rounded up one night, at three in the morning, and told that if they didn't get on the next plane out they would be in deep trouble. The majority complied but at least two managed to stay on for a few more days. For the foreign travellers who were still in Tibet it was no longer possible to get visa extensions and they started to leave in increasing numbers. The word among the foreigners was that Tibet would close down forever. Angri La and his boss from the Deng She came to see me and said:

- You must stop teaching until this trouble ends. You must get out of that room you are staying in.

The padlock to my little room was changed but I managed to get hold of a key from one of the neighbours in the Shata building, so I remained there until I could find somewhere else to live. Nobody came to check on me and I hoped to avoid the crackdown; after all I did have a long time left on my visa, had only been an observer in the protest and had no idea it was even happening until hours after it started.

Rumours were flying around – people were being taken away from their homes in the night. I half expected to be caught up in the police trawl, but continued to hope for the best. I felt determined to stay in Tibet for as long as I could, all my life if possible, and I wasn't going to leave with all the other travellers. What I had seen at the protest made me realise that the faith I had placed in Chinese Communism, a belief that China was the one country where Communism had worked, was based on a false hope that Communism could work somewhere. This naïve view was based on my ignorance of China but since getting to Tibet I had been reading about the history of Chinese Communism, and listening to people, and I gradually realised how appalling Communism had been for both China and Tibet. After this protest I felt that the Tibetans were in fact the subject people of a brutal colonial power.

Robbie Barnett and Nick Howen met up in Lhasa at the time of the protest. They had seen everything and were deeply involved in the collection of information for the newspapers and, later on, for Amnesty International. Nick was a lawyer, Robbie was an actor and they had both learned quite a lot of Tibetan in the short time they had been there. Robbie's manner was serious and he genuinely wanted to help the Tibetans. He was far more intelligent and perceptive than most of the foreign travellers I had come across. He could also be really funny sometimes and he could transform the atmosphere. I decided to trust them, gave them the names of the local people I knew and told them the rumours I was hearing. Robbie was from London and for years had lived on the breadline as a circus performer, eventually getting work with famous stars like Barbara Streisand.

Nick was from Australia. He took himself more seriously than Robbie and sometimes he seemed fierce while at other times he seemed as gentle as a lamb. His face was almost completely hidden by a huge red beard that seemed to grow outwards rather than down, and all you could see were two piercing eyes, almost hidden by a wide-brimmed hat that he always wore. He thought that he looked inconspicuous and perhaps even local, but you could tell he was an eccentric foreigner from fifty paces away. Nick knew a bit of first aid and was working with some foreign doctors who were in town. They would seek out Tibetans who had been wounded in the protest and try to help them. This was a dangerous mission: their medical help was all that was available to the wounded protesters; none of the victims could have gone to the public hospital without facing immediate arrest.

Every morning Robbie and Nick came to Isabella's place for their breakfast meeting. Porridge and tea were consumed slowly as we shared yesterday's discoveries. Stories of torture in the prison were on everyone's lips and a routine procedure for dealing with monks was described: they would be chained to a wall and heavy weights would be placed round their necks so they would have to stoop continually. Was it true that the prison diet consisted of one steamed roll a day? Apparently several bodies were found in the police station after the debris was finally cleared and there was even a rumour that one of them was a foreigner.

When the deadline for the amnesty period passed the crackdown intensified. More people started disappearing in the night. I heard about a woman who was approached by the police at two in the morning and asked to accompany the police to identify a body. They were polite and helpful until they got her into the car and then they drove directly to the prison where she was locked up. Her family heard nothing more about her and the police claimed to know nothing about her whereabouts.

I heard various estimates about how many people had been arrested: from two hundred up to nine hundred. The official version was that thirty people had been detained for questioning after the protest and all were released within 24 hours. Some of the monks I knew had disappeared and I feared for their lives. A nurse from the People's Hospital had reported a story that spread round town like wildfire; two monks had been hanged in their cells and were lying in the hospital refrigerator.

One evening I ran into Nick whom I hardly recognised:

- What happened to your beard? I asked, I don't recognise you without it. You're not so bad looking after all.

- This is my disguise, he replied, I shaved it off.

- Why?

- I went to Drepung Monastery to find out how many monks had disappeared.

- And what happened?

- As I was leaving a young monk ran up to me and told me to run away as fast as I could as the police had spotted me and were after me. The monks started throwing stones at an upstairs window, it was a toilet, and a scared Chinese face appeared in the window frame. It was a policeman taking a crap and those monks were throwing stones at him to create diversion so that I could get away. I ran into the hills as fast as I could and crept back into town, got to my hotel as discreetly as possible, changed into these trendy clothes and shaved my beard. Barbara and Christa even rubbed beer into my hair to make it stand up! I hate to think what happened to the monks.

Despite these risks, Robbie and Nick stepped up their fact-finding mission, amassing swathes of names and allegations. They widened their network of informants and started to behave more furtively, suspecting that many of the people they were dealing with may have been informers for the Chinese police. They were never sure if they had been given false information. One of the most suspicious characters they met was referred to as Number Three and one of them would meet him every morning on the Kora circuit, where they would walk and talk. They didn't trust him and would never go together. They told me he was a Tibetan exile who had learned English in India. After a week of these morning discussions Number Three invited them to a meeting in a certain house and insisted that they both come together. Neither of them went as they suspected it was a trap. They asked one of their informers to watch the house and, sure enough, later that evening some policemen were spotted leaving it. They avoided Number Three from then on and discarded all the information he had given them.

The more I found out about their information-gathering the guiltier I felt about not doing more to help. After all they were doing it in the name of Human Rights and the dignity of the Tibetan people – but I was afraid

of the terrible risks involved and didn't want to compromise my own plan
to remain in Lhasa. While I was very aware of the risks Robbie and Nick
were taking I was blind to those facing me, and it didn't cross my mind to
destroy all evidence of the bus business that I had been running with Je
Yang. Neither did it occur to me that the Travellers' Co-op could be seen
as a den of foreign subversives, rather than a simple information centre,
and that I might be seen as a suspect. And I ignored Angri La's warning to
get out of the room where I was still sleeping, and stop teaching English
– every afternoon I would hold impromptu English lessons in a teahouse
with anyone who came along.

I went to the Travellers' Co-op one evening and had to get out of the
way of two policemen who were carrying a heavy looking sack that
seemed to contain bricks. I ran up the stairs expecting the worst and, sure
enough, the Co-op was full of policemen. I went into the crowded room
and saw a policeman taking an armful of books off a shelf and stuff them
roughly into a sack. Nobody noticed me. There were a couple of officers
there who were looking through some of the large format photo books,
with incredible photos of the Tibetan landscape and monasteries, and I
assumed they considered them subversive. Isabella later told me about one
policeman who knew the collection, took a copy of 7 Years in Tibet and
used it as an example of the kind of subversive political literature we were
distributing.

Isabella was standing by the window, staring out sadly and ignoring the
proceedings. She looked shattered. I went up to her, put my arm round
her and said:

- You okay Isabella? She smiled wistfully and tried to hold back the tears.

- It's not so bad what they're doing here. The books are replaceable.
What breaks my heart is all those young Tibetans we've got to know, and
love. And the monks? What will happen to them? And to think that our
contact with them could make their punishment worse, it just doesn't bear
thinking about.

- What are you going to do?

- I'm going back to Hong Kong.

- By the way, where's Roger? Don't tell me he's still on that trip to Mount
Kailash.

- Yes he is. I wish he was here. He's been away so much this year and
I'm fed up with it, I really am. What are you going to do Rupert? You can't
possibly stay here.

- Why not? This is my home now and I want to stay here for as long as I can. I've still got my residence permit and plenty of time left on my visa.

- If they let you stay you'll probably be the only foreigner left in Lhasa. I doubt they will.

- I don't see how they can stop me.

Isabella didn't wait for Roger to come back from his trek, she left a few days later carrying just a rucksack. She kept her departure low key – no going away party – but it was tearful and emotional. I could tell that the highly charged atmosphere of Lhasa was grinding her down, making her sad and she didn't have my sense of anger towards the Chinese, an emotion that was giving me energy, making the idea of staying seem like a feasible one. I took over her apartment, which was still jam packed full of stuff, and started hanging out with the neighbours more than I had ever done before.

Kaysang, a middle-aged alcoholic who seemed to be going through a dry period, lived along the corridor from Isabella's flat in the Shata building. He was the uncle of Lakdrun, my beautiful teenage student, so I had a soft spot for him. Kaysang's father had apparently been a high lama who was murdered by his own people for betraying secrets to the Chinese. I didn't really trust Kaysang and didn't tell him anything relevant but I did enjoy spending evenings at his place, where he would imitate a yak and other animals and make everyone fall about laughing. It was also the one place where I could hear international news; Kaysang had a powerful radio set and I would listen to news reports from a radio station in Bangladesh.

I assumed the police would come round to Roger and Isabella's flat in the Shata building before long so I searched it for incriminating material. There was so much stuff that it was hard to know where to start. Roger's collection of audio tapes was vast and I had no intention of going through it. They had a superb collection of photo books, probably borrowed from their own library, and I wasn't sure what to do with them. Every wall was covered with Tibetan paintings, fabrics and wall hangings. Boxes of junk were stacked against every wall. Eventually I found what I was looking for among Roger's stuff – something incriminating – a stack of postcards that showed the Dalai Lama, in sunglasses, standing in the foreground and behind him the Tibetan national flag. Roger had probably been given these cards by a traveller and he would have had no idea that they were now incendiary. If the police found these they would suspect us of distributing them and we'd be in big trouble. I had to get rid of them and my first thought was to burn them, but that seemed wrong as Tibetans consider this kind of thing sacred and I didn't want to build up bad karma. So I decided to give them away to the various foreigners I knew, all of whom were happy to take a few, and I also gave one to my neighbour Kaysang.

Robbie and Nick continued to come round for their breakfast meetings and I took over Isabella's role as Mother, cooking the porridge and listening to the latest news. One morning, exactly twenty-two days after the protest, the police burst in. Four of them were in green police uniforms and four were in civilian clothes – a Chinese interpreter and three Tibetan witnesses from the Deng She, the Political Consultative Conference. The leader of the group was young, intelligent-looking and had thin lips and dark glasses. He seemed both pleased with himself and pent up with frustration and I wondered if he was a psychopath. The interpreter was friendly and chatty and behaved as if it were a routine social call. The Tibetans said nothing, as did Robbie and Nick who stayed in the kitchen. The police didn't seem to pay them any attention and I whispered urgently to them:

- This is almost certainly about me. Get out of here as soon as you can. If you stay quiet and act dumb you should be okay.

We gathered round a table in the main room. I was keen to get them away from the kitchen so Robbie and Nick could get away. The lead policeman laid a photograph on the table; it was one of Roger's postcards of the Dalai Lama in front of the Tibetan national flag. Oh my God! Was it one of those I had handed out? It didn't look like one of them – it was too thin.

- Mister Policeman would like you to tell him about this photograph, said the interpreter.

- Never seen it before, I said, looking into the eyes of the lead policeman. A momentary grin passed across the policeman's thin lips, like the smile of a snake, and he shouted a command. The door was opened and, to my horror, my neighbour Kaysang was ushered in.

- Who gave you this photo? The policeman asked Kaysang in Chinese, showing another brief grin of satisfaction. Kaysang, his chest puffed up in pride, didn't hesitate. He pointed at me and said in Chinese:

- Him! He gave it to me.

- Did you give it to him? asked the interpreter. I hung my head in shame and nodded. The policeman talked furiously to the interpreter, who said to me in English:

- Do you know that this symbol is illegal? It is a symbol for those who want to split the Motherland. We now have the right to search this apartment. I didn't say anything. The policeman thrust a piece of paper in front of me and the interpreter said:

- You must sign this.

- What is it? It's in Chinese and I can't understand it.

- It's a search warrant. We are going to search this apartment.

- I can't sign that. And it's not even my apartment. This seemed to infuriate the policeman who shouted at the interpreter.

- Mister Policeman says that you will be in much worse trouble if you don't cooperate. And if you will not sign it they will search the apartment anyway. You are not allowed to leave.

I didn't sign it.

I sat on a chair and watched the policemen go through all of Roger and Isabella's possessions. There were only two things that could still lead to trouble, a small book called Tibetan Songs for Independence, which I slipped into my pocket, and a large format book of beautiful old black and white photos of aristocratic Tibetan houses – taken long before the Chinese invasion – the sort of material that would incense the police as it showed a country with its own unique culture, while the Chinese version of history is that Tibet was a cruel, medieval quagmire before they liberated it. This photo book was propped on a high shelf and seemed incredibly visible. How could they not see it? They were too busy going through all the stuff on the floor, on shelves, under the bed, in boxes – and were looking down.

The interpreter sat with me and tried to make conversation. I tried to keep them away from the kitchen and noted with satisfaction that Robbie and Nick had managed to slip out – God knows what would have happened to them if the police had found out what they were up to. The interpreter was chatting away as if we were in a teahouse, asking endless questions in a friendly way: How long had I been in Tibet? Did I like it here? How long would I stay? How did I get here? Where had I been? Who are my students? Where are Roger and Isabella? I knew he was working for the police and I knew that it would be foolish to answer any of his questions so I remained silent.

- What are these? Said the police leader aggressively, holding a handful of rock samples in one hand and a small sack with more rocks in the other.

- Those are rock samples, I replied.

- Why do you collect rocks?

- I don't.

- Whose are they?

- Roger's.
- Where's Roger?
- I don't know.
- Why does an English teacher collect rocks?
- I don't know.

Four hours later they had finished, leaving with sack loads of stuff. The caretaker of the building, an old man who had, until now, been like a friendly uncle to me, turned up with a new padlock in his hand. He changed the lock to Roger and Isabella's flat and we all trooped down into the yard. They had told me to take my personal clothes, which I stuffed into my rucksack. I wasn't sure what was going on so I said:

- I have been sleeping in this apartment. Where am I supposed to go now?

- You cannot stay here any longer, said the interpreter, without even referring to the policeman. You must come with us.

- Where to?

- You must stay in a hotel. Not here.

- I have permission to be here. I am an English teacher.

- Now we must look in the little room over there that you have been using. Where is the key for that lock? They were gathered round the door of my previous room, where I had a desk and where I kept my papers. The policeman shouted at the interpreter who said to me:

- Where is the key to this room?

- I don't have it.

- That is no problem.

The old caretaker who, along with some of the other neighbours, had been watching this exchange, hurried off to get a hammer and some pliers. He seemed to move with a spring in his step and I wondered if he was enjoying it. Within seconds the pathetically small padlock had been prised off the wooden door frame, where it had been held by a little metal ring. They poured into my room and threw all my stuff into a couple of cardboard boxes. They were in a hurry. The only thing I was really concerned about was my diary, a leather-bound page-a-day volume in which I had written my impressions on each and every day. There was nothing incriminating in it but I didn't want the police going through it. I had slipped into the room alongside them and, as a diversion, I threw a Tibetan-English dictionary on the desk. This attracted their attention for a few moments, and I realised they had probably never seen one before. As they were poring over the dictionary I slowly took the diary and slipped it into the little shoulder bag that I always carried.

Within twenty minutes they were done; all my stuff was in boxes and they were changing the locks. They seemed glad to have finished. They took my passport, ordered me to check into the Kirey Hotel and report to the police station every day. I sat on the steps of the Shata School not knowing what to think. Confusing feelings of despair, disappointment, anger and defiance were surging through my body. I didn't know what to do and didn't want to speak to anyone. The neighbours had gathered in the yard and were looking at me silently. I tried to ignore them. They were moving towards me slowly. There seemed to be some sympathy in their look but I detected a note of greedy patience too, as if they were vultures who had seen their victim move one step closer to death.

Then the lead policeman and the interpreter hurried back into the yard. I stood up to meet them and noticed that the policeman seemed to have mellowed a bit, perhaps he was feeling a sense of satisfaction at a job well done. The interpreter spoke:

- You must write a self-criticism.
- What's that?
- You must write on a paper the story of what you did.
- What do you mean?
- You must explain exactly when you gave that man the illegal photograph, where you got it from, how many others you had given out and – most importantly – what was in your mind when you gave it to him.
- You want this now?
- No, you can do it tomorrow. We will come to Kirey Hotel tomorrow morning and get it from you.

I left the yard and wandered round the Kora, pondering this. I had read about self-criticisms and knew that they were important tools in the Cultural Revolution, when people who had been accused of being associated with anything traditional, cultural or non-Communist would have to write a part confession, part apology. In the worst days of Mao Tse Tung's terror these were read out publicly before the hapless victims were tortured or killed. But in this day and age? Mao Tse Tung was long dead, China had opened up and mellowed out. Surely they weren't going to hold an impromptu court in the Shata yard and have all the neighbours denounce me – which I'm sure they would have happily done.

And then it struck me – they needed this document so they could close the case. The police obviously had an open file on me, they had raided my apartments, caught me lying about that wretched photograph and had confiscated a load of stuff. I could see the logic now: if I gave them a detailed explanation about handing out that photo, and a confession of my guilt, it would probably tie up the file nicely. My sense of defiance surged to the surface and I made the decision not to help them. Why should I? I wasn't guilty of anything. I was angry with the Chinese police for torturing monks and terrorising the people I had grown to love, so why should I help them? Not to mention the fact that I had wanted to settle in Tibet and this now looked impossible. I was pretty sure they would expel me from China but felt confident they weren't going to jail me – they would have done it by now if that was their intention – so why should I cooperate? What did I have to lose?

I managed to find a bed in a shared room at the Kirey Hotel that didn't cost much. The next morning the police were back, the same team but without the Tibetan witnesses from the Deng She. They had set up the former Travellers' Co-op as an interrogation room and it looked suitably empty and harsh. I was sent for. The interpreter spoke:

- Where is the paper?

- What paper?

- The paper we told you to write yesterday. Where you must explain why you were distributing illegal propaganda photographs.

- Er...I haven't written it yet.

- Why not?

- Well, first of all I want my passport back. And I want my English class back too. When this was translated to the policeman his face reddened with anger. He screamed at the interpreter who then said:

- It will be much better for you if you write the self-criticism.

- Why?

- Things will be much clearer.

- How?

- You must write it. In your country you do not behave with such impertinence with the police.

- It's different in my country. If we are charged with something we are assumed innocent until proven guilty and we are allowed a defence lawyer.

- If you want a lawyer we will get you one. This will mean big trouble for you. And he was right. The role of defence lawyers in China is to apologise for the accused and plea for a lesser sentence.

For several days this performance continued. We would sit round the table and the questions and answers would fly back and forth. A routine developed. I sat with my back to the wall and my arms folded on the table, opposite me sat the interpreter who had taken to staring at me continually, like a snake hypnotizing its prey. The two junior officers sat in the corner staring into space and the leader marched up and down, shouting long angry tirades. We remained at loggerheads. I refused to write a self-criticism until my passport was returned and they kept refusing to do this. Before our daily meetings I felt horrible surges of fear, my stomach would churn and my hands would shake. What was I doing? I was afraid. Once I got into the room with them my confidence returned, I started to feel as if I was in control of the situation and the angrier and more frustrated they got the more determined I became.

Considering that I was under a form of house arrest I had quite a lot of freedom. I was allowed to wander about the streets and go wherever I wanted – which was only to the market and the teahouses – and I was left in peace. If I was being followed it was done very discreetly. The image of the monks being tortured in the prison was always in my mind and this stiffened my resolve, scared me and made me appreciate my liberty more than I had ever done before. I was grateful for the fact that the police had not slung me in jail and were treating me with restraint.

I told everyone I met about my troubles and asked them for advice. The foreign travellers all said that I should comply with the police demands. My Tibetan friends told me to resist. They explained that those who stand up to the police are treated with a certain respect but if you cooperate they walk all over you. They were also vitriolic in their denunciation of the Chinese, more so than I had ever heard before. I attempted to contact the British Embassy in Beijing and sent telexes to them from the Post Office every day. The US Consul, whom I had met, also promised to ask his people at the American Consulate to contact them. After a week I realised that the Brits wouldn't lift a finger to help me and they never replied.

Then Roger came back from Western Tibet and the routine I had developed with the police changed completely. I tried to brief him on the situation and prepare him for what was to come but he didn't seem able to listen. He had spent almost a month in the wilderness and he had apparently lost the habit of speaking with people. When he heard that Isabella had gone, that he was locked out of his flat, had lost his job and his possessions – he went into a state of shock. A strange, distant look came into his eyes, he became very quiet, and I suspected that he had given up. The police were delighted to see him and seemed to lick their lips in anticipation. As soon as he understood what the police wanted he agreed to write a self-criticism and wrote page after page right in front of us. I was furious although I got some satisfaction knowing that whoever dealt with this text would have a big problem understanding his handwriting.

Afterwards, Roger asked the police for access to his apartment so he could take out his personal stuff and this was granted. A crowd of policemen were assembled, I was sent for, and we all trooped off to the Shata Building, which is about ten minutes on foot from the Kirey Hotel. Roger was talking continually even though nobody was listening and the interpreter had long given up translating his words. There were about ten of us walking through the backstreets and, apart from Roger, nobody said a word. The padlock on the apartment was unlocked and Isabella's two cats shot out, yowling in protest and hunger.

The rooms were searched again. Roger was asked to explain why he had so many Tibetan artefacts, where he got them from; why he had so many tapes in the Tibetan language, so much literature on the Dalai Lama, and about his wretched collection of rocks. He answered every question in detail and I started to get bored. Then, to my horror, they found a book of bus tickets that I had been using with Je Yang. This was incriminating evidence as our bus business was probably illegal. For once I was grateful for Roger's verbal diarrhoea as this was taking up all of the police energy and I hoped they wouldn't realise the significance of what they had found.

The next day Roger and I were summoned to the police station. Now that they had my bus tickets and Roger's rambling confession they changed tactics, and I guessed the former Co-op room was no longer required. I tried to brace myself for what was to come but couldn't stop shaking until I got into the police station where my resolve and anger took over. Roger was chatting away cheerfully, assuming that he would be allowed to stay now that he had told all. They ushered us into a small room with dirty white walls and asked us to sit down in front of a table – where the bus tickets had been placed. The lead policeman was flicking through the ticket stubs, something he had obviously done hundreds of times and, without saying a word, showed me the incriminating evidence: ticket prices with the dreaded symbol of the US Dollar next to each number. There was no mention of the self-criticism that day and the interpreter got straight to the point:

- Who is the driver of the bus?

- Er...what?

- We want to know who is the driver of the bus you are selling tickets for?

- I really don't know his name, which was true.

This non-reply didn't seem to bother them as much as I would have expected. The lead policeman was determined to stay on top of the situation, keep his temper under control and not let me have the advantage. He produced a ream of paper, all of which had the letterhead of the Gong Anne Jew, the Public Security Bureau, on it, thumped it onto the table and told me to describe the driver. I refused to write or draw anything. I did tell them that he was young, tall, didn't smoke and came from Southern China. His bus, I told them, was big, modern and foreign. In reality the driver was middle-aged, came from northern China, smoked like a chimney and drove a small, Chinese-made old heap. I was grateful for the driver as he had basically funded my time in Tibet and there was no way I was going to betray him. The police were delighted that they had finally got something from me and couldn't suppress their excitement. Other officers were summoned into the room and I understood enough of what was being said to realise that they were going to head off to the bus station at once to arrest the driver. I hoped that my driver friend had had the foresight to get out of town.

They turned their attention to Roger and asked him lots of new questions. They had been through what he had already written and wanted to know more: what happened when he first came to Tibet? Why did he come here? What had he heard about Tibet in Hong Kong? What were his dealings with the Deng She and the school? Where else had he been in Tibet? How long was he planning to stay? Why did he have a suspicious collection of rocks? Why did he set up the Co-op and where was Isabella? I hissed at him through the side of my mouth that he shouldn't answer any of this as he'd already given them a ton of information. He ignored my advice and cheerily answered each question at length and wrote page after page of detail. The only good thing about this was that the interpreter seemed to be dying of boredom and they gradually realised that having someone spill their guts like this could be overwhelming. On the way back to the hotel Roger seemed to be in a good mood, convinced that he would be rewarded for his cooperation. I was so furious that I couldn't talk to him.

Back at the Kirey Hotel the phone was ringing. Roger went off to his room and I hung around, as I liked to chat in Tibetan with the girls on the reception desk. They were fun and I needed a dose of their light-hearted humour. They were stressing out as there was a foreigner on the phone. Their grasp of English was good enough to deal with the travellers but there was something about the phone that appalled them.

- Mister Rupert, Mister Rupert, please help!

- What is it?

- Telephone for you.

- For me? Nobody had ever telephoned me in Tibet. I took the call willingly.

- Hello.

- Hello there, this is Miles at Reuters in Beijing. Can you help me?

- I don't know.

- Can you tell me what's going on in Lhasa?

- Er...there's not much going on actually. It's pretty quiet around here nowadays.

- Could you please try and find Robbie or Nick?

- Oh yes, of course. Those are the people you need to speak to. I asked the girls if either of them were in the hotel but they shook their heads.

- I'm afraid neither of them are in at the moment.

- Oh dear, that's annoying. It was really difficult to get through to this number. Can you please hold the line for a bit? Don't hang up.

- Ok. I had thought about telling the foreign press about my problem with the police but Nick, who dealt with the press all the time, told me that they wouldn't be interested in my story. He told me they only want information about how many more people have died or been arrested, or if there were any changes to the political situation. My story, he had said, was irrelevant to the press.

- Hello, are you still there? Miles here.

- Hi, yeah, I'm still here. And I was wondering if you would like to hear my story?

- Umm...okay...Sure, go ahead.

- Well, I am under house arrest...

- Really? What happened?

- About a week ago the police took my passport, locked me out of my flat and accused me of distributing Dalai Lama photographs.

- Keep going...I'm noting all this down.

- And there's someone else in the same situation, a guy called Roger Hill. I'm not really sure what he's accused of. He ran a library here in Lhasa and they confiscated all the books which they seem to think are subversive.

- And what are the police going to do?

- I'm not sure. They won't give me back my passport until I write a self-criticism.

- And have you written it?

- No.

- Why not?

- Because I don't want to cooperate with the police after what they did in Lhasa.

- I see. What was your name again?

- Rupert Wolfe Murray.

- And how long have you been in Tibet?

- About nine months. I worked as an English teacher until the protest. Then they closed the school.

- Well, thanks very much Rupert. This is great stuff and I can definitely use it.

- Really? My story is newsworthy? I had no idea.

- Absolutely. It was good speaking to you. I've got to hang up now.

- Bye.

The next day was confrontation day. It had to be. The Public Security Bureau had kept my passport for six days and – according to Nick – if they kept it for another day, without charging me, they would be in breach of China's Consular Agreement with the UK. China had only recently emerged from its Mao-inspired isolation and was just finding its feet on the global diplomatic stage. Surely they didn't want a scandal about a couple of rogue English teachers.

We weren't summoned to the police station until late afternoon and I could sense that the atmosphere had, once again, changed completely. We had been invited into another room, a much more pleasant one, and we were sitting on a comfortable sofa rather than hard-backed chairs. There was a note of panic in the air and policemen I had never seen kept popping their heads in to look at us, as if we had suddenly become of interest. Presumably the Reuters man had written up his news story and I wondered if that had stimulated the British Embassy to contact the Chinese authorities on our behalf. I could tell that the police had lost control of the situation again and this gave me a grim sense of satisfaction.

The interpreter, who was now in police uniform, and another policeman sat facing us. The police leader looked more stressed out than usual and he kept popping in and out of the room, as if someone in the room next door was giving him instructions. When he stepped out we could hear his voice and I realised he was on the phone to Beijing – they were presumably telling him what to do. I knew they had to resolve the case that day and, in order to close the file. They needed my self-criticism. If I held out just a little bit longer I could win this struggle. Since the interpreter had donned his uniform, the nasty side of his personality was coming out. He scowled at me and said:

- You must write the self-criticism.

- I have told you I will not do it until you give me my passport and job back.

- Mister Mullee, if your attitude doesn't improve we will have to punish you. He placed some blank sheets of paper in front of me, and a fountain pen. I ignored them.

Time passed and neither I nor the interpreter spoke, we just stared angrily at one another. The lead policemen came into the room carrying our passports. He had a bitter expression of defeat on his face and he slapped the passports on the table, in front of the interpreter, and stalked out. The interpreter picked them up and spoke to me:

- Mister Mullee, here is your passport.

- Thanks very much.

- Your punishment is expulsion. You must leave the People's Republic of China within four days. Mixed feelings of satisfaction and disappointment surged through me.

- Punishment? What is my crime?

- You have been a bad influence in the capital of the Tibetan province and you are guilty of working in the People's Republic of China without a permit.

- What? Me? Working without a permit? I have a resident's permit and this office issued it.

- Under the Aliens' Regulations foreigners are not allowed to work without a valid residence certificate.

- I have a residence certificate and you gave it to me.

- Ah yes. We have cancelled it.

It was pointless arguing against such logic. I realised that, as far as ordinary people are concerned in China, the law is what the police tell you.

Presumably nobody ever questioned them and I assumed that my approach infuriated them. I took some satisfaction in getting my passport back and looked inside it, where I saw a new stamp that said Must Leave by a date that was just four days away. This was it, the end of the road, time to leave. But how was I going to leave when all the roads to Kathmandu were closed by snowdrifts? I couldn't afford a flight and the journey to Hong Kong would take more than a week. I started thinking about the practicalities of getting my stuff together and hitting the road. The pressure of the last week had been intense and I was glad it was over; I was looking forward to going home for the first time in years.

Then they came to Roger. Having missed the protests and written a detailed self-criticism he was cheerily assuming that they would let him stay. I looked at him and was curious to see where his policy of cooperation would get him.

- Mister Lodger, said the interpreter. When he was speaking with Roger he would smile and show his charming side. He was holding Roger's battered old passport.

- Here is your passport. You must leave China within a week. You must also pay a fine of one thousand yuan. Roger looked stunned and didn't say a word. A thousand yuan was a lot: £160.

- Why is he being fined so much? I asked. The interpreter glanced at me with a look of venom. I could see that he didn't want to explain anything but I kept staring at him.

- Mister Lodger had people to stay in his house on third October. That was not allowed. He also has a suspicious collection of rocks.

- The third of October, said Roger vaguely. His voice was faint and weak. I wasn't in Lhasa on the third of October.

- Aha...you are responsible for the Shata School rooms are you not, Mister Lodger?

- Wrong there, I said. I was responsible for those rooms when Roger was away.

- No Mister Mullee, you were not responsible. You have no papers.

- I did have papers. I got them here.

- You see Mister Mullee you had no official relationship with the Political Consultative Conference. You are an unauthorised English teacher. Illegal.

- That's nonsense, I said angrily, throwing caution to the winds. They have known me over a year and they have asked me to work for them many times. They gave me a job and it was them who asked you for a residence permit.

- The Political Consultative Conference do not know you Mister Mullee. You have no papers.

Roger was awestruck and had sunk into silence. Even though I had warned him what to expect he had placed all his faith in those ridiculous self-criticisms. He was in shock and having problems accepting his fate. He weakly agreed to pay the fine and we were shown out of the police station, free at last. Roger was anything but free and I knew he was wondering where on earth he could get a thousand yuan.

Isabella had gone, the fine was huge and Roger no longer had a forum – the Travellers' Co-op – where he had been quite good at selling second hand stuff to foreigners. I suggested he sold some of the things he had accumulated – camera gear, hi-fi equipment, hundreds of tapes with jazz and rock music, camping equipment, tools, cooking gear, a huge tricycle, a slide projector, clothes and what remained of his book collection. There was no way he could leave Lhasa with all that stuff, unless he hired a truck.

Crucial days passed and Roger didn't ask me, or anyone else, to help him flog his gear – and I was so annoyed with him that I didn't offer to help. I knew that organising a junk sale was easy enough but it did require a certain frame of mind, determination and energy that Roger was probably lacking due to the shock of his losses. If I had been less angry with him I may have felt compassion and done more to help him out, after all he'd always been good to me.

The truth was that my annoyance with Roger was becoming an obsession and I was thinking more about how he would sort himself out than about my own immediate future. Although my preparations for leaving were simple compared to Roger's – all I had to do was grab my rucksack – I didn't want to think about what I would do in Kathmandu. Since my plan to live in Lhasa had been shattered I avoided thinking what I would do next, where I would go or that my money belt was almost empty.

I put a lot of energy into organising a bus to the Nepalese border but this wasn't getting anywhere as the government had clamped down on all overland transport for foreigners. Plus, the road to Kathmandu was blocked by snowdrifts. It was still possible to get a bus to Golmud but getting from there to Hong Kong would take more time than I had available. There were no buses going to the Nepalese border, not even for locals as five-metre snowdrifts were reported from that part of the country.

The police approached me several times and the interpreter said cheerily:

- Tell Mister Lodger that he must pay the fine. Otherwise we will arrest him and we will have to send him to prison.

Although he was broke, Roger tried to make some money to pay his fine. He got hold of an empty room at the Kirey Hotel, filled it with his stuff and he would invite foreigner travellers in, tell them stories and try and sell his things. Problem was there were very few foreigners in Lhasa at that point and those that were there had been around for a while and didn't need any extra stuff.

Then Nick Howen, who worked as a lawyer back in Australia, took pity on Roger and accompanied him to the police station. He started explaining to the interpreter and his chief the concepts of human rights, due process and other western legal standards. They flipped, and Nick was seen racing out of the station with several policemen in hot pursuit. They saw him disappear into the Kirey Hotel, sent for reinforcements, blocked all exits and searched the place from top to bottom. They found him hiding in a toilet, took him to the station where they found that his visa had expired – a minor misdemeanour. Their anger fizzled out when they realised he wasn't hiding some bigger crime and they actually laughed at the expired visa and said the border police can deal with him. He was given an expulsion order and was very lucky that none of them worked out that he had been gathering information for human rights organisations and the press for the last few weeks.

The following day the police came to the Kirey Hotel and summoned Roger and me into the former Travellers' Co-op, a room that only they had the key for. I knew all of them by now – the interpreter, who seemed surprised that I was still around, the Tibetan policeman who stood in the corner and never said anything, the Chinese hardman who waited in the corridor with the guns – and my old friend the team leader. The interpreter told me that they weren't leaving until Roger paid his fine.

Roger was willing to pay it and he pulled out of his various pockets everything he had: two hundred and ninety yuan and ninety fen in grubby notes. He also had some crumpled US and Hong Kong Dollars, a few British pounds and coins in various currencies. Round his neck was a Russian Zenit camera he had been trying to sell and he offered it to them in lieu of the remainder. He invited them to come and see the room where he could offer them more stuff. They looked at him with a mixture of pity, anger and resentment, scooped up the money, grabbed the camera and stalked out. I think they realised that this was all they were going to get and we never saw them again.

Each day that passed seemed more precious than the last; I knew these were my last moments in Tibet and I was determined to savour every impression, every encounter. Tension was building as we needed to get out but didn't know how we could. We were anxiously listening for news from the Nepalese border as that was our route out but it was blocked by snow.

When a group of tourists appeared from Kathmandu by bus we were jubilant: the road was open! The world media was showing the People's Liberation Army rescuing a group of stranded western tourists from a snowy landscape and flying them into Tibet by helicopter. Until then the international media had been portraying the Chinese as monk-killers, so for China this was a coup, as it showed the world that Tibet was open to tourists.

But we soon found out that the group who had just arrived had never been stranded in the snow at all. They were unknowing pawns in China's propaganda campaign directed at the west. They were simply a group of western tourists at the border, where there was snow on the ground, and they were selected by a government TV crew to be given a free helicopter ride into Tibet, where they were transferred onto a bus. In fact, the road wasn't clear at all and there really was a bus full of foreigners stranded in a snowdrift at five thousand metres, but the army hadn't bothered to rescue them. They were left to freeze for several days and eventually managed to make it back to Nepal, without fatalities, thanks to a gang of local Tibetans who dug them out of the snow.

There were scores of foreigners around who were planning to travel down to Kathmandu as soon as the road was cleared, and on November 3rd, just one day before the deadline on my expulsion order, news came through that the road might be open. I went to the bus station, found two big Japanese buses, spoke to the drivers and told them to set a price and sell tickets to each foreigner – I wasn't getting into the bus-ticket business again. I didn't see my old business partner at the garage, didn't look out for him and hoped he had made it out okay.

Last night in Lhasa. I sucked in the clean, sharp air and savoured it for the last time. I spent the evening rushing from house to house, visiting all the kindly people who had been such good hosts over the last few months, seeking out my favourite students so I could say goodbye. In a way I couldn't believe I was leaving. I was mentally gearing up for a period of uncertainty;

I didn't know what I was going to do next or where I would go. They asked when I would be coming back and all I could say was maybe one day. The snow in Lhasa had melted enough to permit cycling and I was riding round town like a dervish. The streets at night seemed deserted apart from the odd army patrol, young Chinese soldiers in groups of ten, each holding an AK47 machine gun as if they were expecting to be attacked at any minute.

At one point I saw a crowd of Tibetans outside a tea shop. The place was so packed that people were standing on the street so they could watch the TV that was playing inside. I forced my way in to see what was on and saw that it was the old Russian version of War and Peace, in black and white with Chinese subtitles.

It must have been almost midnight by the time I got back to the Kirey Hotel. Normally everyone would be asleep by this hour; the altitude in Tibet is draining and makes you appreciate early nights. I could hear a commotion from Roger's junk room and I slipped by invisibly, or so I thought. I had been spotted and Roger started shouting for me. I didn't reply and tried to find somewhere to hide. He soon tracked me down and I could see a desperate look on his face.

- What's so urgent? I asked. Why are you making such a racket? It's midnight and people are trying to sleep.

- I need your help, he said meekly.

- Oh yeah?

- Can you help me move house? Please!

- You've got to be joking. You haven't moved your stuff from the Shata Building yet? You've had ages. We're leaving tomorrow morning.

- We can do it now. It shouldn't take long. I've got a handcart and my trike. Robbie and Nick will help and so will Jenny and June. We need you too in case we get stopped by the police. We all agree that you're the best at talking to the police.

- This is madness, I said, but as the others came up the corridor to where we were I realised that I couldn't get out of it.

- Hang on, I'll come, but I have one question. Why the hell hasn't this been done already? Everyone glanced at Roger but he didn't reply.

We set off to the Shata building like a gang of thieves in the night, watching out for police patrols and trying not to arouse the dogs. It was quite exciting. Roger had somehow managed to get the key for his old apartment from the police and when we got in I realised that he had only moved a fraction of his stuff to his junk room in the Kirey and he hadn't even put stuff into boxes or bags. I had been in situations like this before, in Edinburgh, when I worked with my Dad moving furniture from house to house. Some people would have had their belongings neatly stacked in boxes, ready to be moved. In other houses we would have to carefully wrap each breakable item – crockery, ornaments, glasses – in newspaper before packing them tightly in tea chests.

I took charge, told Robbie to pack the books into a trunk and Nick to stuff clothes into rucksacks. I sent June into the kitchen and told her to pack up whatever she felt was worth keeping, and I helped Jenny stuff another trunk with bric-a-brac. We worked well as a team, made jokes and soon the room was clear – but there was a mountain of luggage to be moved. We needed a truck and there was no way we could move it all in one go. The neighbours had come out to watch the spectacle and were licking their lips in anticipation. I knew they would be in the apartment as soon as we left and they would strip the place clean in minutes, grabbing whatever was left behind. The one item that Roger was keen not to let fall into the hands of these vultures were his home-made speakers, each one made of plywood and almost two metres tall. He carried them down to the yard and said he would wait there until we came back for a second trip. I said there was no way I was coming back. One trip was enough for me and I was fed up to the back teeth with Roger.

We piled four big trunks, several rucksacks and scores of boxes and bags onto the hand cart. I tied it down with some string I had found in the apartment but it was far too weak and I knew it would all come crashing down at the slightest mishap. I looked out into the deserted street and prayed our luck would hold and we wouldn't stumble across a police or army patrol. With some straps and a belt, I pulled as hard as I could on the handcart, an ancient construction with wooden wheels and two large wooden handles that Robbie was grappling with. Just to get the thing moving took four of us. It seemed to weigh several tons and the problem was steering such an unwieldy, overloaded beast.

Right outside the Shata building was a huge pile of human manure, the result of twelve months of excrement that had been piling up in a room on the ground floor. The men who empty these places had only just shovelled it up onto the street, where it stood waiting to be collected for the nearby fields. We did our best to avoid it but it had leaked an evil smelling black liquid across the width of the alley and we couldn't avoid the wheels going through it. It was only after we got back to the hotel that I realised that the contaminated wheels had touched my trousers, which then stank to high heaven. At the Kirey Hotel the door was locked. The friendly porter who had let us out without question an hour earlier was now refusing to open up. I thumped on the door and shouted in Tibetan:

- Open up! We've got Roger's stuff.
- Who's there?
- It's Rupert.
- You said it's Roger?
- No, I said it's Roger's stuff.
- Why are you carrying Roger's stuff?
- That's a damn good question, I said quietly to myself, and then shouted at the door again:
- Just open the bloody door before the police come. The grumpy old porter relented, opened the door, looked at us in horror, let us in and quickly bolted it up again.
- You know what's funny, said Robbie.
- What?
- Roger only has one ticket on the bus.
- So?
- How's he going to get all this stuff on?

By this stage I was so fed up with Roger that I refused to go back to the Shata building for his wretched speakers, but Robbie went and I persuaded the porter to open up for him again. I felt guilty about not helping them – I was being lazy and selfish, and if the police had stumbled across them I would have been dragged into it anyway. I paced around the hotel restlessly. They returned quickly and this time I was the one who opened the door. Leaving Roger re-arranging his pile of junk, I crept off to bed for a couple of hours of sleep.

At dawn the next day there was a crowd of travellers outside the Kirey Hotel, crowding round the two old Japanese buses that were going to take us to the Nepalese border. There was an air of excitement in the frozen air and we were all glad to be getting away from the tension of Lhasa. We had one rucksack each and we stowed them in the small luggage area under the bus and on the roof rack. I climbed up on top and helped to tie down the rucksacks and fit a big tarpaulin over them. I noticed that Roger hadn't yet put in an appearance and I didn't want to think about what would happen if he missed this bus. Just as I was lashing down the tarpaulin Nick shouted at me and I looked over, he was coming out of the hotel with

Robbie and they seemed to be imploring Roger to follow:

- Don't tie the tarp down yet. Roger's got loads of stuff to get on.

I climbed down to help, asked the driver to hang on for a few minutes and we both looked on in horror as we saw what Roger was bringing: four rucksacks and three trunks. The driver shook his head and told me there was no way that he would take all that stuff and I translated the message. As Robbie and Nick turned all their charm and persuasive powers onto him, I was on top unlashing the tarpaulin and squeezing the extra gear in.

The driver was furious and it was awkward getting past his glaring face when we eventually boarded the bus, half an hour later. The bus was pointing towards the entrance to the Kirey Hotel and the driver was gunning the engine, ready to go. We were all waiting for Roger who kept popping back in for more stuff. Then he appeared with his vast tricycle, a Heath Robinson contraption that would never have fitted on the roof rack, and the driver lost control: he drove the vehicle at Roger with every intention of hitting him, or at least crushing his infernal trike. I ran up to the driver, implored him to stop and then jumped out. Roger was looking dreamy, evidently not aware of the frustration he was causing.

- Get on the bloody bus! I shouted.

- I can't leave my trike here. I made it myself. It's valuable.

- For Christ's sake Roger, please get on the bus. Now. We're going and you'll be left behind.

- What about the trike?

- There's no way we can get that on board.

- Why not? There must be space on top.

- There's none, I promise you. Leave it right here. Let's go. Robbie and Nick had appeared and they gently took Roger by the arms and led him onto the bus. I lifted the heavy trike onto the pavement and pushed it against the wall, where it fell onto one side.

- Good riddance, I said to it.

The trip to the border was slow and uneventful. We were all too tired and fed up to think about visiting monasteries in the holy cities of Gyantse and Shigatse. We spent our first night in an unheated concrete block which felt like the inside of a deep freeze. Luckily there was plenty of thick bedding and enough bodies packed in to get the temperature above freezing. Everyone was lying down on the huge wooden beds, everyone except Keith, a young sporty-looking Australian guy who was sitting cross-legged, in the lotus position, in his thick down jacket – apparently asleep. When I woke up late in the night he was still sitting there, like a Buddhist statue in a monastery. I had never seen a westerner sleep in the lotus position before and had heard it takes a lot of practice to do so. What was odd was that Keith seemed like the least spiritual person on the bus – he was constantly joking and being crude in the typical Australian way – and here he was showing the discipline that comes with a lifetime of monasticism. I tried talking to him about it the next day but he was dismissive:

- That's just the way I sleep, mate!

By the second night we had reached the entrance to the gorge, which is about twenty kilometres above the Nepalese border. We had to stop as there was a pile of rocks in the road and a sign saying the road was closed. I knew that there were constant landslides along the gorge and believed what the locals were telling us – the road was blocked – and dismissed the suggestion that it was a police tactic to make us walk out of Tibet, as some sort of punishment. I slept with about ten people on a long shelf of wood that was just big enough to accommodate all of us – if we all lay on our sides and crushed up against each other. There were plenty of jokes about smelly feet, homosexuality and unwanted sexual advances but it was surprisingly comfortable and warm and I slept well.

The next morning I managed to scrounge a nourishing breakfast of tsampa flour in yak butter tea, and was ready for the hike down to the border. Although it was downhill all the way the road was rough and so we needed to leave as soon as possible. I wanted to go on my own but there was a big crowd that wanted us all to walk together. The problem was Roger's three trunks and four rucksacks. They were dragged out into the snow, we all looked at each other with a sinking feeling and someone asked the question that was in everyone's head: How the hell are we going to shift this lot?

Fortunately a local herdsman was found and he was willing to hire us four yaks and carry Roger's stuff down the gorge. Roger was flat broke and Robbie had to pay the yak man – on the promise that he would get repaid as soon as Roger could sell his stuff in Kathmandu. Having translated for both parties I was desperate to get away from them and I set off alone, marching as fast as I could, and had a refreshing day walking on my own. The gorge was stunning. Pine trees were growing out of the cliffs in seemingly impossible ways. I could understand how a tree can sprout out of a vertical cliff as it starts off like a tender shoot, with no real weight, but when it becomes a fully grown tree, weighing tens of tons, how can it possibly support itself?

It was still light as I approached the border town and the road looked like it had undergone an aerial bombardment – huge fragments of rocks were lying all over the place. A deep rumbling sound would sometimes come from the mountains above, as if the Gods were angry with us for daring to cross their threshold. Stones would tumble down and spin across the road lethally. At the worst point a landslide had cleared away all vegetation and rocks were cascading down continually. I sheltered behind a massive boulder, looked up, chose my moment and then sprinted across to the next big rock. I reached the border town, which seemed to be perching on a cliff, checked into a guest-house, went to get something to eat and waited for the others.

As night fell the rest of the bus passengers wandered in. I was comfortably seated in a ramshackle cafe and I could see them straggling along the road, weighed down by their rucksacks. I would pop out into the road, greet them and point out the guest-house and the cafe. One by one they joined me and we became the kind of big, noisy mob that I would usually avoid. It wasn't until almost midnight that Roger turned up with Robbie, Nick and the yaks. We decided to celebrate our last night in Tibet by drinking too much bad Chinese spirits, listening to Robbie's jokes and giving loud speeches.

The following morning we decided to approach the customs house en-masse, hoping that our expired visas would be treated more leniently in this way (I was beyond my four day expulsion order and many of the others had expired visas). We had the idea of sending Roger with all his stuff ahead – we all helped carry the trunks – hoping that his mountain of stuff would distract the attention of the border police. It worked, the police spent most of the day searching Roger's possessions, listening to his detailed explanations, and our expired visas seemed to pale into insignificance. Before long we all had exit stamps in our passports and we helped Roger re-pack his trunks, get them back outside and onto the backs of the patient yaks. The yak-owner had spoken to the customs officers and they gave him permission to take Roger's stuff down to the Nepalese border.

We hurried down to the surging river, across the rickety wooden bridge and piled into the Nepalese frontier hut where we were all given an entry stamp in our passports. At that point the group split up – some people managed to get onto the minibus to Kathmandu, others started hitching and I walked ahead of the others as fast as I could, wanting to be alone in the steep mountain gorge. I also had an urge to listen to loud music on my Walkman – I played the album Word Up by Cameo over and over again – to take my mind off things and re-connect to the modern world.

The following day I was in Kathmandu and a week later I met with Roger, who told me gloomily that he'd only got two hundred and fifty dollars for all his stuff. It was just enough to get him a plane ticket to Hong Kong where he hoped to get back with Isabella. I had to admit that Roger was one step ahead of me this time: he had made some money, had a plan and was on his way home; whereas I had still not decided what to do, or where to go. One thing was sure, I didn't have enough money to fly back home to Edinburgh. I didn't fancy the idea of going to Hong Kong or Taiwan, even if I had had the money for the airfare. I felt the need to get out of the orient to go home for a while. But how? For the time being I was stuck in Kathmandu.

One evening I met an Australian journalist in a noodle house and when I told him my story he suggested I offer an article to a British newspaper. I was sceptical. Why would they want anything from me? I had no idea how to write an article. He explained that the newspapers were always on the lookout for eyewitness accounts and the Lhasa protests were still a news item. The next day I sent a telegram to my parents about this and my Mother replied quickly. My Dad had spoken to Nigel Wade, the Foreign Editor of the Daily Telegraph in London, and they were willing to pay £500 for an article about my recent experiences in Lhasa. Five hundred pounds! That was a fortune, more than enough to get home with.

Writing the article seemed impossible. I spent a week writing draft after draft and realising that each one was worse than the last. They all ended up in the bin and my confidence took a nose-dive; I couldn't do it, I was too stupid, always had been. I could write letters and entries in my diary, and even essays, but articles? How the hell do you write an article? Robbie came to my rescue and helped me structure it into a format that might be acceptable to the newspaper. Eventually we came up with something that we guessed would be suitable – and, to my amazement, it got published in the opinion page of the Telegraph.

The money was paid to my parents who then bought me a ticket home. That was it, end of story, the end of my Asian experience and time to move on to other things. I didn't want to become an obsessive, bookish Tibetan supporter. I had no intention of carrying Tibet with me into the future or being one of those people who look back sentimentally and yearn for those days again. I was supportive of the Free Tibet movement but didn't have the energy to get properly involved. My time in Tibet had been incredible, I had wanted to settle there but it hadn't worked out. No point crying over spilt milk.

The end.

Afterword

My intention with this Afterword is to simply tell the story of 9 Months in Tibet and to thank the people who helped – as well as those who read it. I would also like to acknowledge all those people I met in Eastern Europe and Asia who were stuck where they were by Communism, a creed that forbade the kind of freewheeling travel that I did. To them I probably seemed very privileged.

I remember feeling a sense of resentment towards those authors whose acknowledgment sections are packed with names of publishers, editors, friends and family who all seem to be cheering them on. When I started writing this book I felt very much alone, as if nobody gave a damn whether I did it or not. But the more I got into it the more I realised that I was quite wrong about this. Having kept it hidden from friends and family for as long as possible I eventually shared it and they were very supportive. This process had been necessary as I needed to withdraw into a dark and lonely place from where I could actually start re-writing the damn thing.

The origins of this book go back to late 1987: I had been kicked out of Tibet and was twiddling my thumbs in Kathmandu. I needed cash and my father suggested I write a short testimonial about my experiences for the Daily Telegraph, whom he had called on my behalf. To my surprise they published the article and paid me the vast sum of £500. That was the money that got me home and, first of all, I need to thank my parents – Angus and Stephanie Wolfe Murray.

Stewart Anderson also deserves an honourable mention as he was the chap who found me blind drunk one night in 1986 and decided to put me on a plane to Thailand the following morning (see Chapter One). At that point in my life my aim was to travel to Latin America where I would learn the languages, get a job, fall in love and never leave. If it wasn't for Stewart I may never have reached Asia at all.

After Tibet I got back to Edinburgh and had no idea what to do with myself, but I did know that I should avoid what happened to me the first time I got back from the Orient when I became a pub bore on the subject of Asia. I tried to avoid talking about my experiences, but I needed to get them out. Every traveller does.

Then I got a letter from a London-based literary agent – Caroline Dawnay – who is a distant family relative. Caroline had read my article in the Daily Telegraph and she asked me if I had considered writing a book. All you need to do, she wrote, is write a synopsis and the first chapter.

One of the few things that I picked up from my parents, who had set up Canongate Publishing in 1974, was that the famous London publishers paid generous cash advances. And I knew that Caroline Dawnay was big league.

Now it was my turn to earn a bit of real money. I had a great story, how could I not earn a fortune? I sent off the precious first chapter and started planning what I would do with the advance on sales revenue (should I buy a house in the country or a car?) By the end of 1988, a year later, I had finished the book and, despite the fact that I still hadn't heard back from Caroline, sent her the full manuscript.

After a month or so I was struck by the obvious: perhaps it wasn't the international bestseller I had so fervently imagined; maybe she wasn't playing off one publisher against the other. I wrote her another letter and she replied with a friendly note saying the book wasn't suitable for mainstream publishers and I should insert more historical information about Tibet.

I got over the collapse of my illusions relatively quickly and wondered what to do with the manuscript. I couldn't accept the idea of inserting historical information -- I had no intention of writing an educational book about Tibet. I just wanted to tell my story.

But I did realise that my book was badly written and, if I was being honest with myself, saw that the literary agent was right: no publisher would touch it with a barge pole. I remember getting to the end the chapter I had just drafted and thinking that was a seriously well-written piece of literature and then looking at it again in the morning and thinking who wrote this crap? I would then study the chapter, learn from the bad writing and then write another chapter – and the same process would repeat itself. The result was that each chapter was stylistically different from the one before and this made the whole manuscript incoherent.

I have to learn how to write properly, I said to myself, and then I will rewrite my book. I came to the conclusion that the best way to learn how to write better was to get into journalism. I proceeded to teach myself how to write articles by copying the style of The Independent, a London newspaper that was superbly edited in the 1980s.

My first big story as a journalist was the Romanian revolution of 1989 and next thing I knew I was in Bucharest. I wrote some good stuff for The Scotsman and Scotland on Sunday but after a few months they stopped publishing my articles. I called the foreign editor of The Scotsman who told me: the public are no longer interested in Romania.

The foreign editor said he wanted stories about Romania's AIDS babies and the terrible situation of the children's homes. I did one story that made the front page of Scotland on Sunday – a moment of glory in my short journalistic career – but I felt it was morally wrong to write about such tragedy without doing something to help. I still have an image in my mind from 1990 that I will never forget: a western news photographer holding his huge camera over the emaciated body of a tiny Romanian baby with AIDS.

In 1990 I moved into one of the terrible children's homes that I was supposed to be writing about, with my brother Magnus who has since become a charismatic leader of humanitarian aid around the world. During the day we would organize the clothing, feeding, heating and washing of over a hundred children who had been abandoned by the system and what started out as a simple task became intensely complicated. My initial plan had been to write articles for newspapers in the quiet evenings but this was an illusion – there were no quiet evenings – and years would pass before I wrote another article.

I was sucked into the frantic world of humanitarian aid and the next few years were a whirlwind of meeting Romanian government and EU officials, hustling journalists to write about us, managing volunteers, negotiating in Romanian (which is a Latin language and easy to learn), begging people back home for money and continually sorting out crises. After a few years I went back to Scotland, set us up as a registered charity (subsequently incorporated into Mercy Corps) and then went to work in Bosnia Herzegovina for a couple of years. This is where I can say none of this [aid work] would have been possible without....my mother Stephanie. She was the one back home who dealt with our continual requests for supplies and money. By the year 2000, I had a well paid job as Team Leader for a hugely ambitious EU project called Improvement of the Roma [gypsy] Situation in Romania.

Every year I told myself I must re-write my book about Tibet but there were always so many other things to do. Three things happened that enabled me to overcome this block and get on with it: some inspiring quotes, a couple of good friends in Romania and the emergence of self-publishing as a serious business proposition.

Considering that everything in this world starts out as an idea, or concept, I think it was the quotes that really broke my 23 years of writer's block. George Orwell wrote something in an essay called Inside the Whale that was particularly enlightening. He said the only books about the Great War that were still in print were: written by common soldiers or junior officers who did not even pretend to understand what the whole thing was about. What Orwell was saying to me was that you don't need to be an expert to write, and you shouldn't tell people what to think. It's best to simply explain what you saw. This gave me the confidence to get on with the big re-write.

Kurt Vonnegut's experience with his first book was similar to mine and he made me realise that it's never too late to publish. In the opening chapter of Slaughterhouse Five, one of my favourite books, he described his illusions of grandeur about his war memoir: it would be a masterpiece or at least make me a lot of money. Vonnegut was describing my own experience and the fact that he kept plugging away at it long after his dreams had been shattered gave me the inspiration I needed to rewrite it.

But I wasn't quite ready yet. I had accumulated what psychologists call unhealthy behaviours, in particular a tendency to be withdrawn, secretive and complacent. I had been through an unhappy marriage and a bruising divorce and I was full of anger as well as sadness at leaving my two wonderful kids. I needed to address these issues if I was going to get creative. This is where my two friends in Romania came in.

Nancy Rice is a retired therapist from San Antonio Texas who lives in a village called Peris (pronounced Perish) just outside Bucharest. She gave me therapy after my divorce, helped me to address my demons and taught me about real love and forgiveness. Manuela Boghian is a good friend, we do creative work together and she helped get me going on the book (since then we have moved to Liverpool together and got engaged). Both of these wise women helped me overcome my complacency and get on with the very time consuming job of re-writing my book.

I wrote the book during 2013, mainly in Romania but also in Crete when I took a month off and lived on a beach. What made it happen was simply dedicating a few hours every morning to the task. Manuela gave me feedback and encouragement at every step of the way and also gave the manuscript a thorough edit when it was ready. But Manuela wasn't the only editor, in fact I couldn't believe how long the editing took (most of 2014).

My mother stepped in and scribbled comments and corrections all over it and then I sent it to Camilla Rooney, a teacher friend in Transylvania who gave it another thorough edit. Kevin Sullivan, a Scottish author who is based in Bosnia came with another set of corrections. An editor friend in Brighton, Chris Allinson, also had a quick look at it and gave me some useful feedback – as did Silvana Prodan, a Romanian who worked with me as a volunteer and then got a job with the European Central Bank in Frankfurt. Each one of these edits took a lot of time to deal with as I needed to carefully think about each and every suggestion, asking myself will it improve the book or compromise it? By the end of 2014 I thought I had finished editing but a good friend – Gabriella Bullock -- sent me a series of subtle observations, and complex grammatical corrections that helped me to fine tune and complete the manuscript.

One of the things that had got me writing again was the so-called revolution in self-publishing. Self-publishing, and especially Vanity Publishing, was a rather sad business until quite recently. Authors would pay to get their book edited, designed and printed – but the sales and distribution links were missing and the hapless authors would end up with stacks of unsold copies. These would become the sort of gift-books that you can never face reading, or throwing away.

The big new ebook distributors -- Amazon, iTunes and Google Play -- have changed the publishing business: they have broken the publishers' monopoly of book distribution (even though their own practices can be rather monopolistic). What the likes of Amazon can't guarantee is that anyone will buy, or even see, your book.

I had a Eureka moment when I realised how easy it is to upload a book onto Amazon – I don't need a publisher after all! I cried – and this gave me the energy to finish the book. But the more I looked into self-publishing the more I realised that it would most likely lead to a dead end. What killed it for me was when I read that the average book only sells 30 copies on Amazon.

There is an entire ecosystem of self-published authors who have "made it" on Amazon and the other networks and many have published books explaining how to do it: get huge followings on social networks, build up a big list of subscribers, produce a blog and tell all your new found friends to buy your masterpiece. I actually went down this road for a while, but remain unconvinced that all (or any) of my friends on Twitter and Facebook will actually buy a copy.

And so I ended up where I started: knocking on the doors of publishers and literary agents and collecting rejection letters. I've come to realise that publishers are in fact curators: they select a handful of manuscripts from the thousands they're offered each year and then put a lot of time into editing, design and promotion. Having organised the editing of my own book I realise how much time, effort and focus is required. So when a publisher offers a new title people take notice, as the chances are it will be damn good.

Although publishers and editors have always been charming to me personally, if I mention my book they would roll their eyes as if to say: Oh God, another one trying to get me interested in his self-indulgent ramblings. J.K. Rowling got rejected twelve times before finding a publisher and Stephen King nailed his rejection slips onto a wooden beam until they totally covered it. I dreaded going through that process.

I used to think that publishers are open to manuscripts from all and sundry and it took me years to work out that this is nonsense. When I was a kid there was a pile of manuscripts in the family toilets and one of the urban legends around publishing is that the only time editors get to read unsolicited manuscripts is when they're taking a crap.

I remember once taking a call when I was about 11 years old. It went something like this:

- Can I speak to Stephanie?

- She's not in.

- Do you know when she'll be back?

- No.

- Can you help me? Please, I'm desperate. I sent her the only copy of my book and I can't get hold of her.

- Er...

- I've written to her, called her many times at Canongate, but I can't get her. She doesn't return my calls or answer my letters. It's a really important book that will have a great influence...

- Um...

- The most important thing is that she hasn't lost the manuscript as it's the only one. I stupidly didn't make a carbon copy.

- Er, well...I'll tell her you called.

When I told my mother about this rather intriguing conversation she slapped her forehead in frustration and said: God, I feel so guilty about these authors. They keep sending me their manuscripts and I can't keep track of it all. I do my best but there's just too many of them. They all seem to think their book is the one that will change the world. It's so hard to publish a book, so much work, and we just don't have time for all these authors.

My problem is enthusiasm, a condition the ancient Greeks used to call an illness. Every time I make contact with a publisher, and they agree to read the manuscript, I think this is it. This one will see its potential and turn my book into a bestseller. And each time they would say no my confidence and momentum would suffer. By the end of 2015 I had run out of steam and just couldn't face talking to another publisher. I was reluctantly coming back round to the option of self-publishing, the last resort. As long as I get the damn thing out there, I thought to myself, I can move on. It's blocking my progress. I've got so many other things to write. I don't care if nobody buys it. My illusions of fame and fortune are long dead.

Then I went to the Highlands of Scotland and visited some old friends called Joe and Leonie Gibbs. They had fundraised for our Romanian project many years ago and are now running an impressive rock festival called Belladrum. At their house I met a lady called Jean Findlay who had just set up a new publishing company called Scotland Street Press in Edinburgh. I told her about my book, she seemed really interested and what really encouraged me was her honesty; she said I can't offer you an advance and I'm not even sure if I can sell many copies, but I can publish a beautiful book.

That was all I needed – a decently made copy of the book, not the sub-standard paperbacks that Amazon's print-on-demand service churn out – and also someone to talk to about editing and publicity. I sent her the manuscript and prepared myself for a charmingly-written rejection letter but, to my surprise, she accepted it and here it is finally published. Thank you Jean and her husband Alastair.

I need to say something about the people I wrote about in 9 Months
in Tibet. I have changed the names of some of the people in the book as
I didn't describe them in very flattering terms. But there are exceptions: I
never knew the surnames of the two Italian women I fell in love with and
didn't feel the need to change their names. I am in contact with the two
Romanians whom I mention at the beginning of the book, as well as the
artist Gwen Vaughan, and I didn't change their names.

I managed to track down the Indian lad I had met in Darjeeling (now
he's a high powered physicist) and he insisted on his name being changed.
I also found Isi Amodu, my black travelling companion, re-established
friendly contact by email and am happy to say that he let me use his name.

I was determined to get back in touch with the two Bettinas and I am
now in friendly relations with both of them. It was probably quite hard for
them to digest this book as it can't be easy to read about a relationship that
you were in. They seemed annoyed with me at first, and probably hurt, but
they forgave me. They both insisted that I change their surnames which is
a shame as they have beautiful family names.

I recently visited Bettina the horse rider in Germany. She's a teacher and
is still mad about riding; she took me out the back to introduce me to her
two horses whom she played with affectionately. She then invited me for
a ride through the woods but I couldn't face the cold weather, was feeling
tired and opted out – all of which reminded me of our ride through Tibet
when she was full of energy and I was just thinking about food and rest.

More recently I was in Vienna where I met up with Bettina Tucholsky,
and her travelling companion Uli, and we had tea together in an old
fashioned cafe. Bettina let me scan the sketches that she had made on her
visit to Tibet and I posted them on the website that accompanies this book:
www.wolfemurray.com. Uli had some rather brilliant photos of Tibet that
she has kindly let me use for the website. They both read the manuscript
and came with some really interesting feedback. Charles Ramble strides
into my narrative with considerable style and, after I tracked him down in
Paris, he continued to dazzle. To my surprise he didn't mind me using his
real name and wrote: I don't mind being portrayed as a derelict. He also
read the manuscript, incredibly fast, when visiting China and he sent me a
plethora of suggestions and a detailed analysis of the book that was both
useful and encouraging.

I didn't contact Robbie Barnett until quite late in the process but he came
back with lots of useful suggestions about the final chapter -- a chapter I

am careful to preserve as my personal memory of the protests and not a historically accurate rendering of various eyewitness accounts. Robbie told me the sad news of his friend in Lhasa, Nick Owen, who recently died of a rare form of cancer. Nick's career as a human rights lawyer on the global stage, after our time in Tibet, was incredible and he left behind a wonderful family. His wife Lucy kindly gave me permission to use his name. She also sent me friendly emails at the end of 2015 when I was ready to give up the whole project.

As you will have realised by now I've done a pretty wide variety of jobs – illegally selling bus tickets in Lhasa, painting frescoes, teaching English, humping furniture, flogging books, working on building sites, aid work, journalism, making documentary films, managing big EU-funded projects, PR consultancy, driving trucks and washing dishes. On the one hand I believe that working is essential for our wellbeing (what would you do with your time if you didn't have a job?) but on the other hand I have been continually disappointed with the chaotic or greedy way that most organisations are run. I moved from journalism, which I felt was corrupting, to international charity work which, in my experience, is badly run, to EU jobs where I saw international consultancy companies that seem only interested in ticking boxes and maximizing profits.

What I'm getting at here is that after 30 years of trying to work out what to do with myself, I have finally worked it out: storytelling. In 2015 Manuela and I set up a company called Untold Stories PR Limited and we offer just one service: telling the stories of people in organisations and families. We aim to change the way that organisations communicate, using real stories on the website rather than puff and blurb written in the third person. My long-term plan is to work with families that want to gather up all the fragments of their story.

A final word of thanks is due to Alexander McCall Smith who, to my surprise and delight, agreed to read the manuscript and write a foreword. He remembered me from many years ago when my mother used to publish his children's books, invited me round to tea at his house in Edinburgh – I had African Rooibos – and gave me some really useful feedback. He also helped me to resolve something that had been bothering me for ages – how to classify my book – by coming up with three key words: memoir, travel and adventure.

Another old friend from the past who deserves a mention here is Jim Hutcheson, who kindly offered to do the layout for the print version of this book. Jim still works in publishing, at Birlinn in Edinburgh, where he is the creative director and he took me out for lunch where we talked about Scottish independence. On the subject of design I'd like to also thank Matei Tudor for doing the jacket design and the website -- and Gabi Poiaru for organising the website.

I would really like to hear from you, the person reading this, especially if you would like to do a long journey, find it difficult to get up and go and need some support. Maybe you're a student thinking about a year abroad but afraid to travel alone (I know I was). Perhaps you can't get away from the loving embrace of your parents. Are you in a job, dreaming about travelling across Asia but feeling trapped by routine, family and mortgage? I sometimes think of retired people who want to travel on their own and get told by everyone around them not to be so irresponsible.

Unless this book is a runaway success and I make enough money to buy a mansion in the countryside, and a flash car to get around with, I'm pretty sure I will still be working in Liverpool by the time you read this. I would really like to hear from you, the person reading this, especially if you would like to do a long journey, are having problems overcoming your fear of travelling alone, are unable to get away from work or overcome your complacency. One of the main reasons I wrote this book was to encourage people to overcome their fear of travelling alone by sharing my story and explaining how I did it.

rupert@wolfemurray.com
www.wolfemurray.com